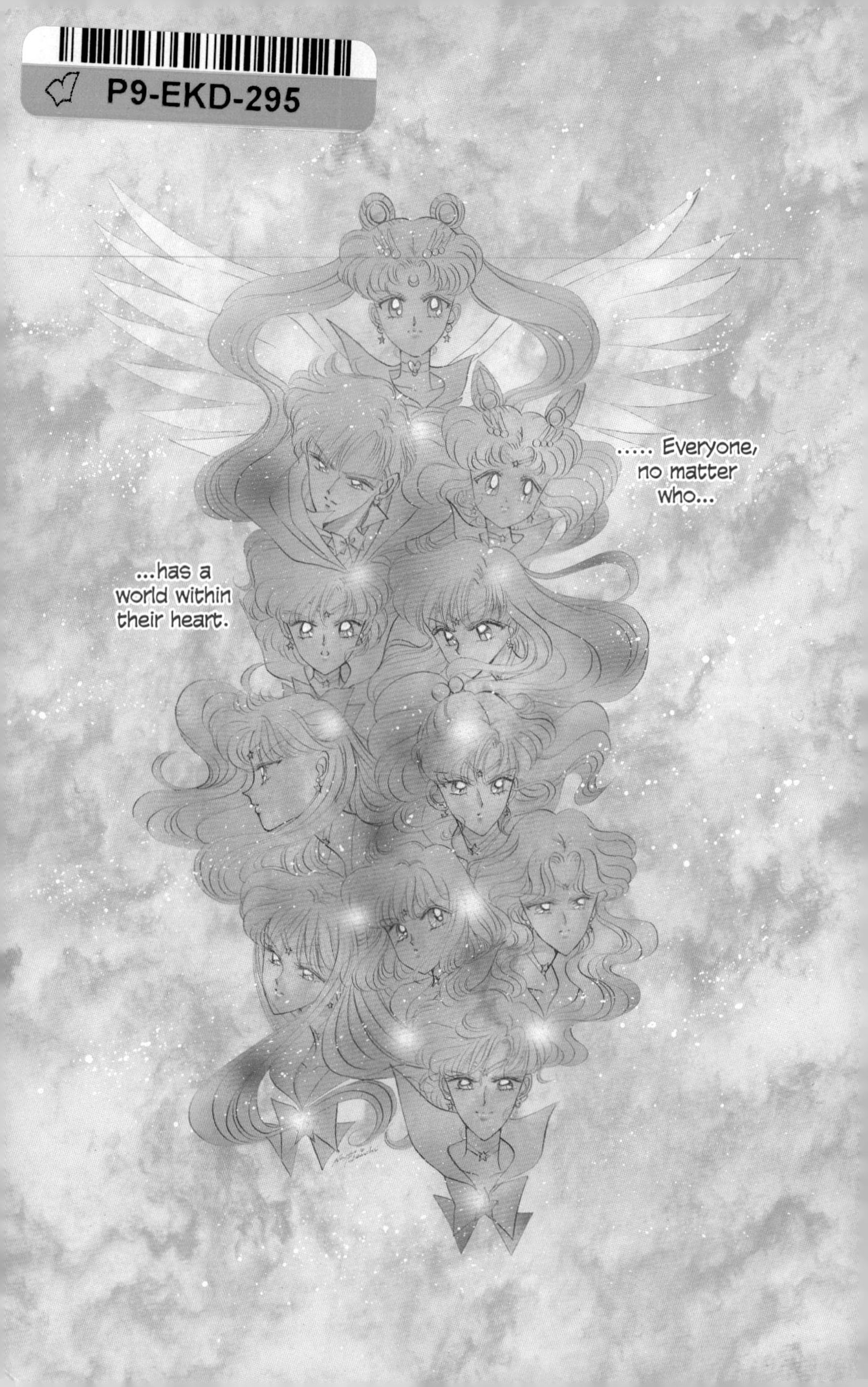
..... Everyone, no matter who...
...has a world within their heart.

Act 50 Stars 1

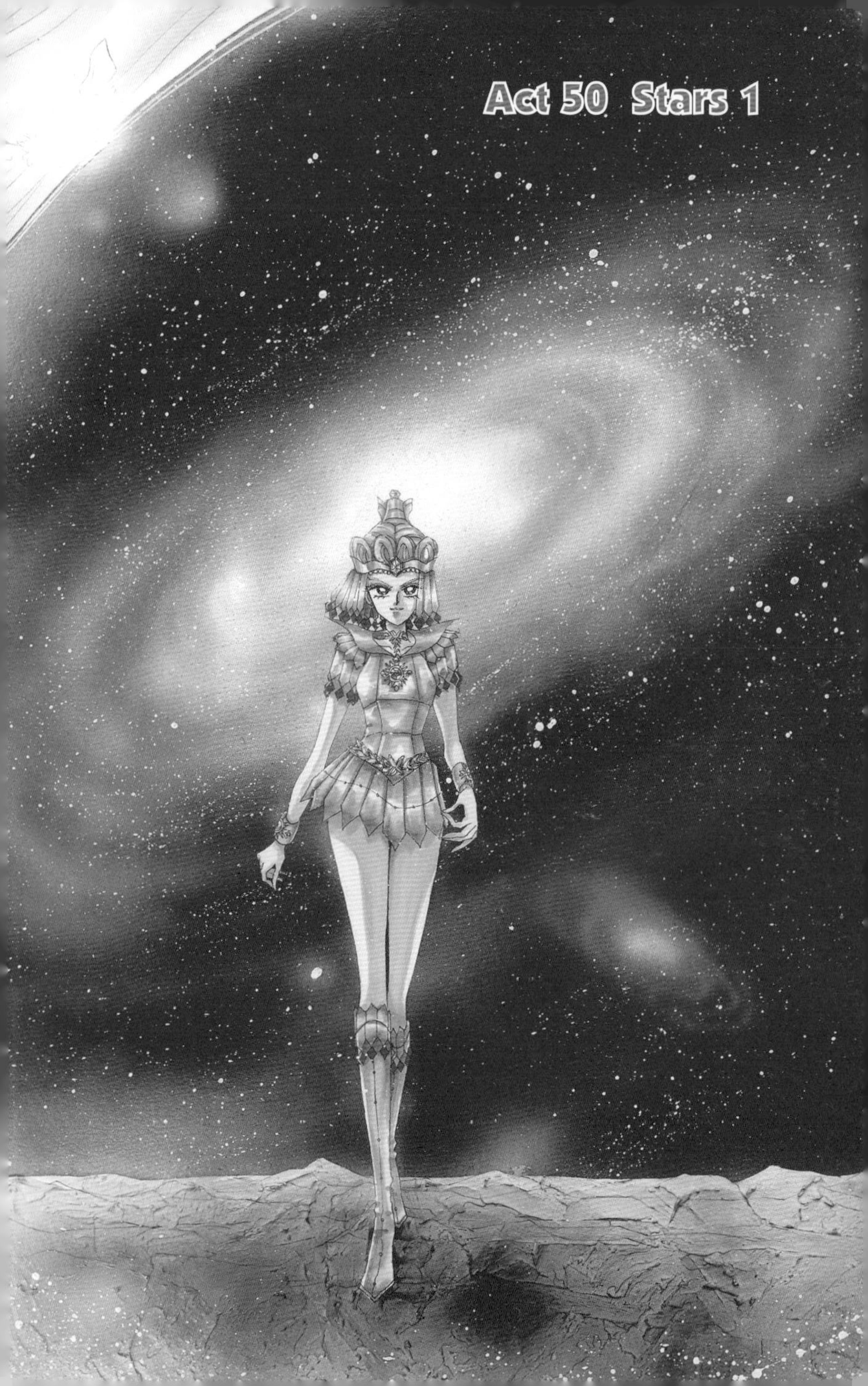

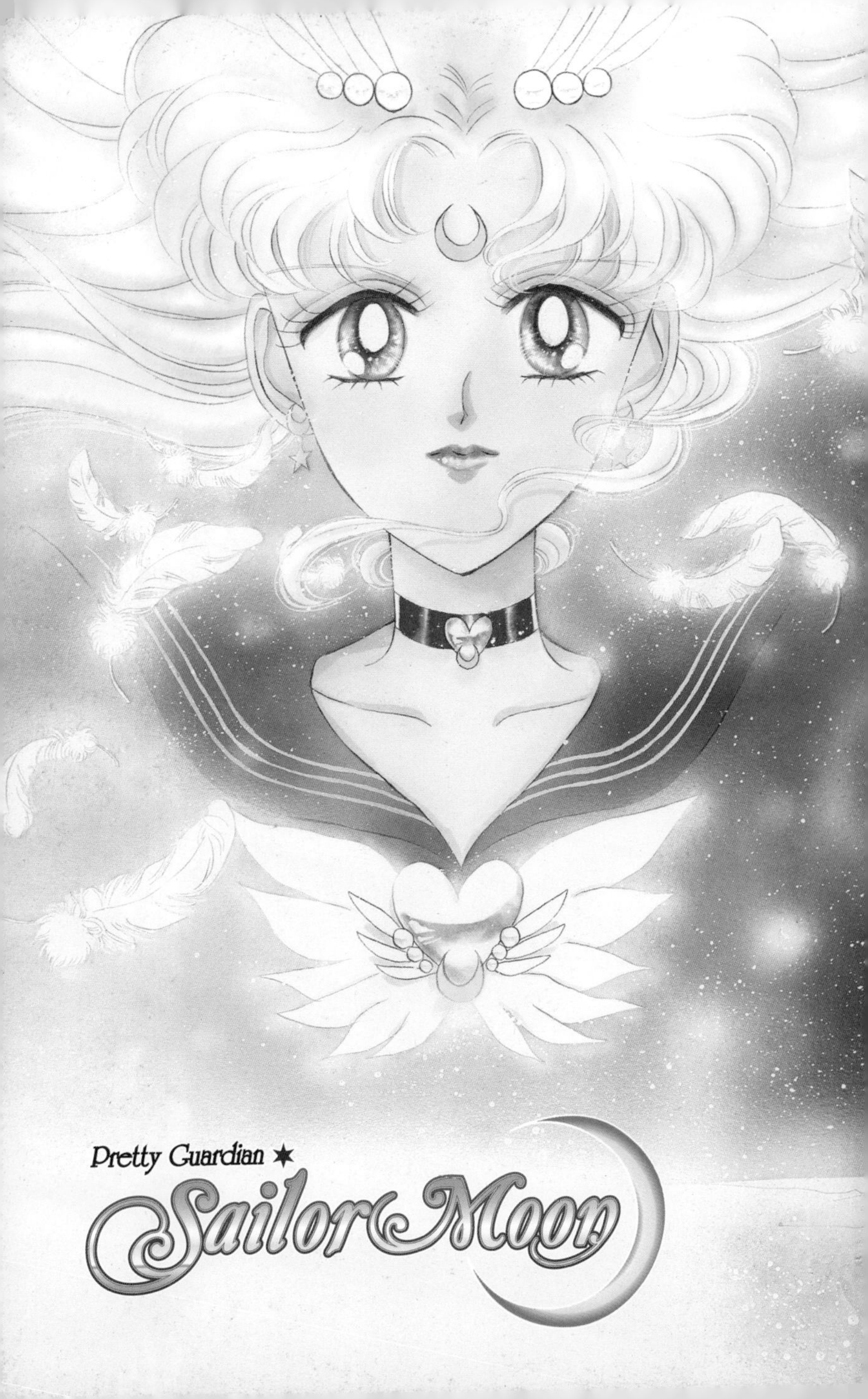
Pretty Guardian ★
Sailor Moon

Pretty Guardian SAILORMOON

CONTENTS

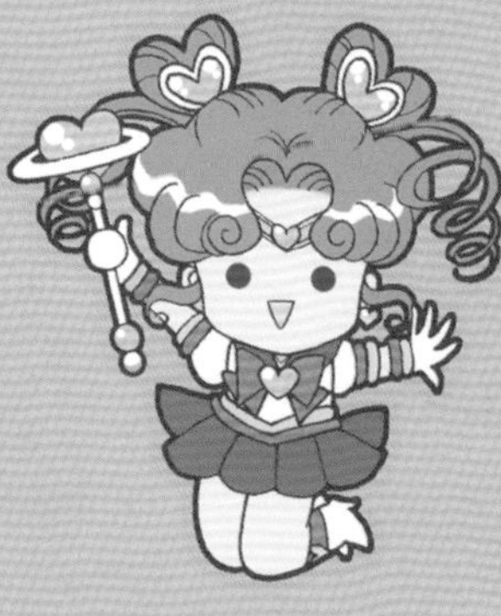

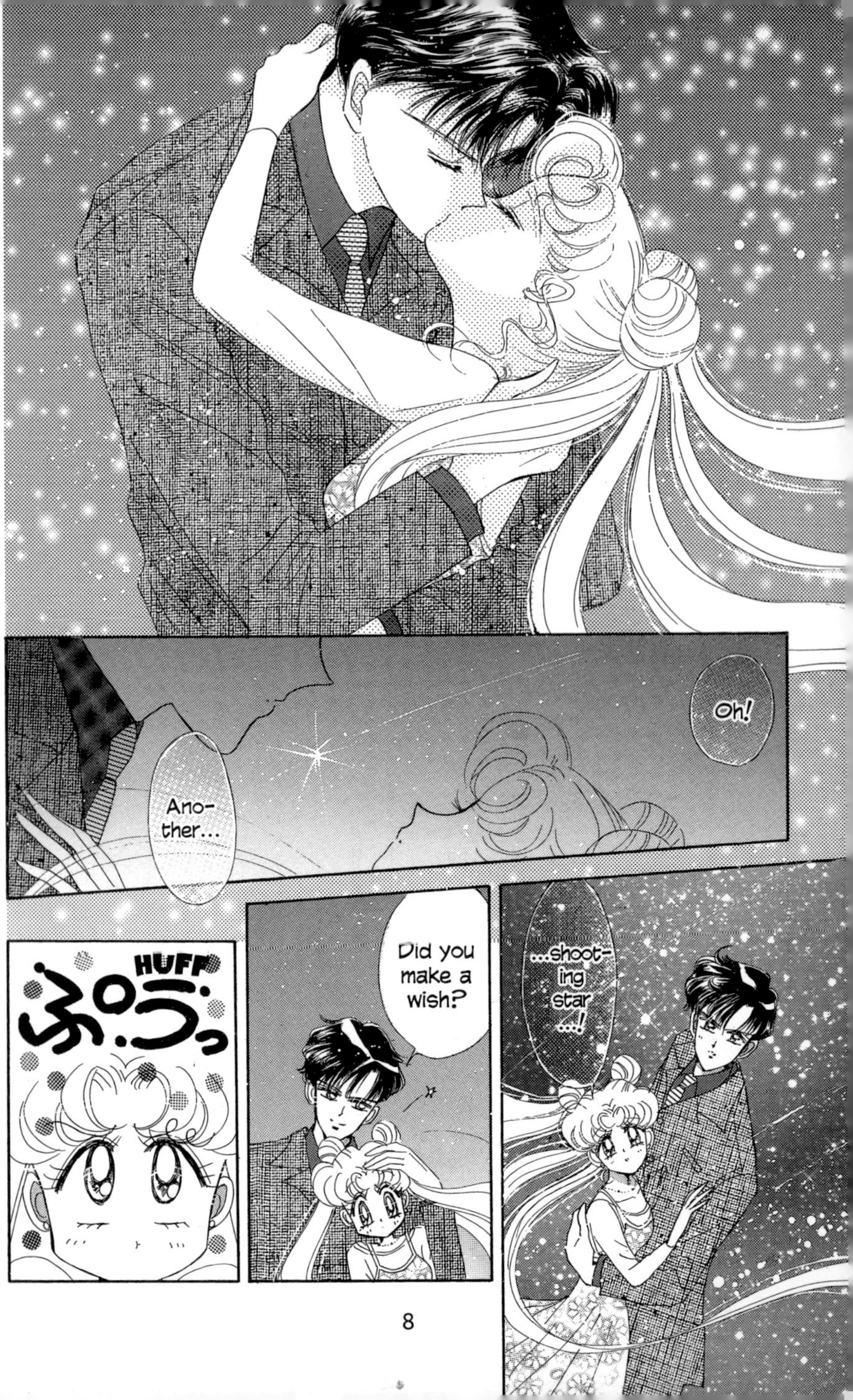
Oh!
Ano-ther...
...shoot-ing star ...!
Did you make a wish?
HUFF
ふぅっ

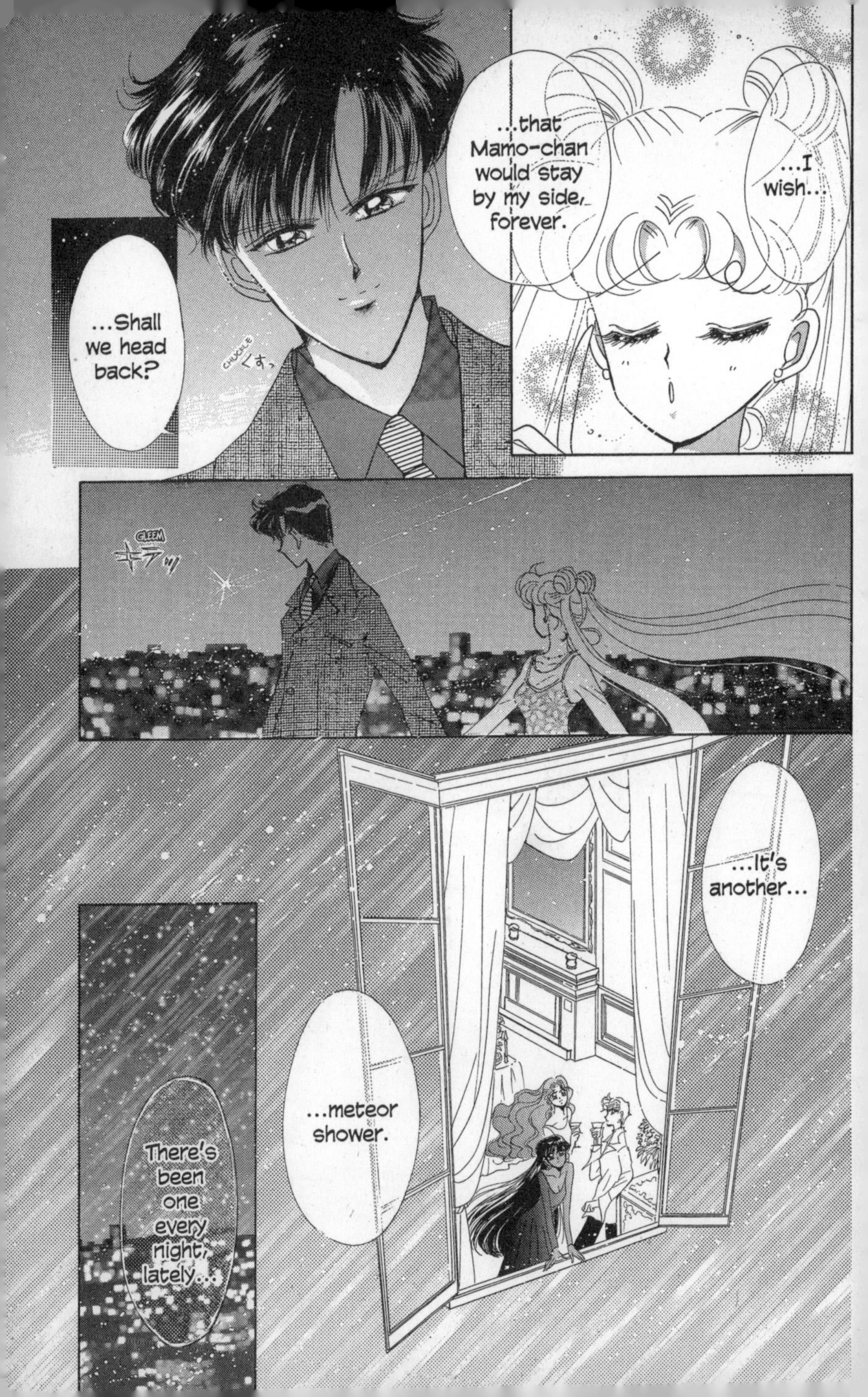
...I wish...
...that Mamo-chan would stay by my side, forever.
...Shall we head back?
CHUCKLE
くすっ
GLEEM
キラッ
...It's another...
...meteor shower.
There's been one every night, lately...

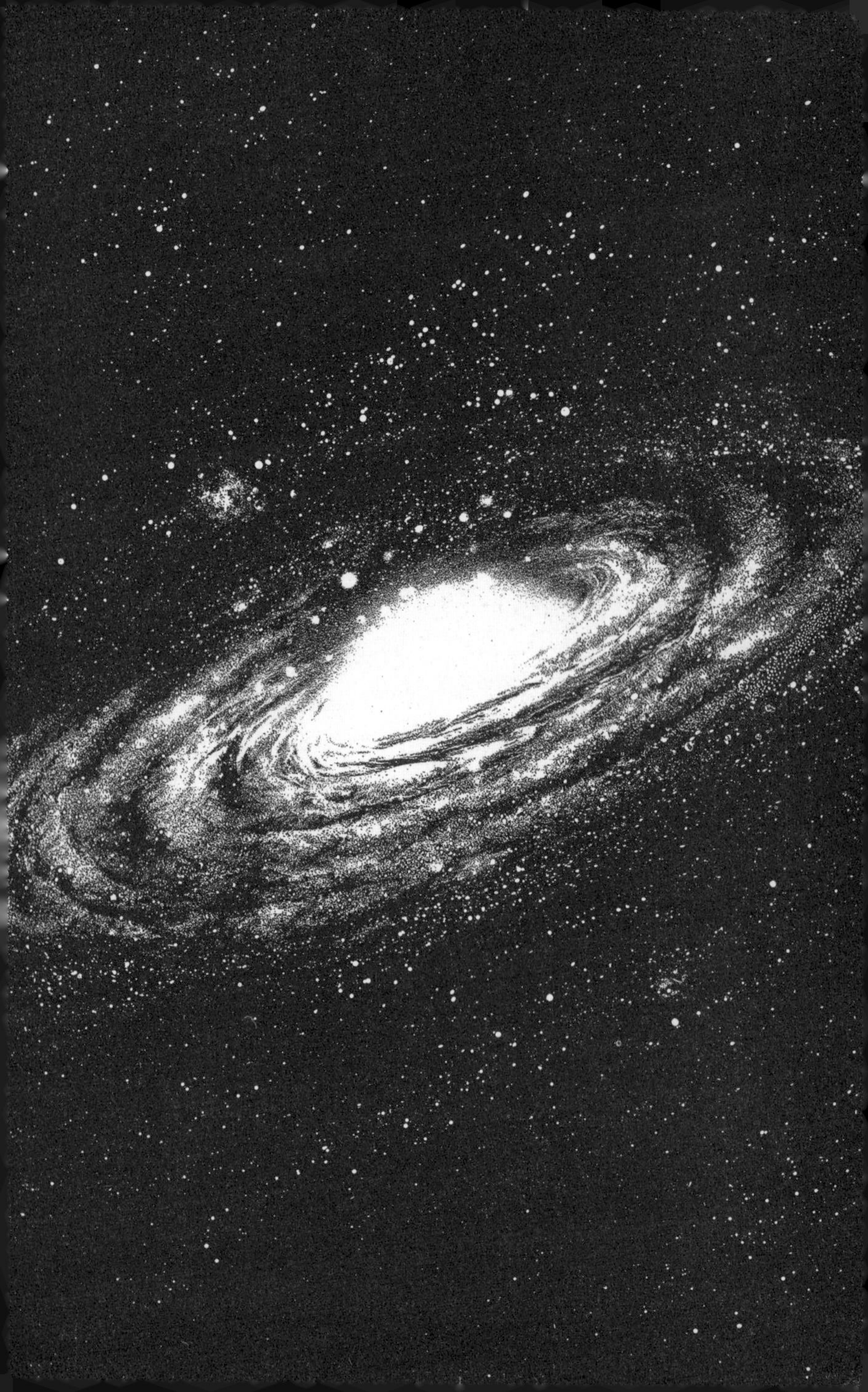

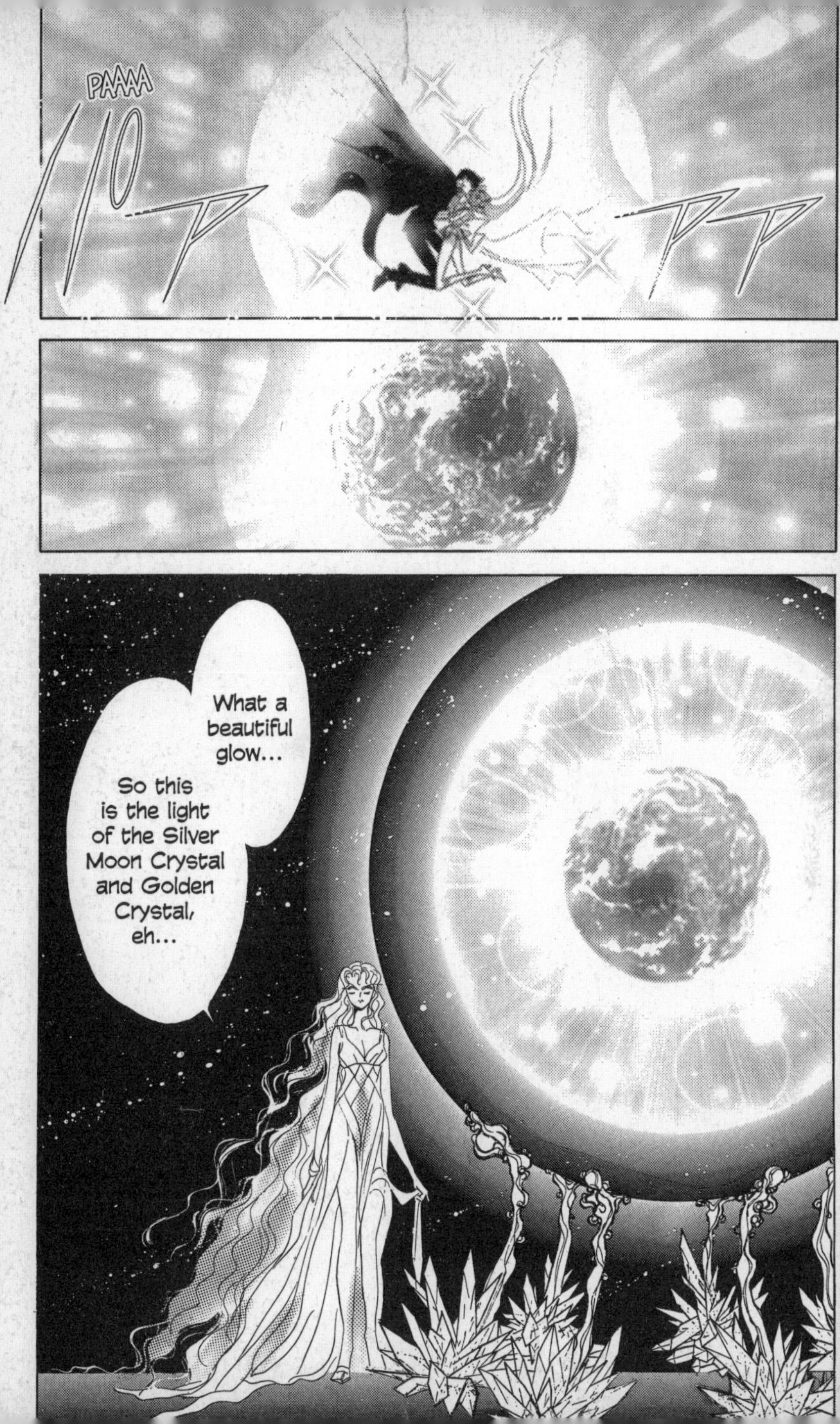
PAAAA
パアアア
What a beautiful glow...
So this is the light of the Silver Moon Crystal and Golden Crystal, eh...

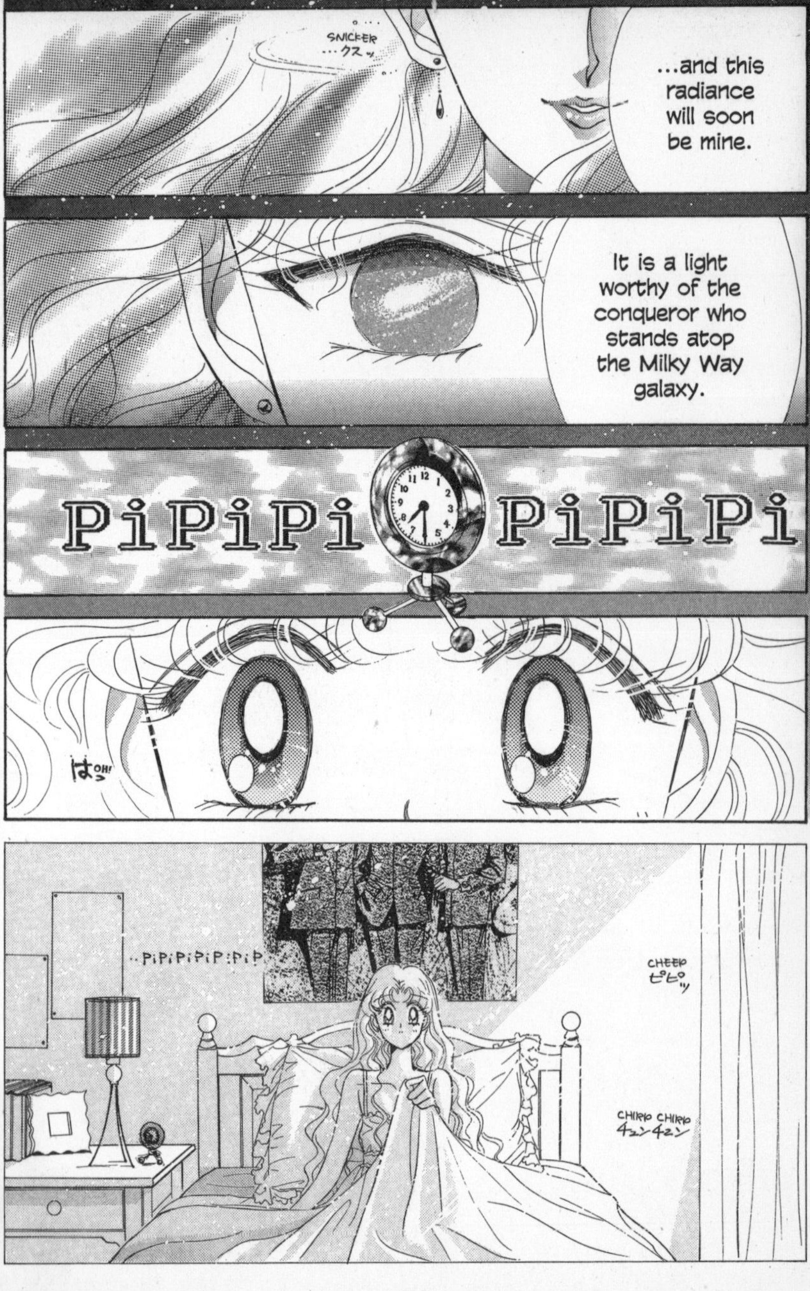
...and this radiance will soon be mine.
SNICKER ...クスッ
It is a light worthy of the conqueror who stands atop the Milky Way galaxy.
PiPiPi PiPiPi
はっ OH!
CHEEP ピピッ
CHIRP CHIRP チュンチュン
..PiPiPiPiP:PiP

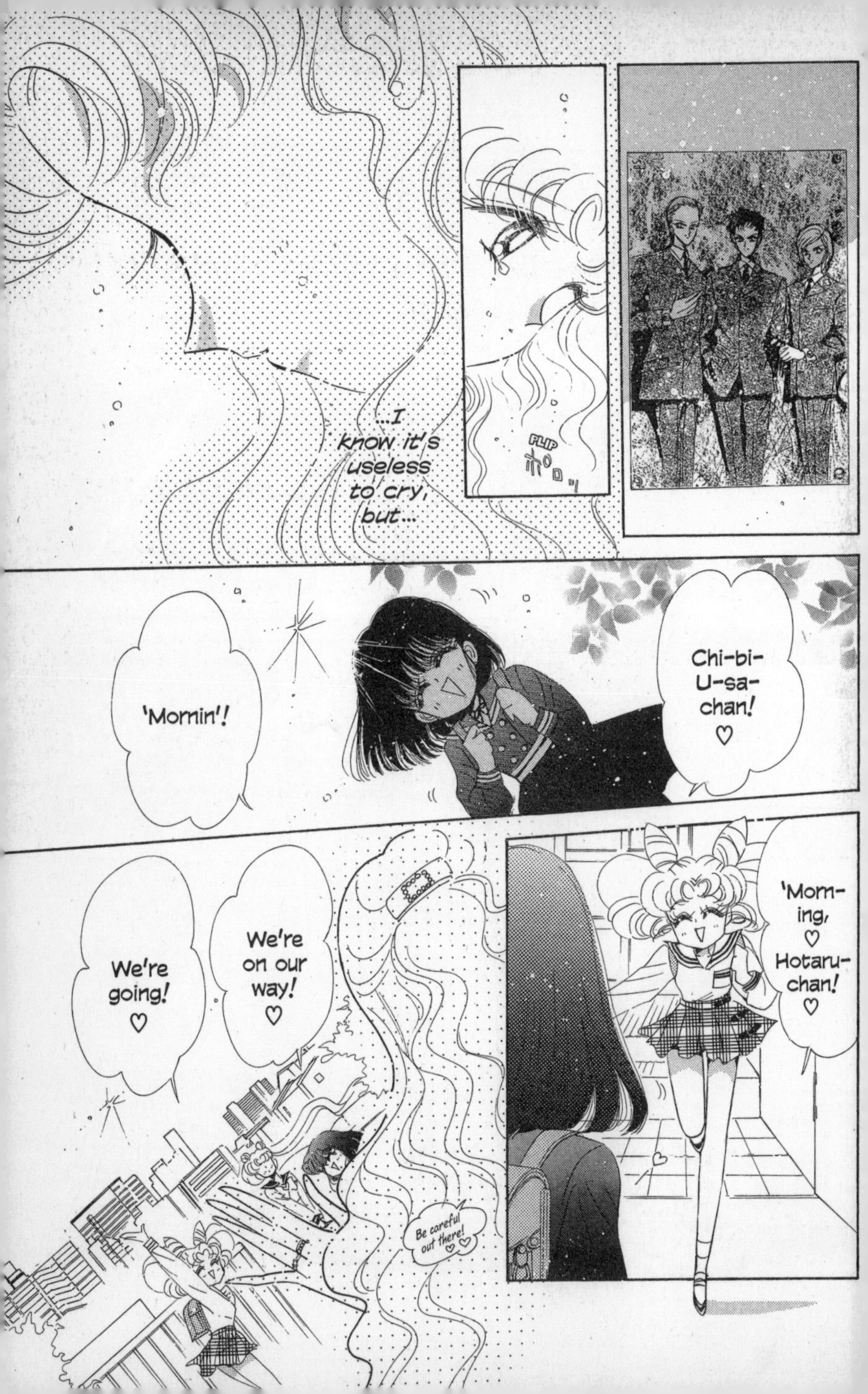
PLIP
...I know it's useless to cry, but...
Chi-bi-U-sa-chan! ♡
'Mornin'!
'Morning, ♡ Hotaru-chan! ♡
We're on our way! ♡
We're going! ♡
Be careful out there! ♡♡

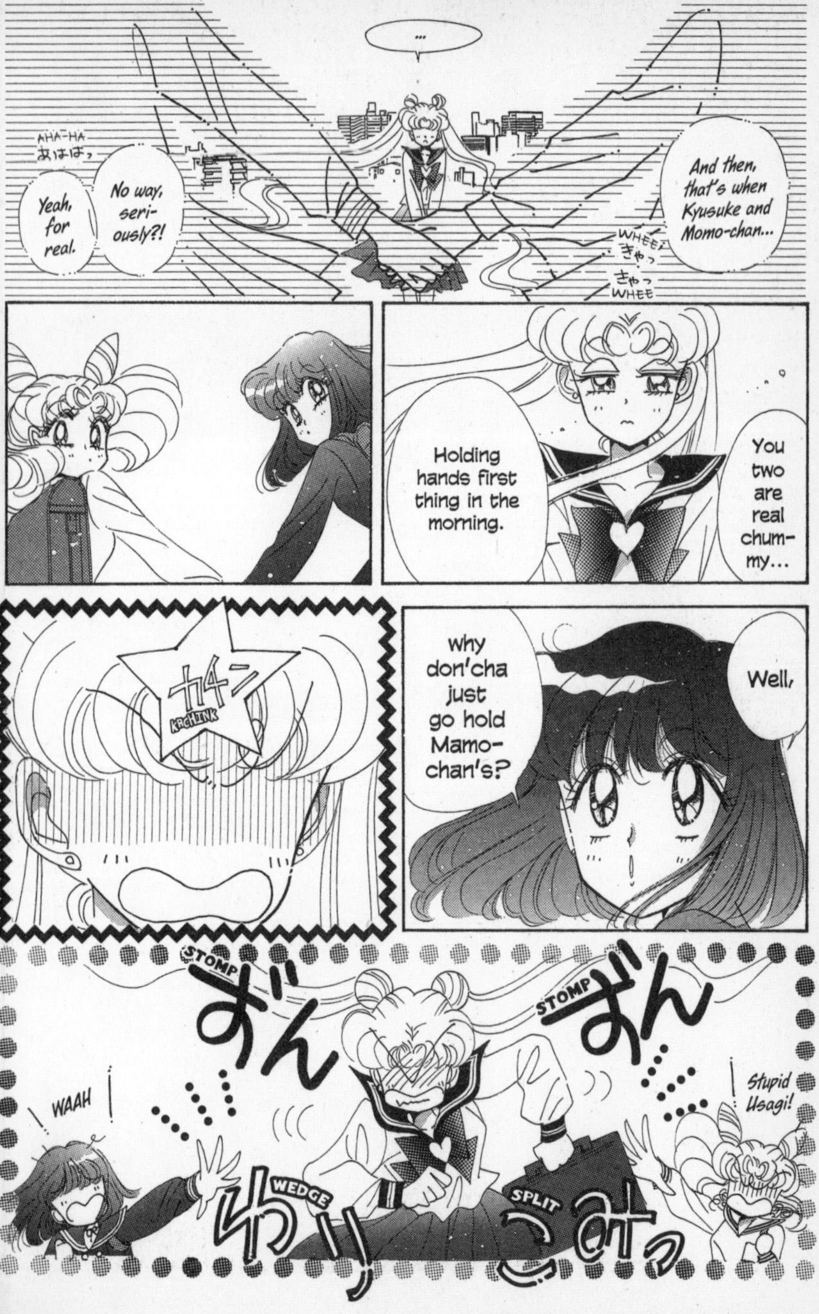
And then, that's when Kyusuke and Momo-chan...
WHEE! きゃっ
きゃっ WHEE
...
No way, seri-ously?!
Yeah, for real.
AHA-HA あはは
You two are real chum-my...
Holding hands first thing in the morning.
Well,
why don'cha just go hold Mamo-chan's?
カチン KACHINK
STOMP ずん
STOMP ずん
Stupid Usagi!
WAAH
SPLIT こみっ
WEDGE わり

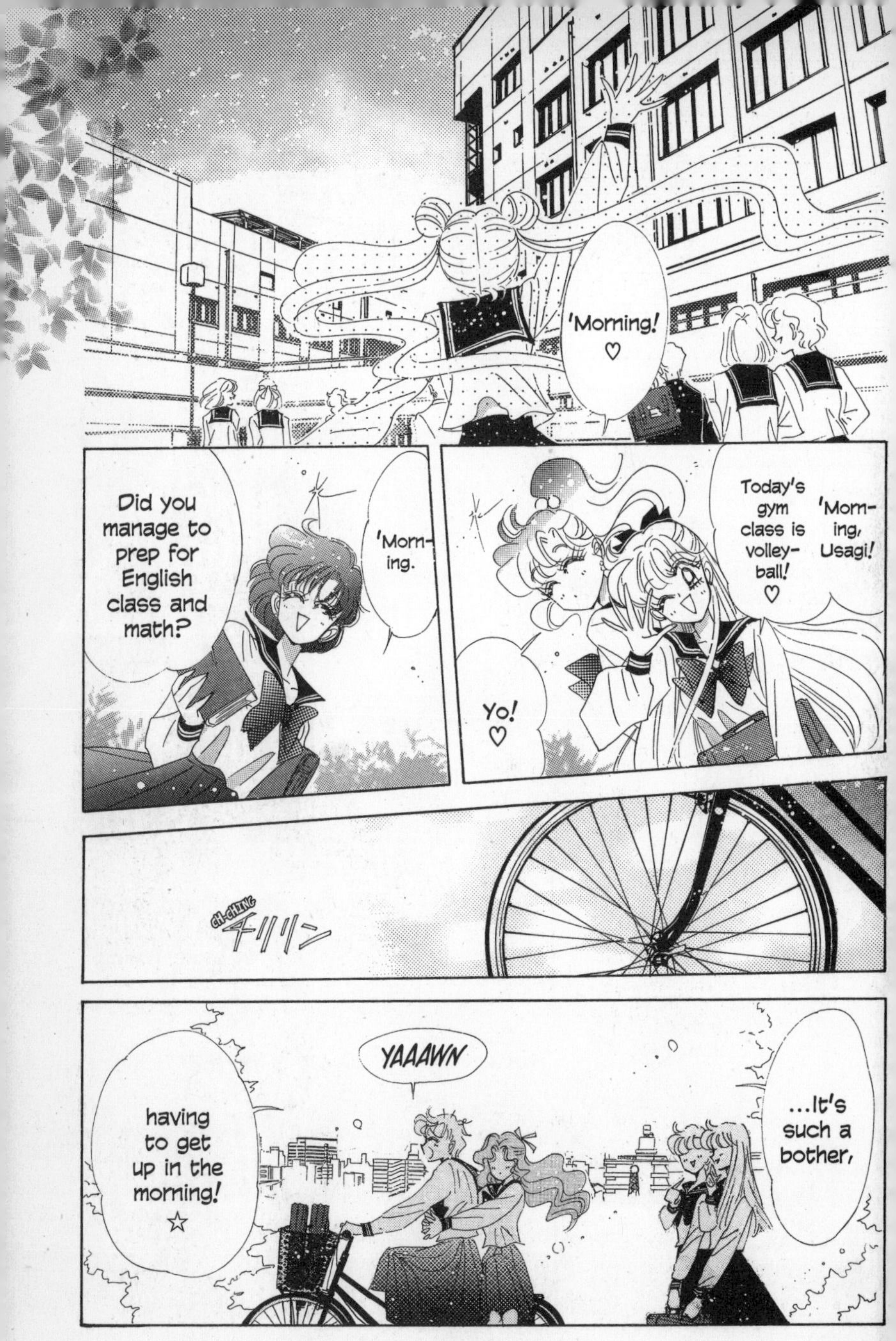
'Morning! ♡
'Morn-ing, Usagi!
Today's gym class is volley-ball! ♡
Yo! ♡
'Morn-ing.
Did you manage to prep for English class and math?
CH-CHING チリリン
...It's such a bother,
YAAAWN
having to get up in the morning! ☆

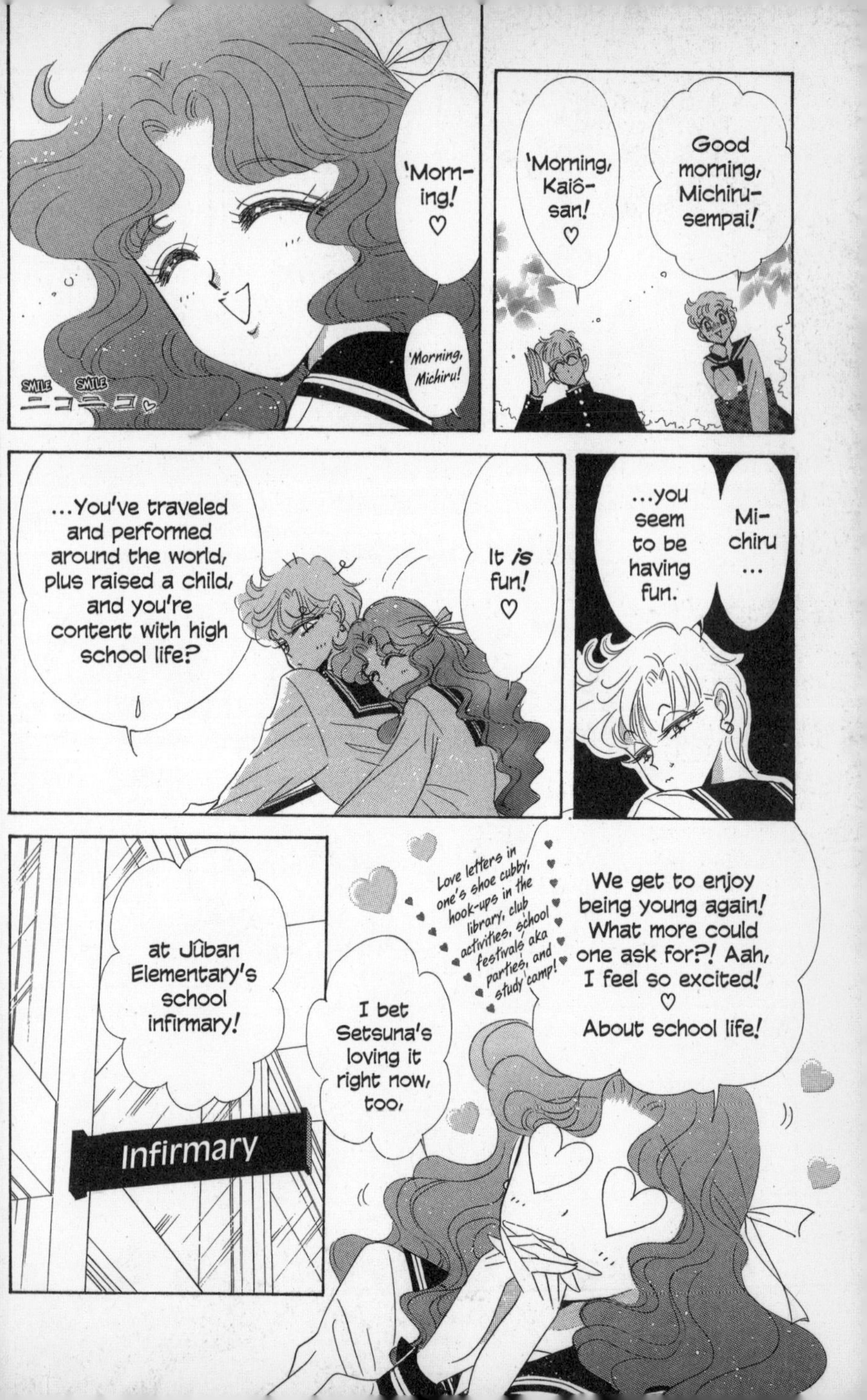
Good morning, Michiru-sempai!
'Morning, Kaiô-san! ♡
'Morn-ing! ♡
'Morning, Michiru!
SMILE SMILE
Mi-chiru ...
...you seem to be having fun.
It *is* fun! ♡
...You've traveled and performed around the world, plus raised a child, and you're content with high school life?
We get to enjoy being young again! What more could one ask for?! Aah, I feel so excited! ♡ About school life!
Love letters in one's shoe cubby, hook-ups in the library, club activities, school festivals aka parties, and study camp!
I bet Setsuna's loving it right now, too,
at Jûban Elementary's school infirmary!
Infirmary

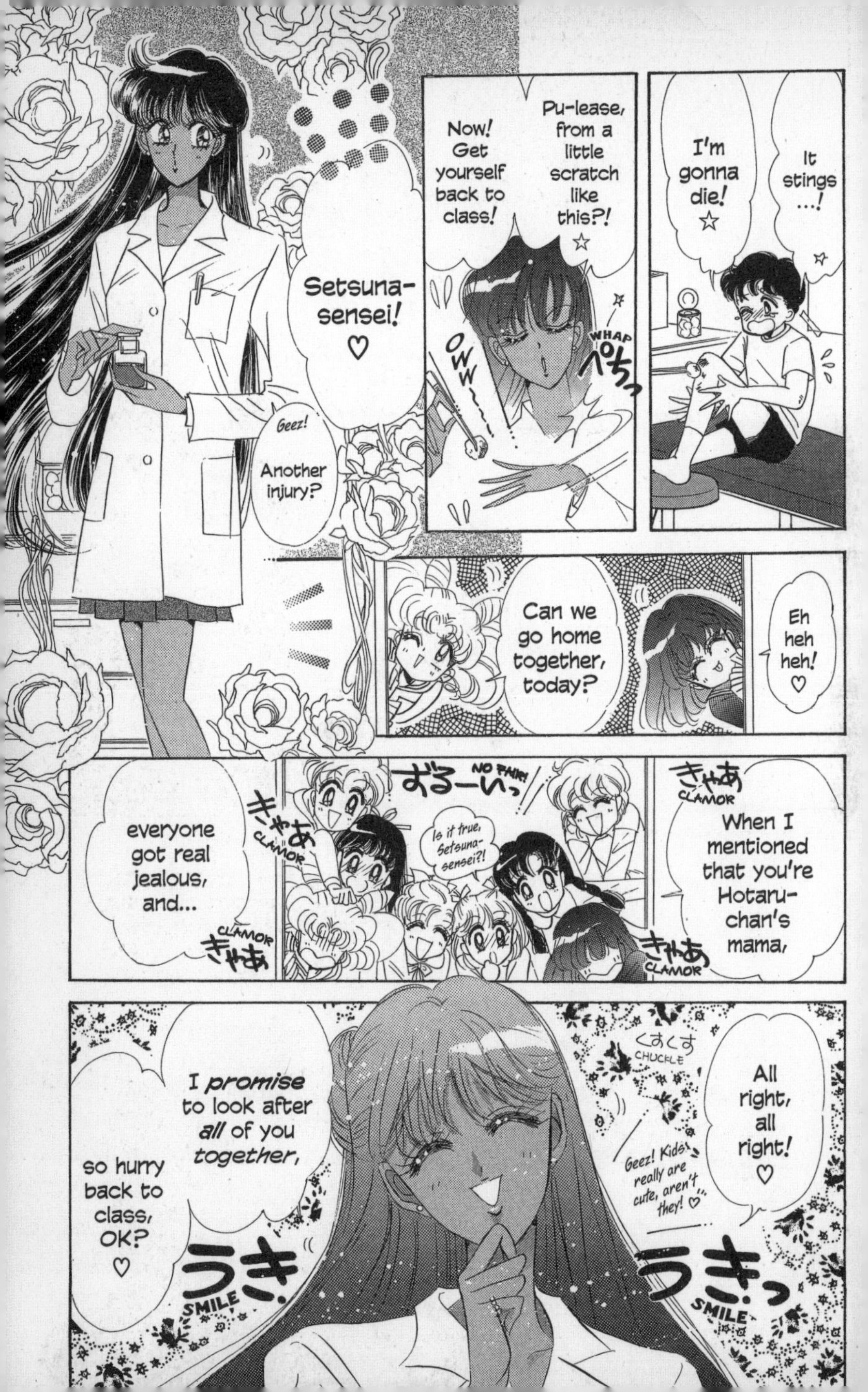
It stings ...!
I'm gonna die! ☆
Pu-lease, from a little scratch like this?! ☆
Now! Get yourself back to class!
ぺちっ WHAP
OWW~~
Eh heh heh! ♡
Can we go home together, today?
Setsuna-sensei! ♡
Geez! Another injury?
きゃあ CLAMOR
When I mentioned that you're Hotaru-chan's mama,
きゃあ CLAMOR
ずるーいっ NO FAIR!
Is it true, Setsuna-sensei?!
きゃあ CLAMOR
きゃあ CLAMOR
everyone got real jealous, and...
All right, all right! ♡
くすくす CHUCKLE
Geez! Kids really are cute, aren't they! ♡
I *promise* to look after *all* of you *together*,
so hurry back to class, OK? ♡
うきっ SMILE
うき SMILE

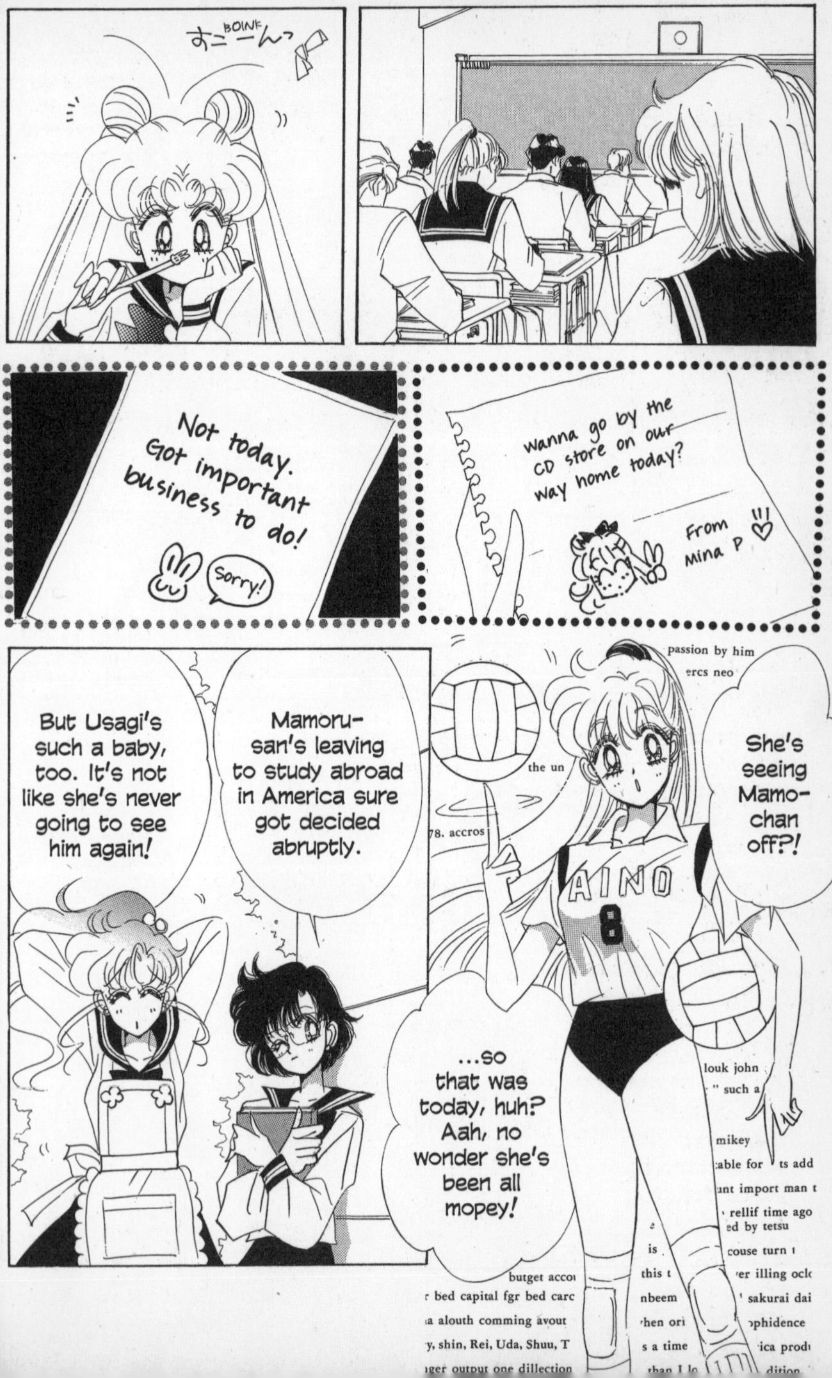

すこーんっ
BOINK
wanna go by the CD store on our way home today?
From Mina P
Not today. Got important business to do!
Sorry!
She's seeing Mamo-chan off?!
...so that was today, huh? Aah, no wonder she's been all mopey!
Mamoru-san's leaving to study abroad in America sure got decided abruptly.
But Usagi's such a baby, too. It's not like she's never going to see him again!

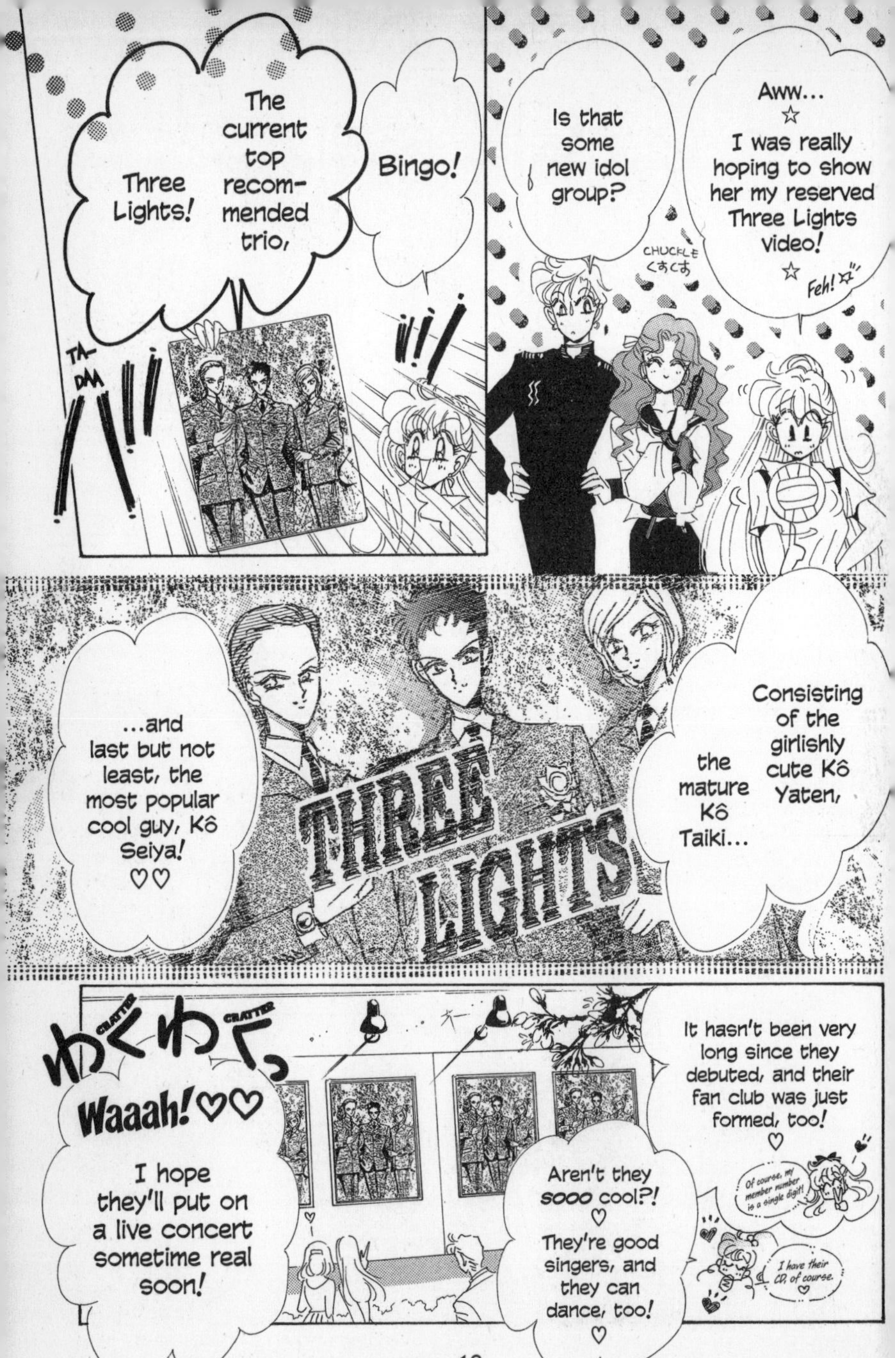
Aww... ☆ I was really hoping to show her my reserved Three Lights video! ☆
Feh!
CHUCKLE くすくす
Is that some new idol group?
Bingo!
The current top recommended trio,
Three Lights!
TA-DAA
Consisting of the girlishly cute Kô Yaten,
the mature Kô Taiki...
THREE LIGHTS
...and last but not least, the most popular cool guy, Kô Seiya! ♡♡
It hasn't been very long since they debuted, and their fan club was just formed, too! ♡
Of course, my member number is a single digit!
I have their CD, of course.
Aren't they sooo cool?! ♡ They're good singers, and they can dance, too! ♡
Waaah! ♡♡
I hope they'll put on a live concert sometime real soon!
わくわく
CHATTER CHATTER

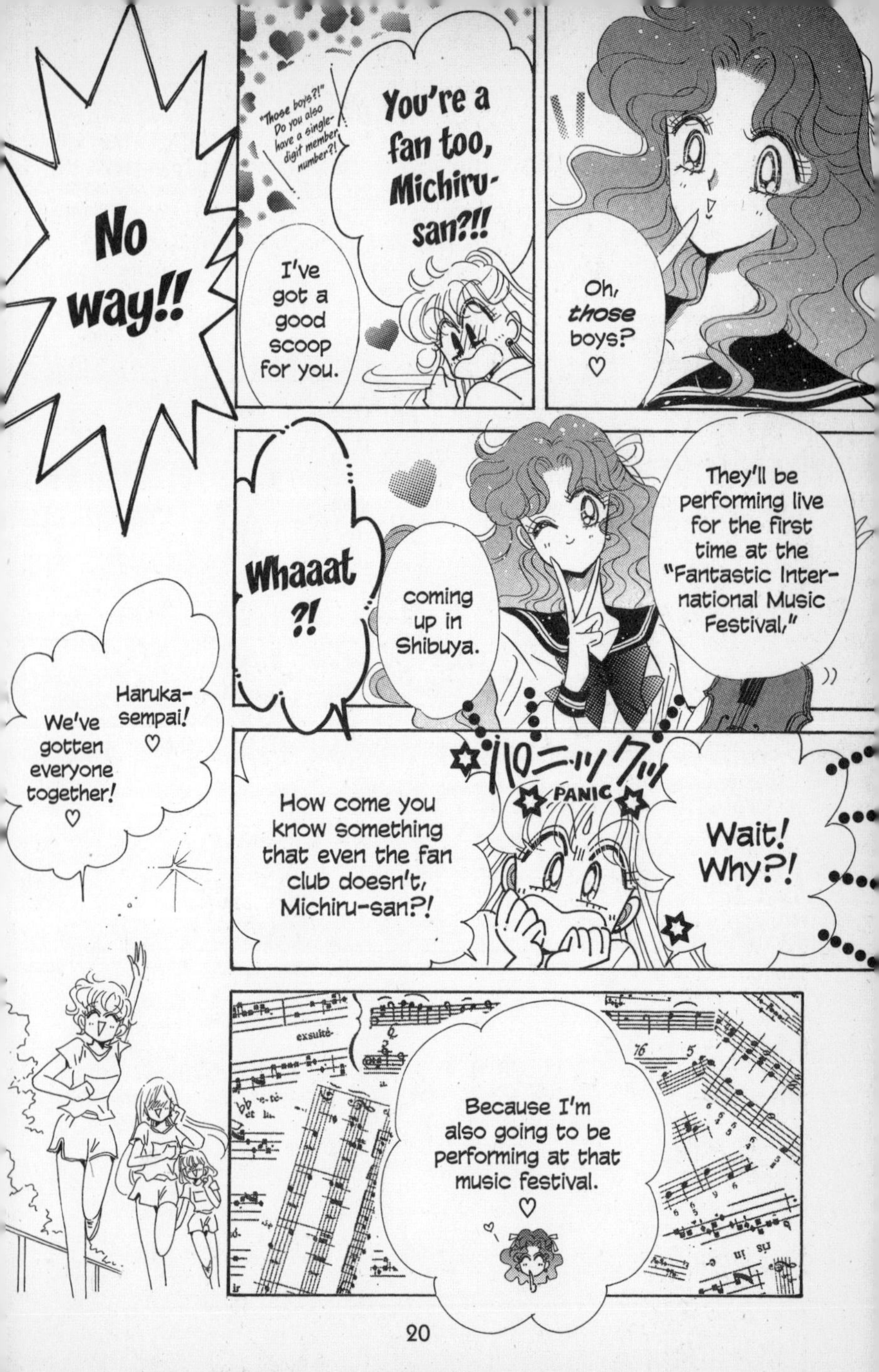
Oh, *those* boys? ♡
You're a fan too, Michiru-san?!!
"Those boys?!" Do you also have a single-digit member number?!
I've got a good scoop for you.
They'll be performing live for the first time at the "Fantastic International Music Festival,"
coming up in Shibuya.
Whaaat ?!
Wait! Why?!
パニックッ
PANIC
How come you know something that even the fan club doesn't, Michiru-san?!
Because I'm also going to be performing at that music festival. ♡
No way!!
Haruka-sempai! ♡
We've gotten everyone together! ♡

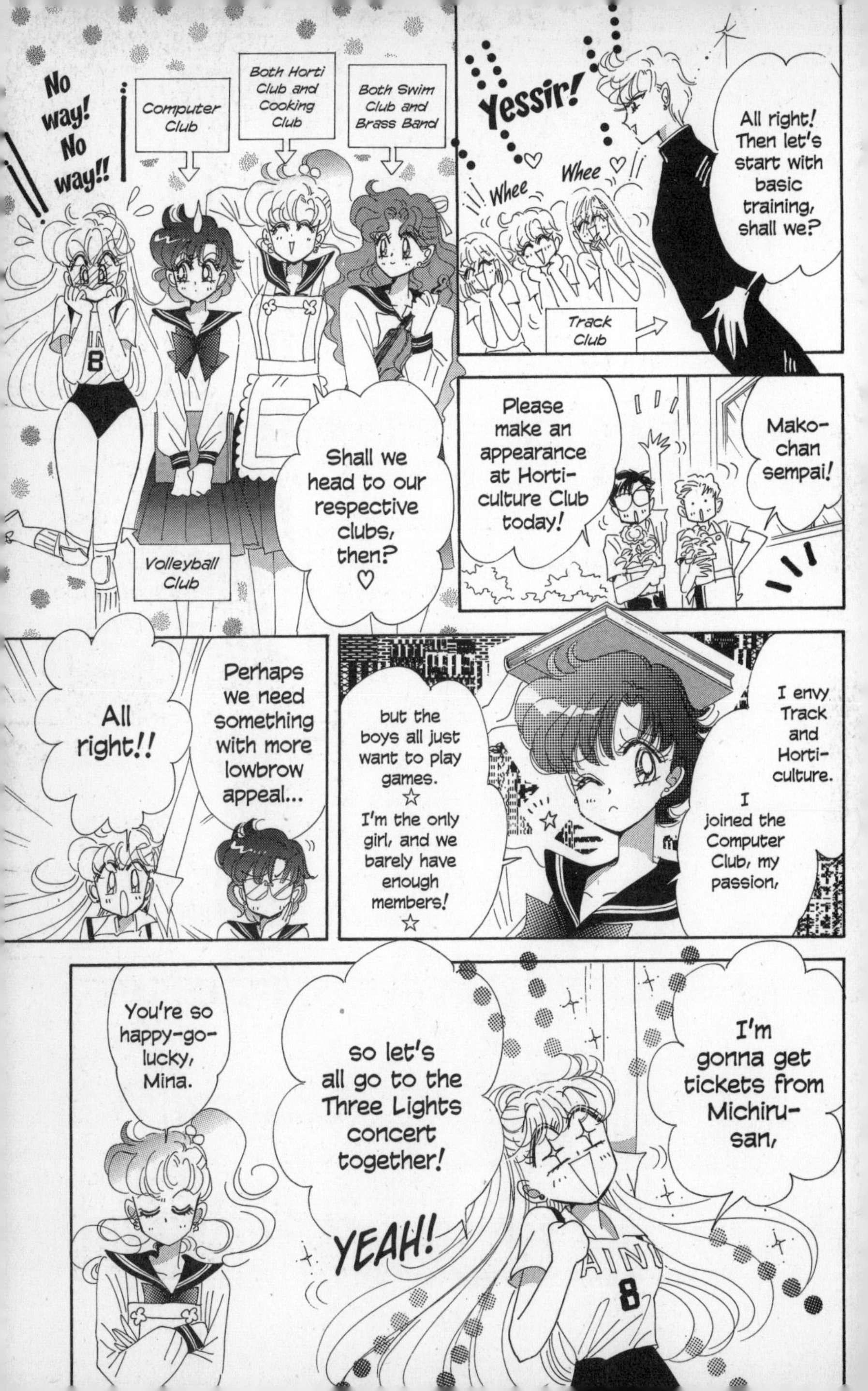
All right! Then let's start with basic training, shall we?
Yessir!
Whee ♡
Whee
Track Club
Mako-chan sempai!
Please make an appearance at Horticulture Club today!
Both Swim Club and Brass Band
Both Horti Club and Cooking Club
Computer Club
No way! No way!!
Shall we head to our respective clubs, then? ♡
Volleyball Club
I envy Track and Horticulture.
I joined the Computer Club, my passion,
but the boys all just want to play games. ☆ I'm the only girl, and we barely have enough members! ☆
Perhaps we need something with more lowbrow appeal...
All right!!
I'm gonna get tickets from Michiru-san,
so let's all go to the Three Lights concert together!
YEAH!
You're so happy-go-lucky, Mina.

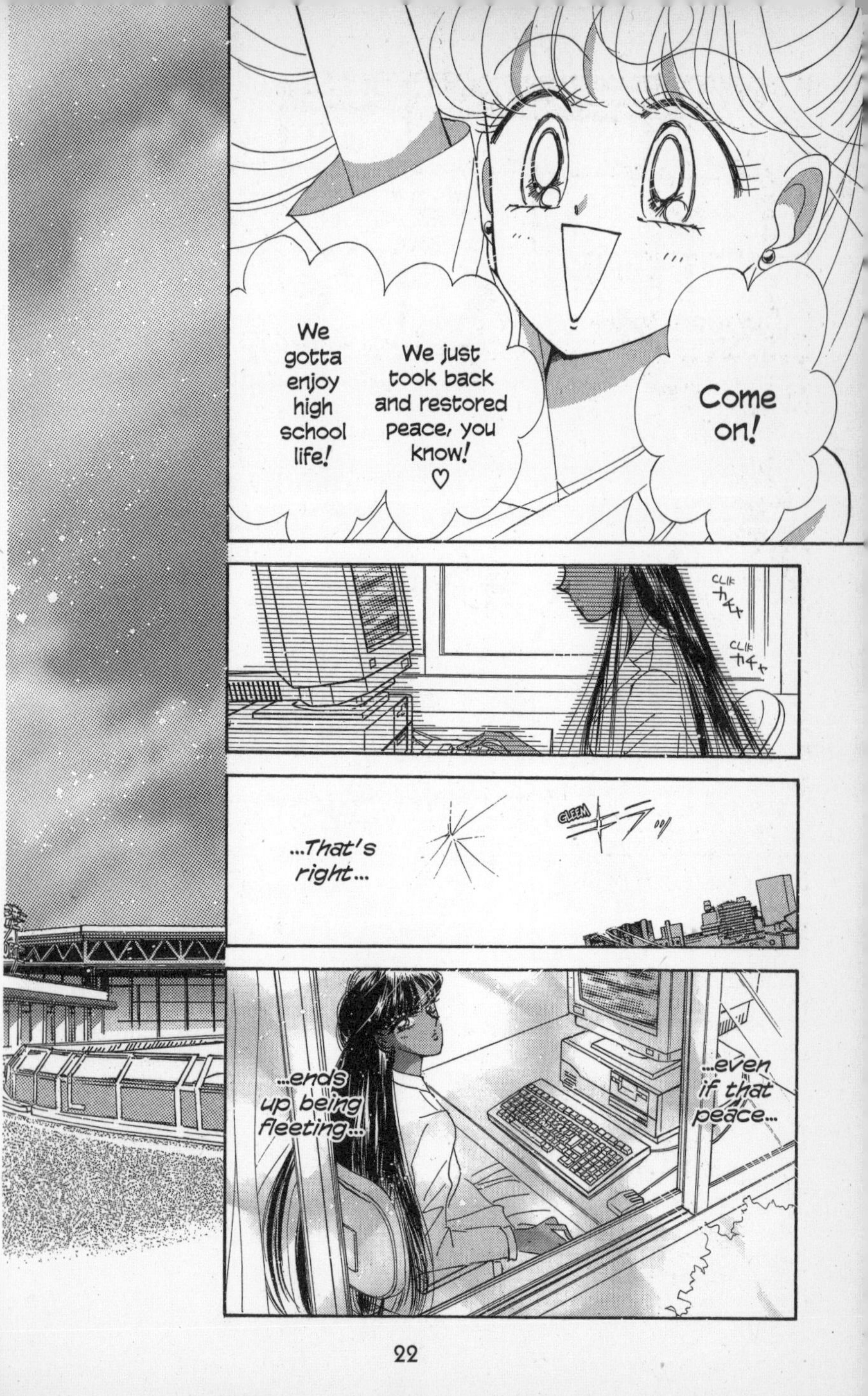
Come on!
We just took back and restored peace, you know! ♡
We gotta enjoy high school life!
CLIK
CLIK
GLEEM
...That's right...
...even if that peace...
...ends up being fleeting...

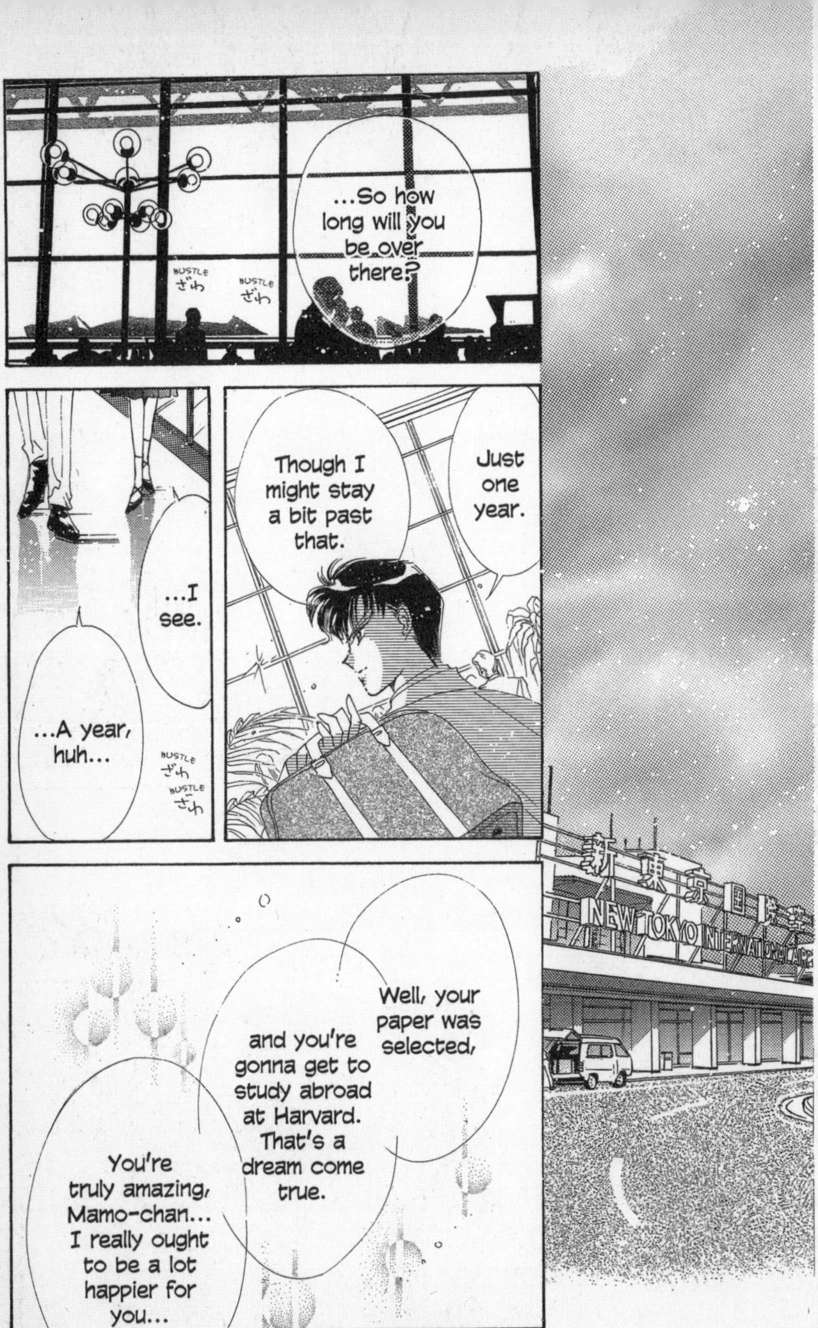
新東京国際空
NEW TOKYO INTERNATIONAL AIRP
...So how long will you be over there?
BUSTLE ざわ
BUSTLE ざわ
Just one year.
Though I might stay a bit past that.
...I see.
BUSTLE ざわ
BUSTLE ざわ
...A year, huh...
Well, your paper was selected,
and you're gonna get to study abroad at Harvard. That's a dream come true.
You're truly amazing, Mamo-chan... I really ought to be a lot happier for you...

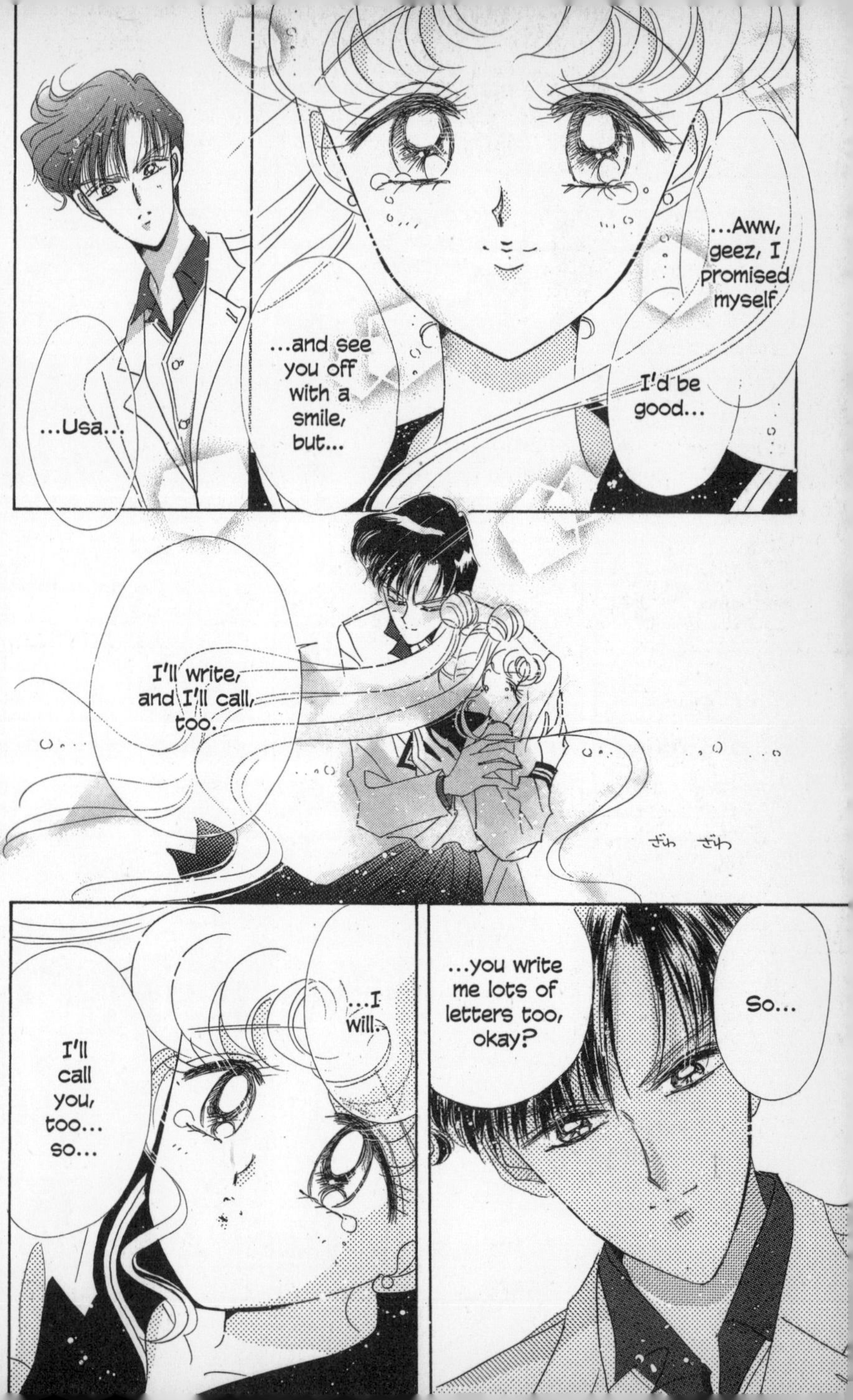
...Aww, geez, I promised myself
I'd be good...
...and see you off with a smile, but...
...Usa...
I'll write, and I'll call, too.
ざわ ざわ
So...
...you write me lots of letters too, okay?
...I will.
I'll call you, too... so...

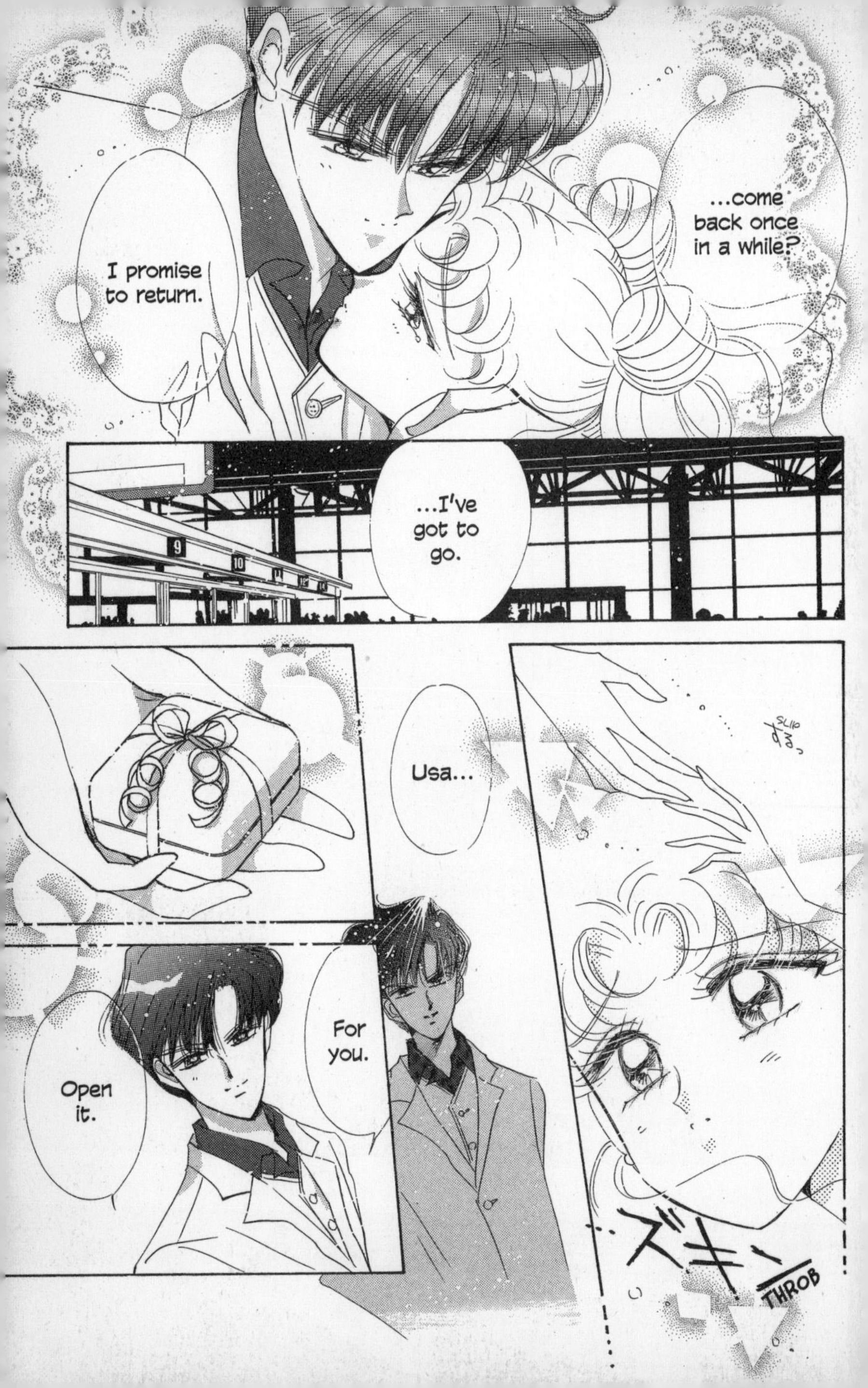
...come back once in a while?
I promise to return.
...I've got to go.
Usa...
SLIP
THROB
For you.
Open it.

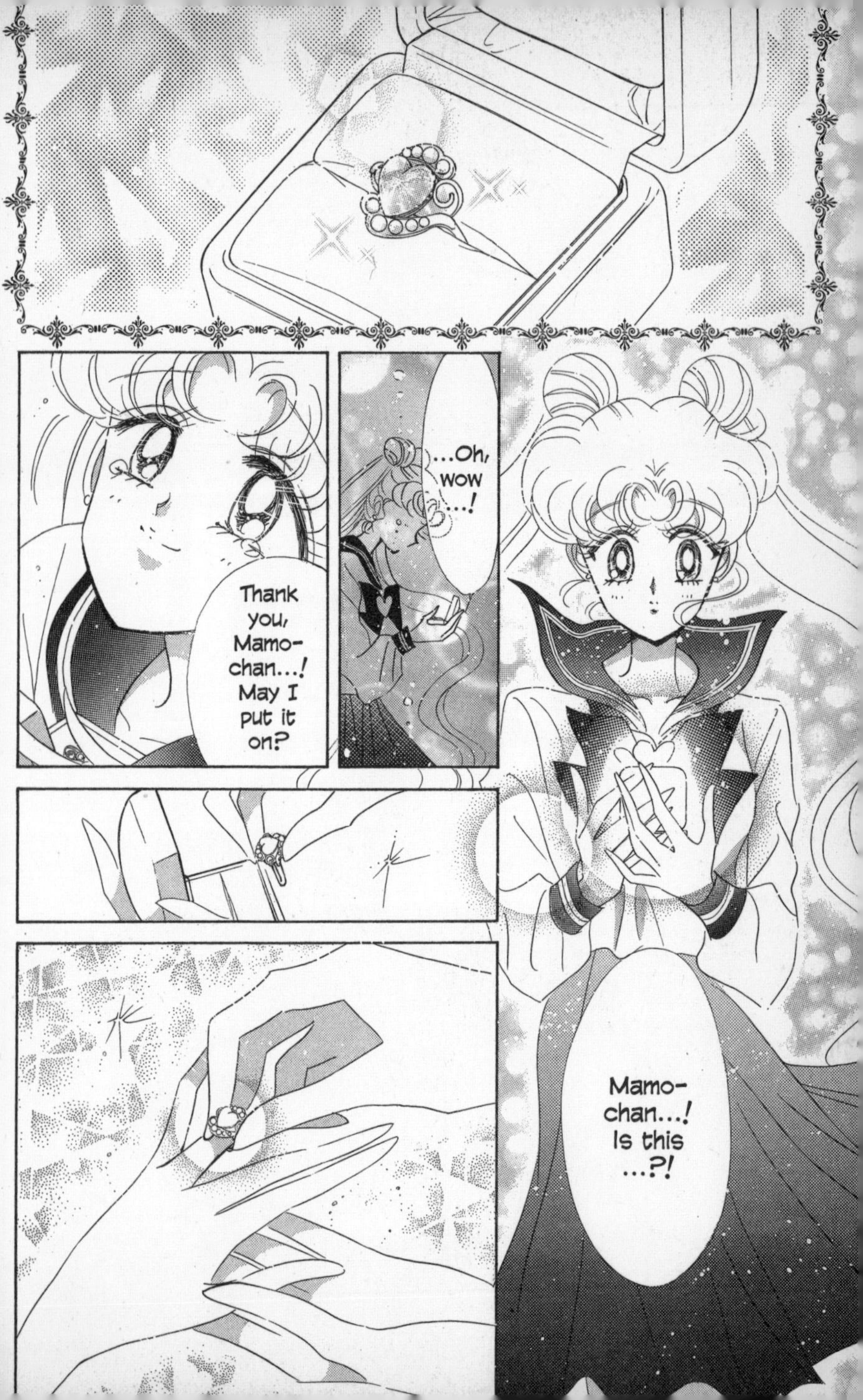
Mamo-chan...! Is this ...?!
...Oh, wow ...!
Thank you, Mamo-chan...! May I put it on?

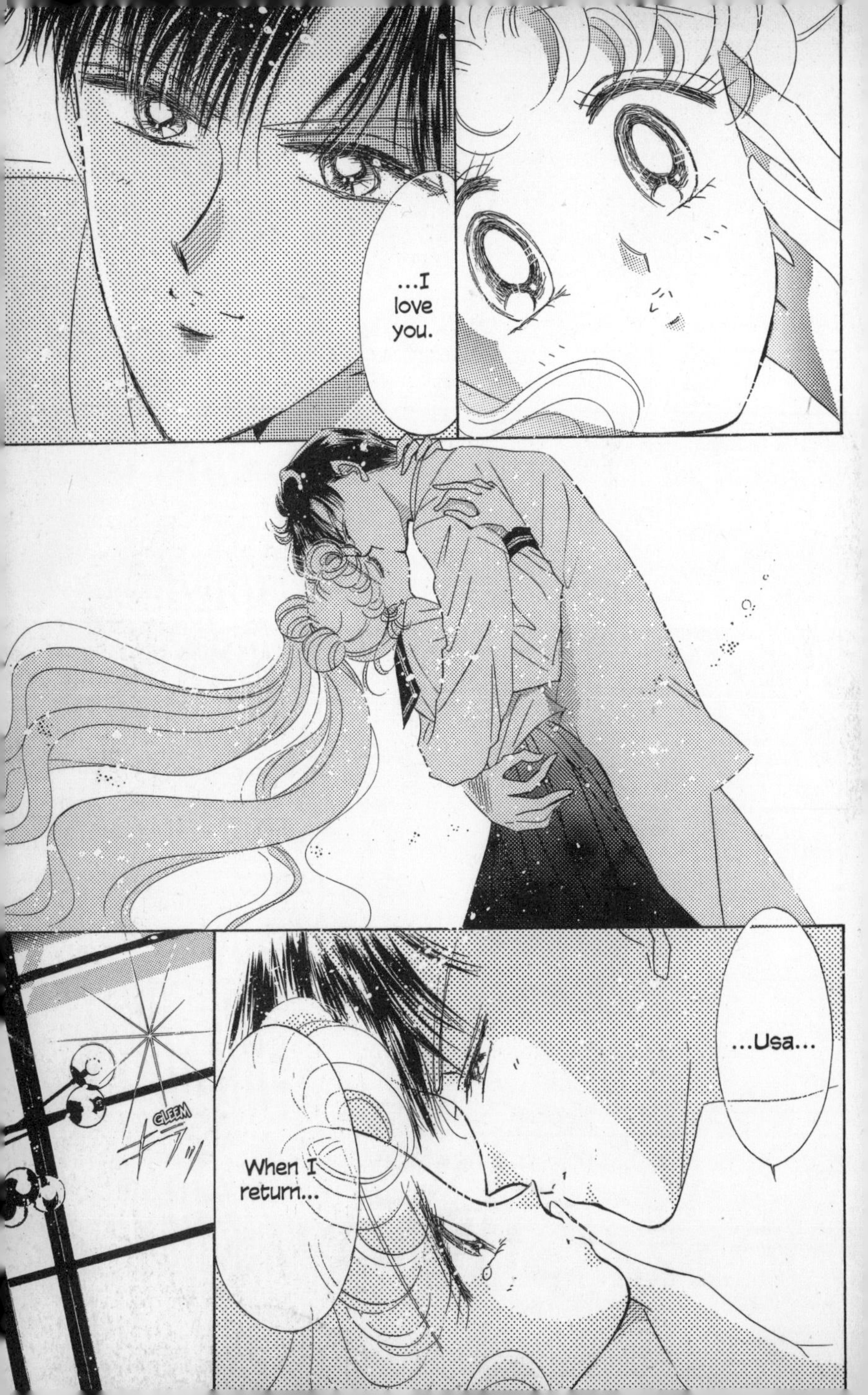
...I love you.
...Usa...
When I return...
GLEEM

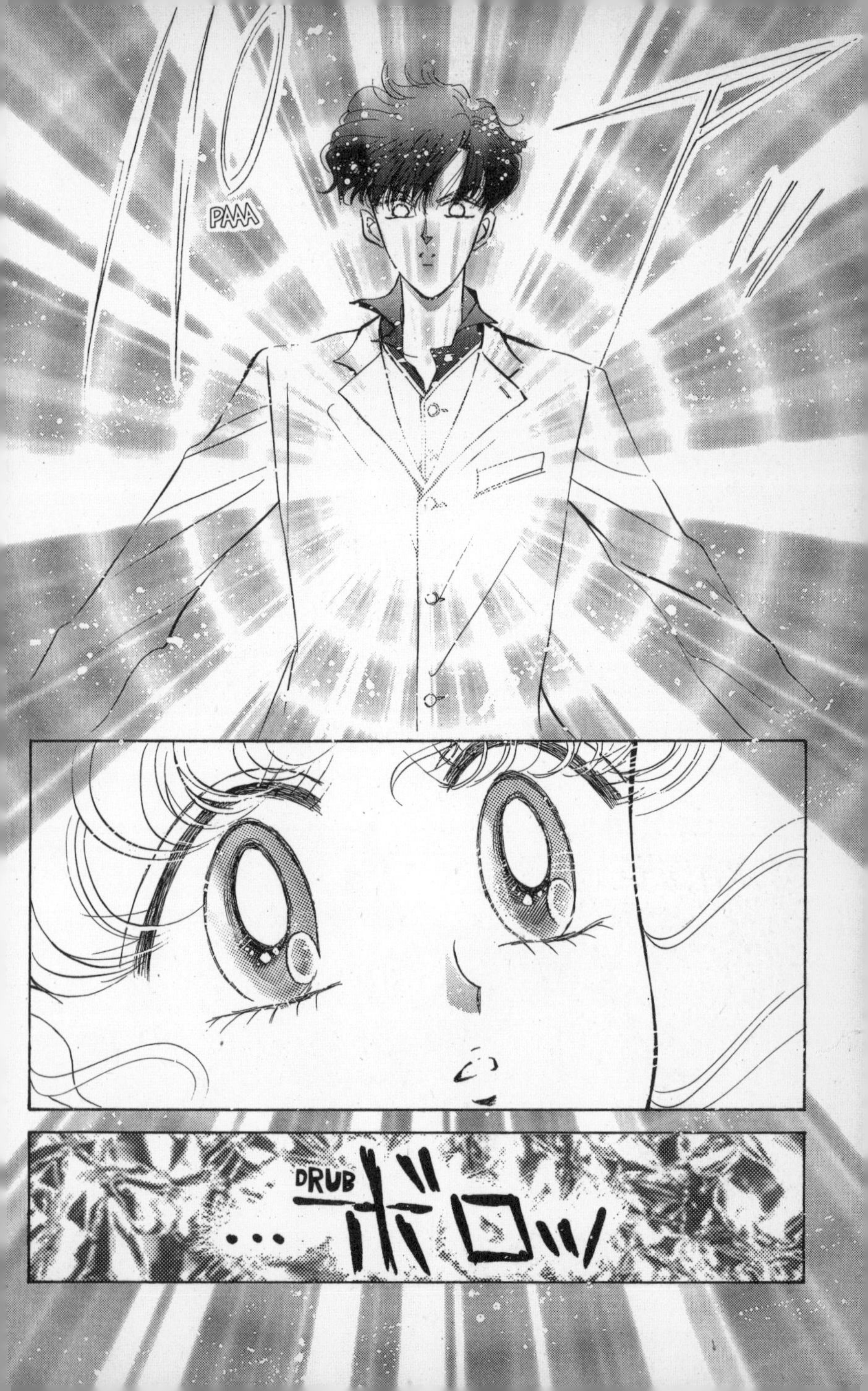
PAAA
DRUB
...ボロッ

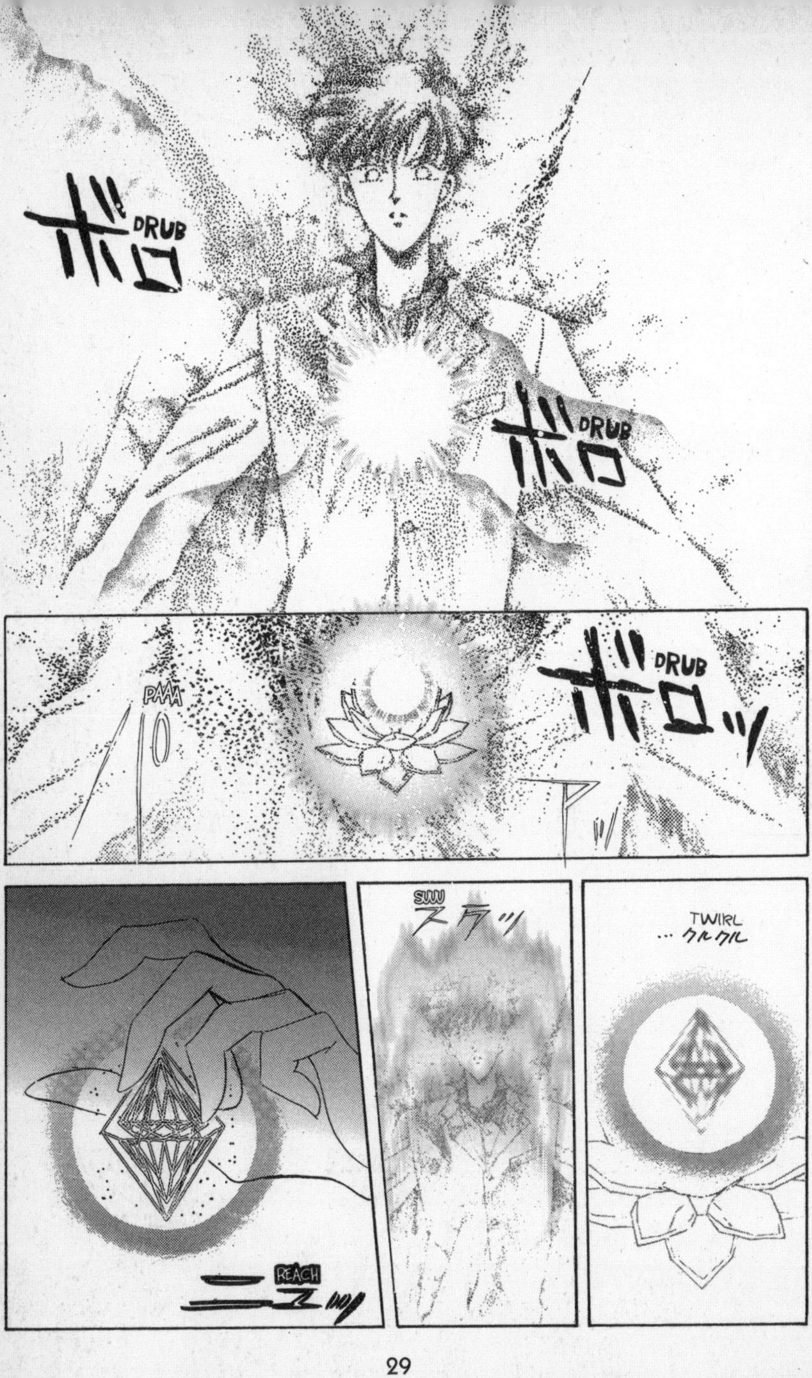

DRUB
ボロ
DRUB
ボロ
DRUB
ボロッ
アッ
PAAA
パ
TWIRL
…クルクル
SWW
スラッ
REACH
ニュッ

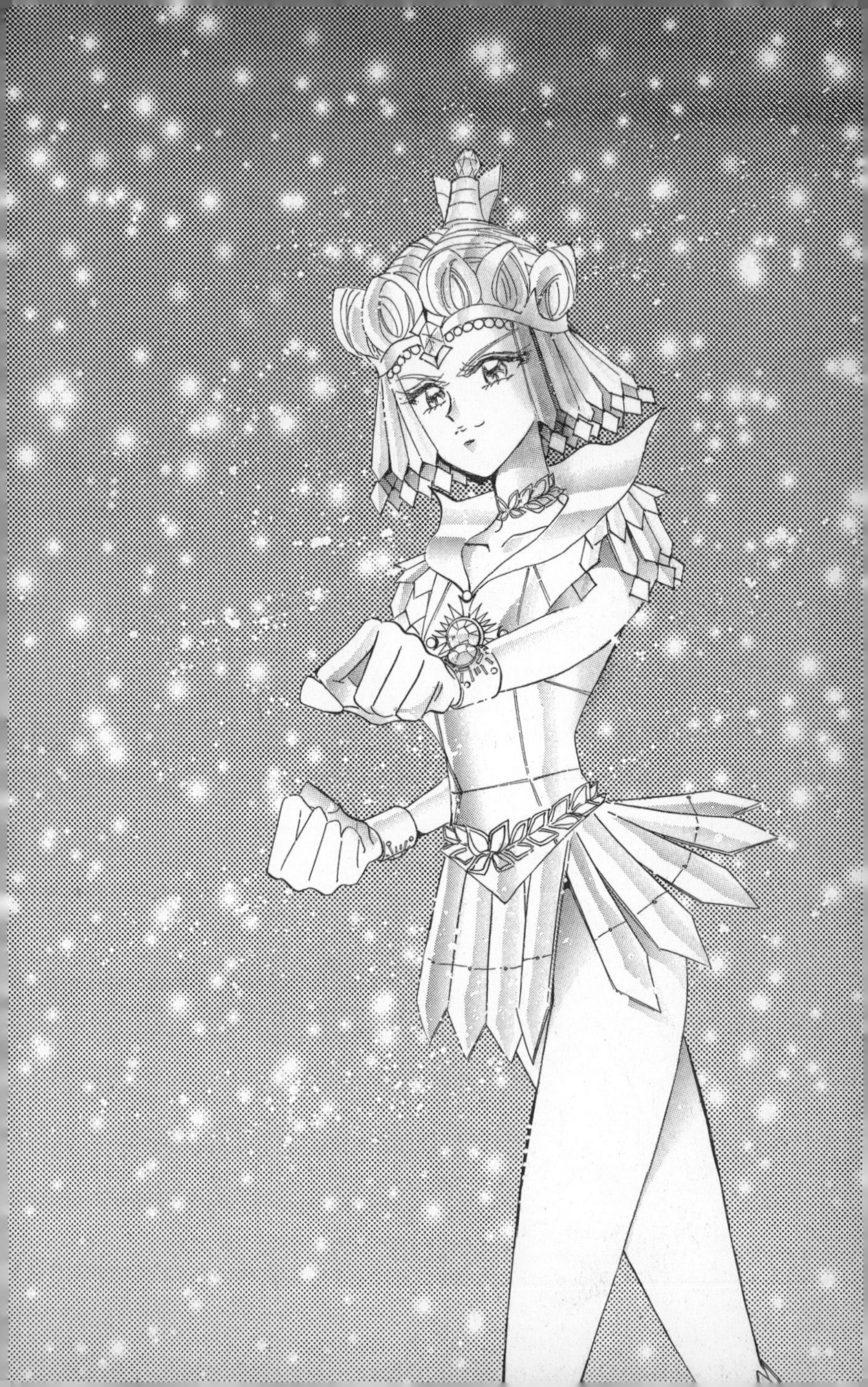

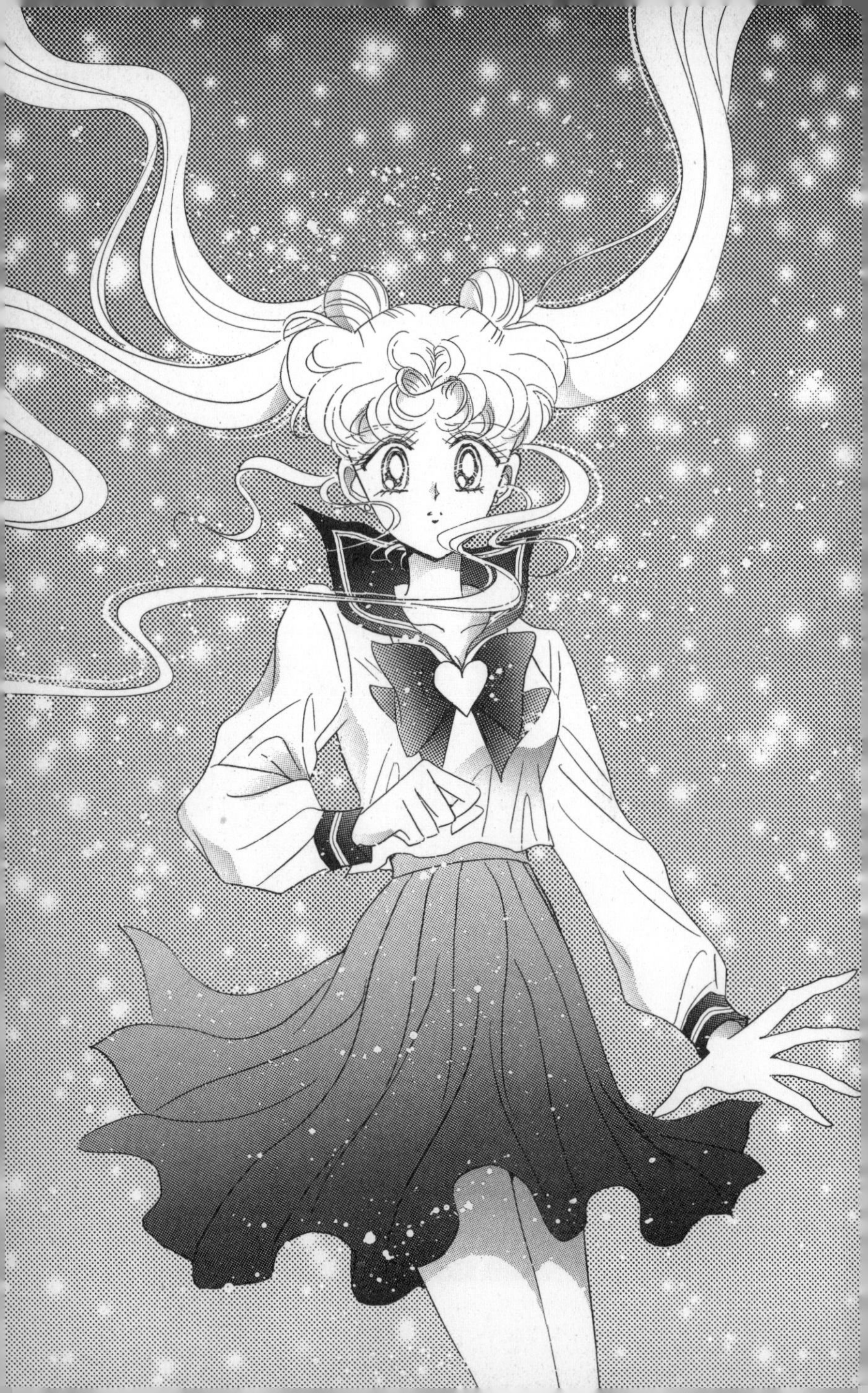

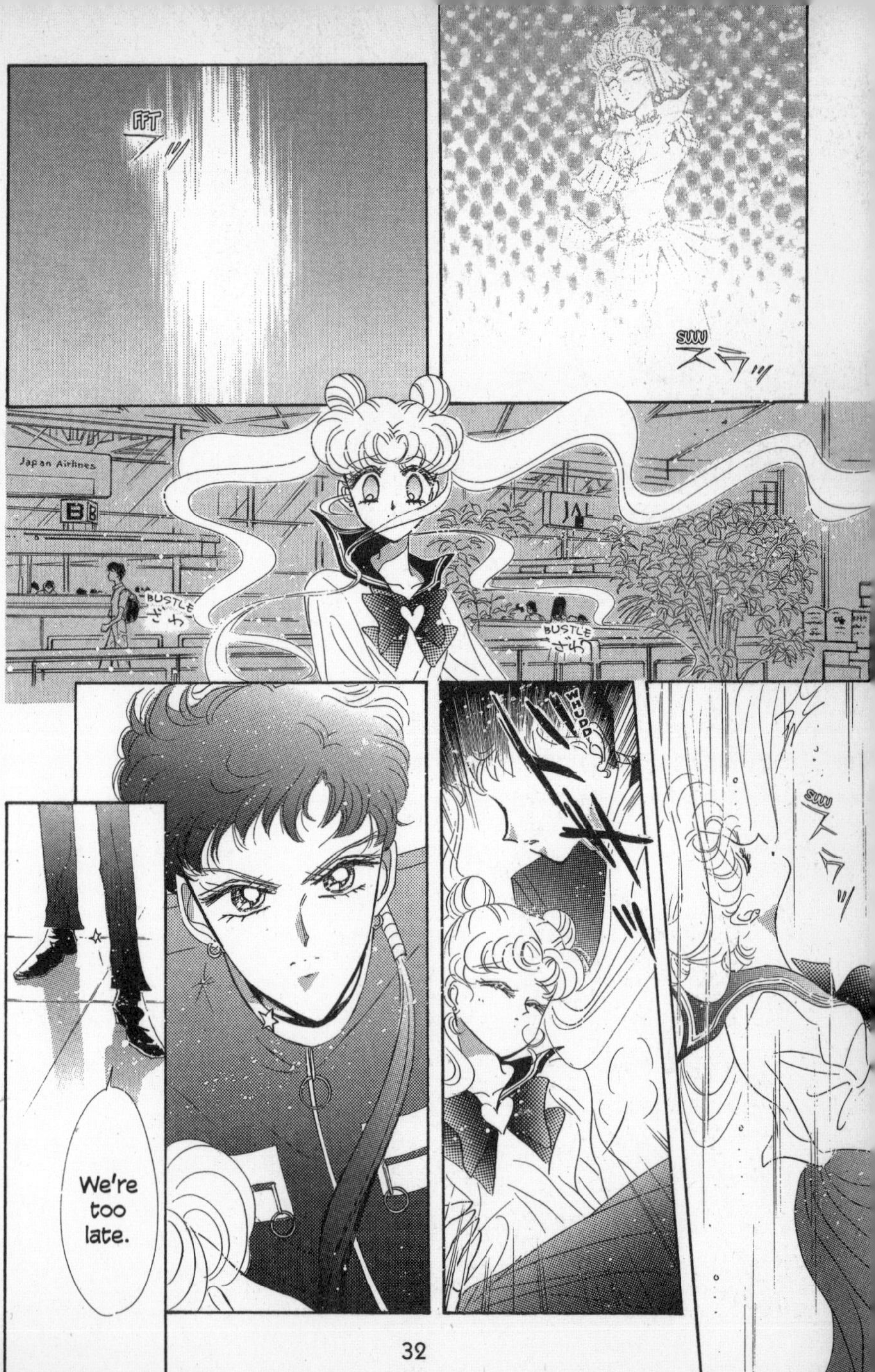
SUW
スラッ
FFT
ブッ
JAL
BUSTLE
ざわ
B
Japan Airlines
BUSTLE
ざわ
SUW
スラッ
WHUDD
We're too late.

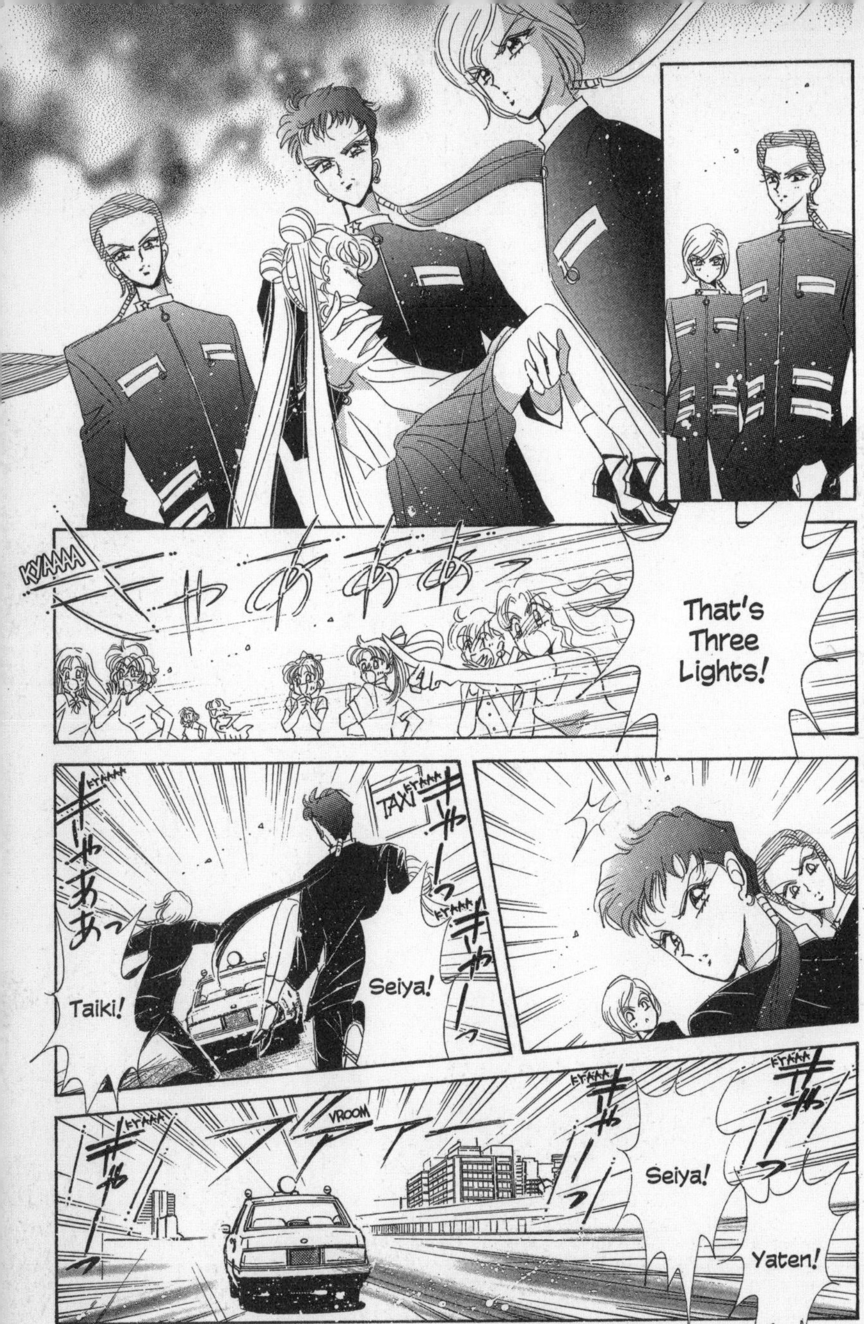
That's Three Lights!
KYAAAA
TAXI
KYAAA
KYAAA
Seiya!
KYAAA
Taiki!
KYAAA
KYAAA
Seiya!
Yaten!
VROOM
KYAAA

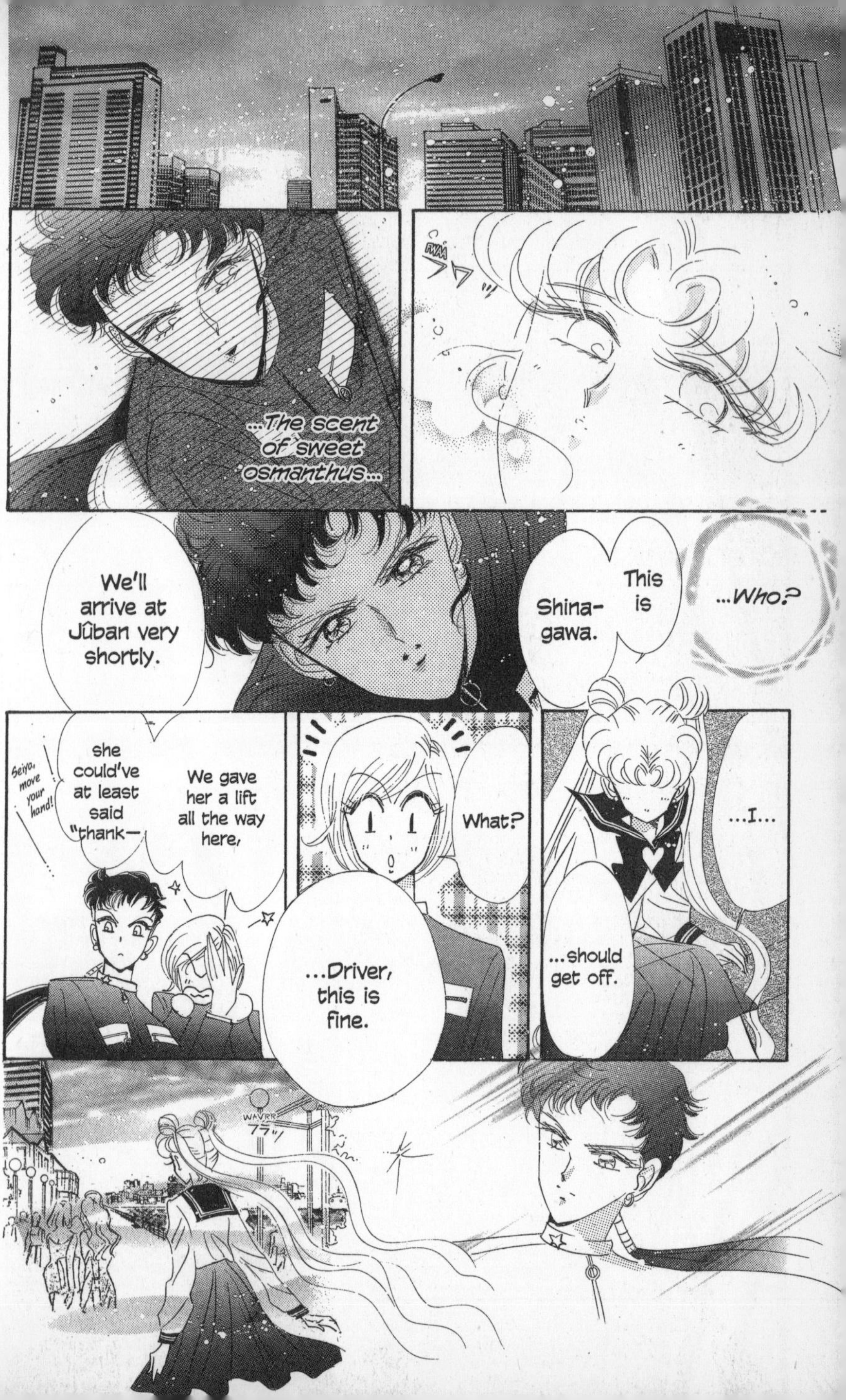
FWAA
...The scent of sweet osmanthus...
...Who?
This is Shina-gawa.
We'll arrive at Jûban very shortly.
...I...
...should get off.
What?
...Driver, this is fine.
We gave her a lift all the way here,
she could've at least said "thank—
Seiya, move your hand!!
WAVRR

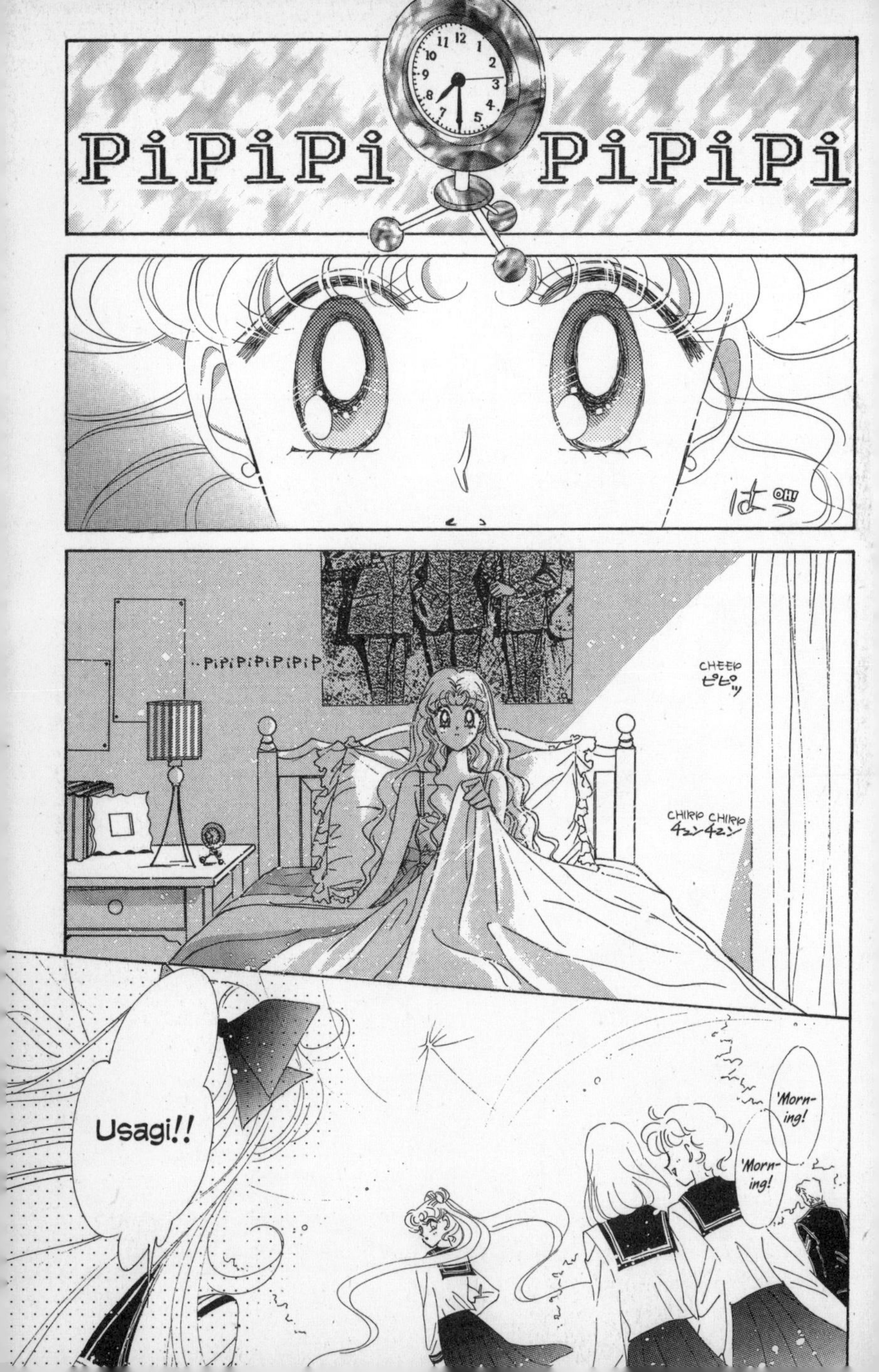
PiPiPi PiPiPi
はっ
OH!
CHEEP
ピピッ
CHIRP CHIRP
チュンチュン
..PiPiPiPiPiPiP
'Morning!
'Morning!
Usagi!!

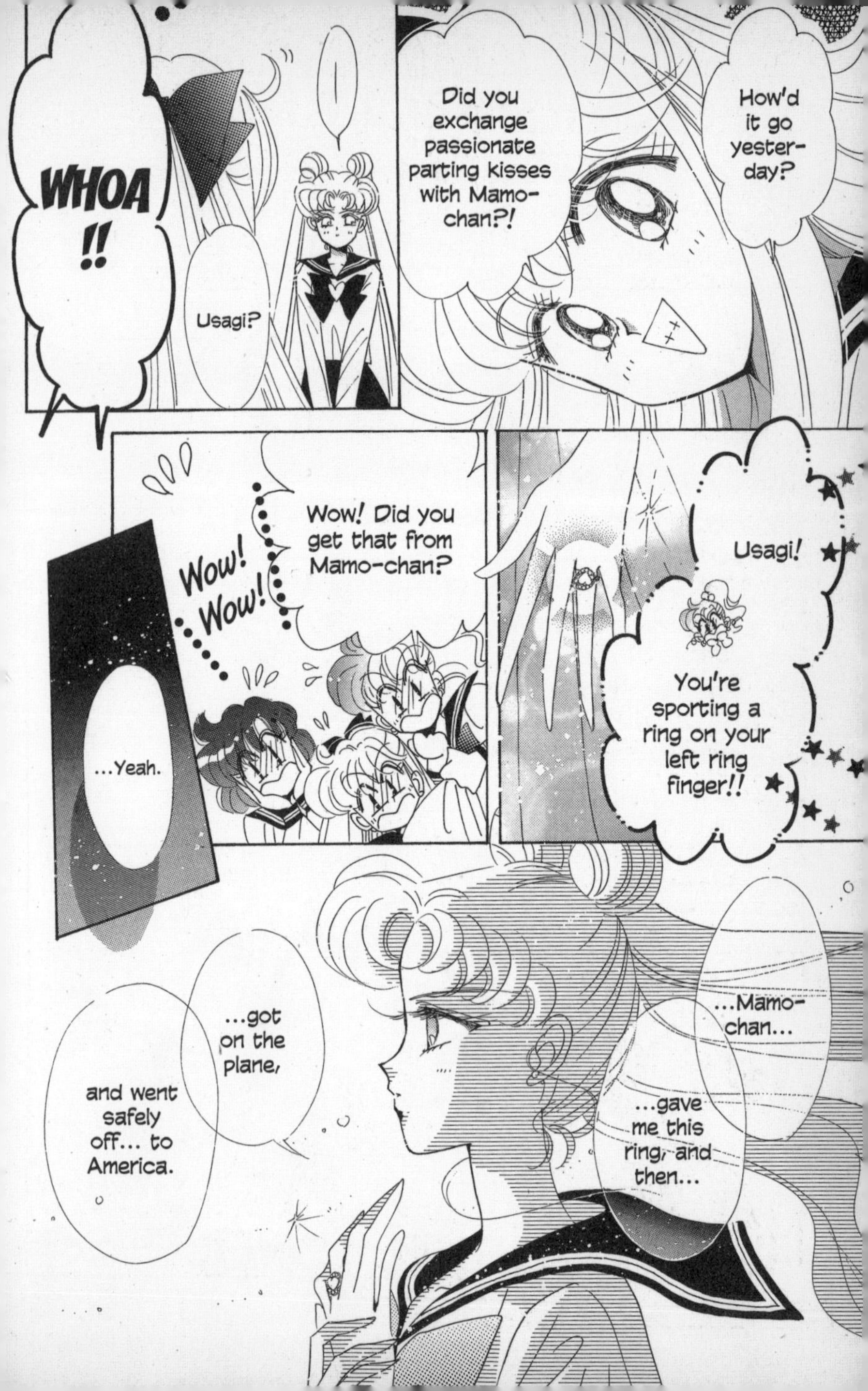
How'd it go yesterday?
Did you exchange passionate parting kisses with Mamo-chan?!
Usagi?
WHOA!!
Usagi!
You're sporting a ring on your left ring finger!!
Wow! Did you get that from Mamo-chan?
Wow! Wow!
...Yeah.
...Mamo-chan...
...gave me this ring, and then...
...got on the plane,
and went safely off... to America.

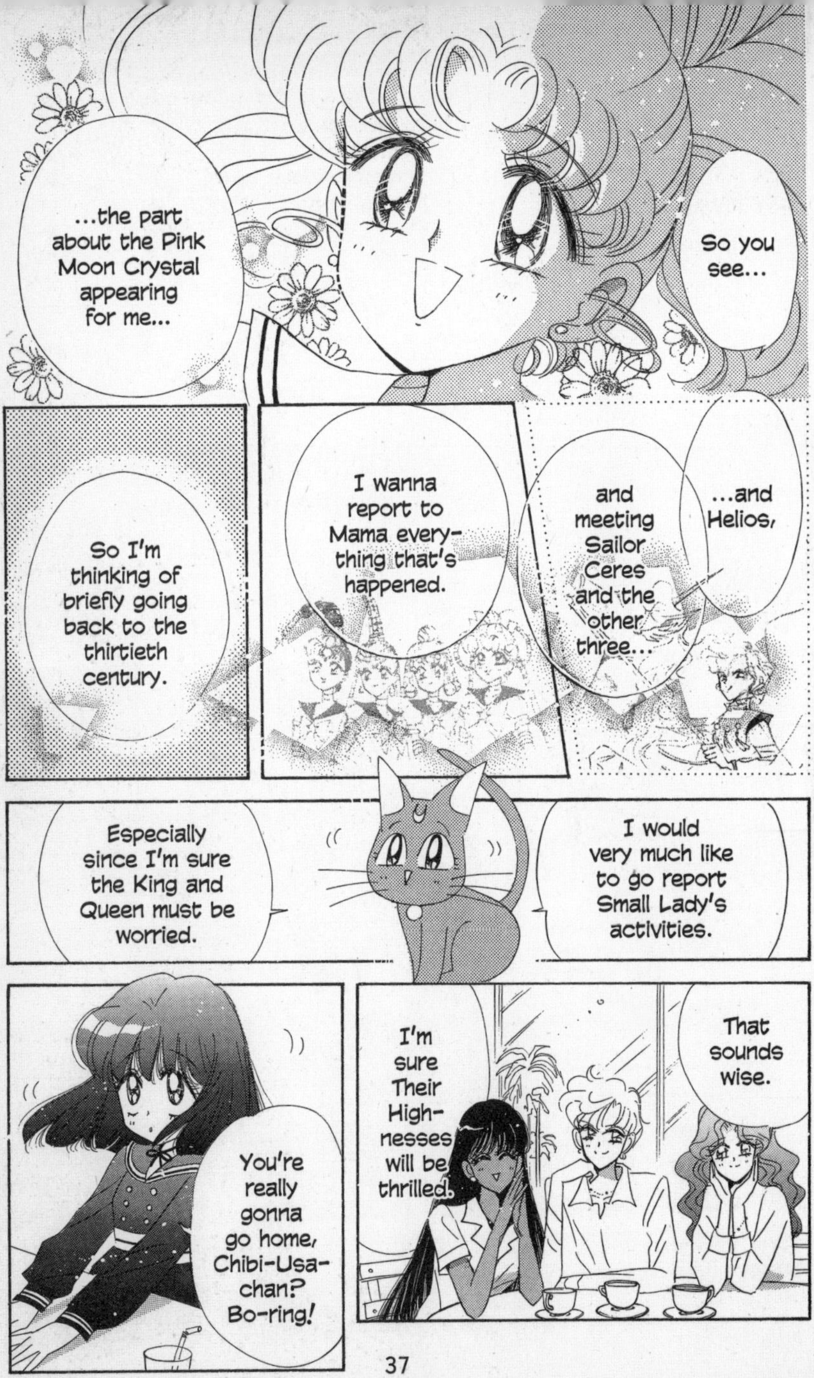
So you see...
...the part about the Pink Moon Crystal appearing for me...
...and Helios,
and meeting Sailor Ceres and the other three...
I wanna report to Mama everything that's happened.
So I'm thinking of briefly going back to the thirtieth century.
I would very much like to go report Small Lady's activities.
Especially since I'm sure the King and Queen must be worried.
That sounds wise.
I'm sure Their Highnesses will be thrilled.
You're really gonna go home, Chibi-Usa-chan? Bo-ring!

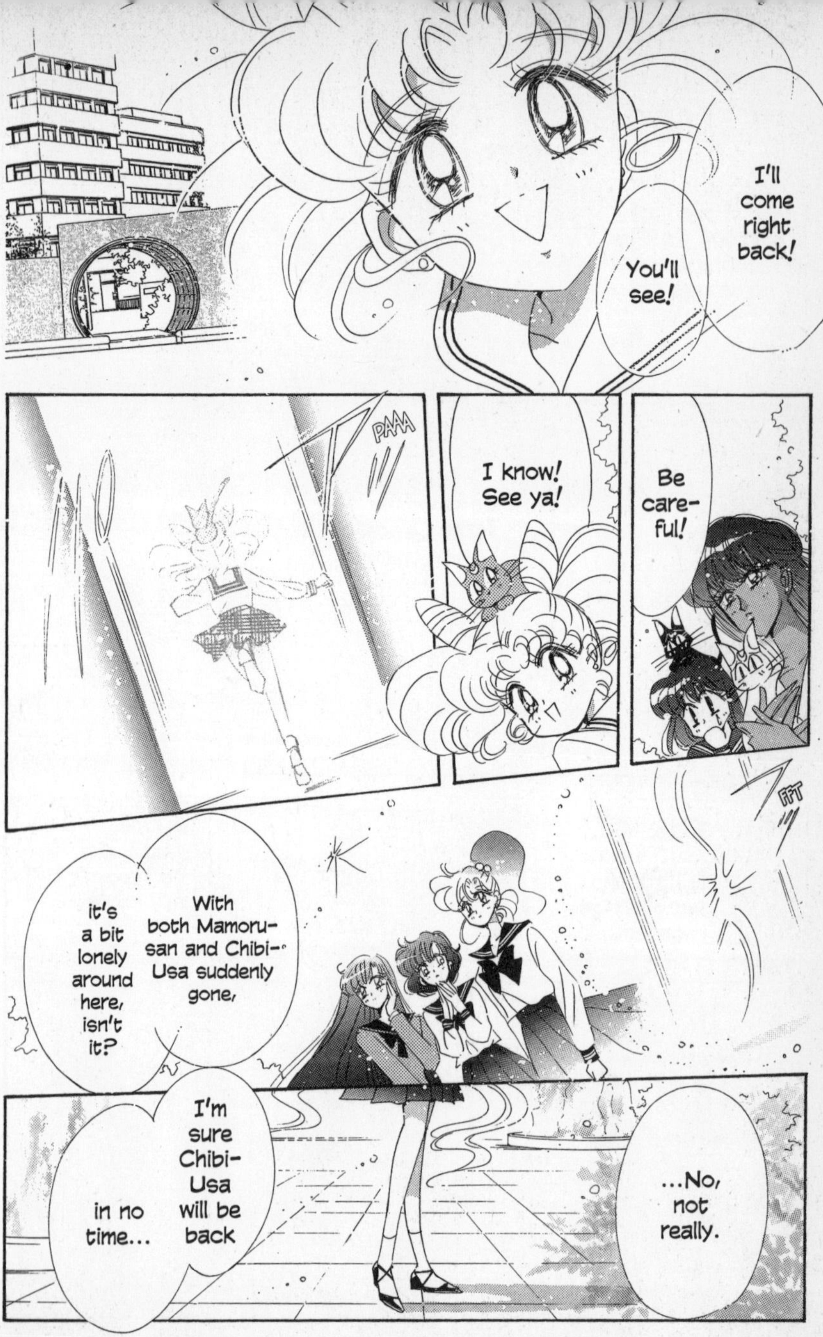
I'll come right back!
You'll see!
Be care-ful!
I know! See ya!
PAAA
FFT
With both Mamoru-san and Chibi-Usa suddenly gone,
it's a bit lonely around here, isn't it?
...No, not really.
I'm sure Chibi-Usa will be back
in no time...

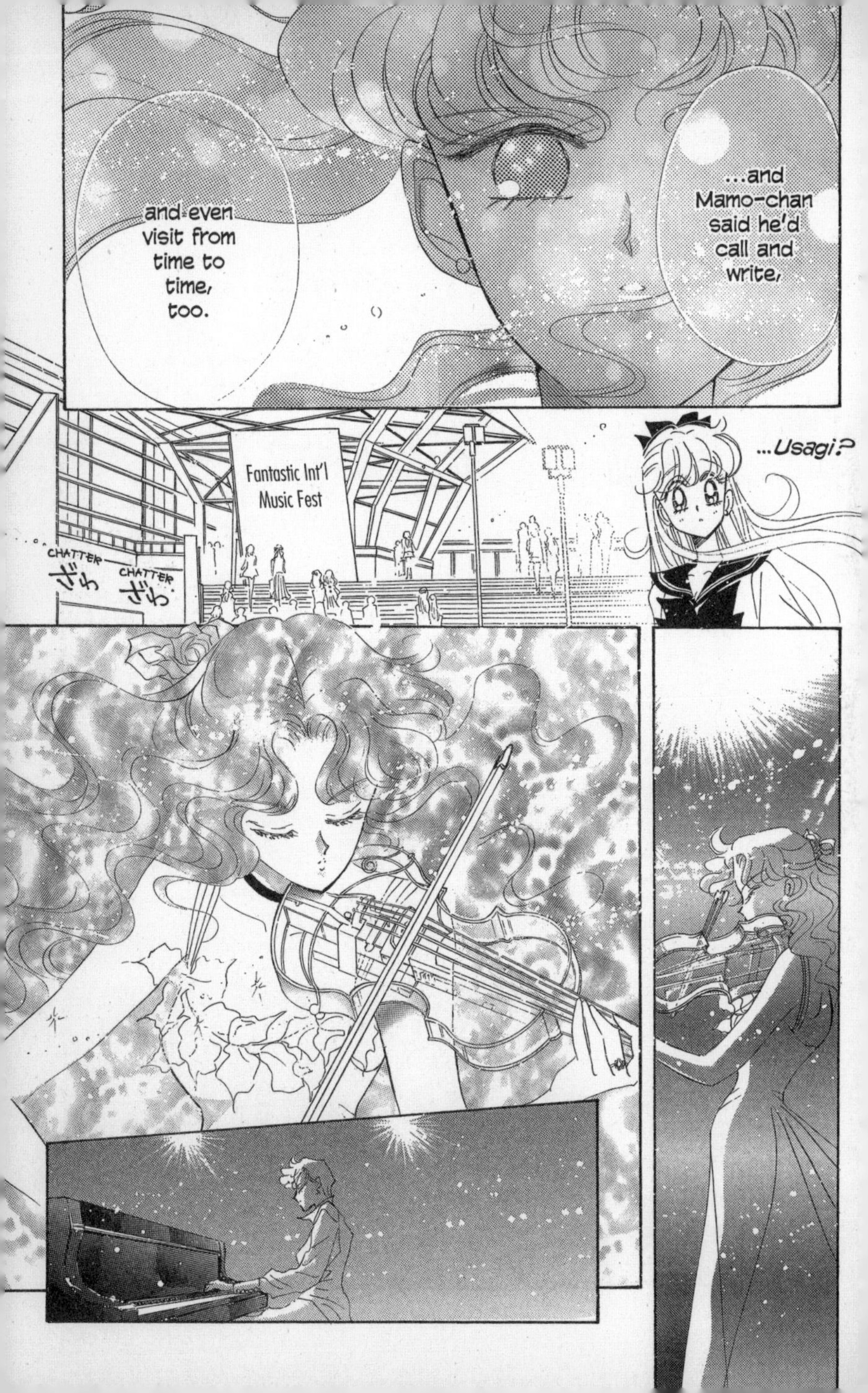
...and Mamo-chan said he'd call and write,
and even visit from time to time, too.
...Usagi?
Fantastic Int'l Music Fest
CHATTER
ざわ
CHATTER
ざわ

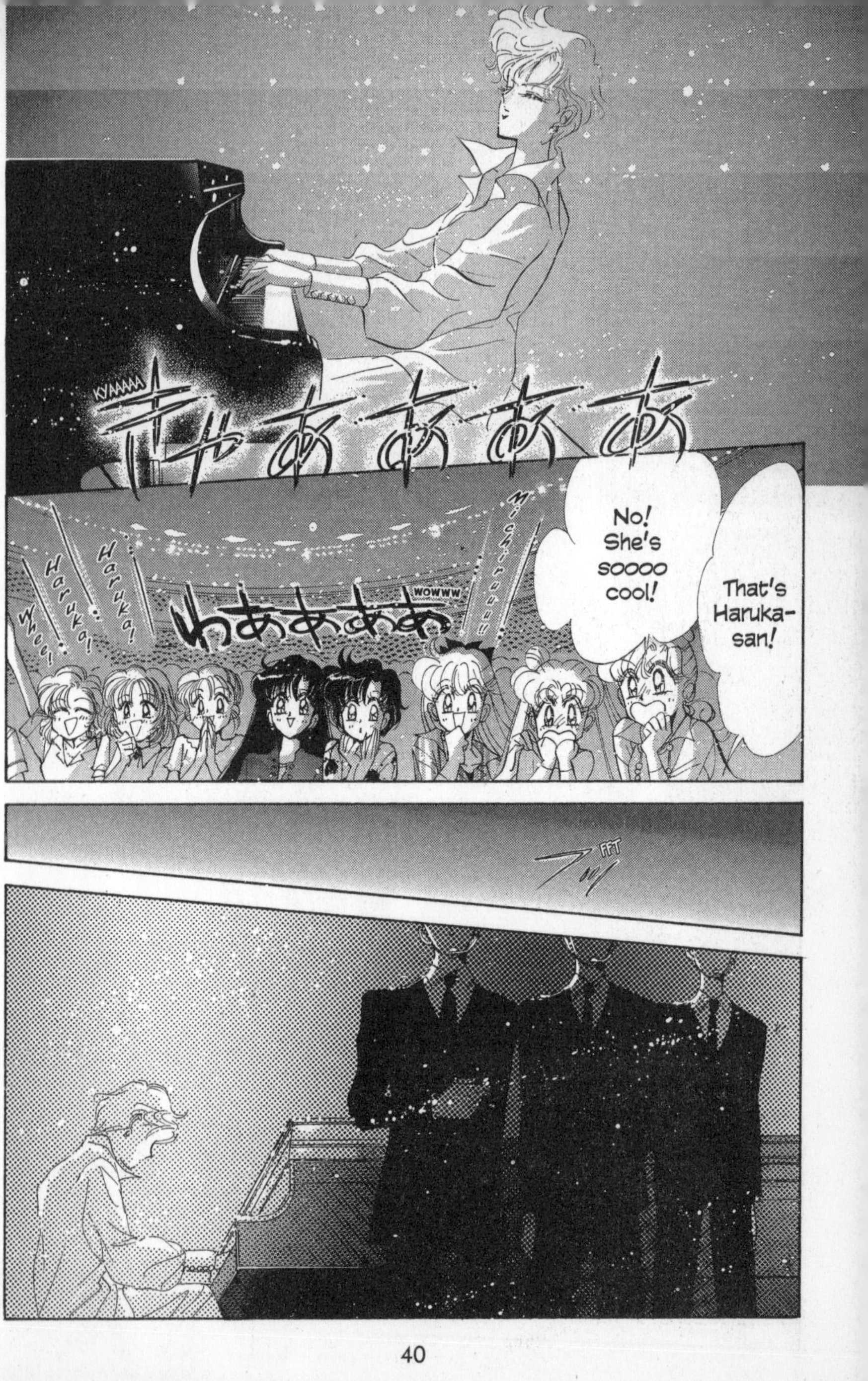
KYAAAAA
That's Haruka-san!
No! She's soooo cool!
Michiruuuu!!
WOWWW
Haruka!
Haruka!
Wheee!
FFT

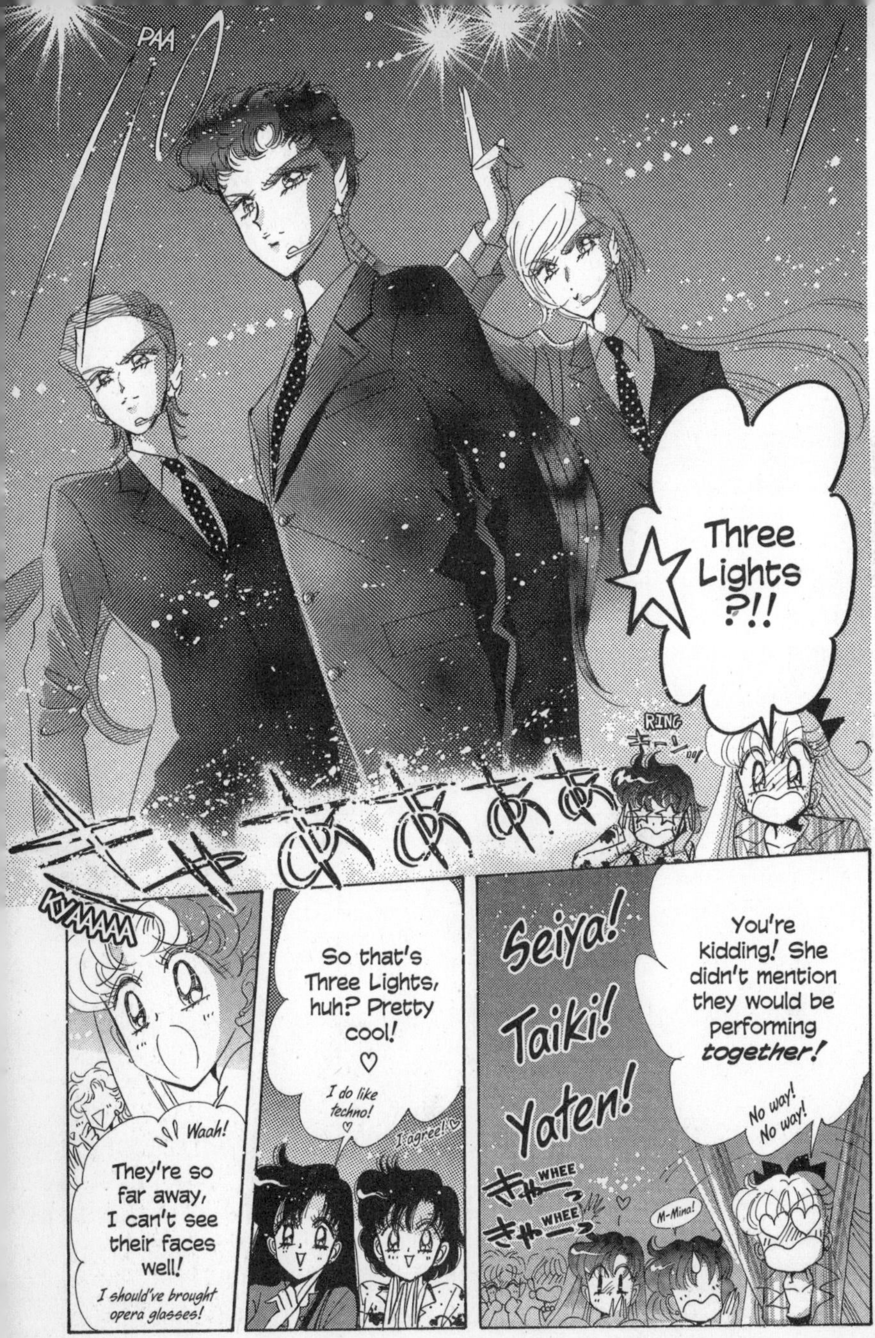
PAA
Three Lights ?!!
RING
KYAAAAA
Seiya!
Taiki!
Yaten!
You're kidding! She didn't mention they would be performing ***together!***
No way! No way!
WHEE
WHEE
M-Mina!
So that's Three Lights, huh? Pretty cool! ♡
I do like techno! ♡
I agree! ♡
Waah!
They're so far away, I can't see their faces well!
I should've brought opera glasses!

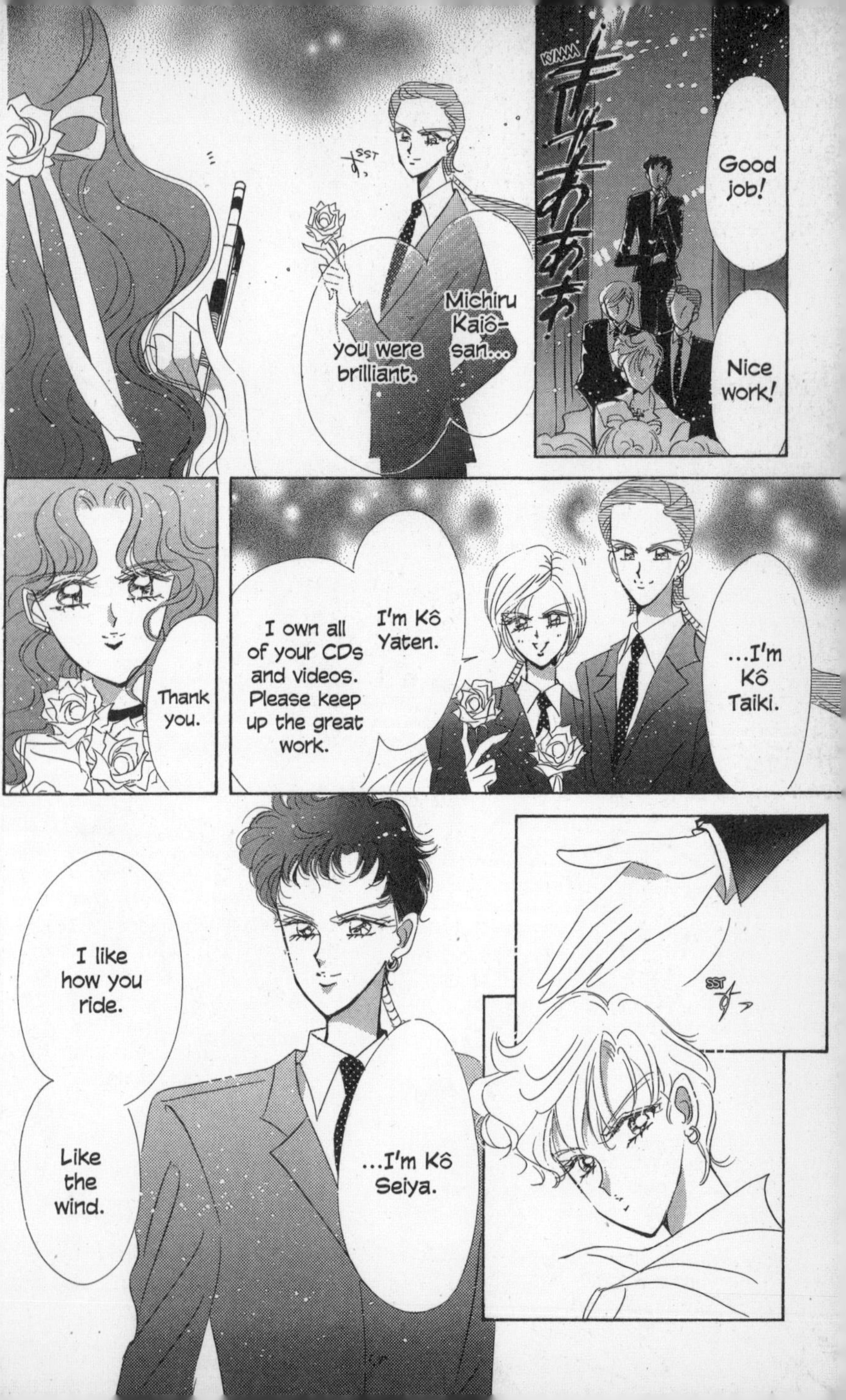
KYAAA
Good job!
Nice work!
Michiru Kaiô-san...
you were brilliant.
SST
...I'm Kô Taiki.
I'm Kô Yaten.
I own all of your CDs and videos. Please keep up the great work.
Thank you.
SST
...I'm Kô Seiya.
I like how you ride.
Like the wind.

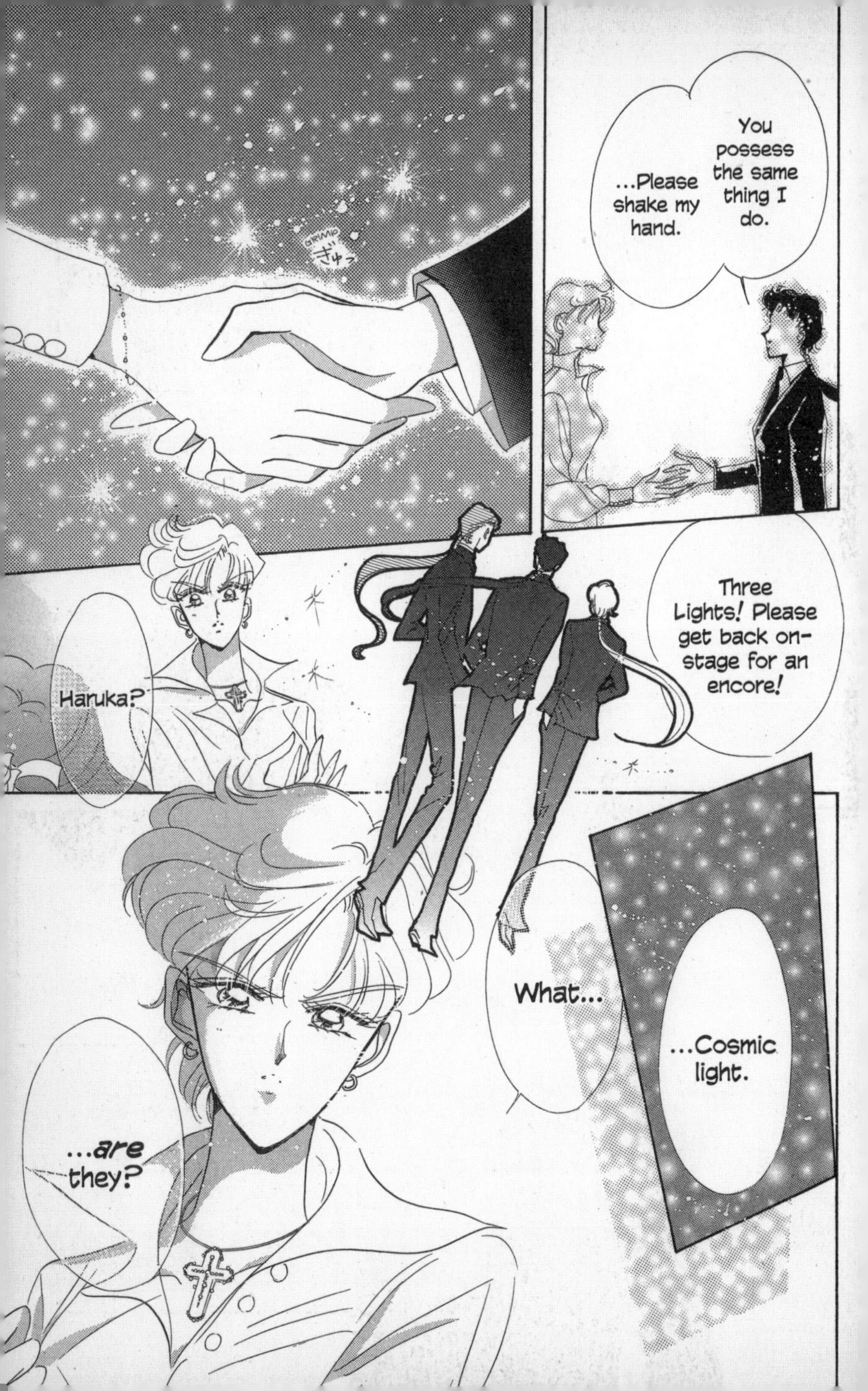
You possess the same thing I do.
...Please shake my hand.
GRIMP
ぎゅっ
Three Lights! Please get back on-stage for an encore!
Haruka?
...Cosmic light.
What...
...are they?

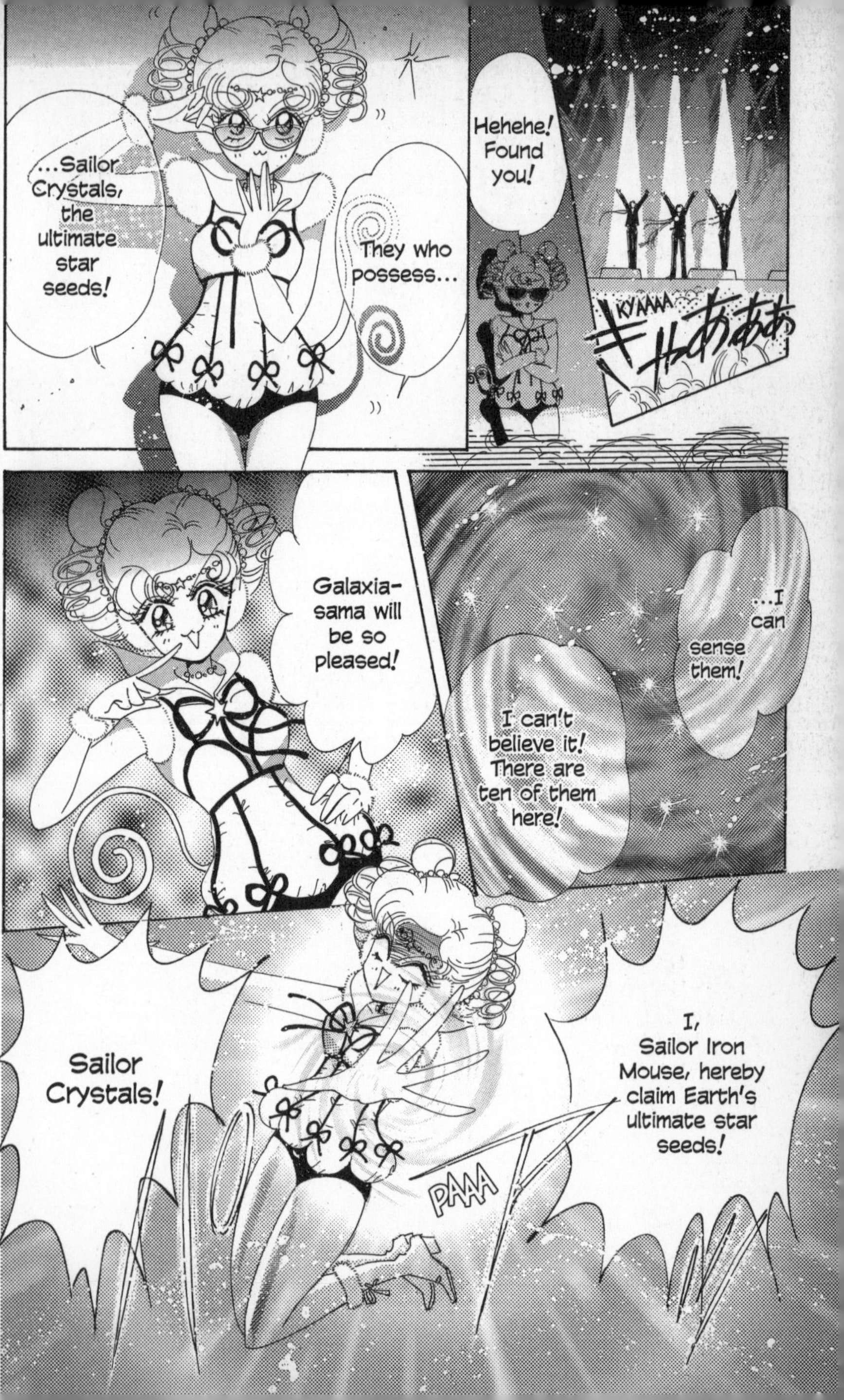
Hehehe! Found you!
KYAAAA
They who possess...
...Sailor Crystals, the ultimate star seeds!
...I can sense them!
I can't believe it! There are ten of them here!
Galaxia-sama will be so pleased!
I, Sailor Iron Mouse, hereby claim Earth's ultimate star seeds!
PAAA
Sailor Crystals!

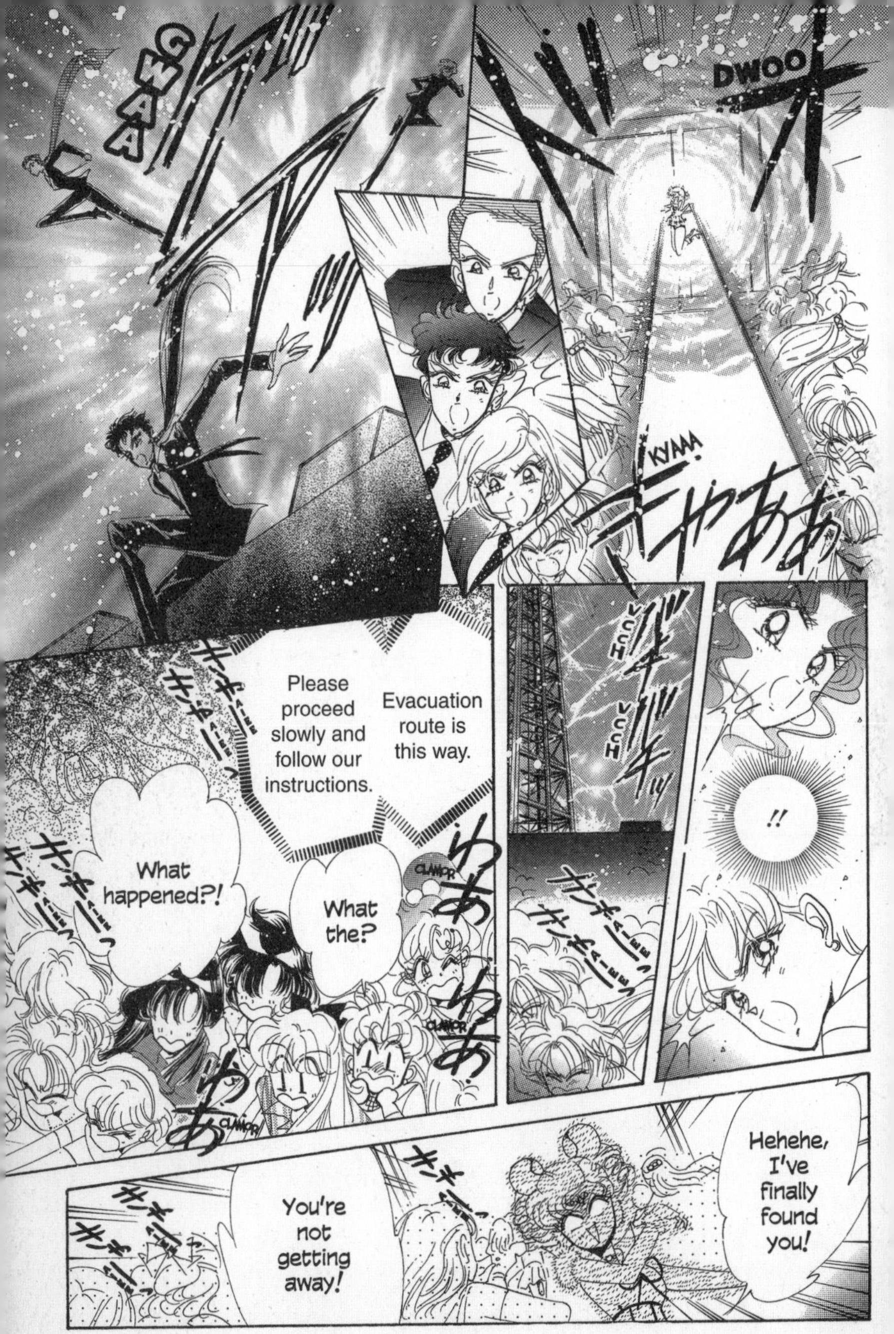
DWOO
GWAAA
KYAAA
!!
VCCH VCCH
Evacuation route is this way.
Please proceed slowly and follow our instructions.
CLAMOR
What the?
What happened?!
CLAMOR
CLAMOR
Hehehe, I've finally found you!
You're not getting away!

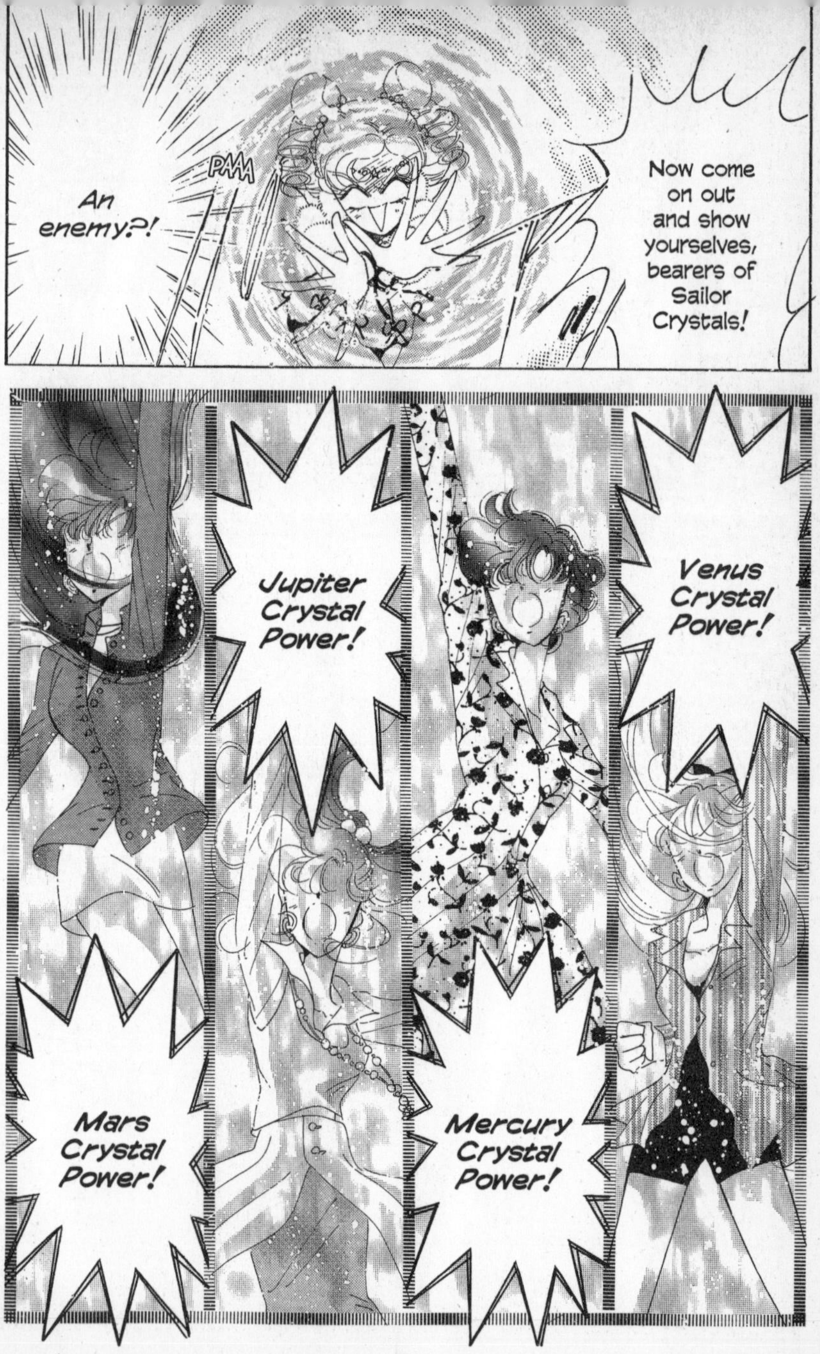
Now come on out and show yourselves, bearers of Sailor Crystals!
PAAA
An enemy?!
Venus Crystal Power!
Mercury Crystal Power!
Jupiter Crystal Power!
Mars Crystal Power!

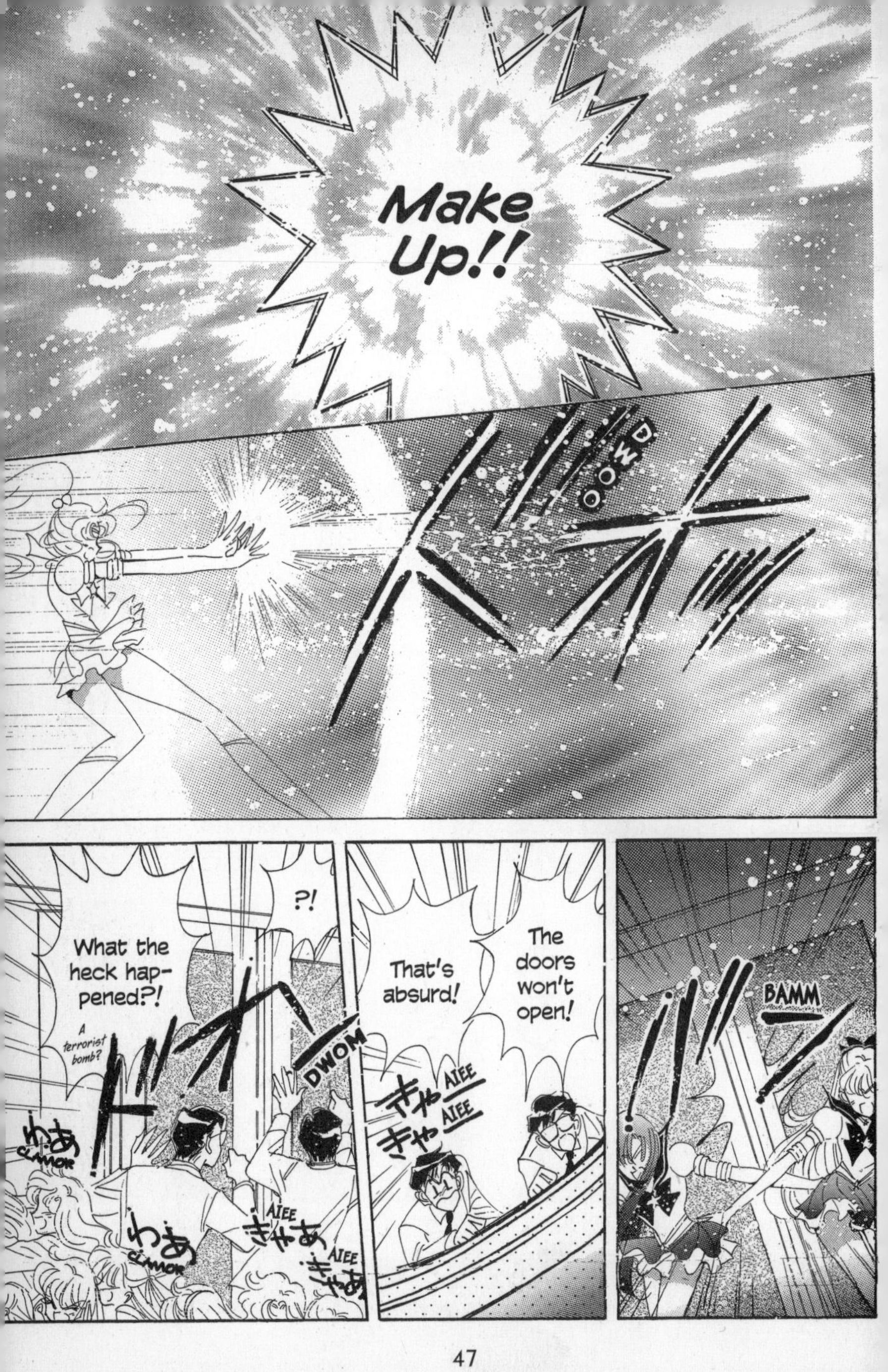
Make Up!!
DWOOO
BAMM
The doors won't open!
That's absurd!
AIEE
AIEE
?!
What the heck hap-pened?!
A terrorist bomb?
DWOM
CLAMOR
AIEE
CLAMOR
AIEE

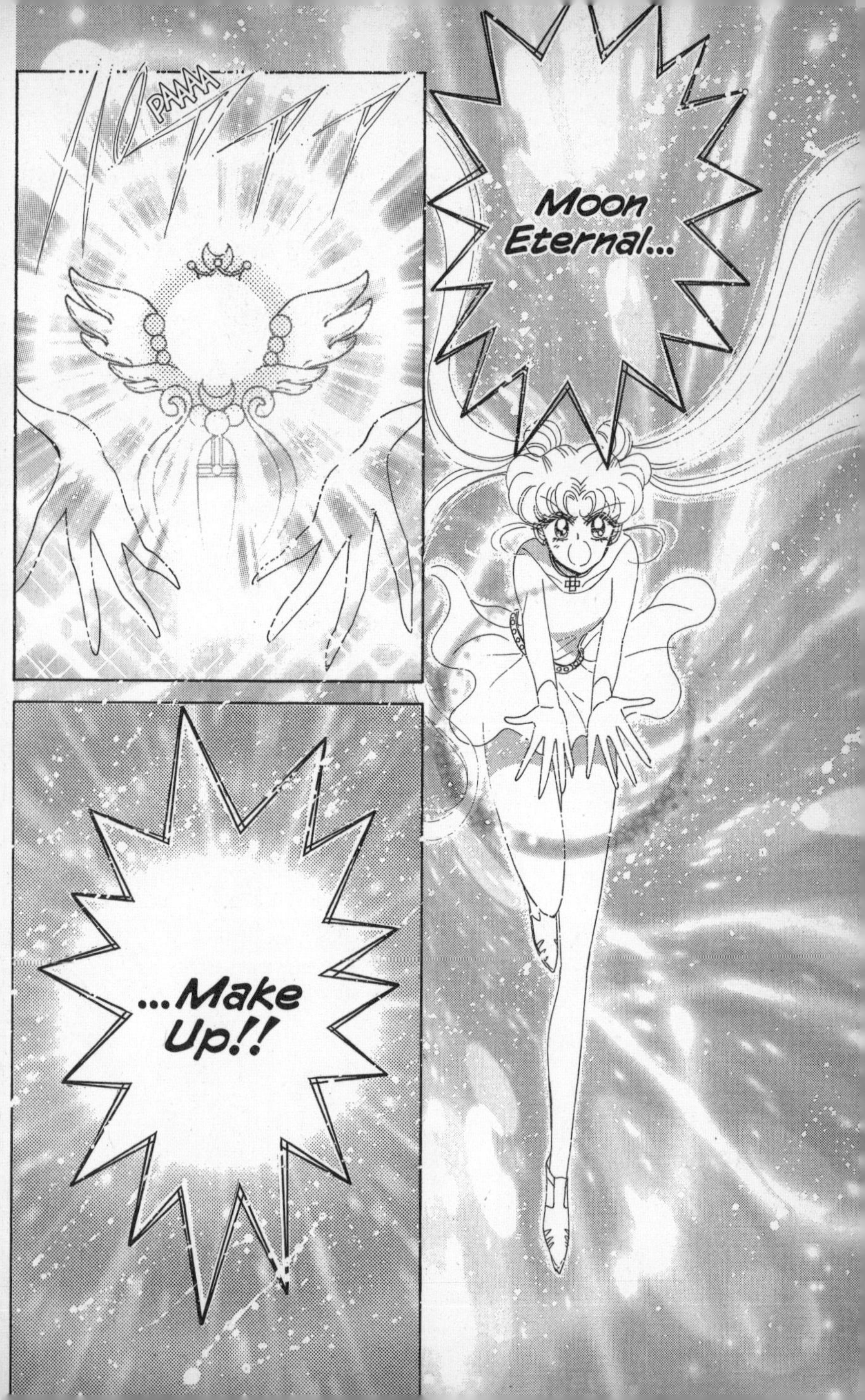
Moon Eternal...
PAAAA
...Make Up!!

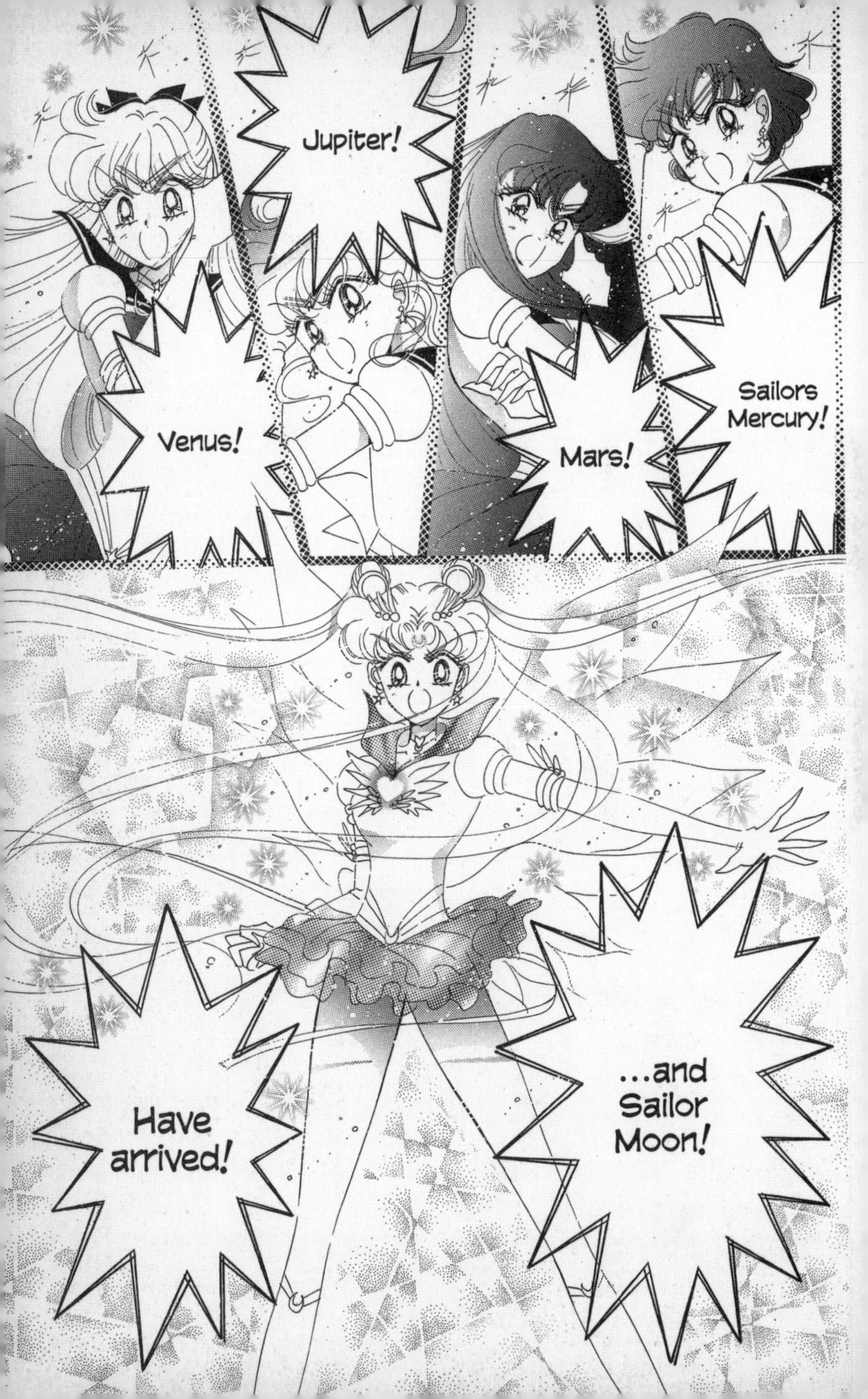
Sailors Mercury!
Mars!
Jupiter!
Venus!
...and Sailor Moon!
Have arrived!

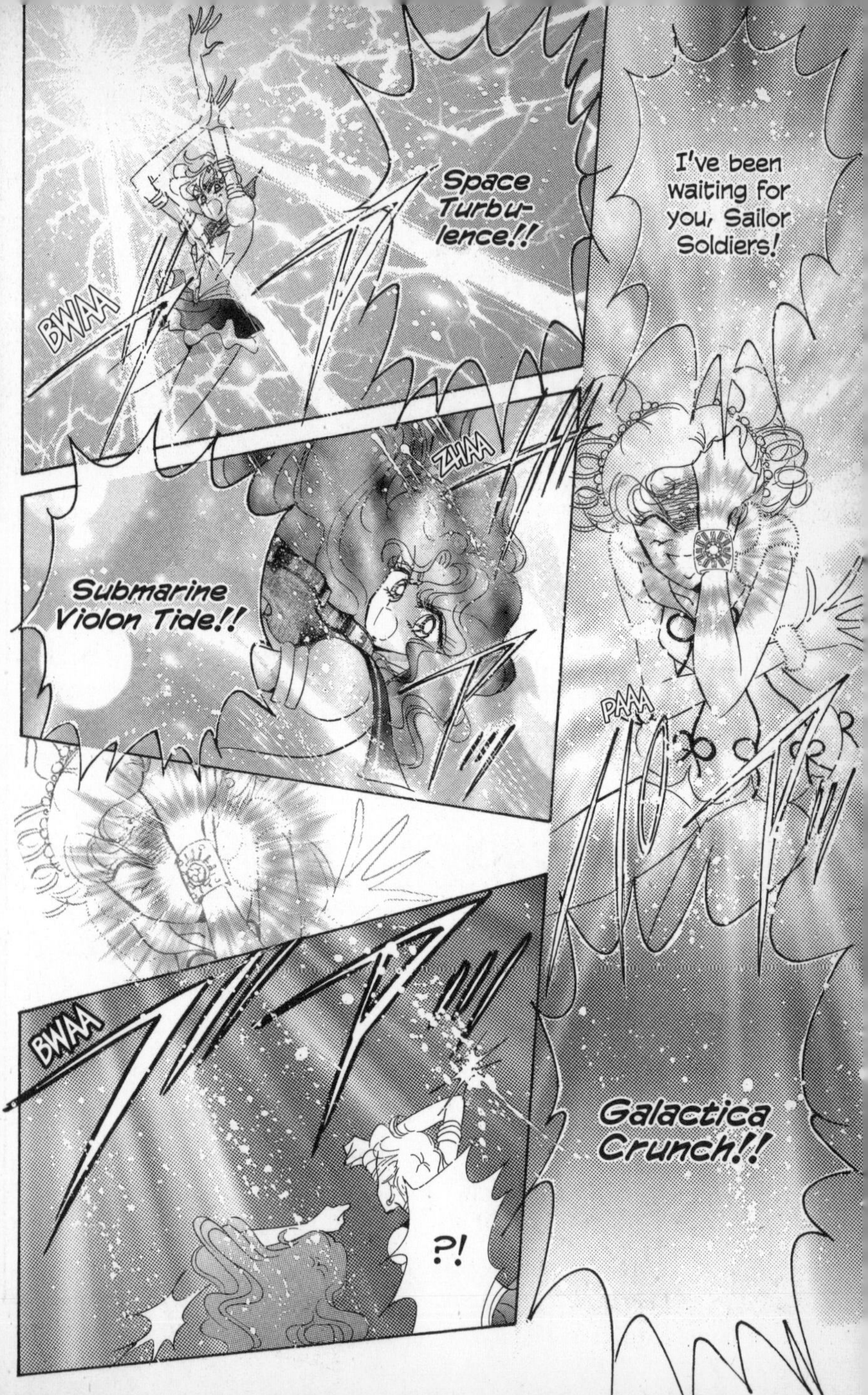
I've been waiting for you, Sailor Soldiers!
PAAA
Galactica Crunch!!
Space Turbu-lence!!
BWAA
ZHAA
Submarine Violon Tide!!
BWAA
?!

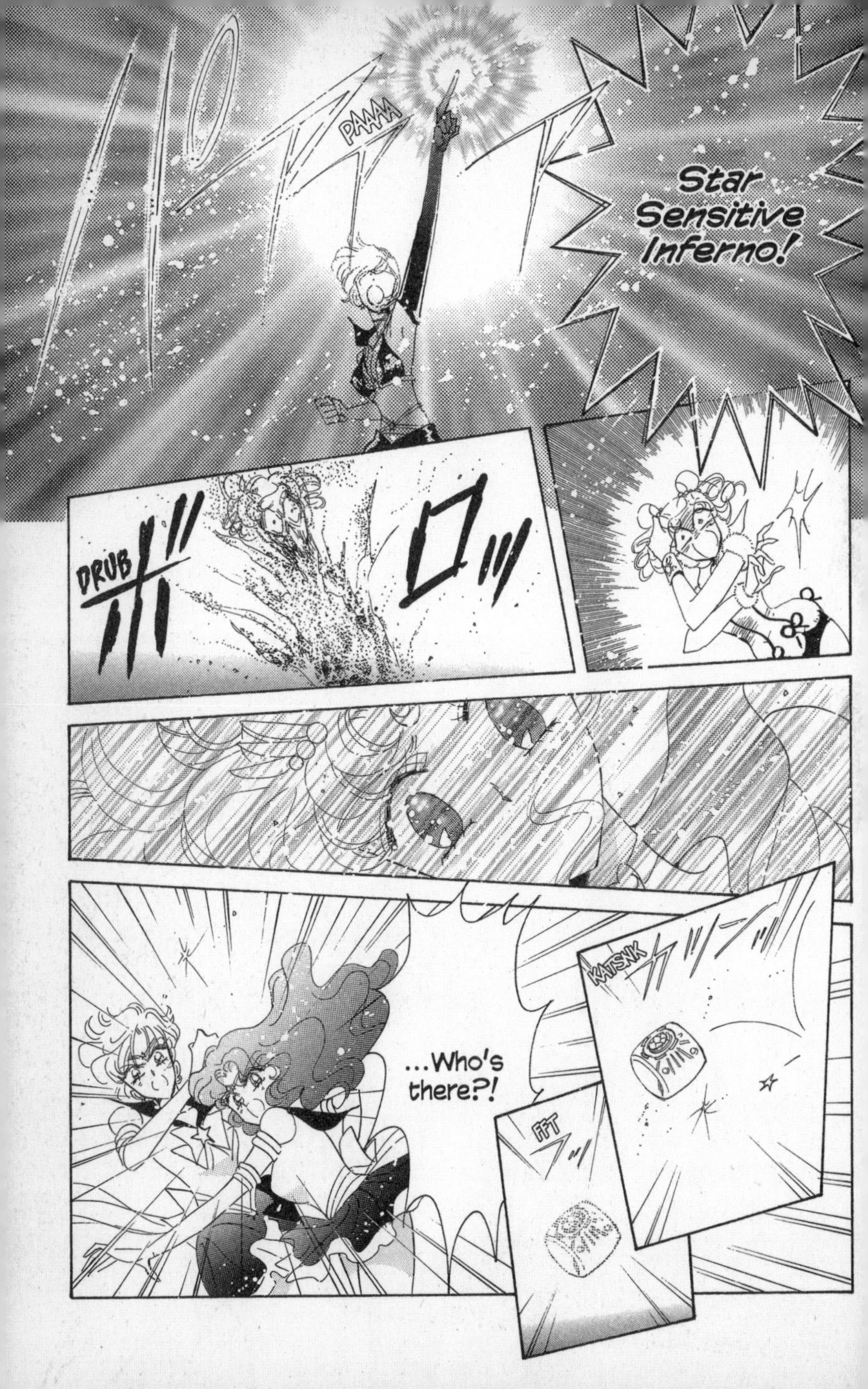
Star Sensitive Inferno!
PAAAA
DRUB
KATSNK
...Who's there?!
FFT

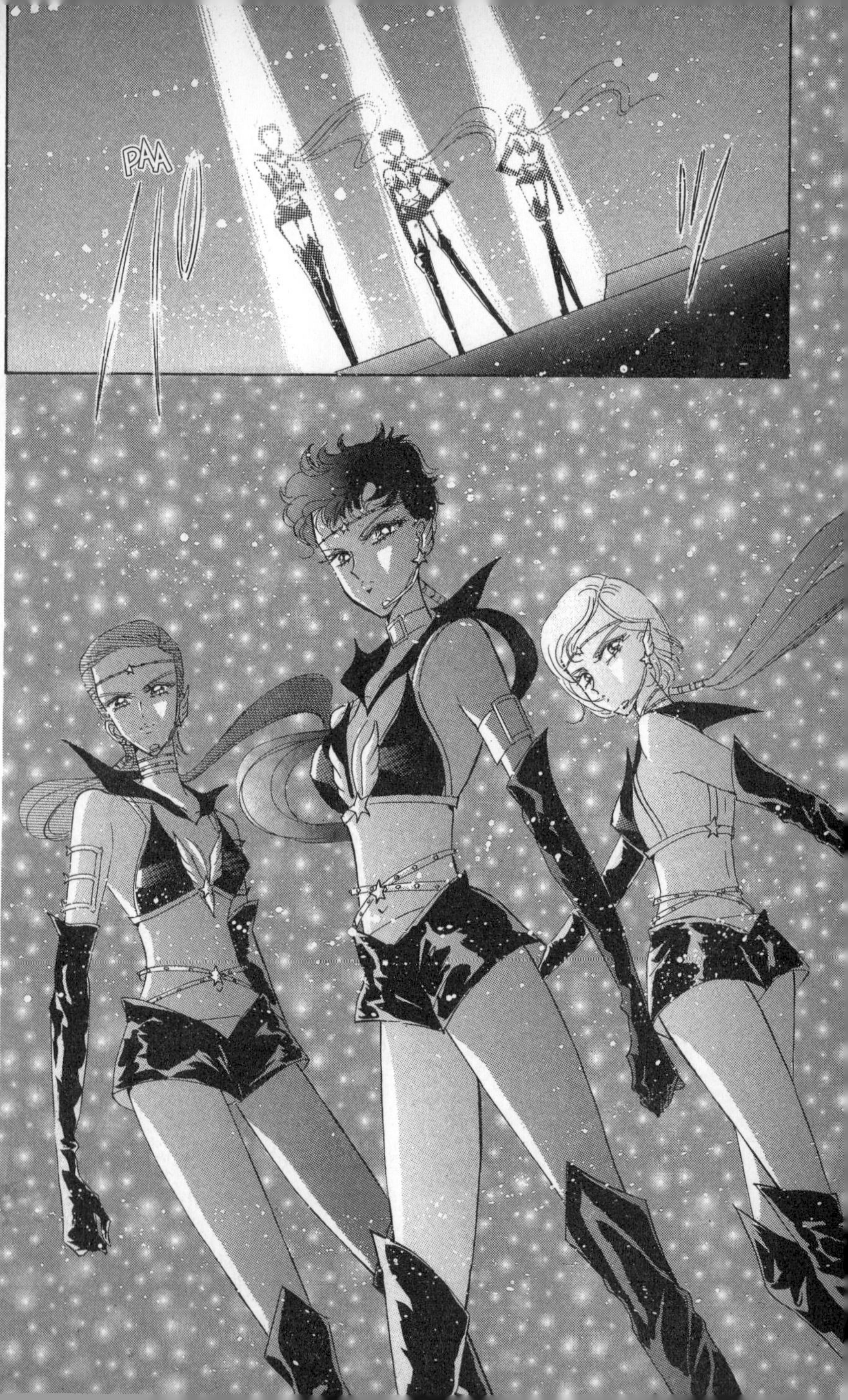
PAA

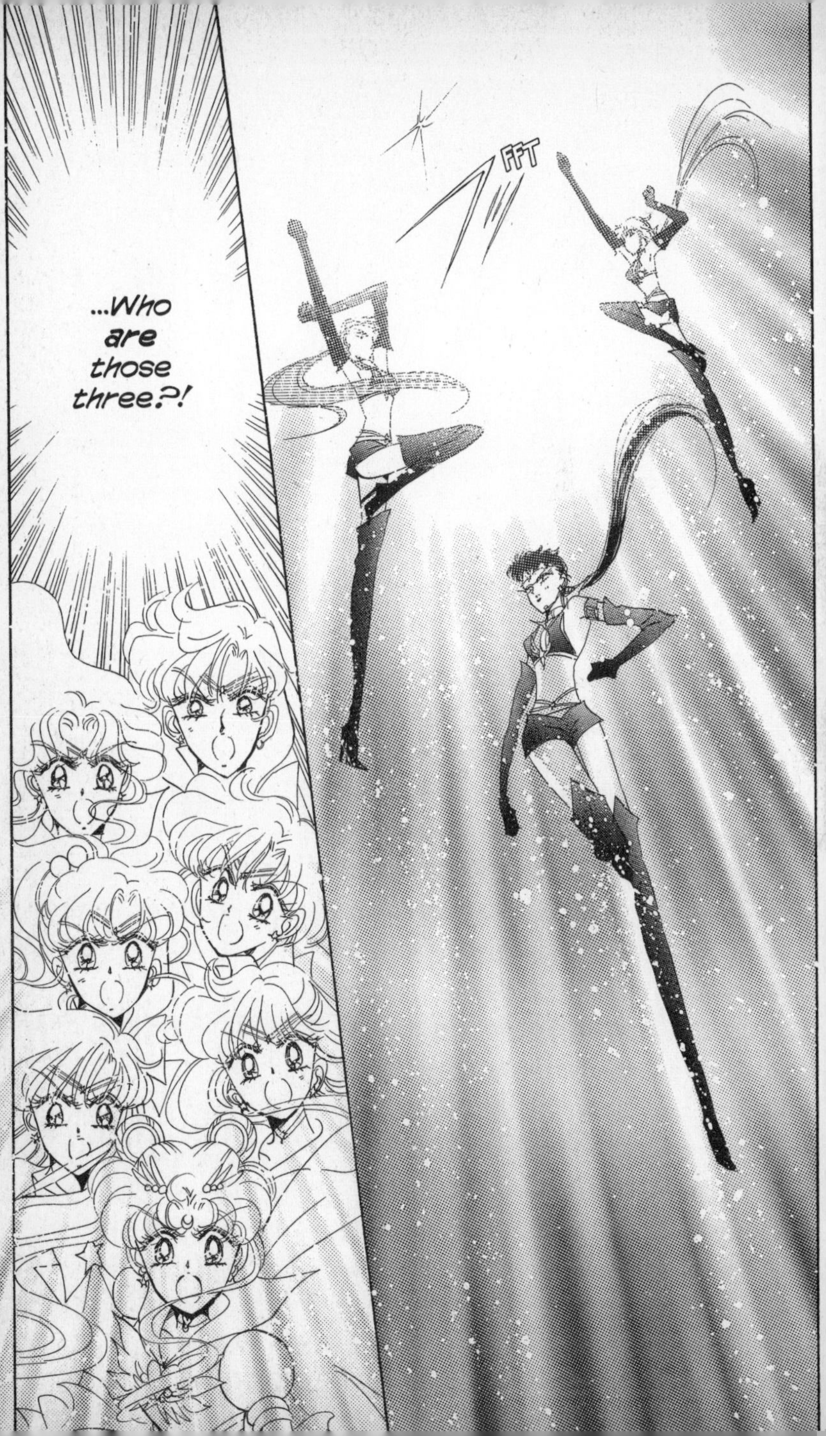
FFT
...Who are those three?!

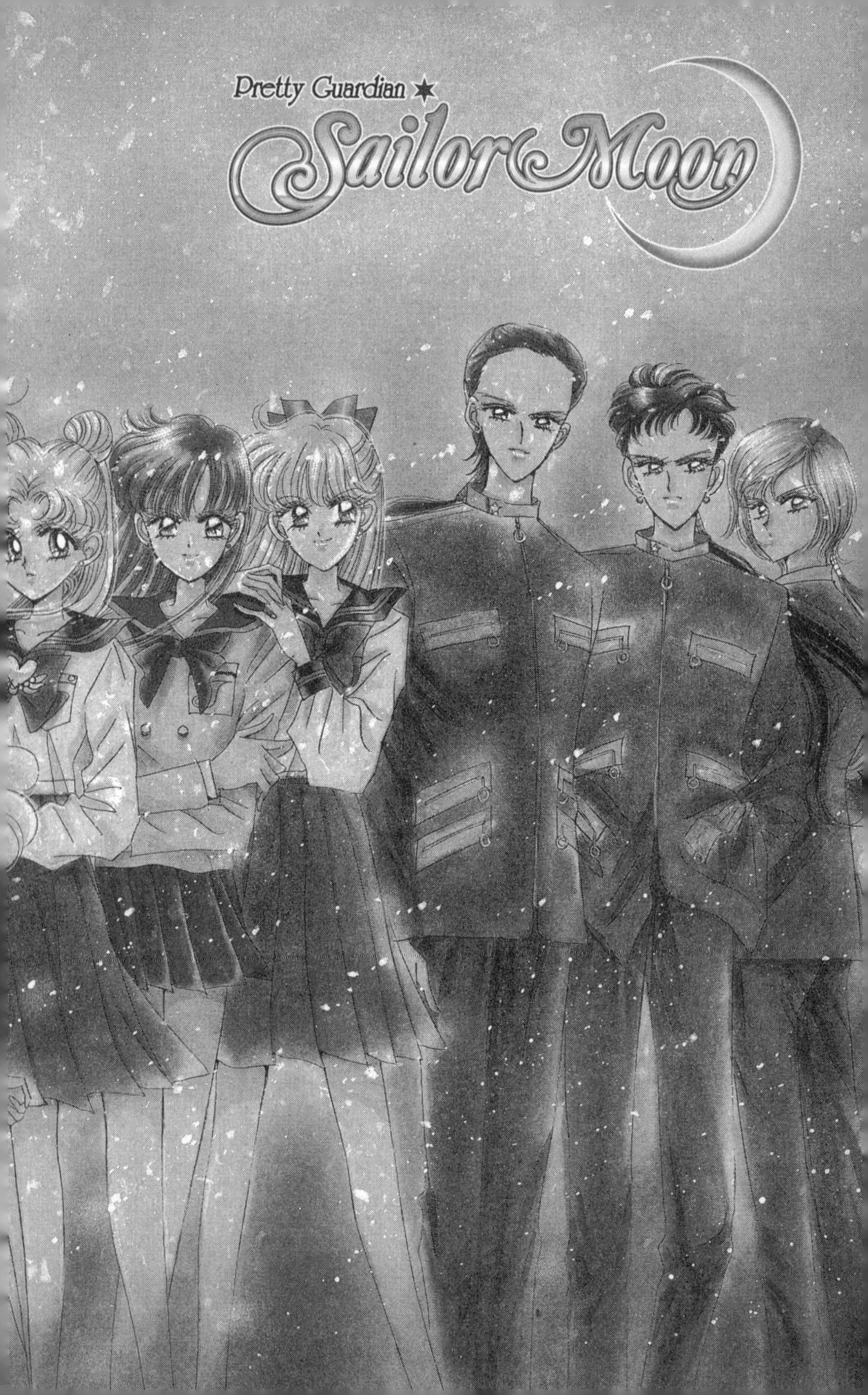
Pretty Guardian
Sailor Moon

Act 51 Stars 2

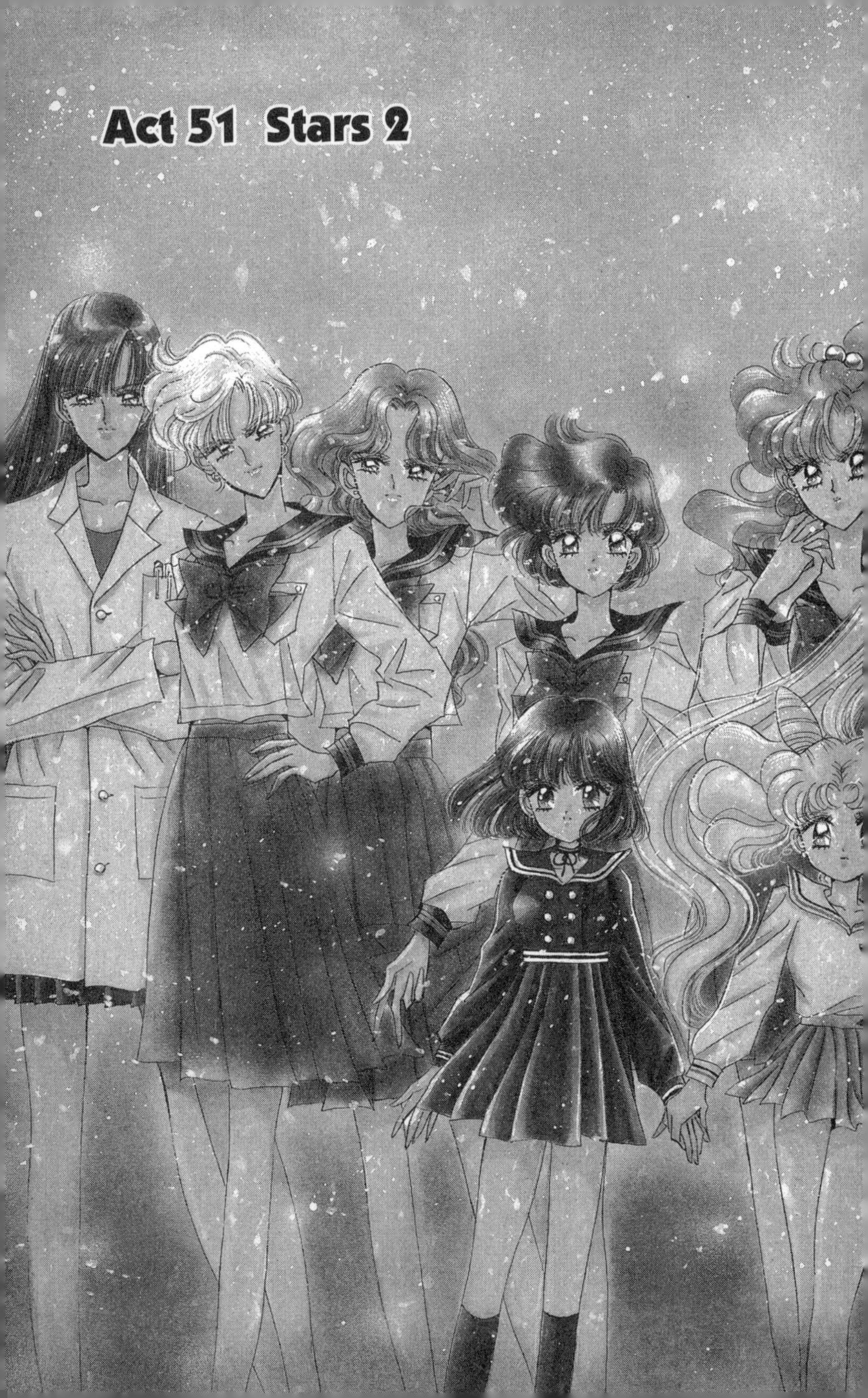

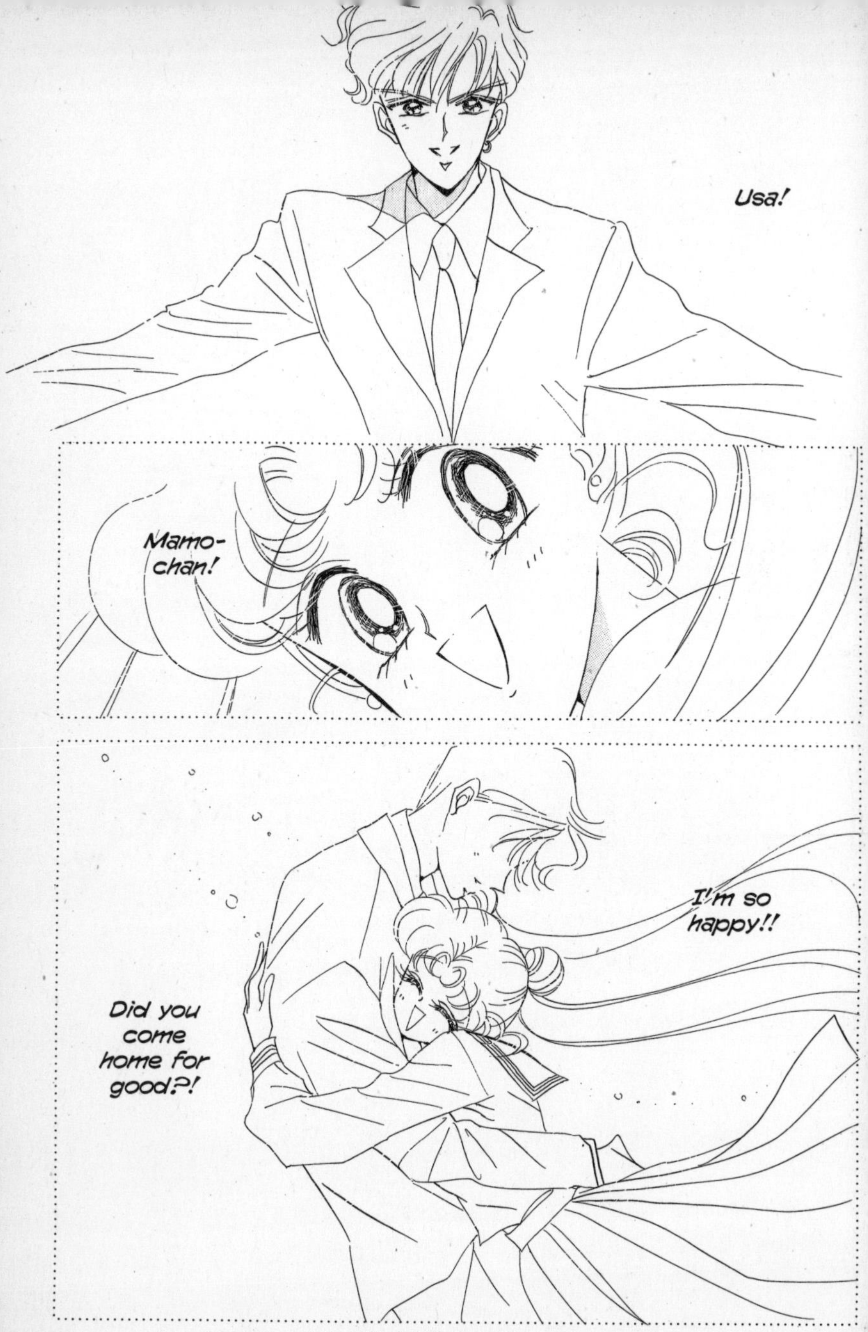
Usa!
Mamo-chan!
I'm so happy!!
Did you come home for good?!

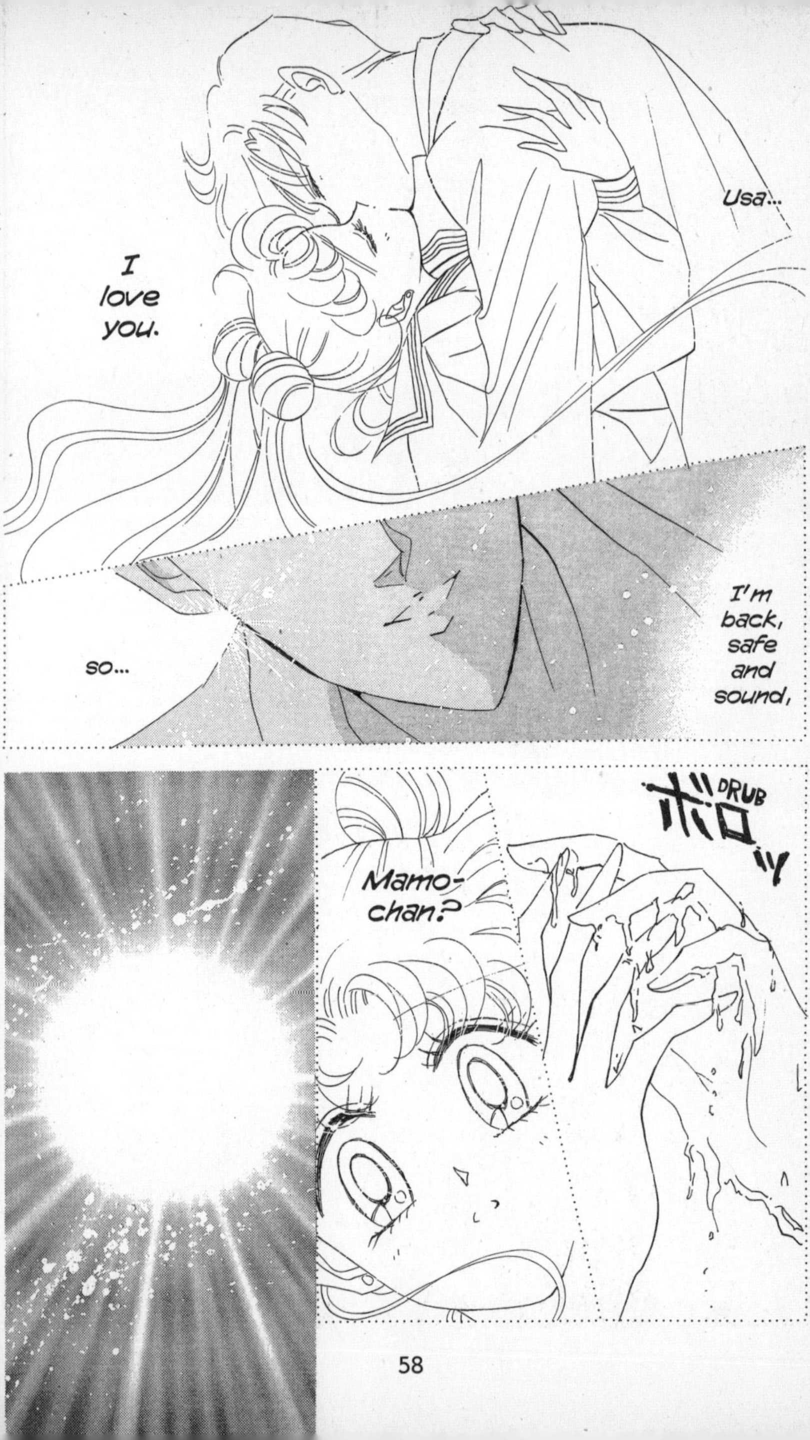
Usa...
I love you.
I'm back, safe and sound,
so...
DRUB
Mamo-chan?

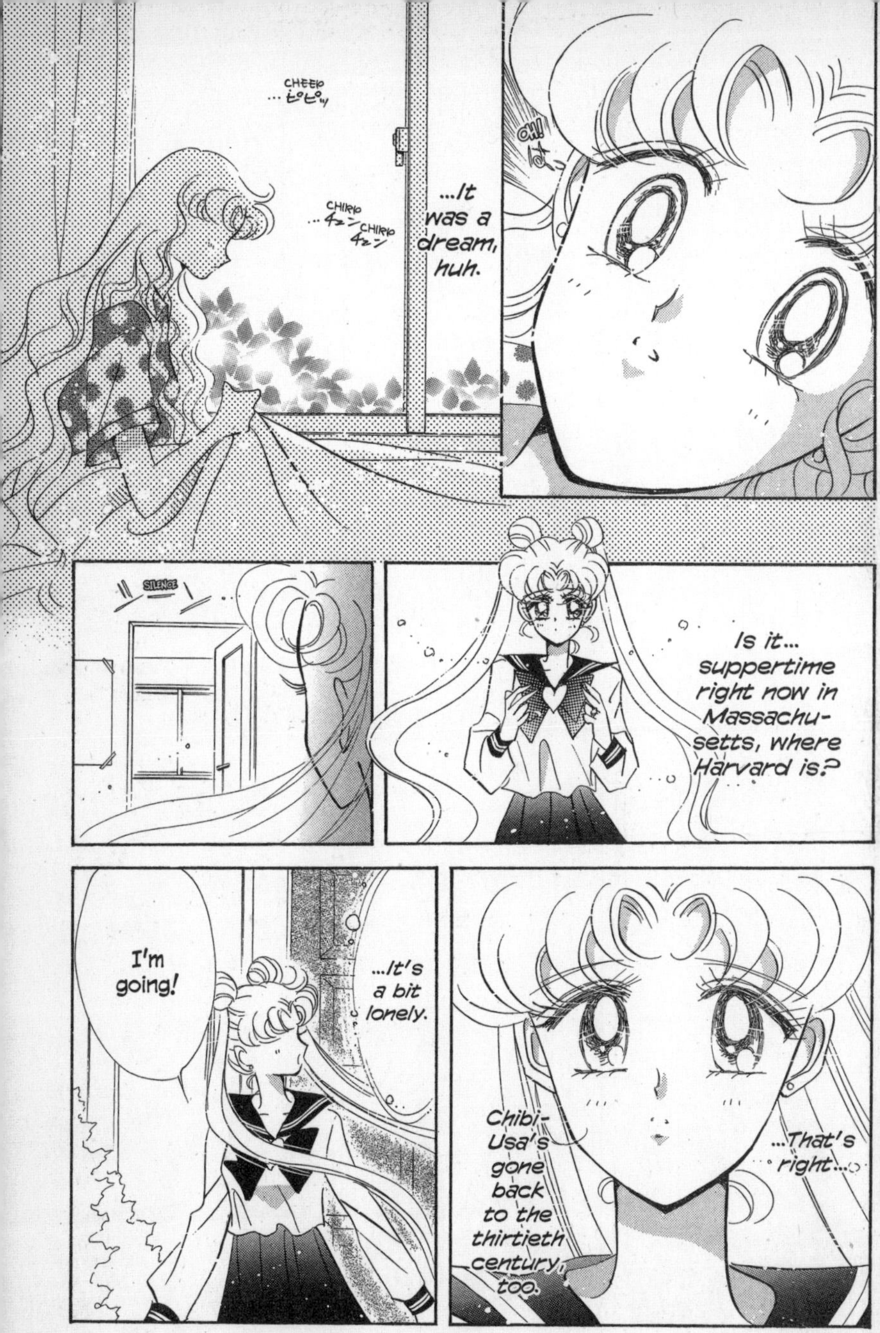
OH!
はっ
CHEEP
...ピピッ
...It was a dream, huh.
CHIRP ...チュン CHIRP チュン
Is it... suppertime right now in Massachusetts, where Harvard is?
SILENCE
...That's right...
Chibi-Usa's gone back to the thirtieth century, too.
...It's a bit lonely.
I'm going!

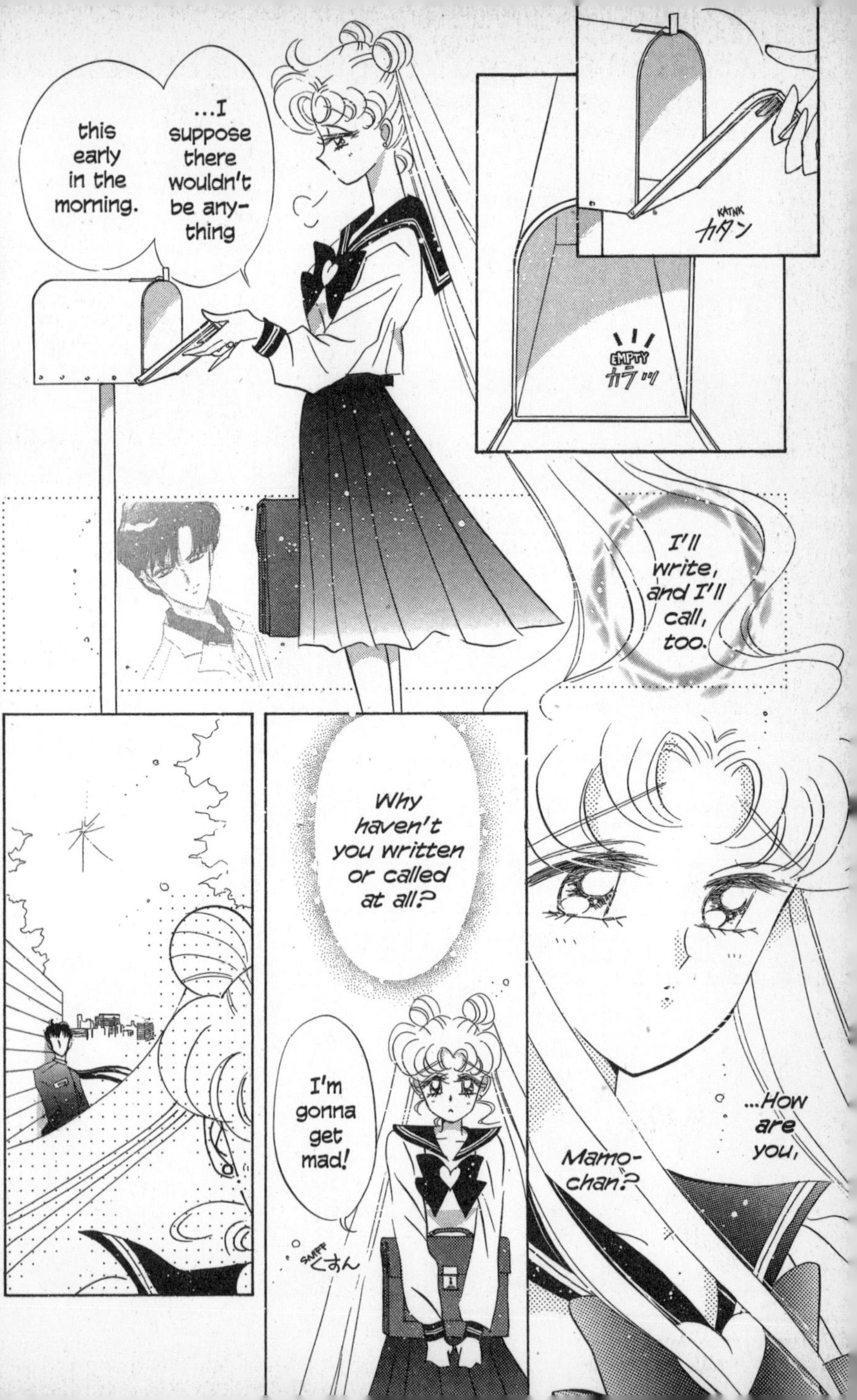
KATNK
カタン
EMPTY
カラッ
...I suppose there wouldn't be any-thing
this early in the morning.
I'll write, and I'll call, too.
...How are you,
Mamo-chan?
Why haven't you written or called at all?
I'm gonna get mad!
SNIFF
くすん

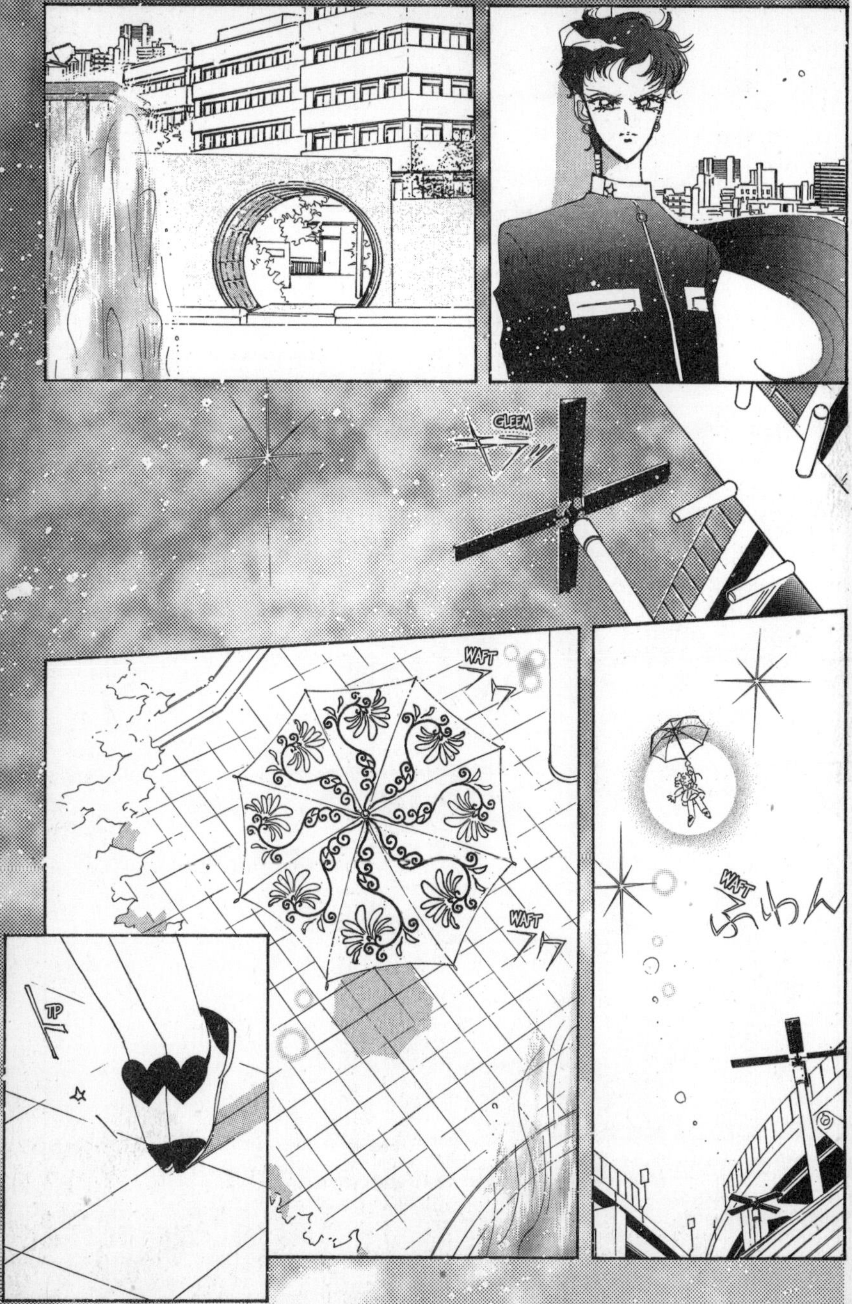
GLEEM
キラッ
WAFT
ふわん
WAFT
フワ
WAFT
フワ
TP

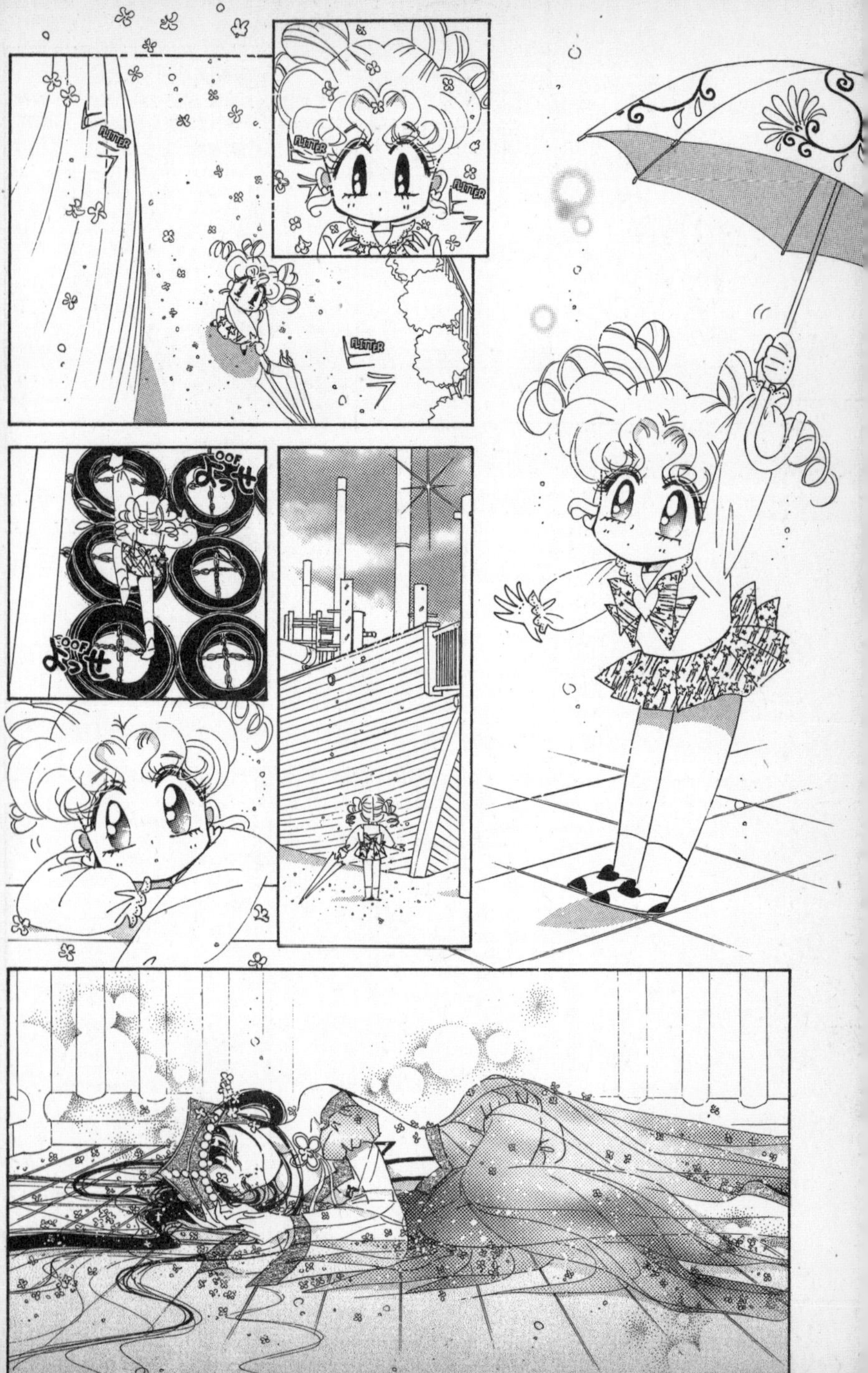
FLITTER ヒラ
FLITTER ヒラ
FLITTER ヒラ
FLITTER ヒラ
OOF よっせ
OOF よっせ

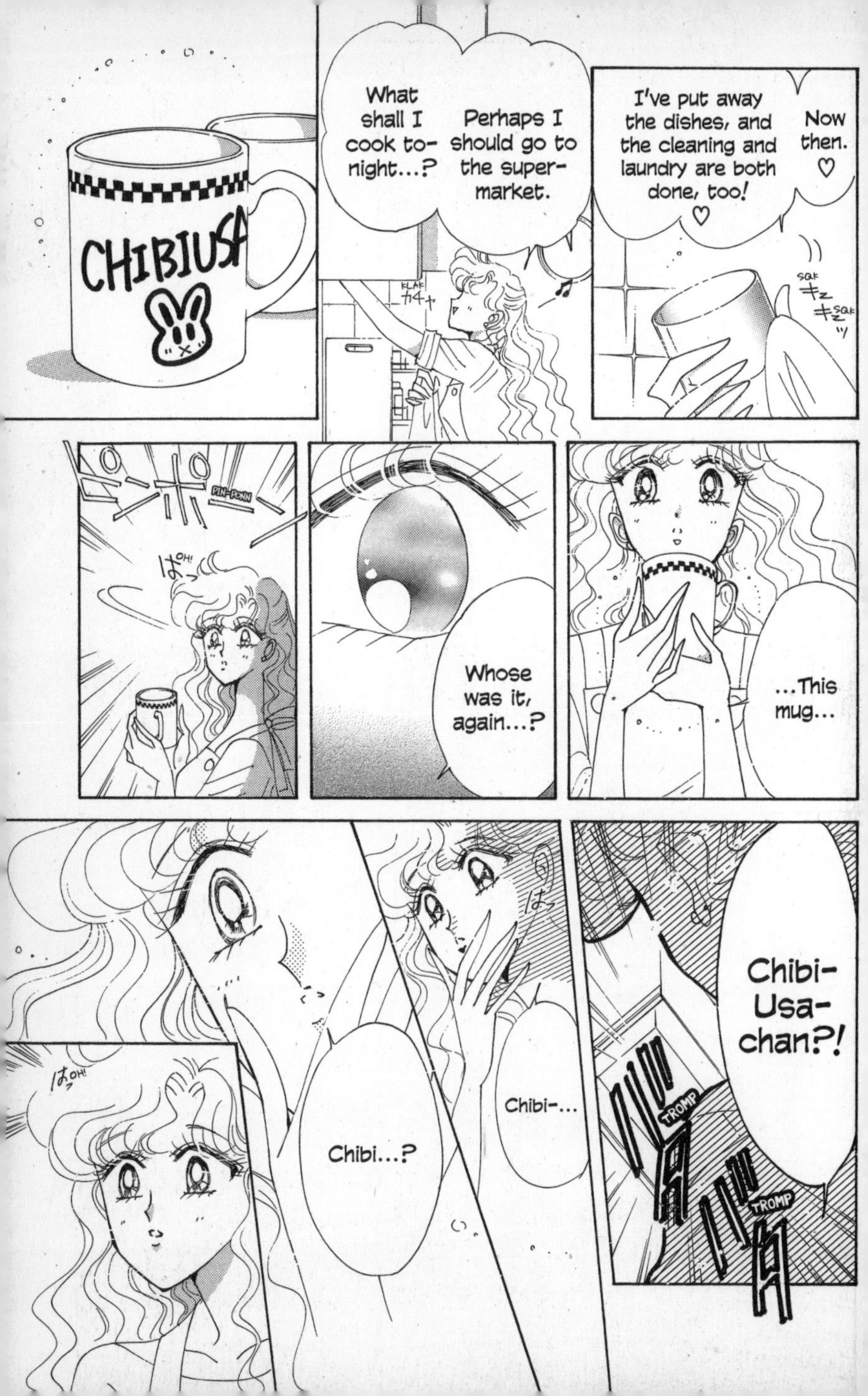
Now then. ♡
I've put away the dishes, and the cleaning and laundry are both done, too! ♡
SQK
SQK
What shall I cook to-night...? Perhaps I should go to the super-market.
FLAK
CHIBIUSA
...This mug...
Whose was it, again...?
PIN-PONN
OH!
Chibi-Usa-chan?!
TROMP
TROMP
Chibi-...
Chibi...?
OH!

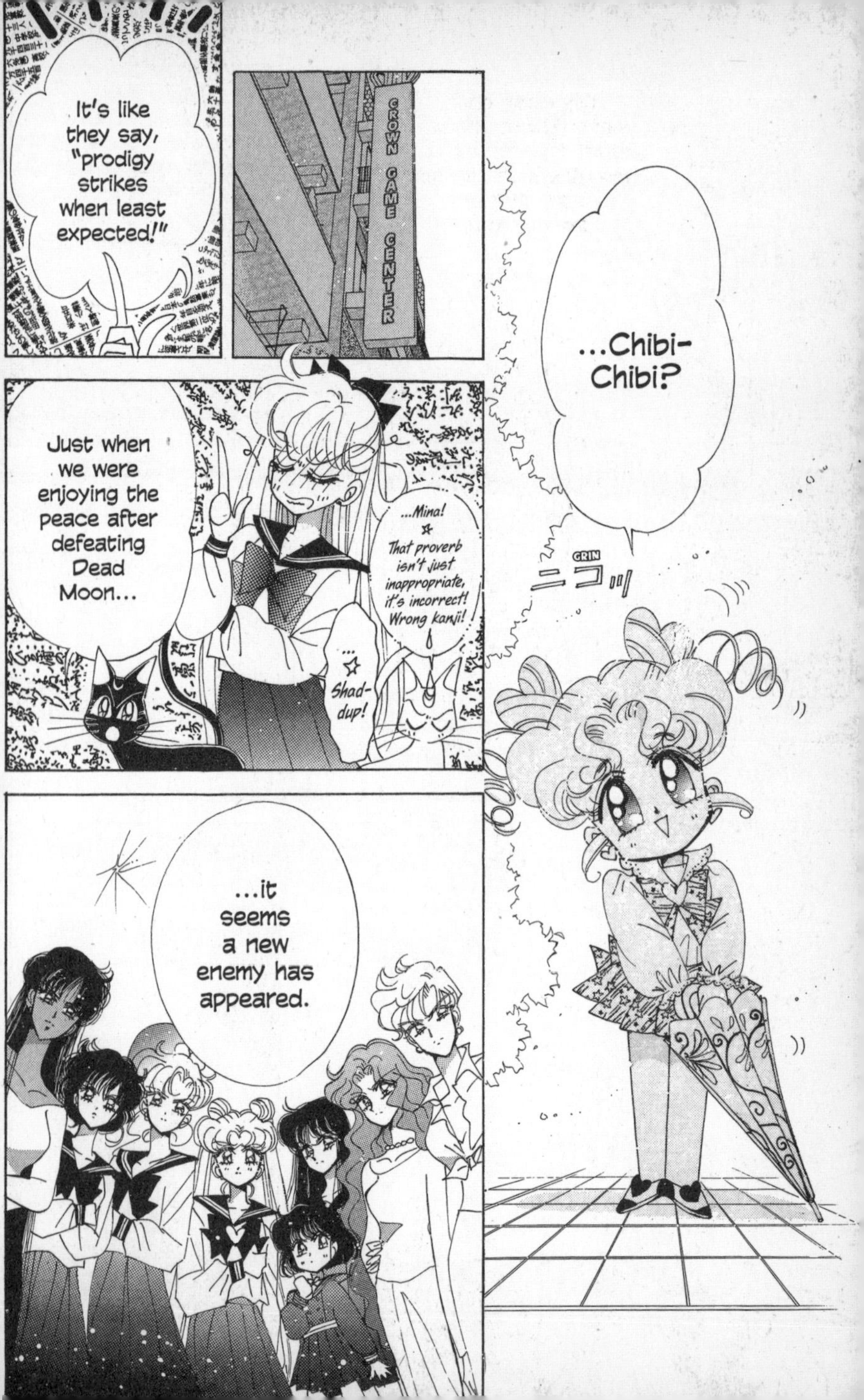
...Chibi-Chibi?
GRIN
ニコッ
CROWN GAME CENTER
It's like they say, "prodigy strikes when least expected!"
Just when we were enjoying the peace after defeating Dead Moon...
...Mina! ☆ That proverb isn't just inappropriate, it's incorrect! Wrong kanji!
...☆ Shad-dup!
...it seems a new enemy has appeared.

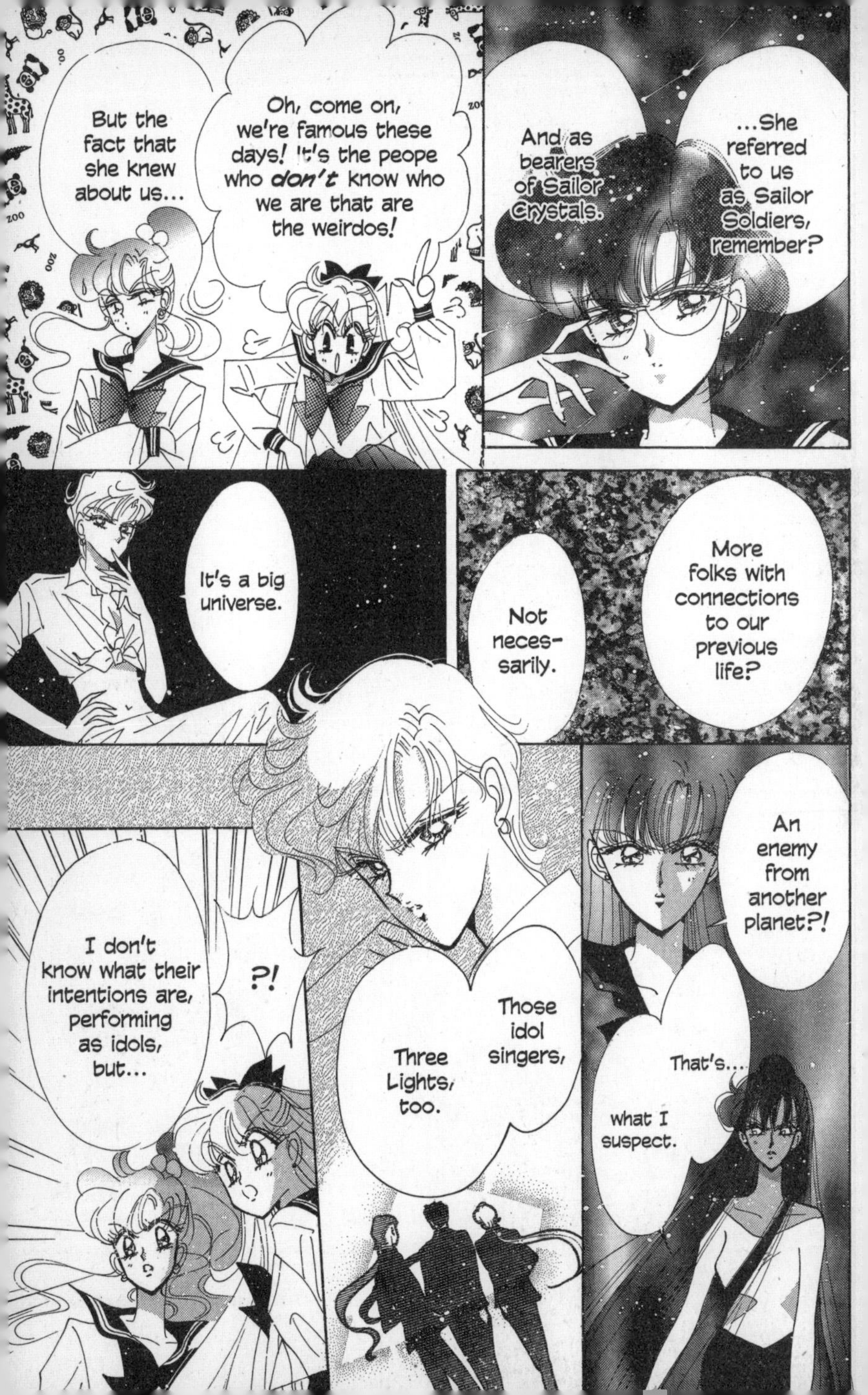
...She referred to us as Sailor Soldiers, remember?
And as bearers of Sailor Crystals.
But the fact that she knew about us...
Oh, come on, we're famous these days! It's the peope who *don't* know who we are that are the weirdos!
More folks with connections to our previous life?
Not neces-sarily.
It's a big universe.
An enemy from another planet?!
That's...
what I suspect.
Those idol singers,
Three Lights, too.
?!
I don't know what their intentions are, performing as idols, but...

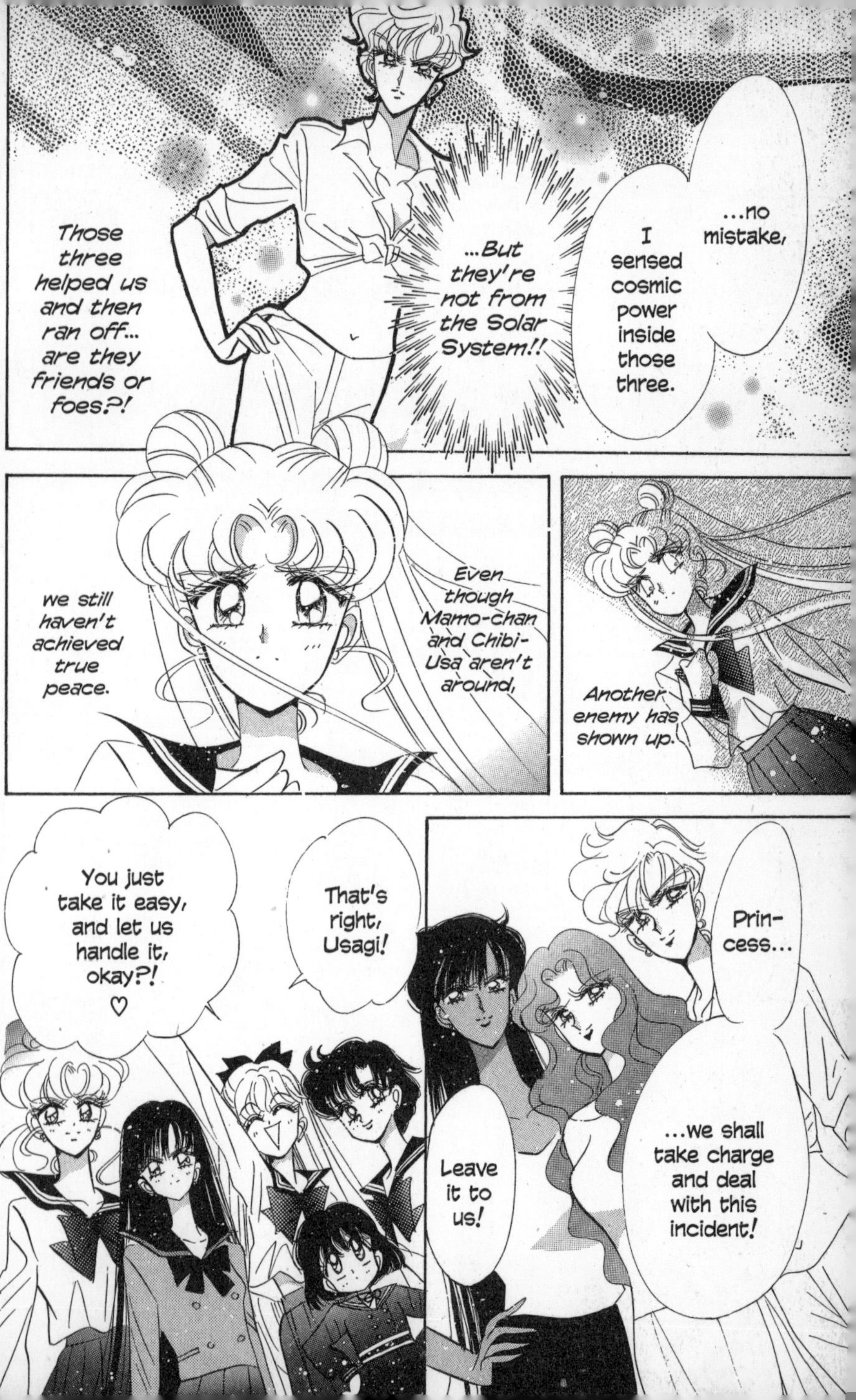
...no mistake,
I sensed cosmic power inside those three.
...But they're not from the Solar System!!
Those three helped us and then ran off... are they friends or foes?!
Another enemy has shown up.
Even though Mamo-chan and Chibi-Usa aren't around,
we still haven't achieved true peace.
Prin-cess...
...we shall take charge and deal with this incident!
Leave it to us!
That's right, Usagi!
You just take it easy, and let us handle it, okay?! ♡

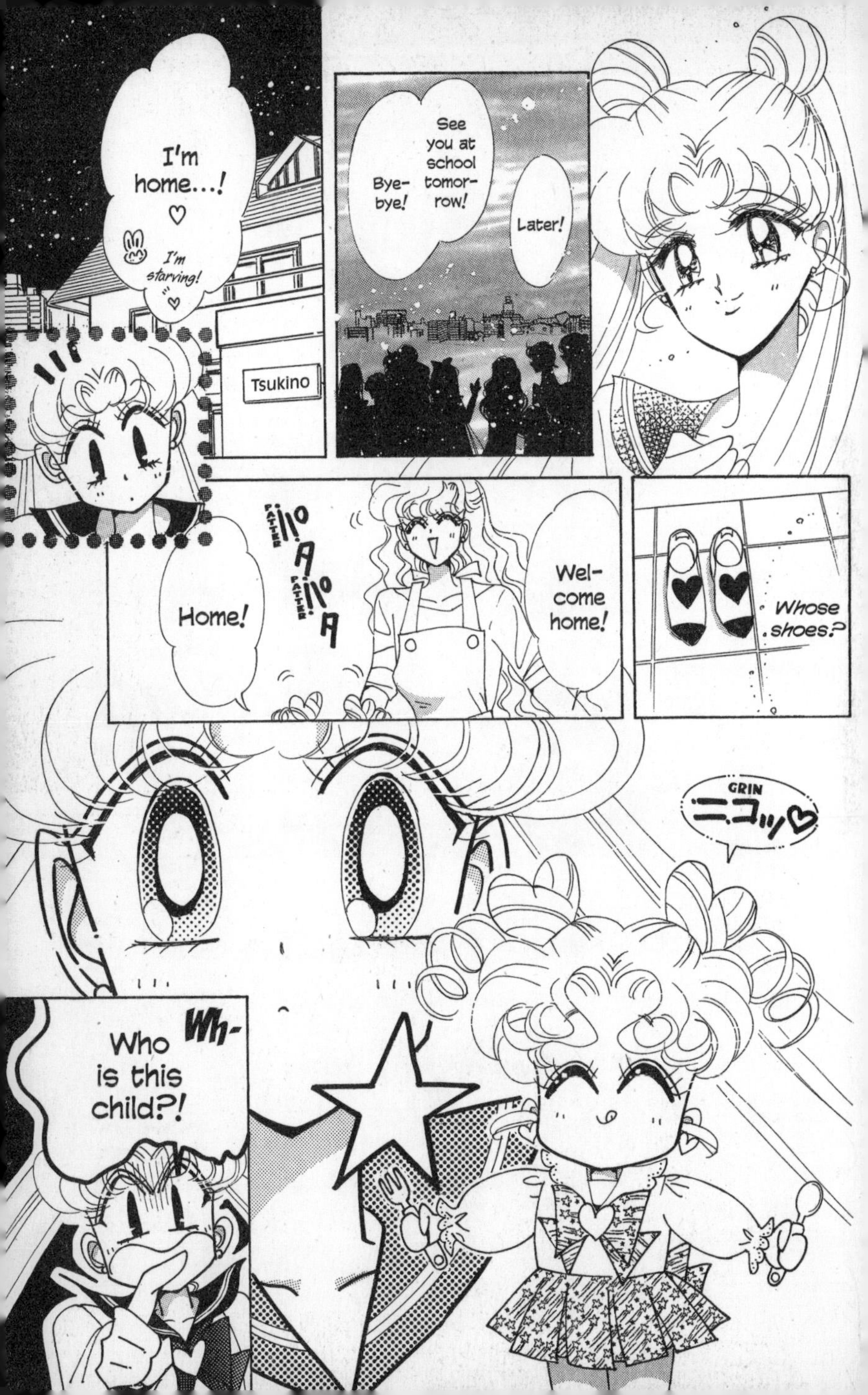

Later!
See you at school tomorrow!
Bye-bye!
I'm home...! ♡
I'm starving! ♡
Tsukino
Whose shoes?
Welcome home!
PATTER PATTER
Home!
GRIN
Wh-
Who is this child?!

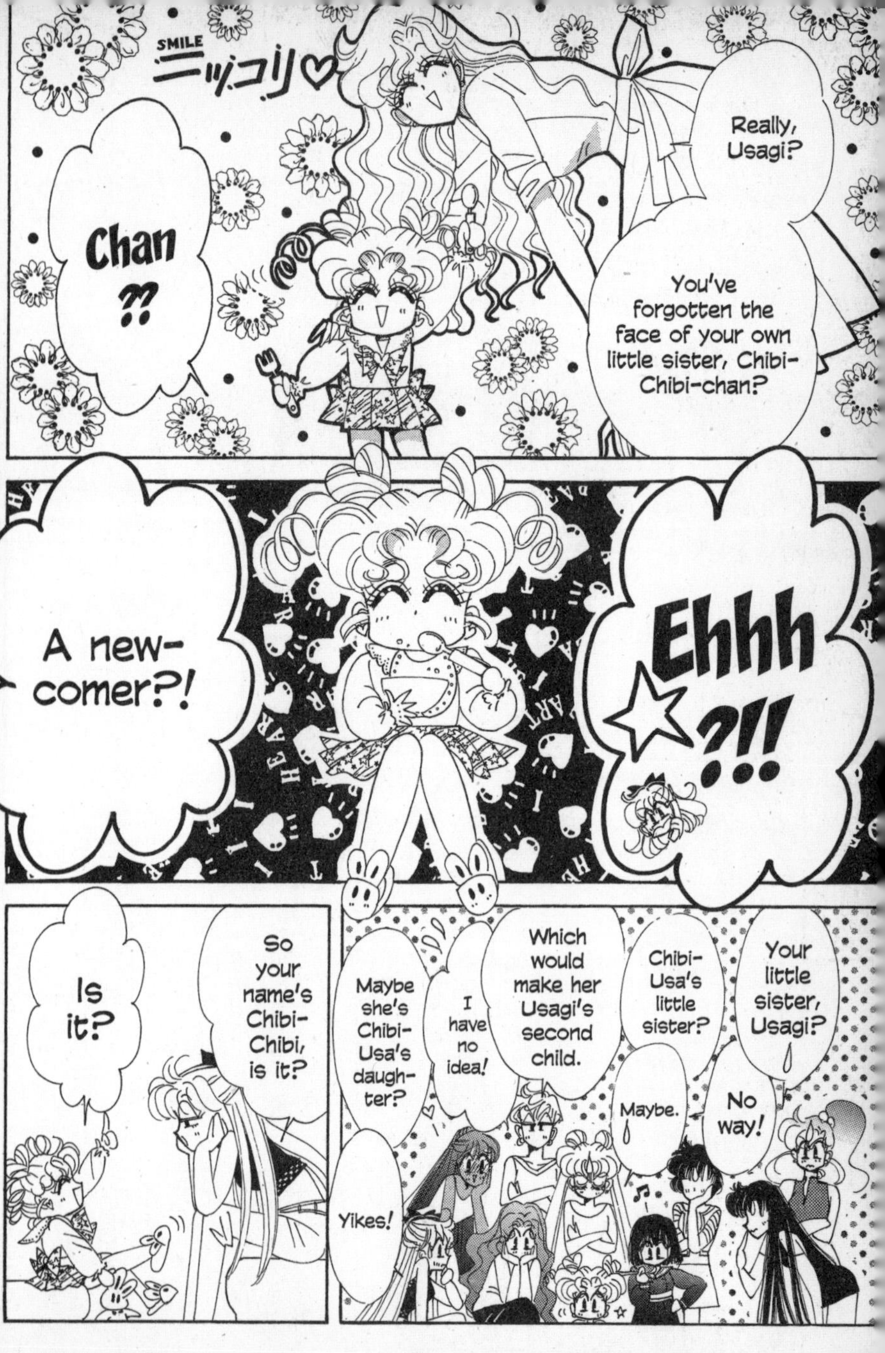
Really, Usagi?
You've forgotten the face of your own little sister, Chibi-Chibi-chan?
SMILE ニッコリ♡
Chan ??
Ehhh ☆ ?!!
A new-comer?!
Your little sister, Usagi?
No way!
Chibi-Usa's little sister?
Maybe.
Which would make her Usagi's second child.
I have no idea!
Maybe she's Chibi-Usa's daughter?
Yikes!
So your name's Chibi-Chibi, is it?
Is it?

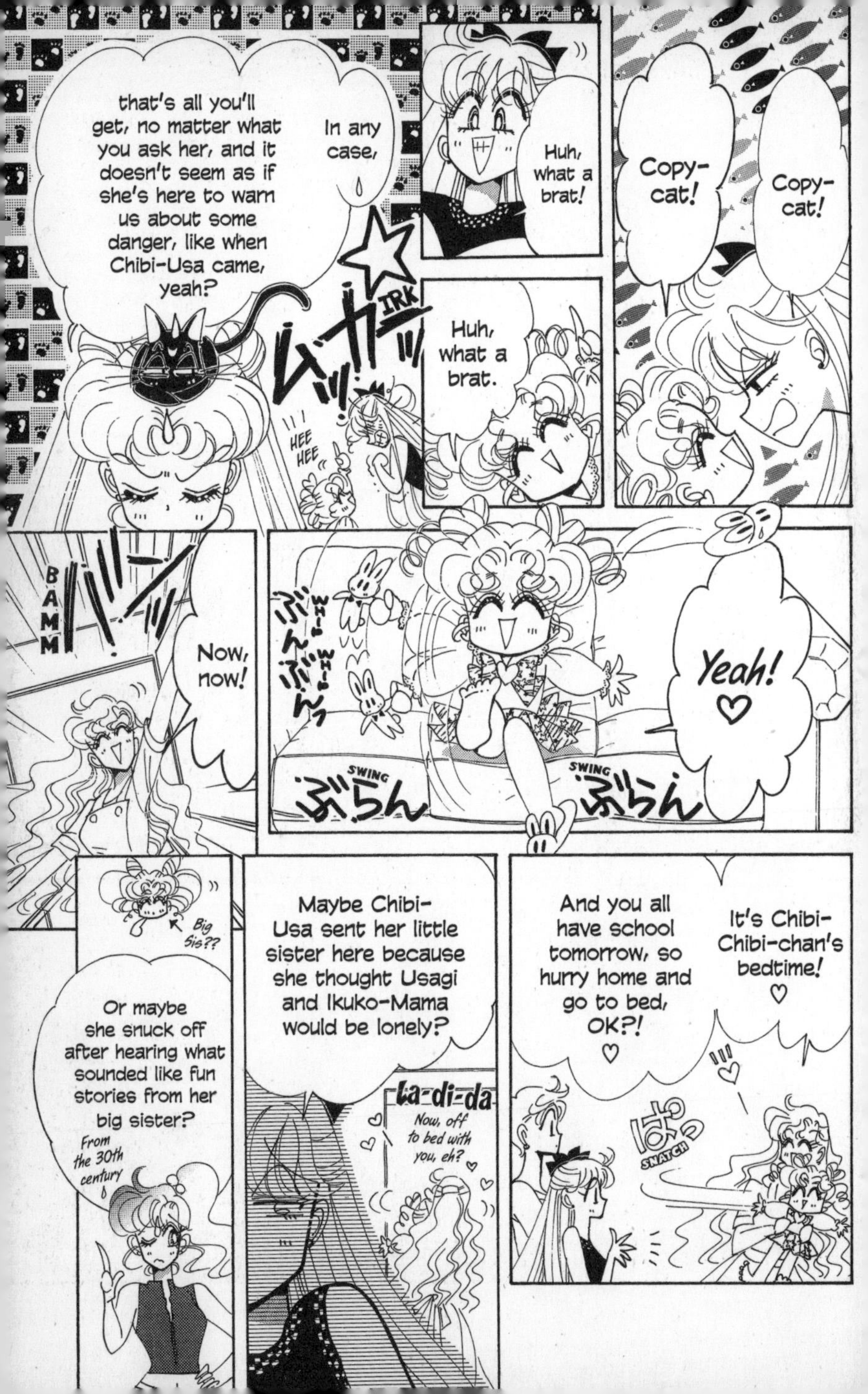
Copy-cat!
Copy-cat!
Huh, what a brat!
Huh, what a brat.
IRK
HEE HEE
In any case,
that's all you'll get, no matter what you ask her, and it doesn't seem as if she's here to warn us about some danger, like when Chibi-Usa came, yeah?
Yeah! ♡
WHI WHI
SWING
SWING
BAMM
Now, now!
It's Chibi-Chibi-chan's bedtime! ♡
And you all have school tomorrow, so hurry home and go to bed, OK?! ♡
SNATCH
Maybe Chibi-Usa sent her little sister here because she thought Usagi and Ikuko-Mama would be lonely?
la-di-da
Now, off to bed with you, eh?
Big Sis??
Or maybe she snuck off after hearing what sounded like fun stories from her big sister?
From the 30th century

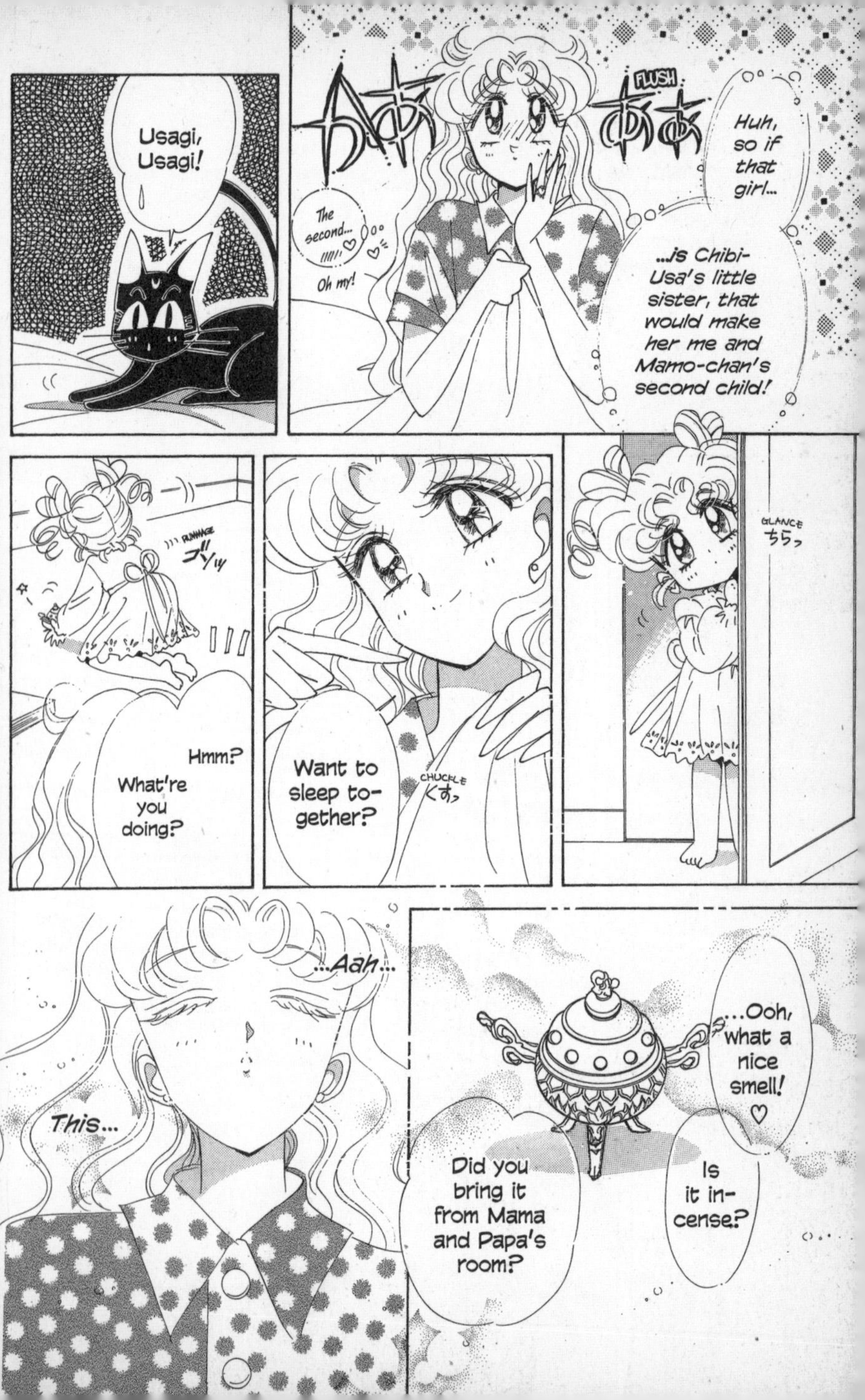
FLUSH
Huh, so if that girl...
...is Chibi-Usa's little sister, that would make her me and Mamo-chan's second child!
The second... !!!!!
Oh my!
Usagi, Usagi!
GLANCE
ちらっ
Want to sleep together?
CHUCKLE
くすっ
RUMMAGE
ゴソッ
Hmm?
What're you doing?
...Ooh, what a nice smell! ♡
Is it incense?
Did you bring it from Mama and Papa's room?
...Aah...
This...

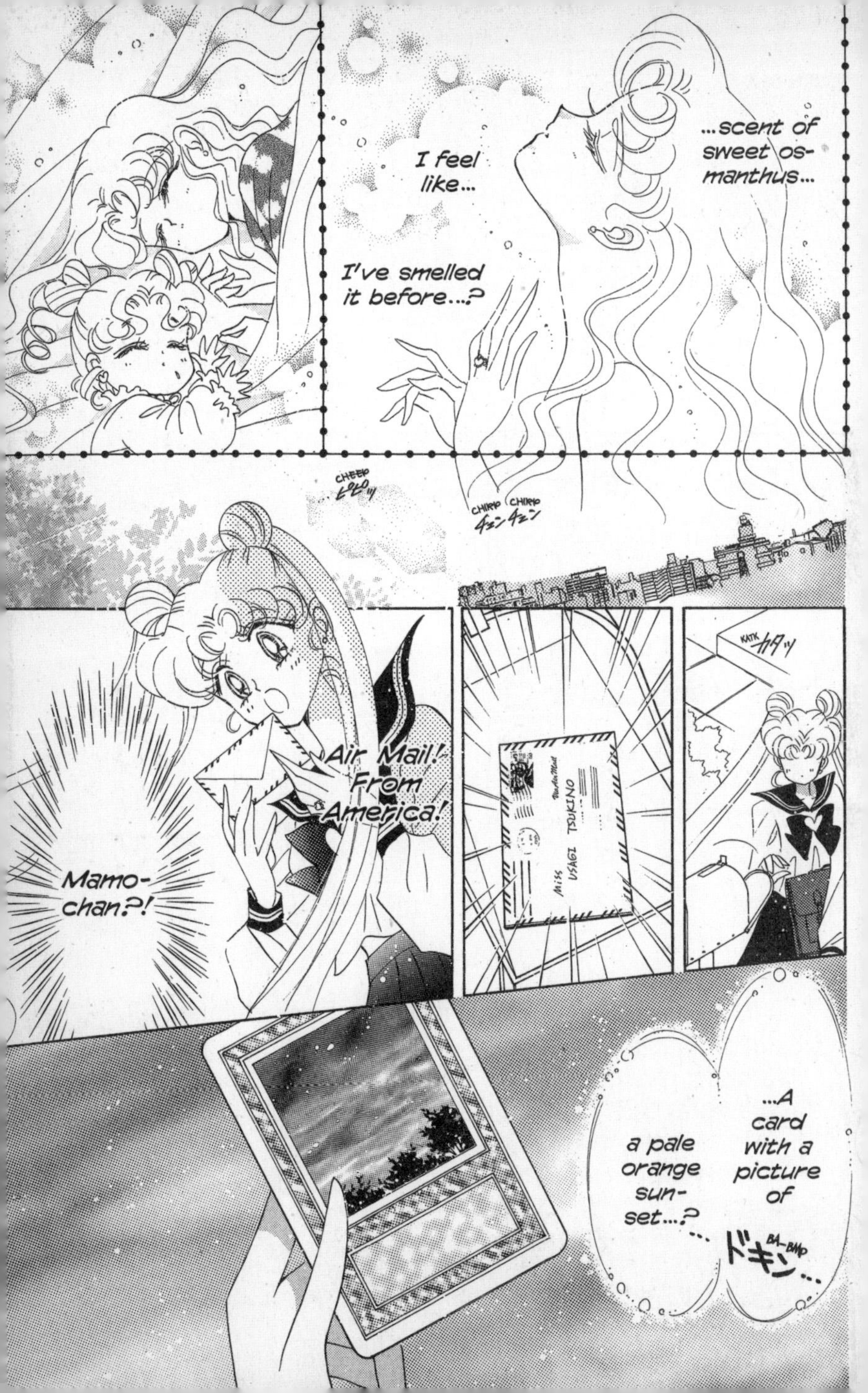
...scent of sweet os-manthus...
I feel like...
I've smelled it before...?
CHEEP
CHIRP CHIRP
KATK
Miss USAGI TSUKINO
Air Mail! From America!
Mamo-chan?!
...A card with a picture of
a pale orange sun-set...?
BA-BMP

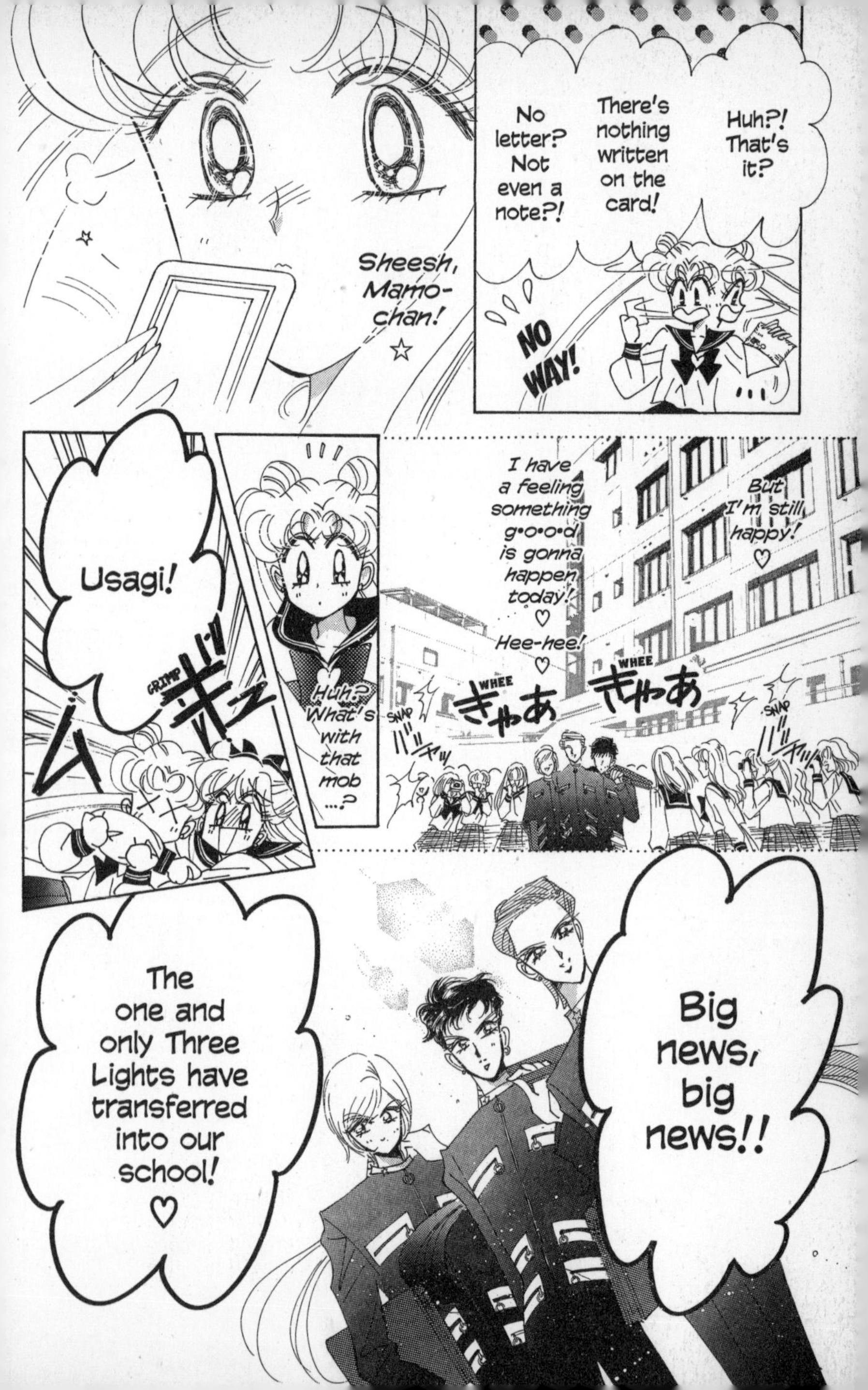
Huh?! That's it?
There's nothing written on the card!
No letter? Not even a note?!
NO WAY!
Sheesh, Mamo-chan! ☆
But I'm still happy! ♡
I have a feeling something g-o-o-d is gonna happen today! ♡
Hee-hee! ♡
WHEE きゃあ
WHEE きゃあ
SNAP バシャッ
SNAP バシャッ
Huh? What's with that mob...?
Usagi!
GRIMP ムギュ
Big news, big news!!
The one and only Three Lights have transferred into our school! ♡

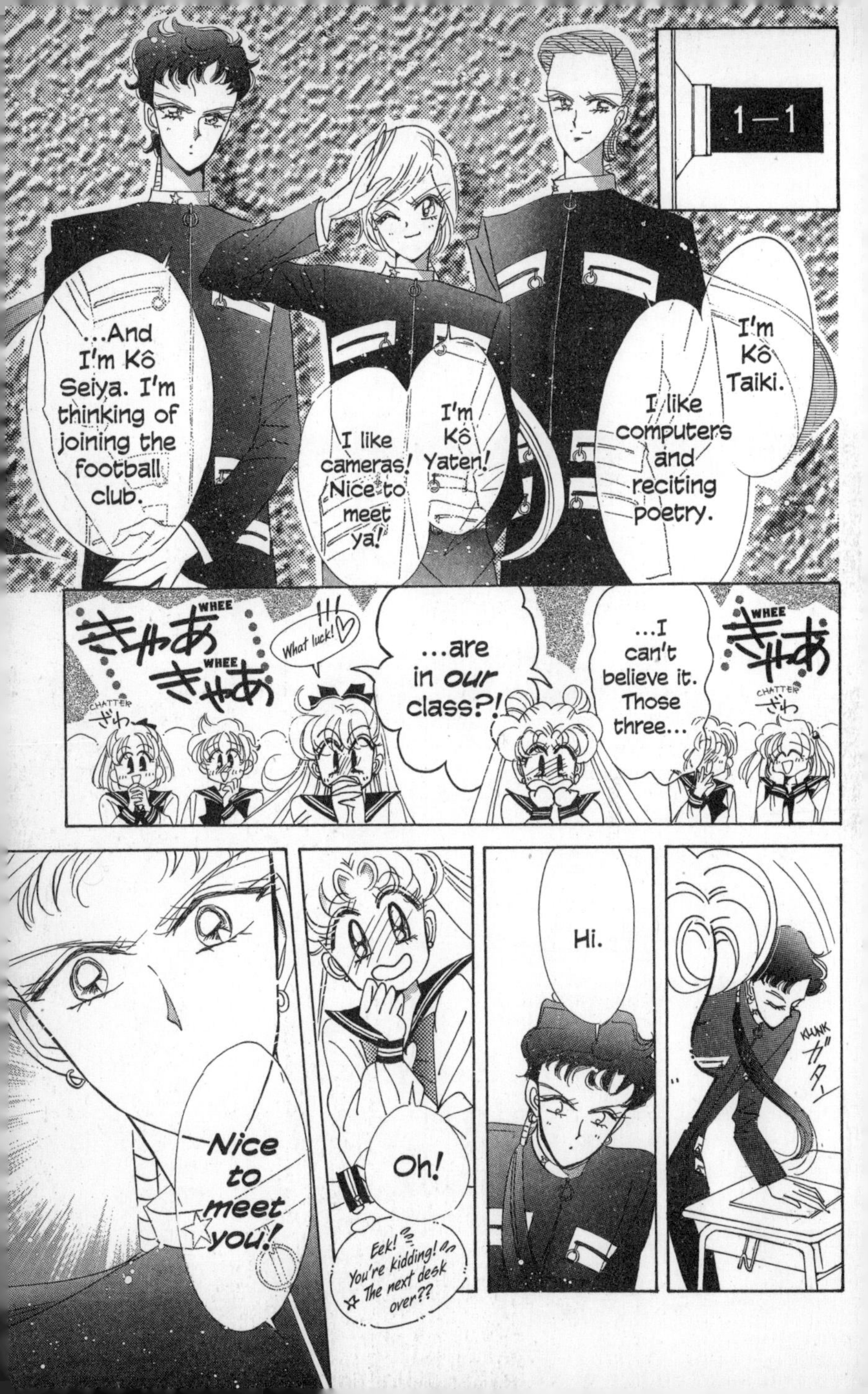
1—1
I'm Kô Taiki.
I like computers and reciting poetry.
I'm Kô Yaten!
I like cameras! Nice to meet ya!
...And I'm Kô Seiya. I'm thinking of joining the football club.
WHEE
きゃあ
CHATTER
ざわ
...I can't believe it. Those three...
...are in our class?!
What luck!
WHEE
きゃあ
WHEE
きゃあ
CHATTER
ざわ
KLUNK
ガタ
Hi.
Oh!
Eek! You're kidding! The next desk over??
Nice to meet you!

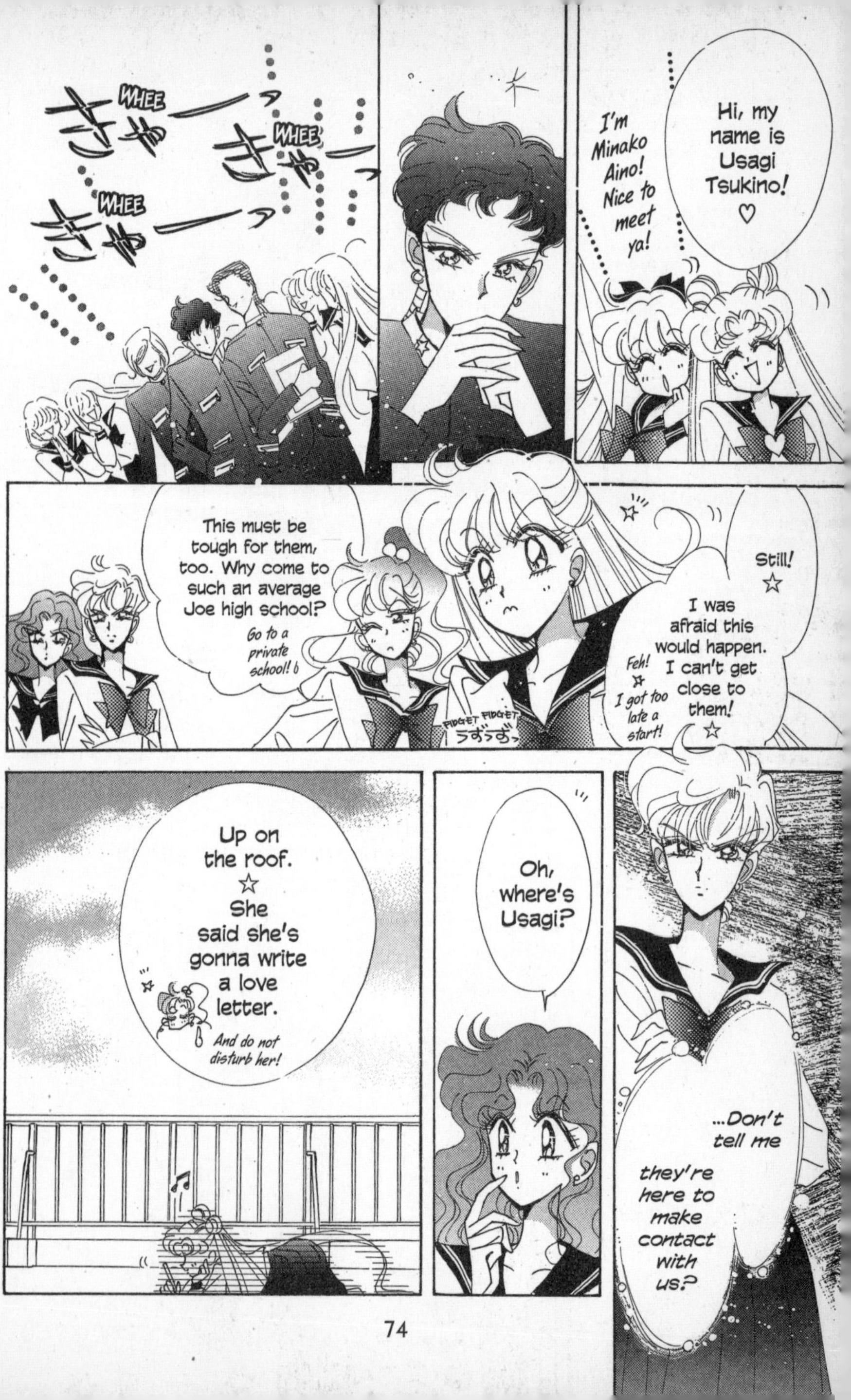
Hi, my name is Usagi Tsukino! ♡
I'm Minako Aino! Nice to meet ya!
WHEE きゃーっ
WHEE きゃーっ
WHEE きゃーっ
Still! ☆
I was afraid this would happen. I can't get close to them! ☆
Feh! ☆ I got too late a start!
FIDGET FIDGET うずうずっ
This must be tough for them, too. Why come to such an average Joe high school?
Go to a private school!
...Don't tell me they're here to make contact with us?
Oh, where's Usagi?
Up on the roof. ☆ She said she's gonna write a love letter.
And do not disturb her!

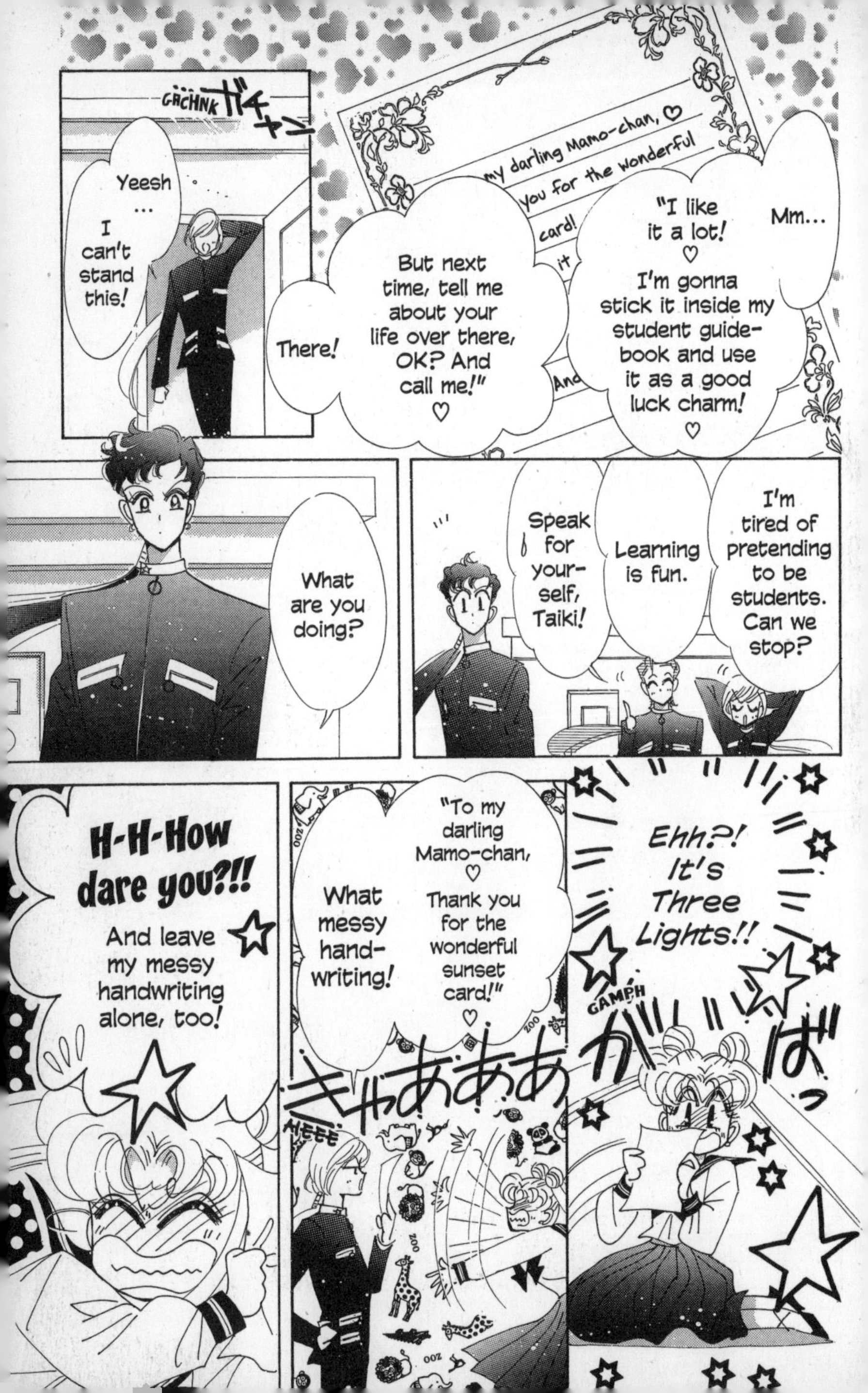
my darling Mamo-chan, ♡
you for the wonderful
card!
it
And
Mm...
"I like it a lot! ♡ I'm gonna stick it inside my student guidebook and use it as a good luck charm! ♡
But next time, tell me about your life over there, OK? And call me!" ♡
There!
GACHNK ガチャン
Yeesh... I can't stand this!
I'm tired of pretending to be students. Can we stop?
Learning is fun.
Speak for yourself, Taiki!
What are you doing?
Ehh?! It's Three Lights!!
GAMPH がばっ
"To my darling Mamo-chan, ♡ Thank you for the wonderful sunset card!" ♡
What messy handwriting!
AIEEE きゃあああ
H-H-How dare you?!!
And leave my messy handwriting alone, too!

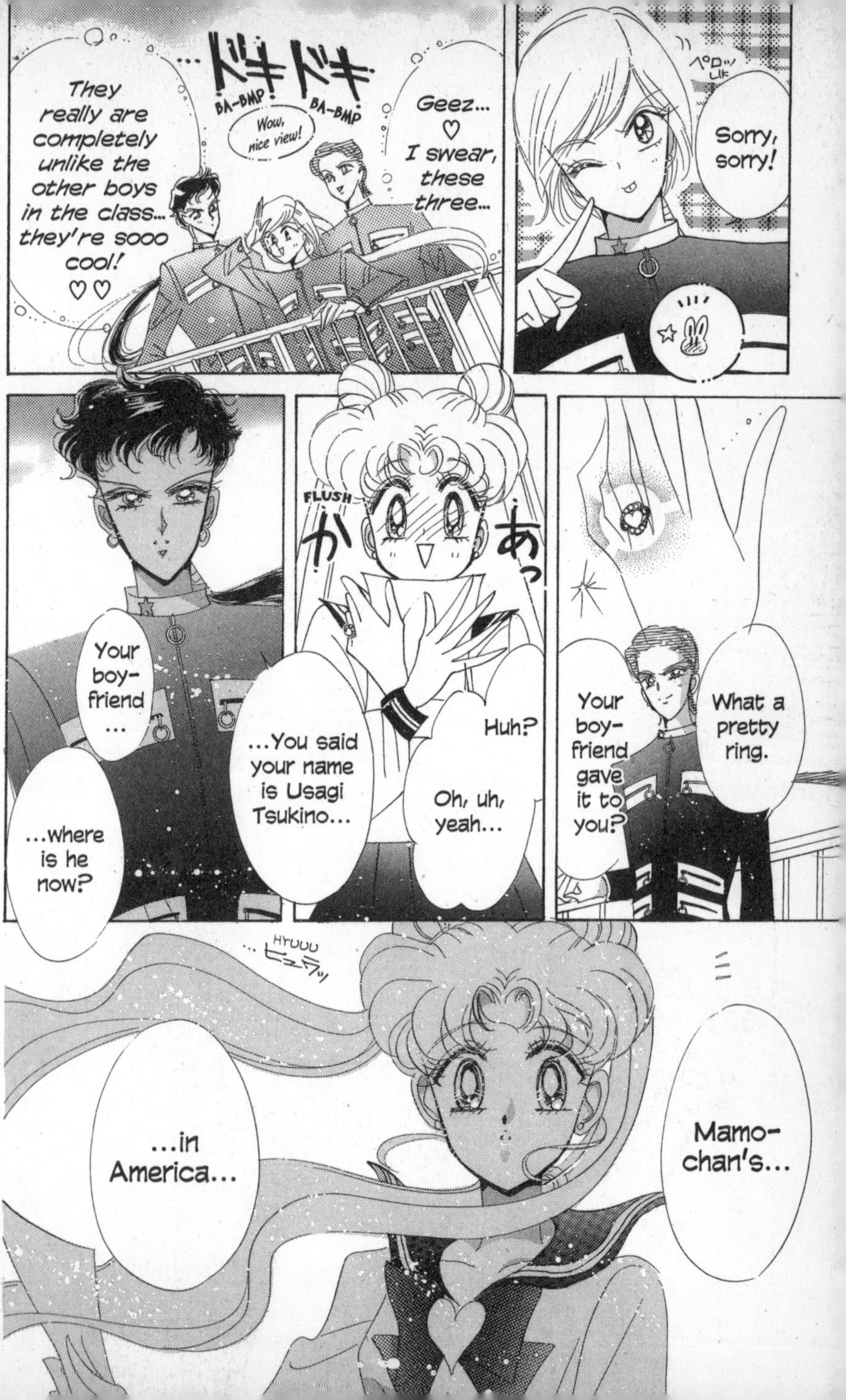
ペロッ
LIK
Sorry, sorry!
Geez... ♡ I swear, these three...
ドキドキ
BA-BMP BA-BMP
Wow, nice view!
...They really are completely unlike the other boys in the class... they're sooo cool! ♡ ♡
What a pretty ring.
Your boy-friend gave it to you?
あっ
か
FLUSH
Huh?
Oh, uh, yeah...
...You said your name is Usagi Tsukino...
Your boy-friend...
...where is he now?
Mamo-chan's...
...in America...
ヒューッ
HYUUU

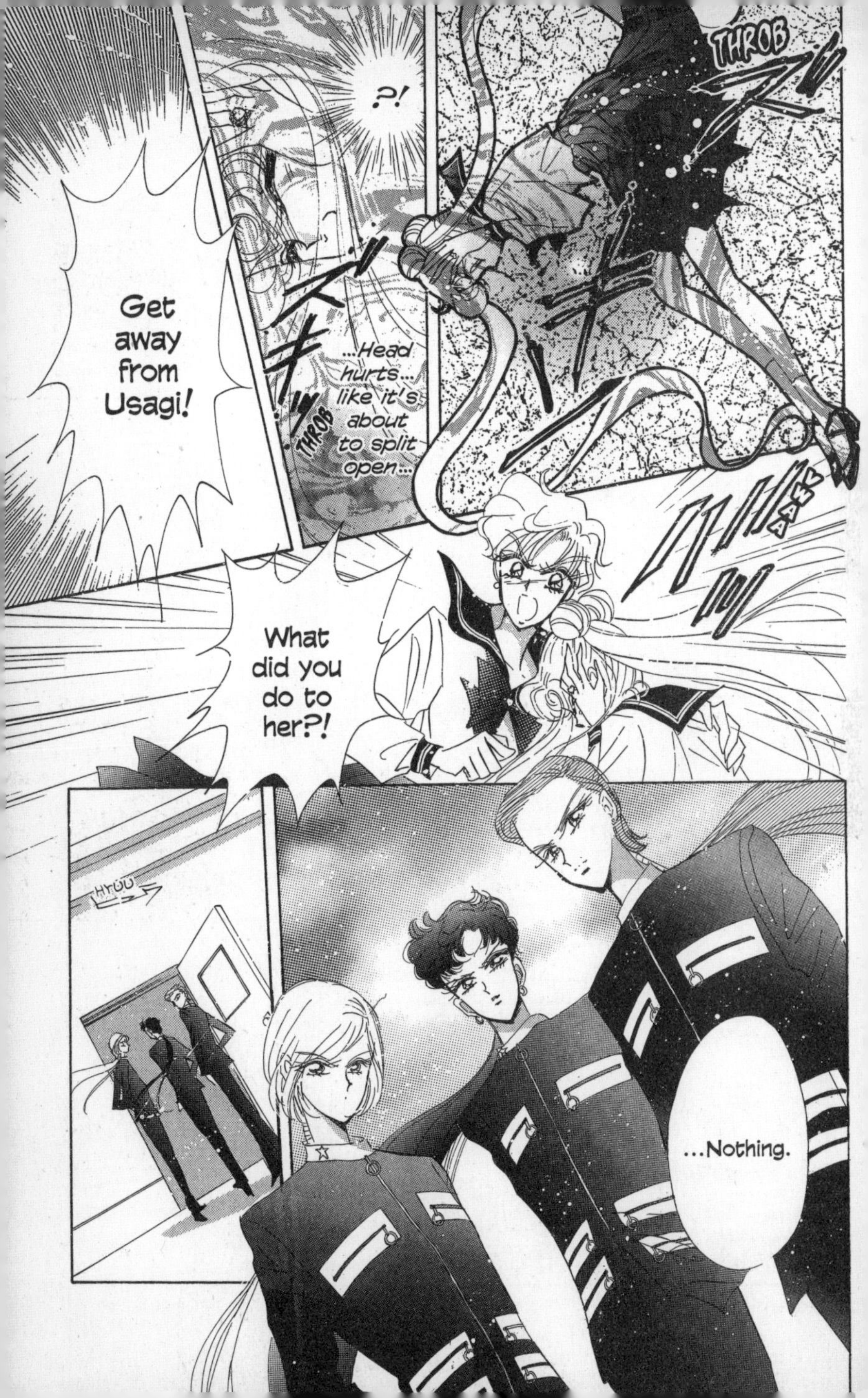
THROB
?!
THROB
...Head hurts... like it's about to split open...
Get away from Usagi!
What did you do to her?!
HYUU
...Nothing.

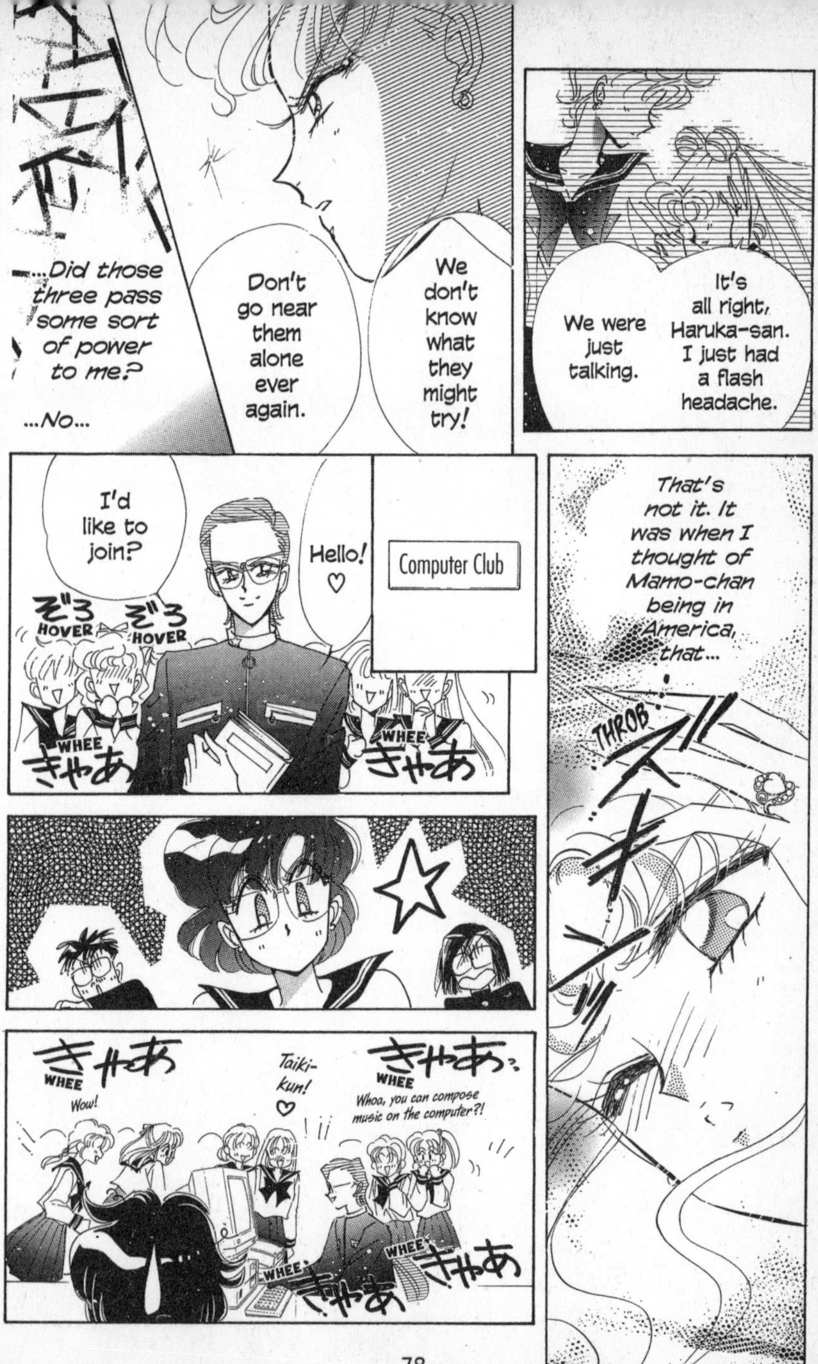
It's all right, Haruka-san. I just had a flash headache.
We were just talking.
We don't know what they might try!
Don't go near them alone ever again.
...Did those three pass some sort of power to me?
...No...
That's not it. It was when I thought of Mamo-chan being in America, that...
THROB
Computer Club
Hello! ♡
I'd like to join?
ぞろ HOVER
ぞろ HOVER
きゃあ WHEE
きゃあ WHEE
きゃあ WHEE
Whoa, you can compose music on the computer?!
Taiki-kun! ♡
きゃあ WHEE
Wow!
きゃあ WHEE
きゃあ WHEE

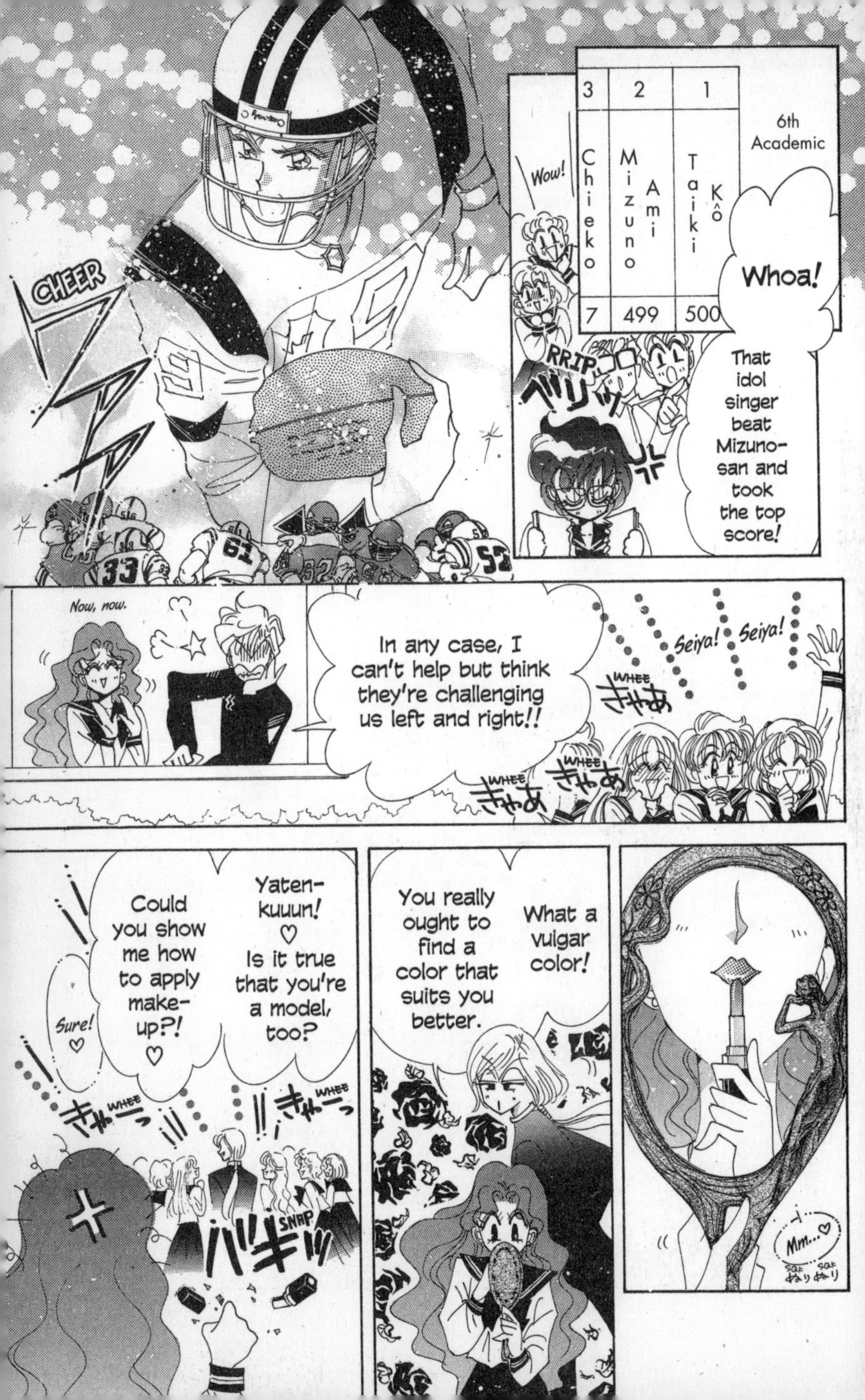
6th Academic
1 Taiki Kô 500
2 Mizuno Ami 499
3 Chieko 7
Whoa!
Wow!
RRIP
That idol singer beat Mizuno-san and took the top score!
CHEER
Seiya!
Seiya!
WHEE
WHEE
WHEE
In any case, I can't help but think they're challenging us left and right!!
Now, now.
Mm...♡
SQK SQK
What a vulgar color!
You really ought to find a color that suits you better.
Yaten-kuuun! ♡ Is it true that you're a model, too?
Could you show me how to apply make-up?! ♡
Sure! ♡
WHEE
WHEE
SNAP

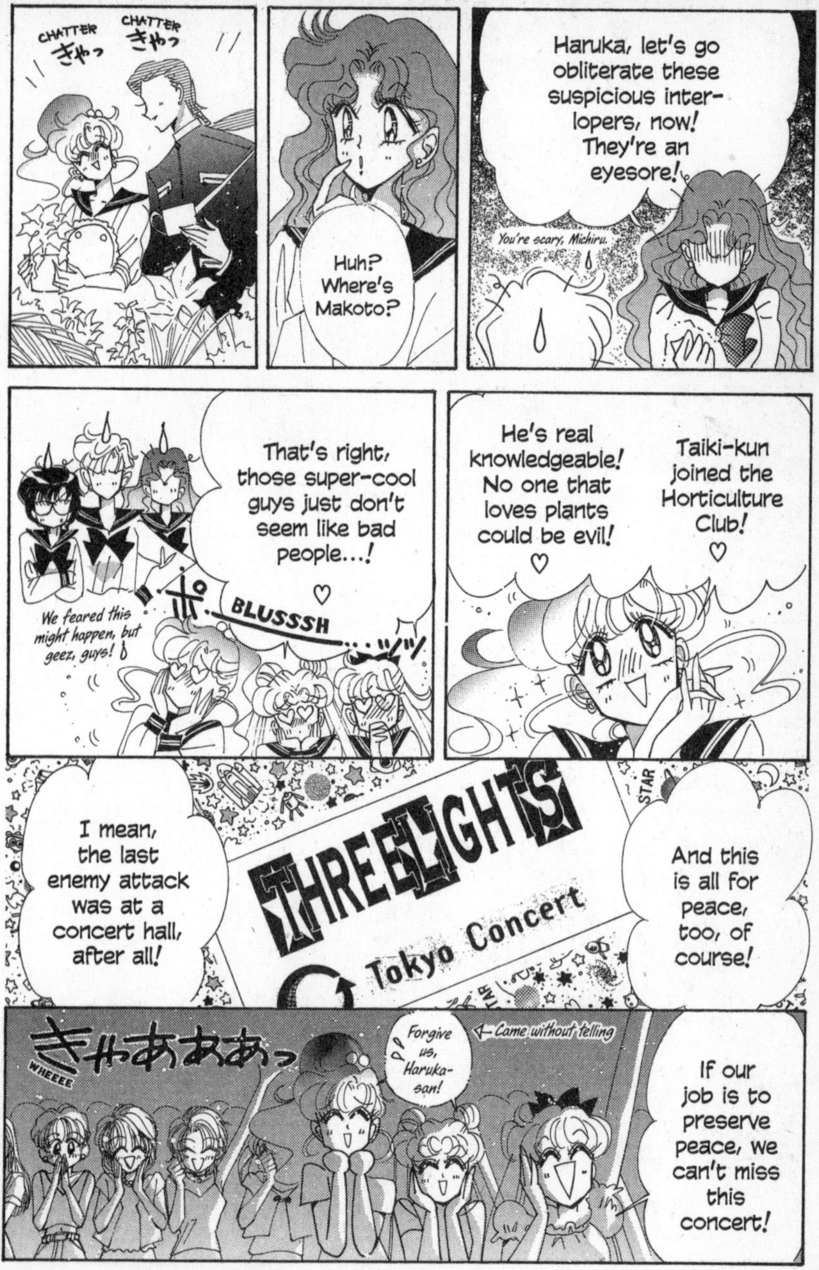
Haruka, let's go obliterate these suspicious inter-lopers, now! They're an eyesore!
You're scary, Michiru.
Huh? Where's Makoto?
CHATTER
きゃっ
CHATTER
きゃっ
Taiki-kun joined the Horticulture Club! ♡
He's real knowledgeable! No one that loves plants could be evil! ♡
That's right, those super-cool guys just don't seem like bad people...! ♡
ポ
BLUSSSH
We feared this might happen, but geez, guys!
And this is all for peace, too, of course!
STAR
THREELIGHTS
Tokyo Concert
I mean, the last enemy attack was at a concert hall, after all!
If our job is to preserve peace, we can't miss this concert!
← Came without telling
Forgive us, Haruka-san!
きゃあああっ
WHEEEE

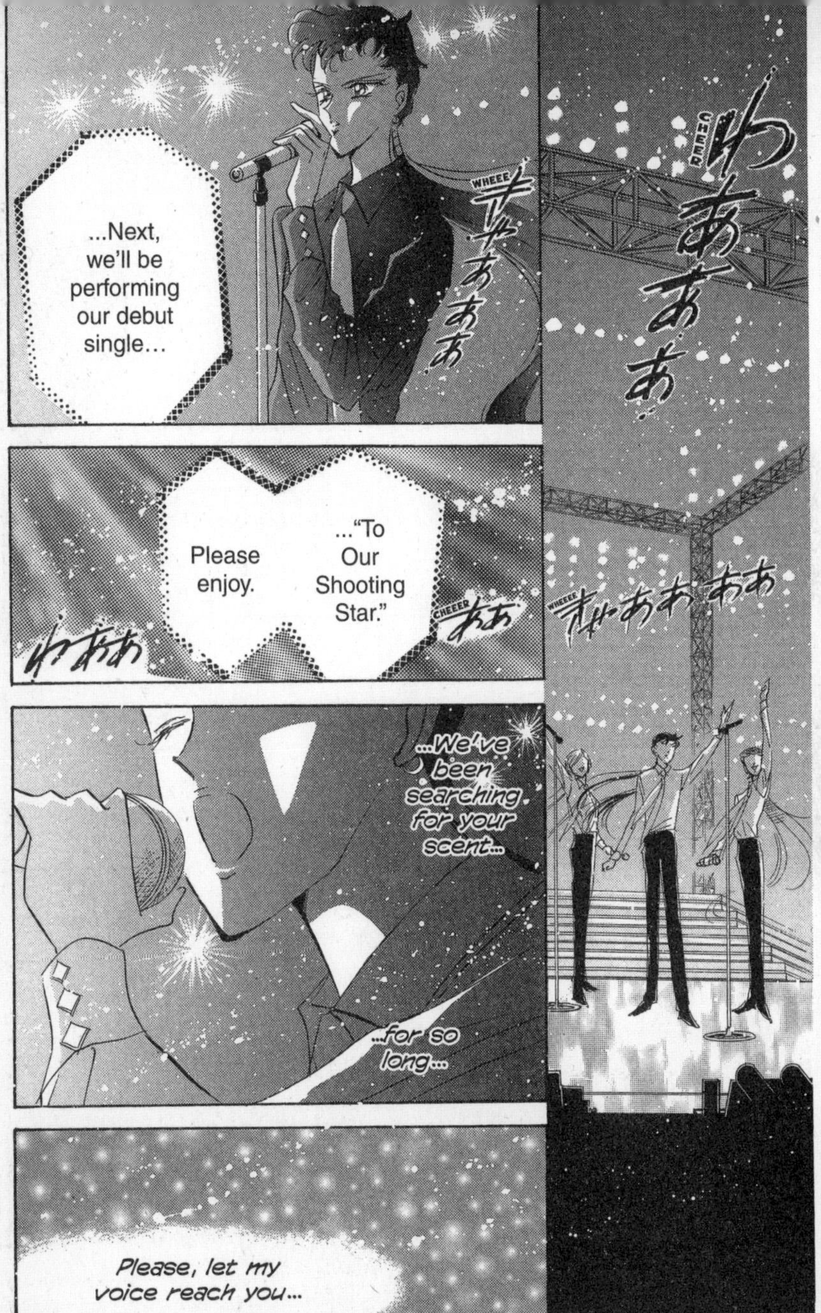
CHEER
わあああ
WHEEE
キャーああ ああ
...Next, we'll be performing our debut single...
WHEEE
キャーあああ
..."To Our Shooting Star."
Please enjoy.
CHEEER
ああ
わああ
...We've been searching for your scent...
...for so long...
Please, let my voice reach you...

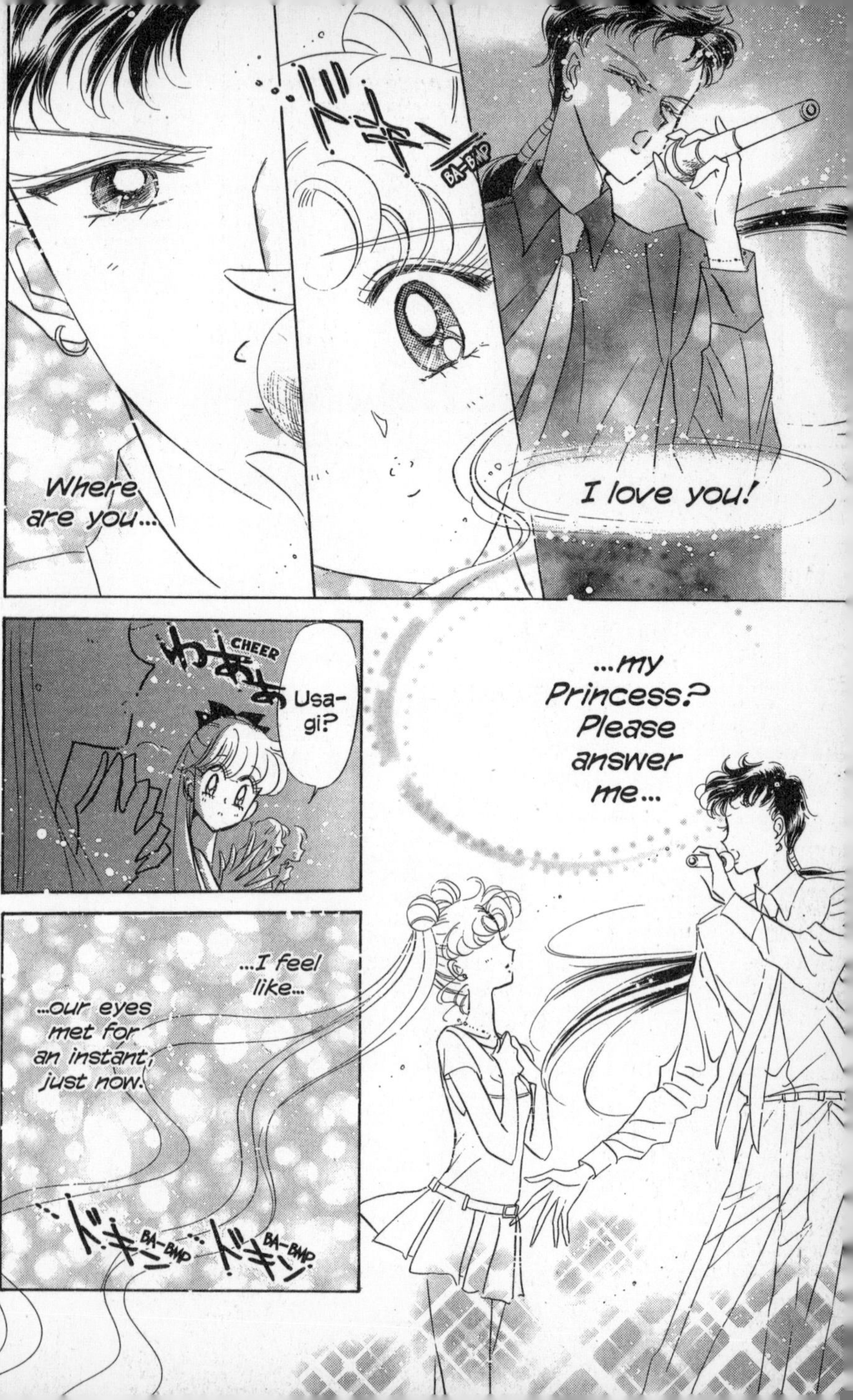
I love you!
ドキン
BA-BMP
Where are you...
...my Princess? Please answer me...
わあぁ
CHEER
Usa-gi?
...I feel like...
...our eyes met for an instant, just now.
ドキン
BA-BMP
ドキン
BA-BMP

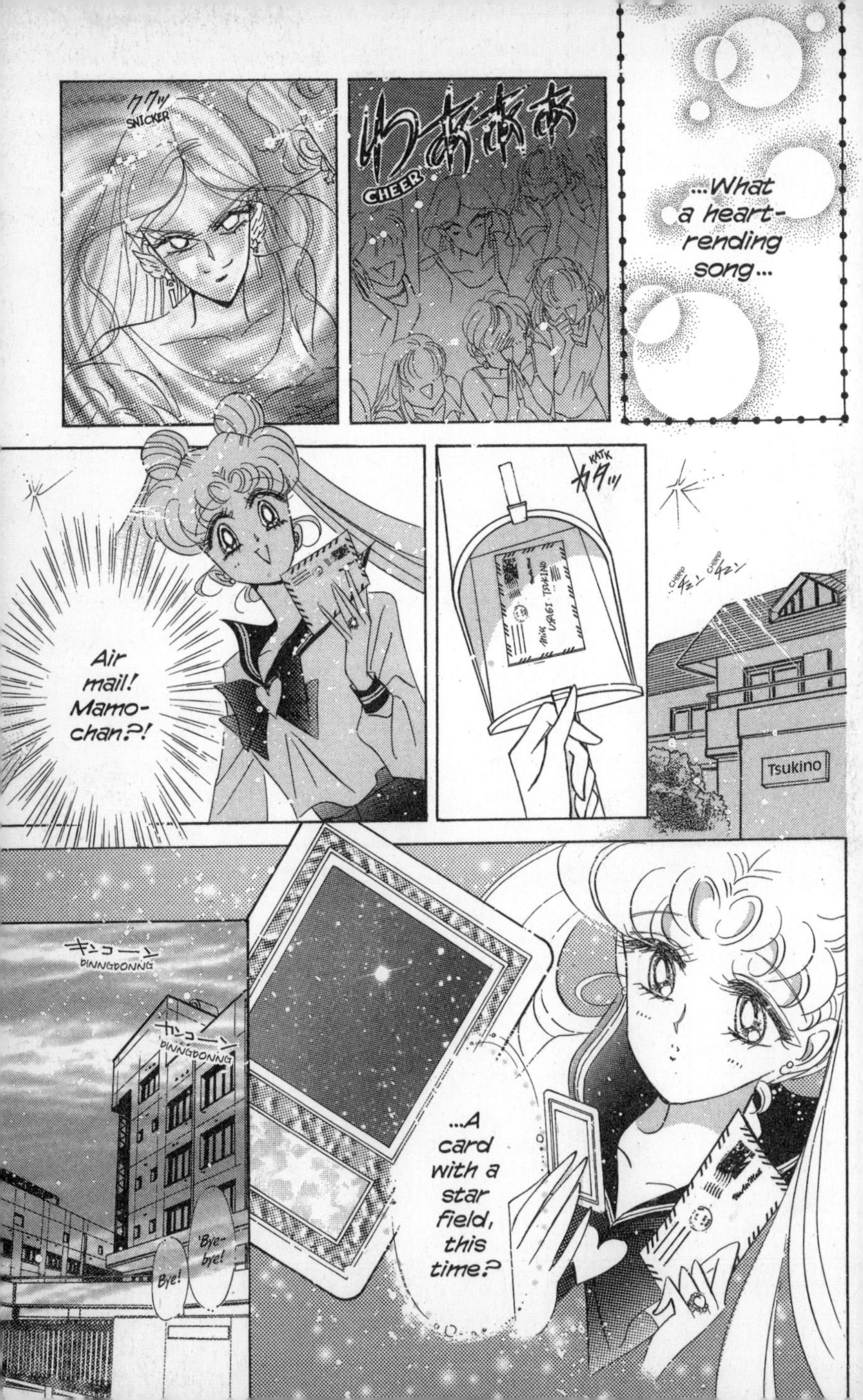

...What a heart-rending song...
CHEER
SNICKER
CHIRP
CHIRP
Tsukino
KATK
Ms. Usagi Tsukino
Air mail! Mamo-chan?!
...A card with a star field, this time?
DINNGDONNG
DINNGDONNG
'Bye-bye!
Bye!

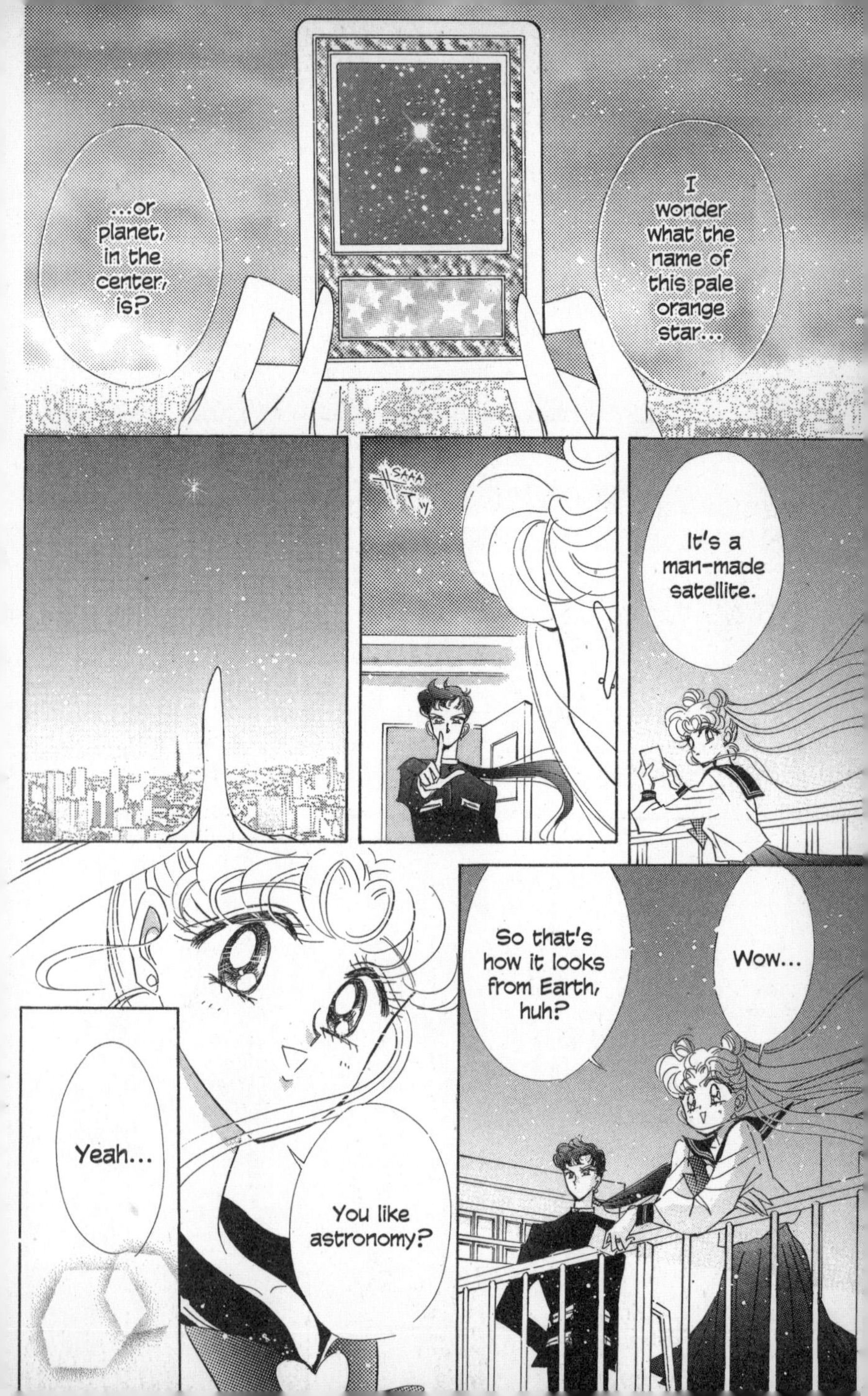
I wonder what the name of this pale orange star...
...or planet, in the center, is?
It's a man-made satellite.
Wow...
So that's how it looks from Earth, huh?
You like astronomy?
Yeah...

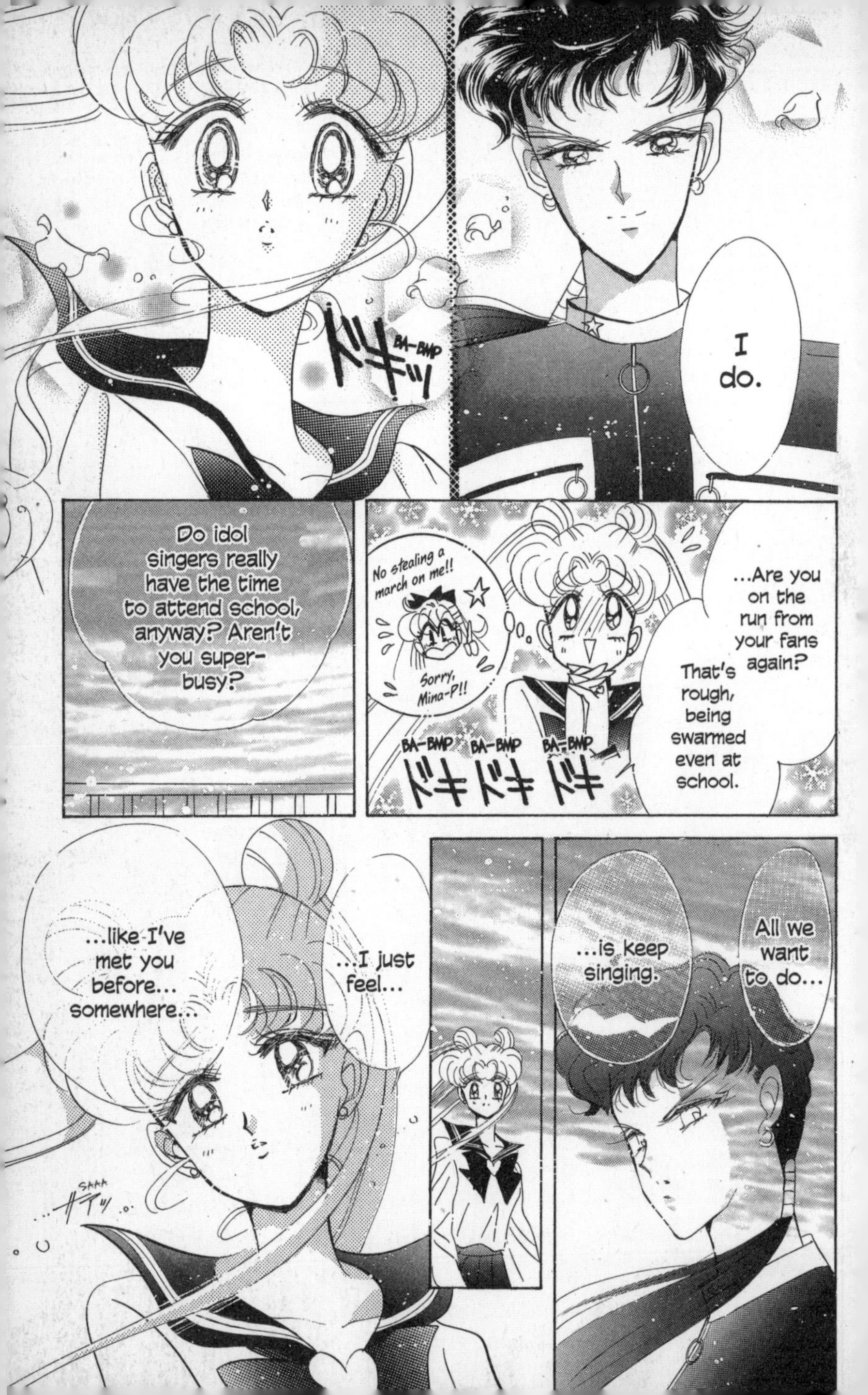
I do.
ドキッ
BA-BMP
...Are you on the run from your fans again?
That's rough, being swarmed even at school.
No stealing a march on me!!
Sorry, Mina-P!!
BA-BMP BA-BMP BA-BMP
ドキドキドキ
Do idol singers really have the time to attend school, anyway? Aren't you super-busy?
All we want to do...
...is keep singing.
...I just feel...
...like I've met you before... somewhere...
SAAA

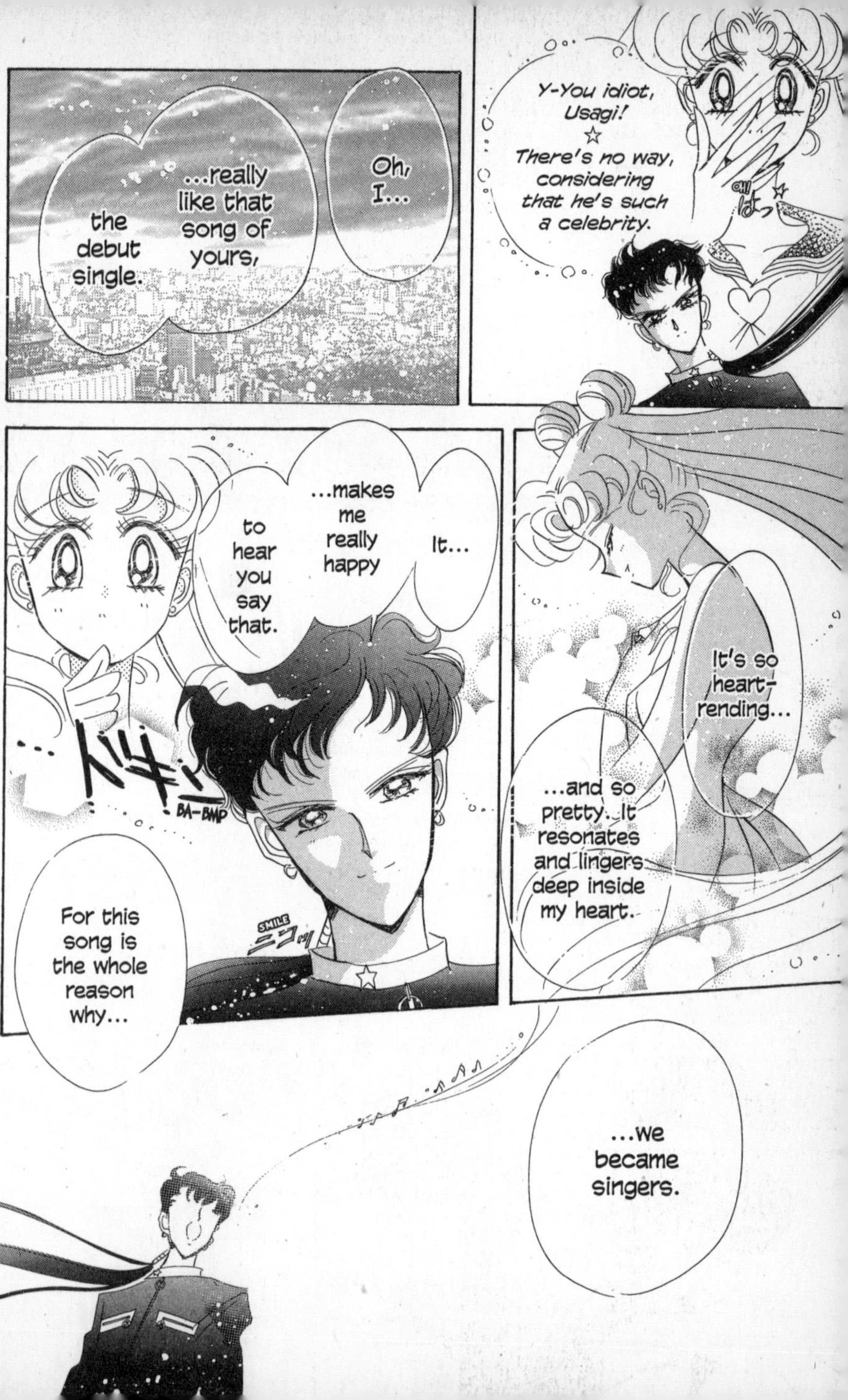
Y-You idiot, Usagi! ☆ There's no way, considering that he's such a celebrity.
OH! はっ
Oh, I...
...really like that song of yours,
the debut single.
It's so heart-rending...
...and so pretty. It resonates and lingers deep inside my heart.
It...
...makes me really happy
to hear you say that.
ドキッ BA-BMP
ニコッ SMILE
For this song is the whole reason why...
...we became singers.

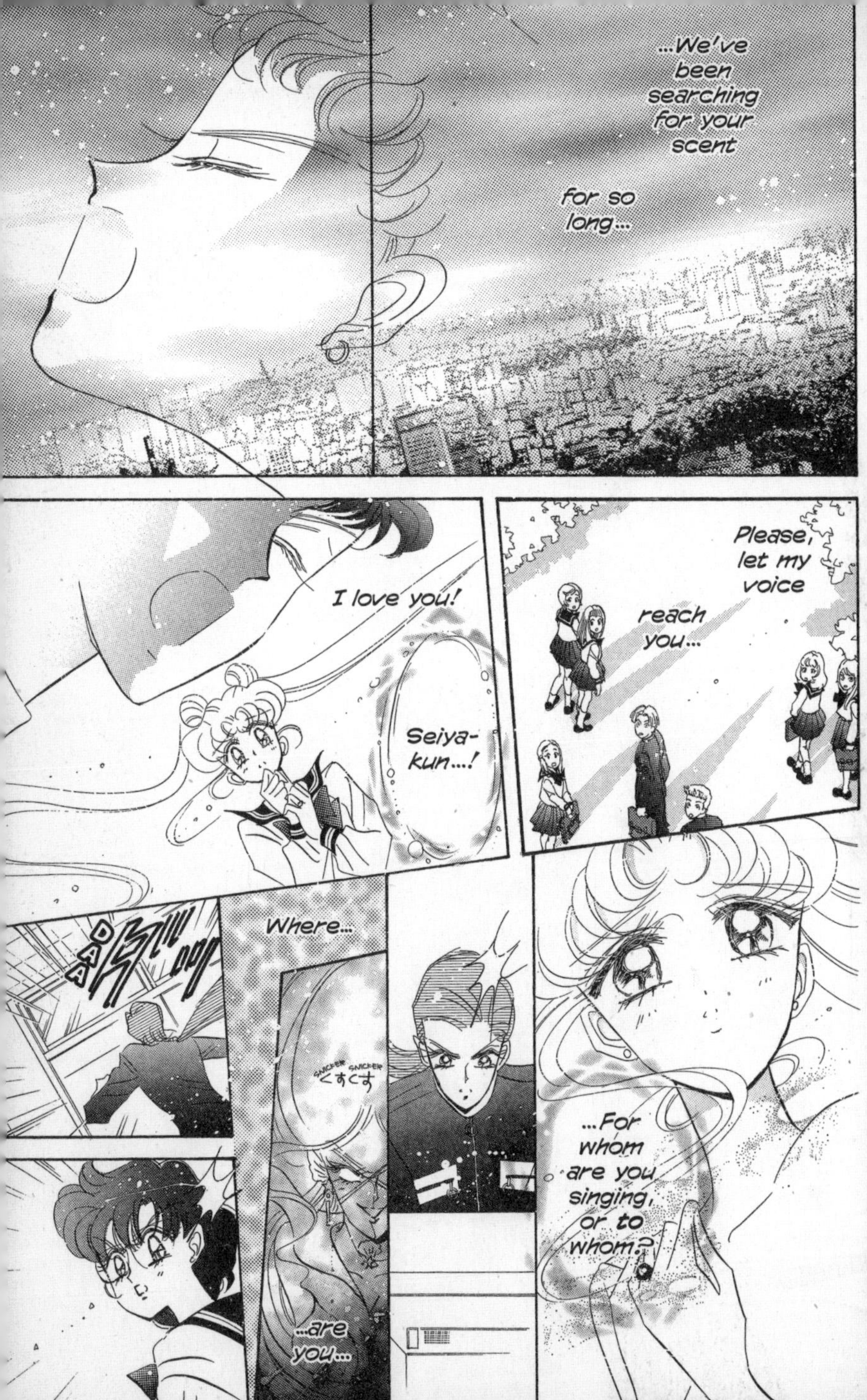
...We've been searching for your scent
for so long...
Please, let my voice
reach you...
I love you!
Seiya-kun...!
...For whom are you singing, or to whom?
Where...
SNICKER SNICKER くすくす
...are you...
DAA

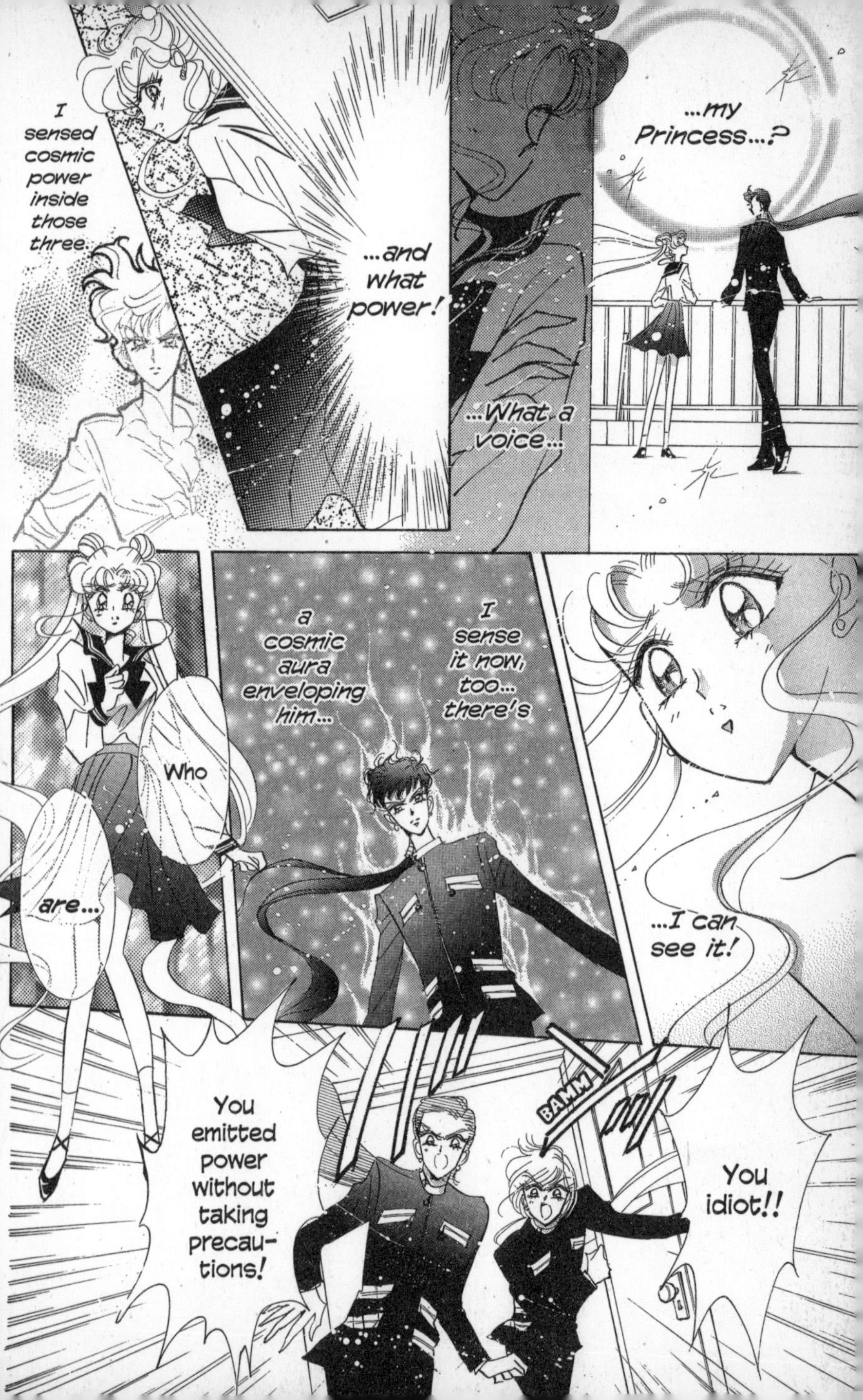
...my Princess...?
...What a voice...
...and what power!
I sensed cosmic power inside those three.
...I can see it!
I sense it now, too... there's
a cosmic aura enveloping him...
Who
are...
You idiot!!
BAMM
You emitted power without taking precautions!

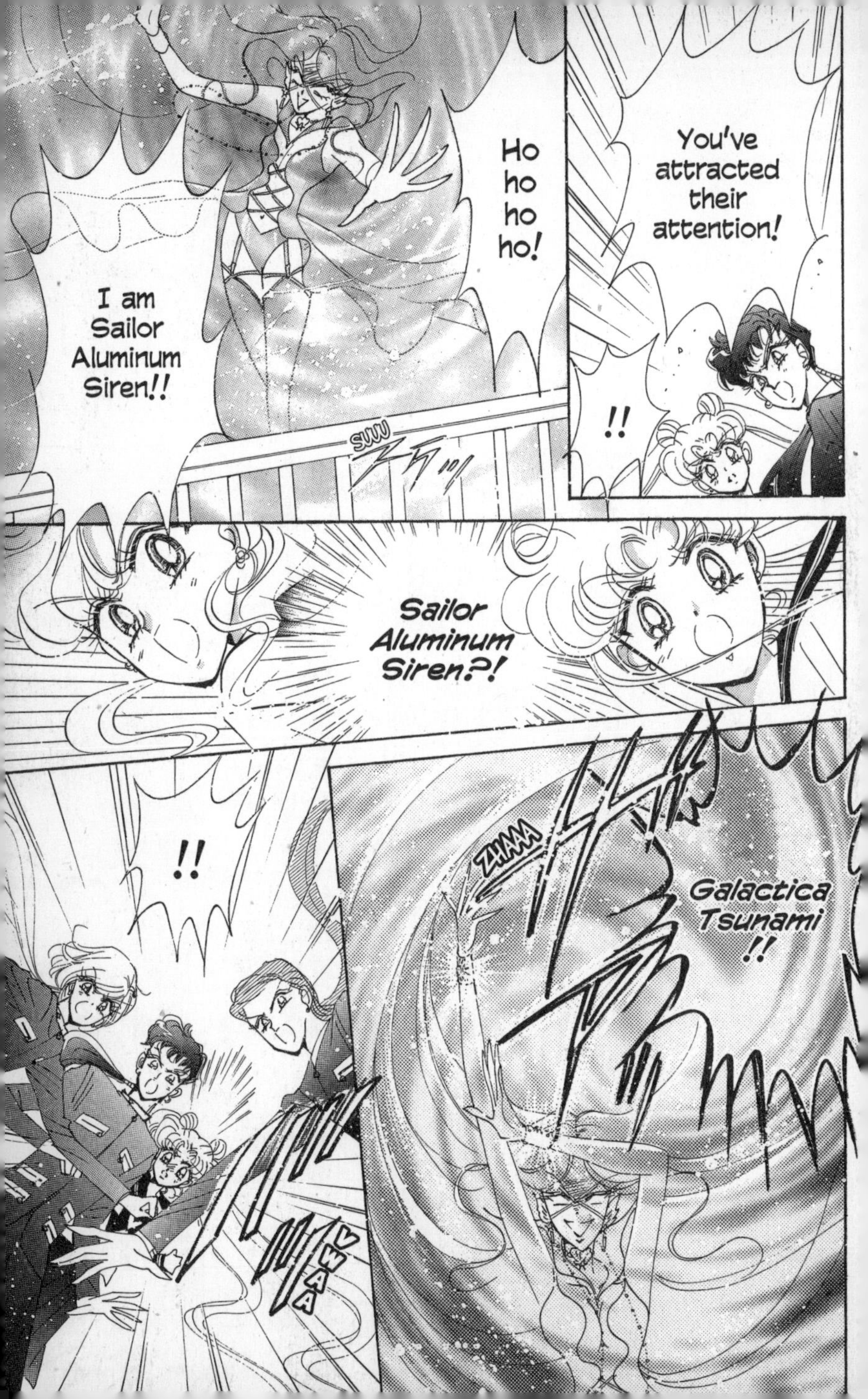
You've attracted their attention!
!!
Ho ho ho ho!
I am Sailor Aluminum Siren!!
SUUU
Sailor Aluminum Siren?!
Galactica Tsunami!!
ZHAAA
!!
VWAA

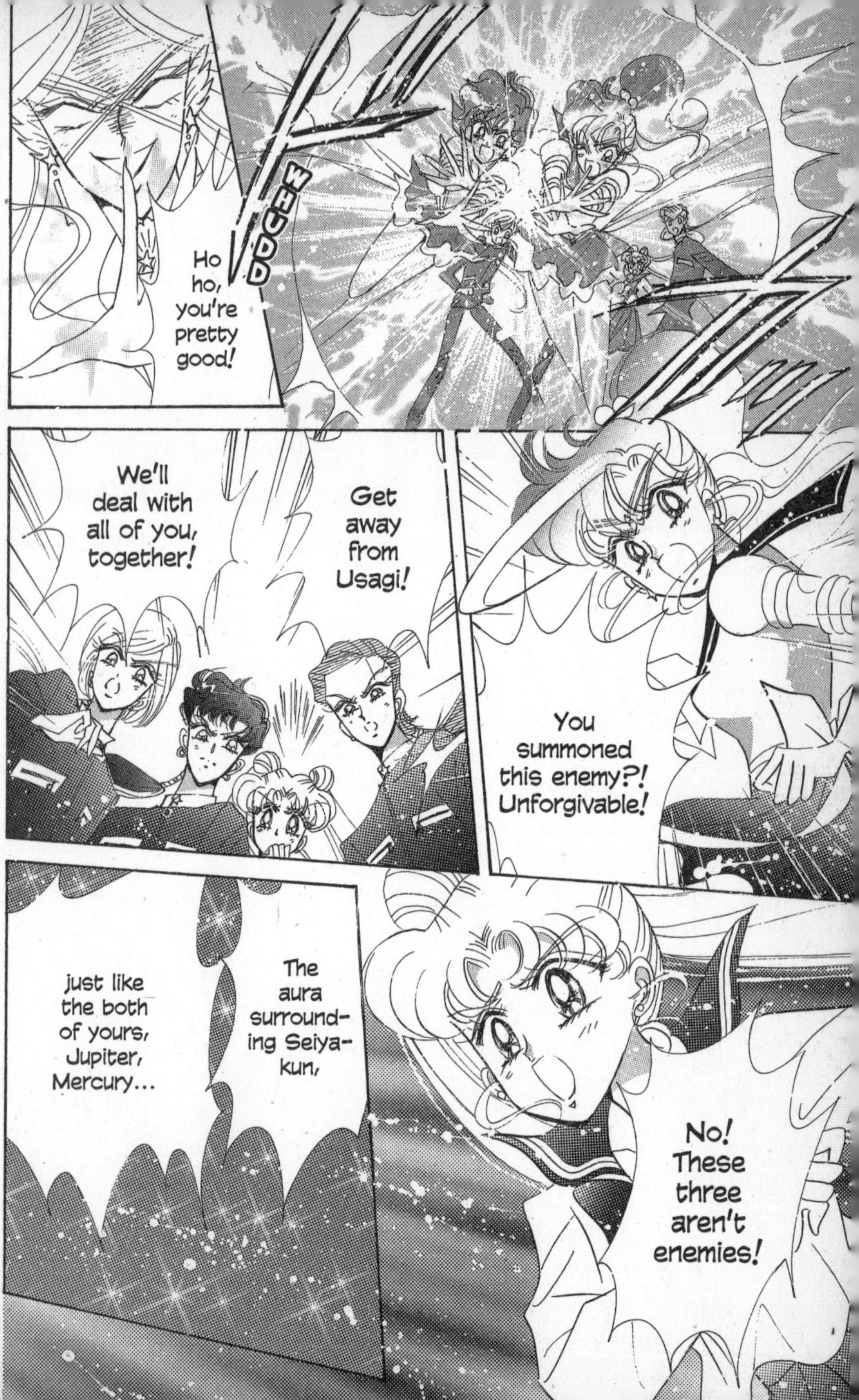
WHUDDD
Ho ho, you're pretty good!
You summoned this enemy?! Unforgivable!
Get away from Usagi!
We'll deal with all of you, together!
No! These three aren't enemies!
The aura surround-ing Seiya-kun,
just like the both of yours, Jupiter, Mercury...

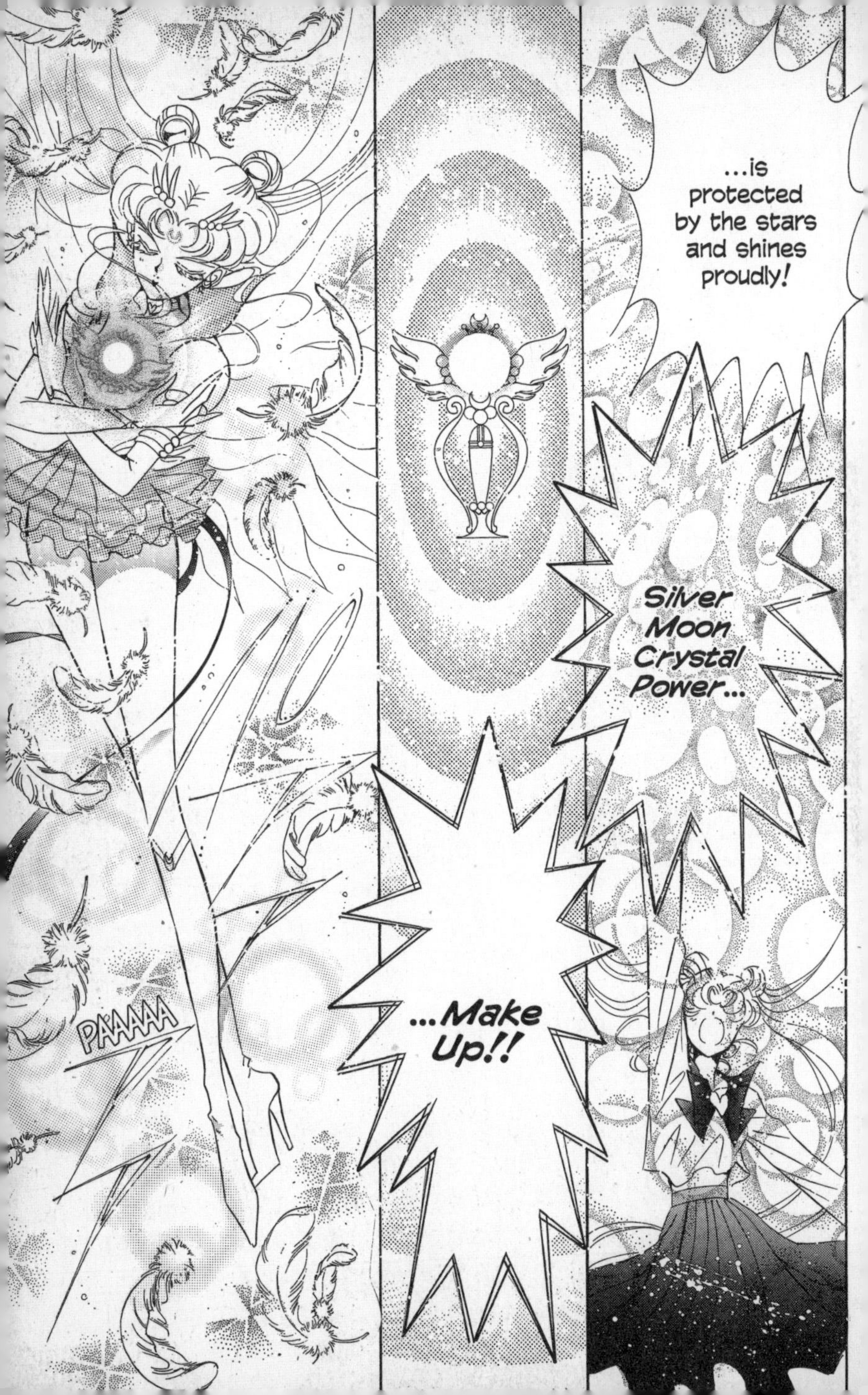
...is protected by the stars and shines proudly!
Silver Moon Crystal Power...
...Make Up!!
PAAAAA

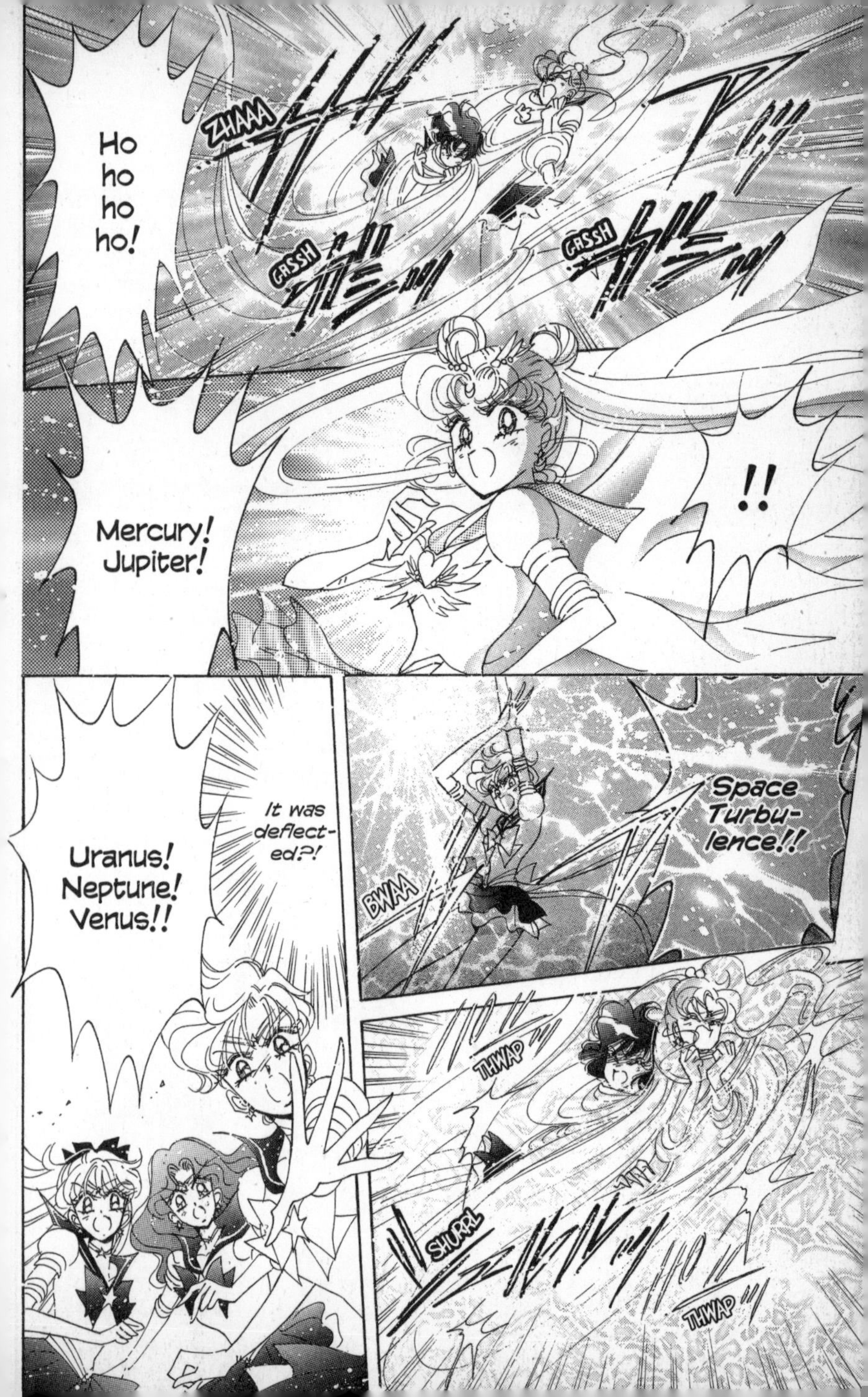
ZHAAA
GASSH
GASSH
Ho ho ho ho!
!!
Mercury! Jupiter!
Space Turbulence!!
BWAA
THWAP
SHURL
THWAP
It was deflected?!
Uranus! Neptune! Venus!!

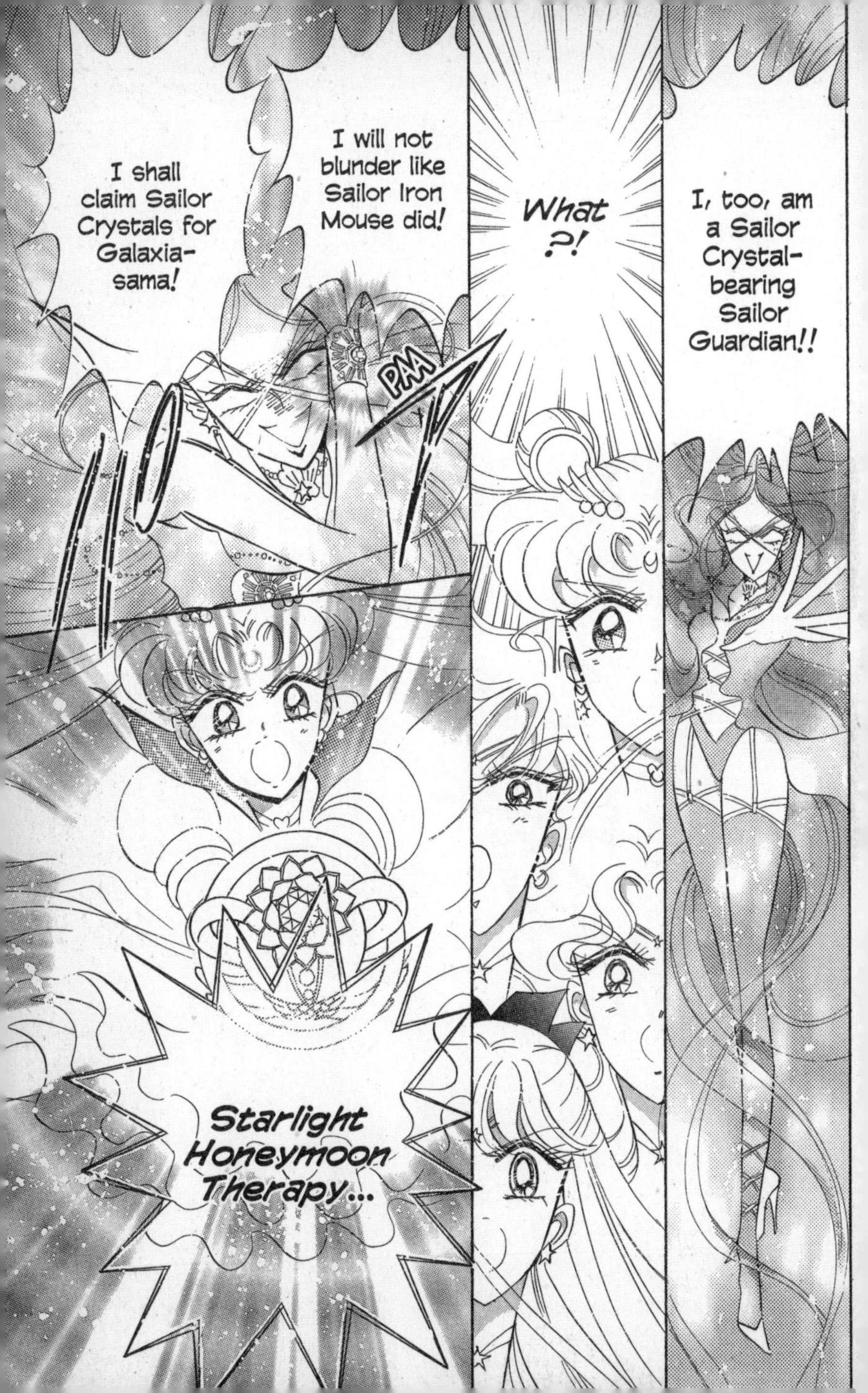
I, too, am a Sailor Crystal-bearing Sailor Guardian!!
What ?!
I will not blunder like Sailor Iron Mouse did!
I shall claim Sailor Crystals for Galaxia-sama!
PAA
Starlight Honeymoon Therapy...

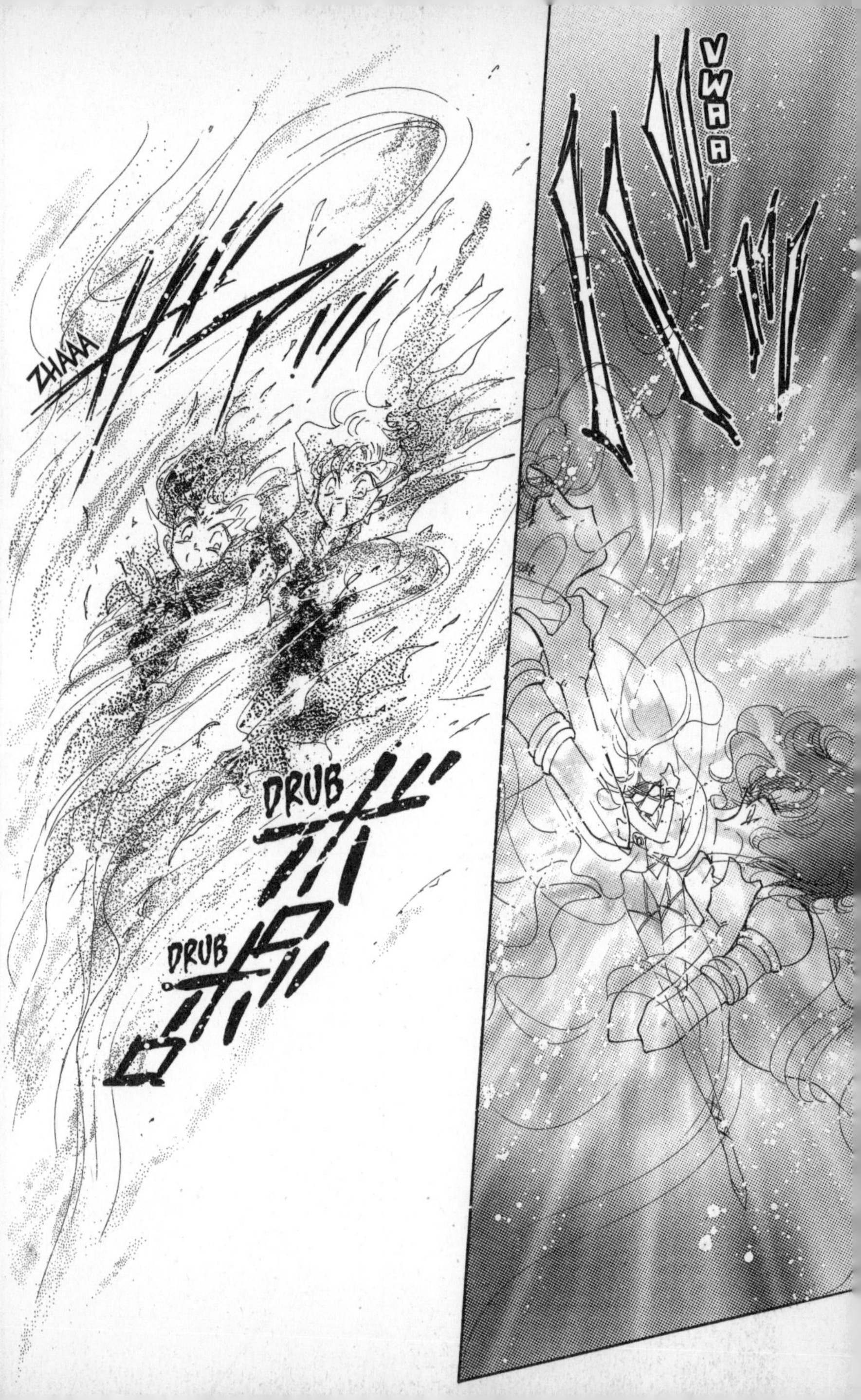
VWAA
ZHAAA
DRUB
DRUB

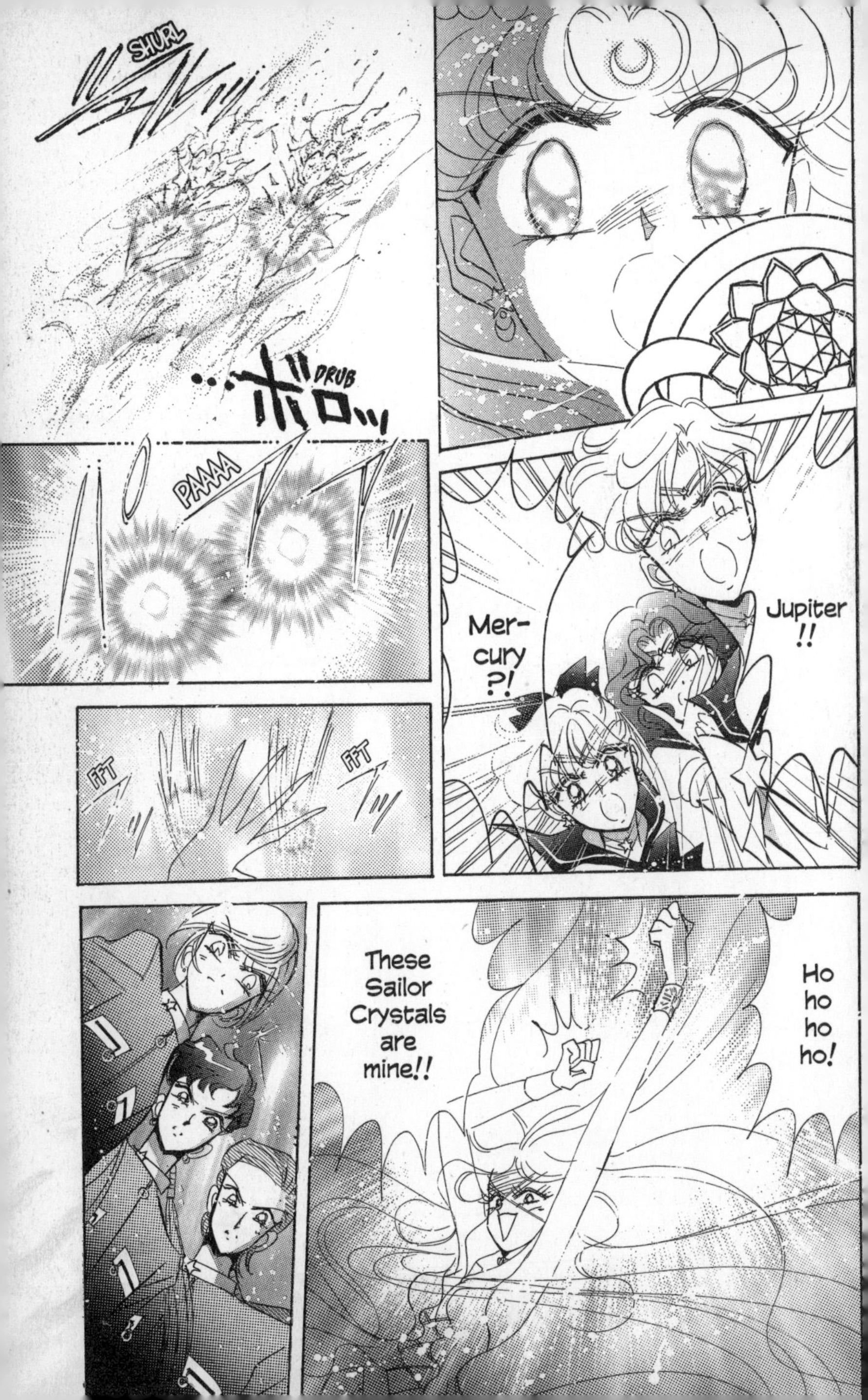
SHURL
DRUB
…ボロッ
Jupiter!!
Mer-cury?!
PAAAA
FFT
FFT
Ho ho ho ho!
These Sailor Crystals are mine!!

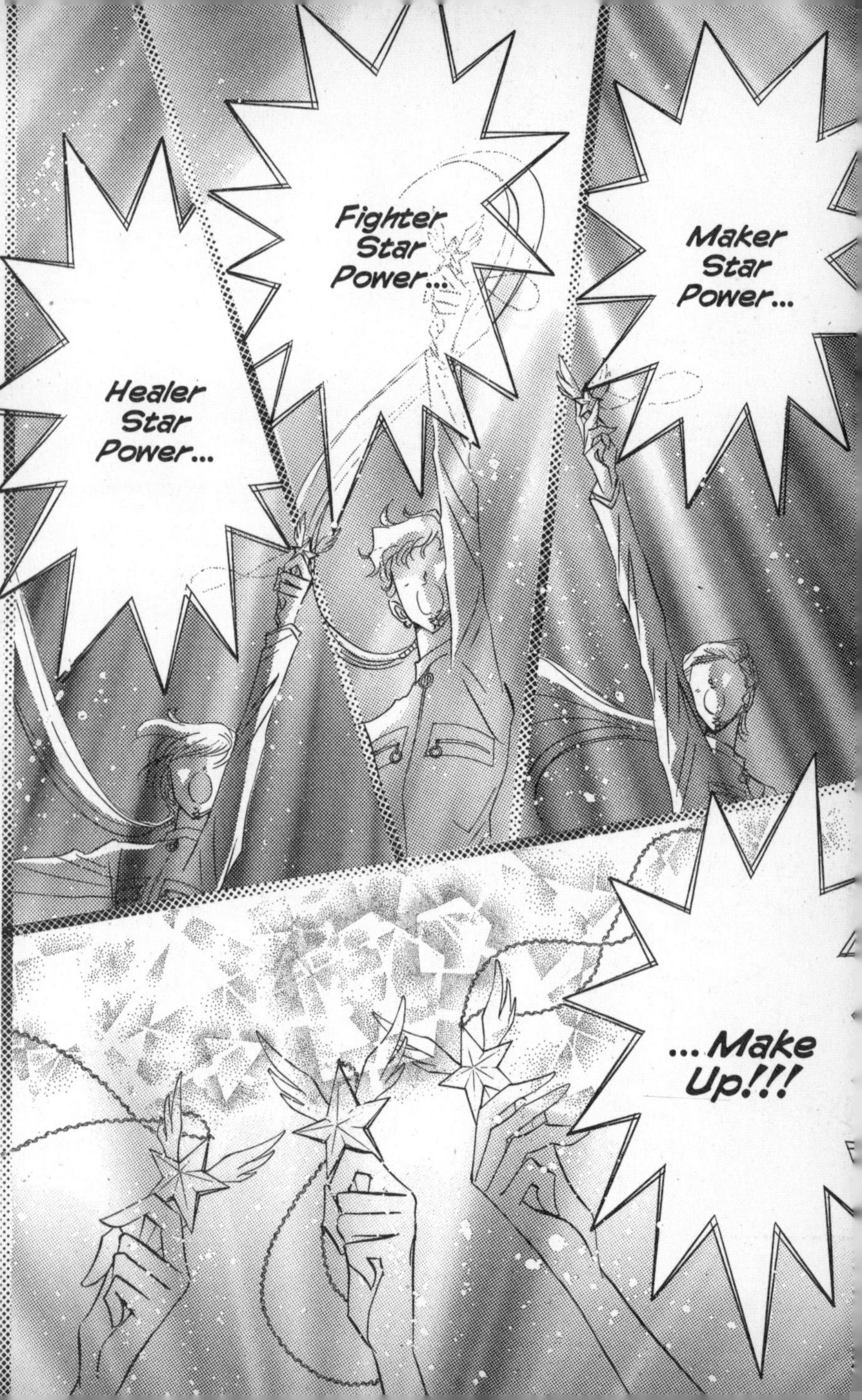

Maker Star Power...
Fighter Star Power...
Healer Star Power...
...Make Up!!!

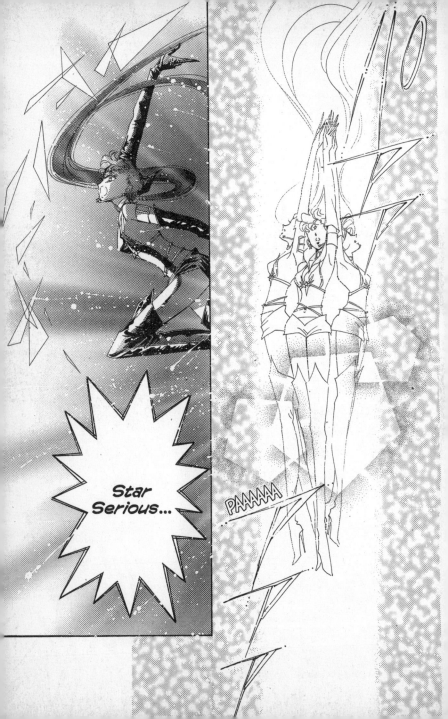

Star
Serious...

PAAAAAA

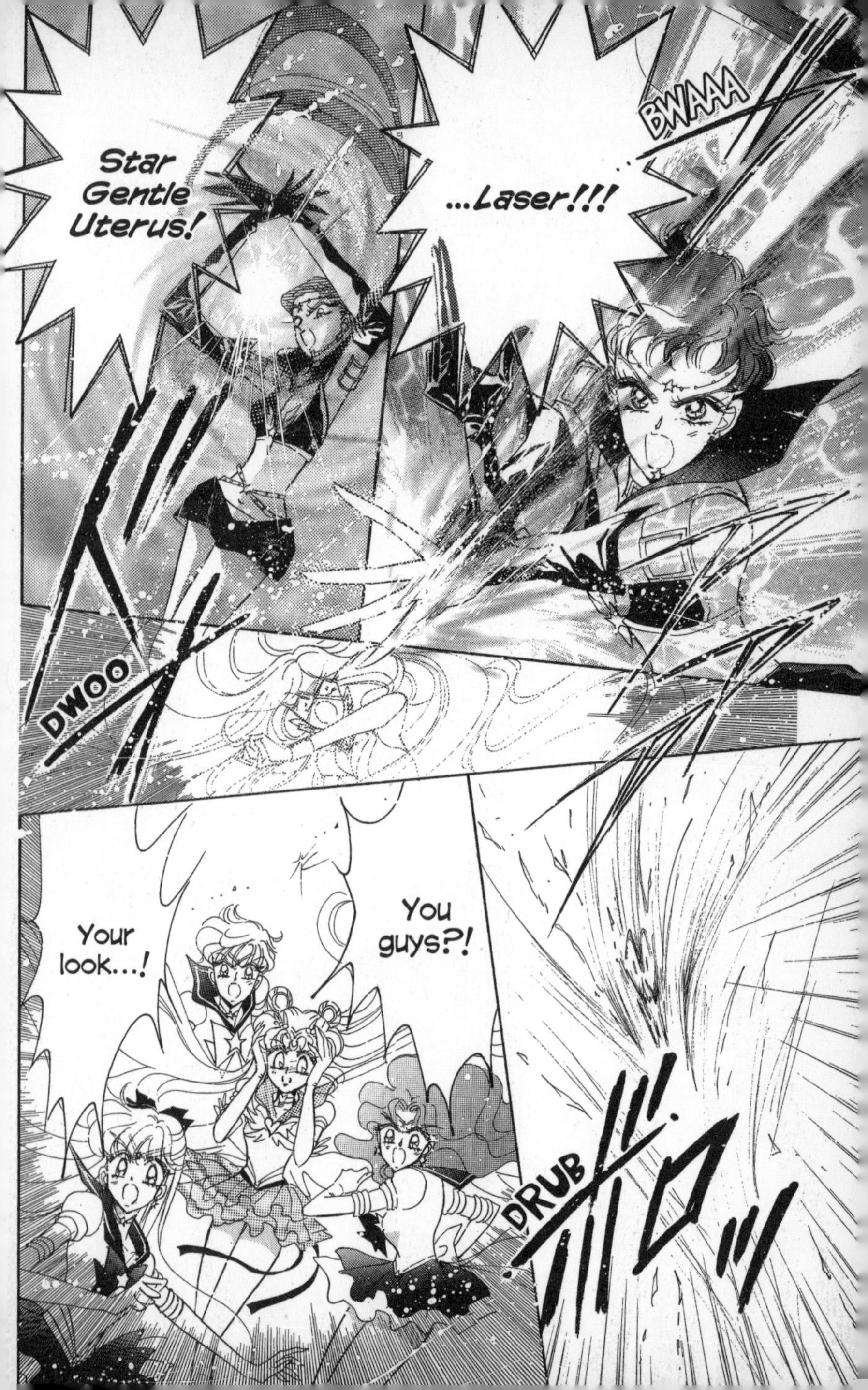
BWAAA
Star Gentle Uterus!
...Laser!!!
DWOO
DRUB
You guys?!
Your look...!

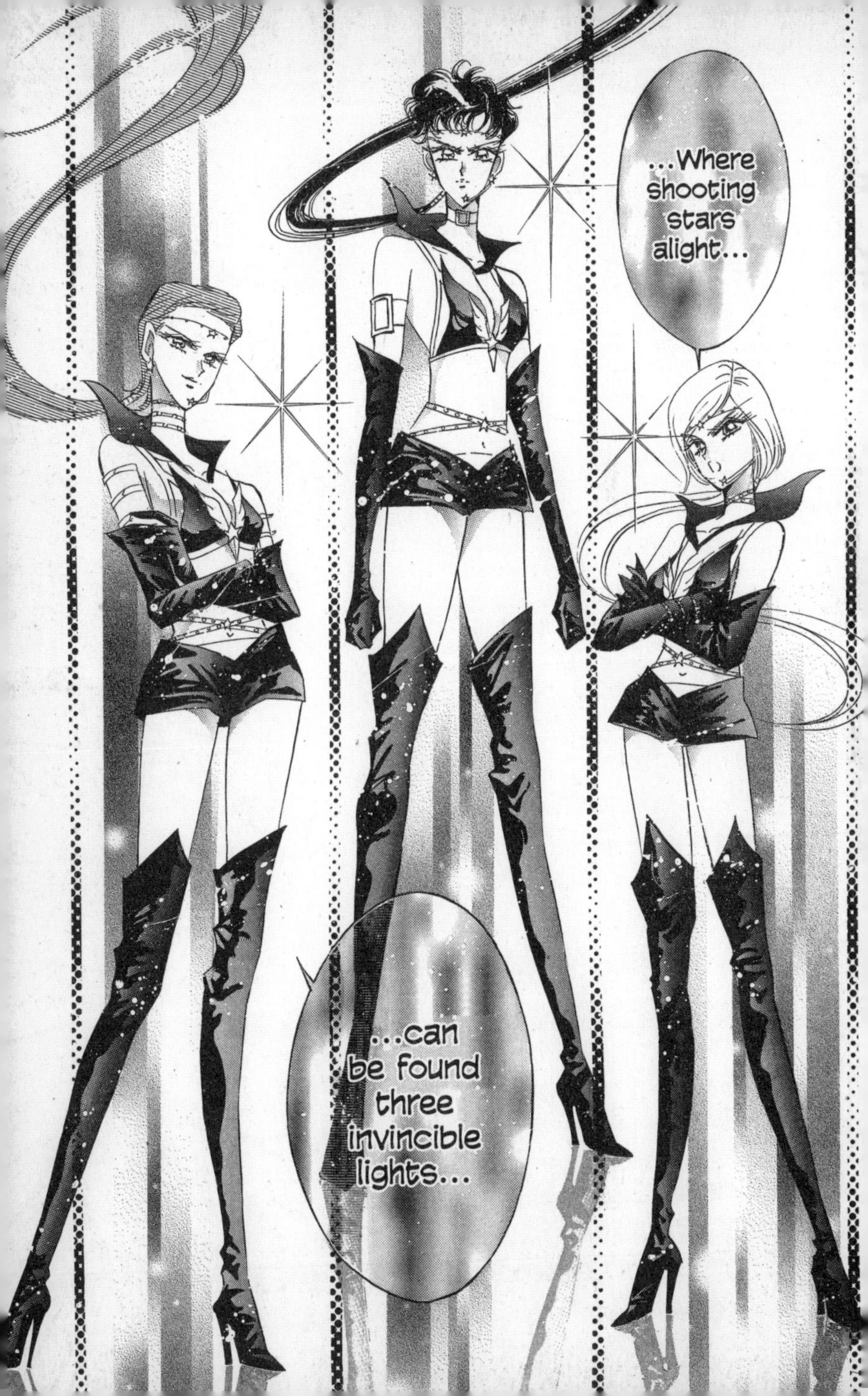
...Where shooting stars alight...
...can be found three invincible lights...

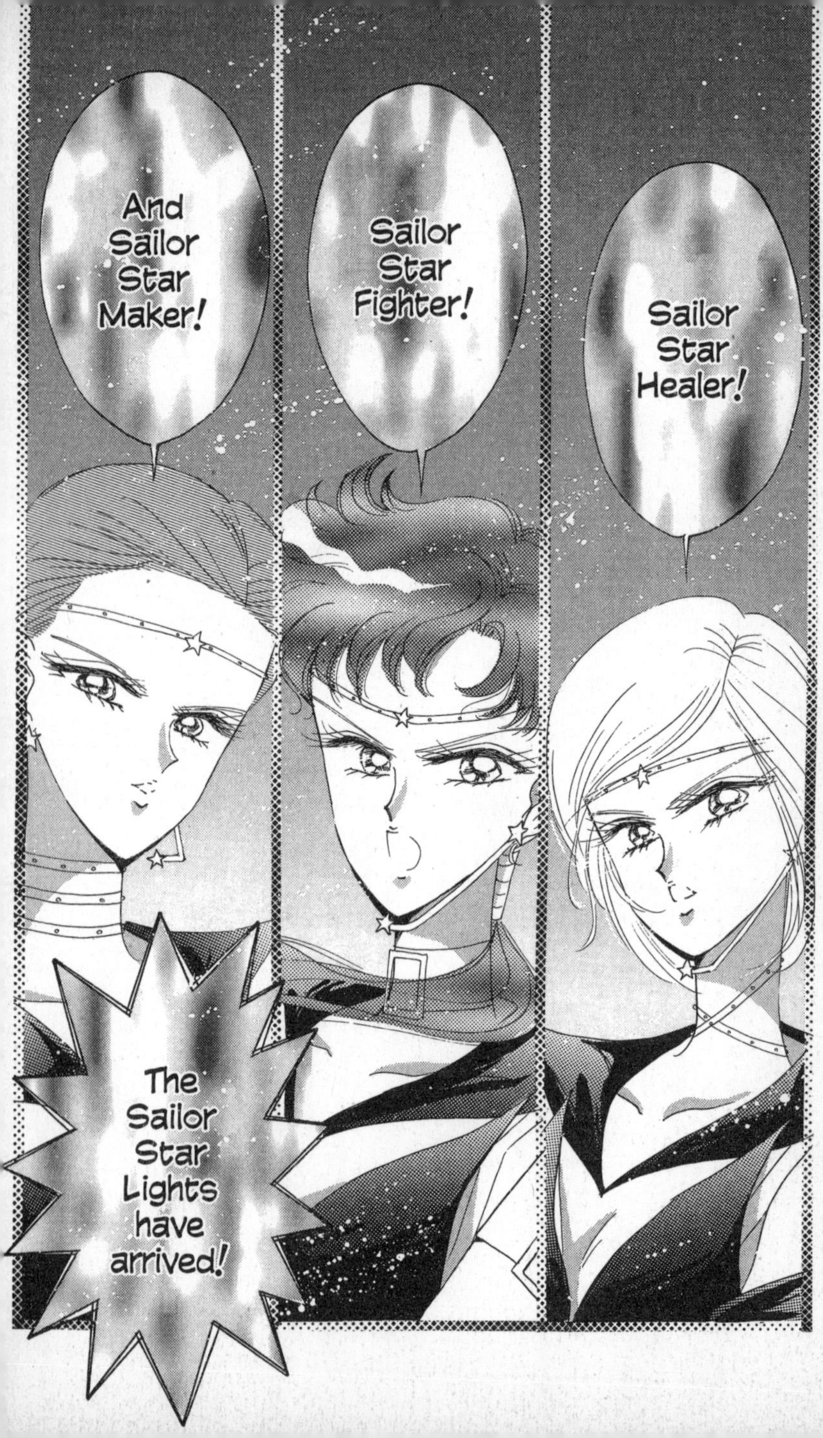
Sailor Star Healer!
Sailor Star Fighter!
And Sailor Star Maker!
The Sailor Star Lights have arrived!

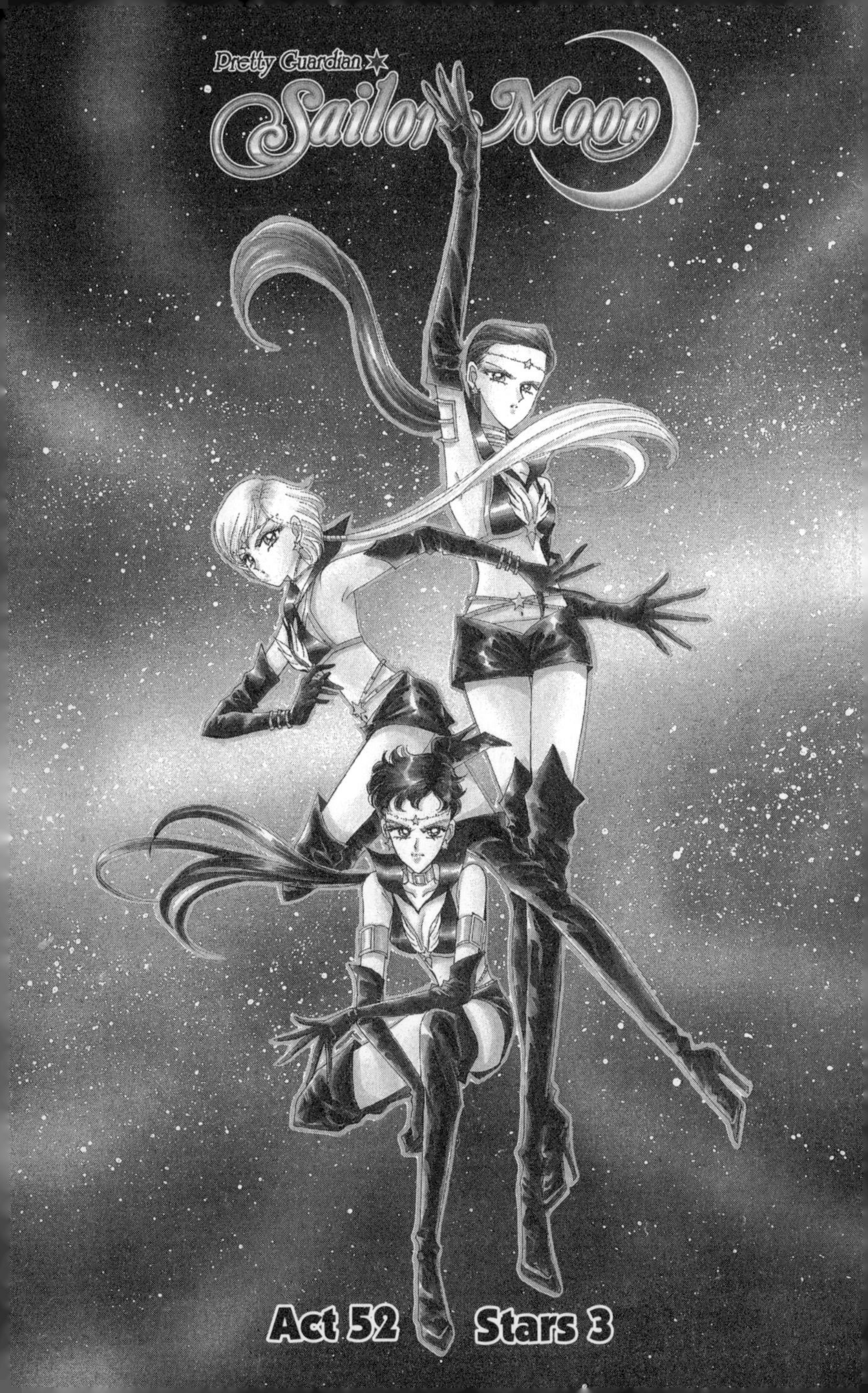
Pretty Guardian
Sailor Moon

Act 52 Stars 3

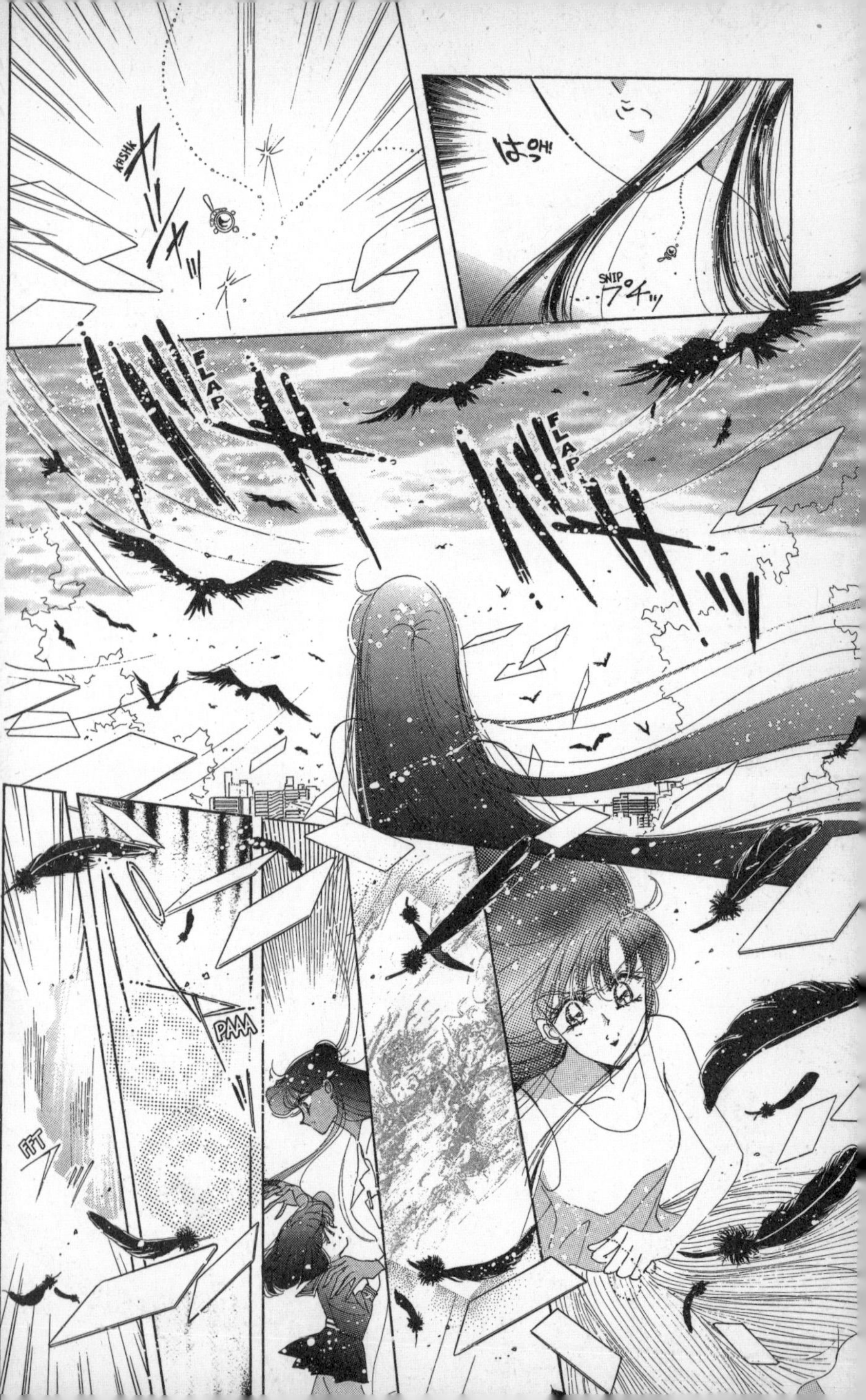
はっ OH!
SNIP プチッ
KRSHK
FLAP
FLAP
PAAA
FFT

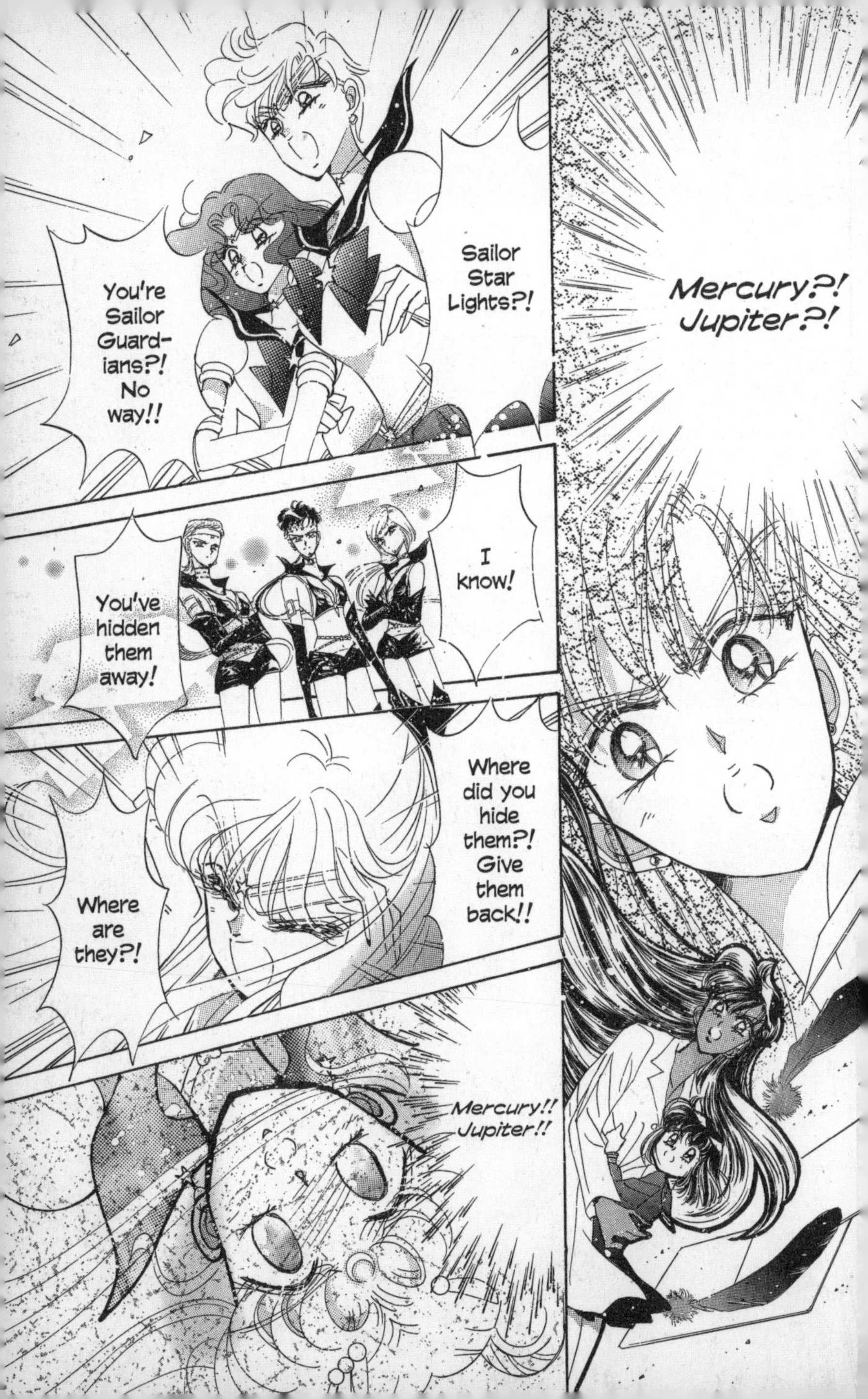
Mercury?! Jupiter?!
Sailor Star Lights?!
You're Sailor Guard-ians?! No way!!
I know!
You've hidden them away!
Where did you hide them?! Give them back!!
Where are they?!
Mercury!! Jupiter!!

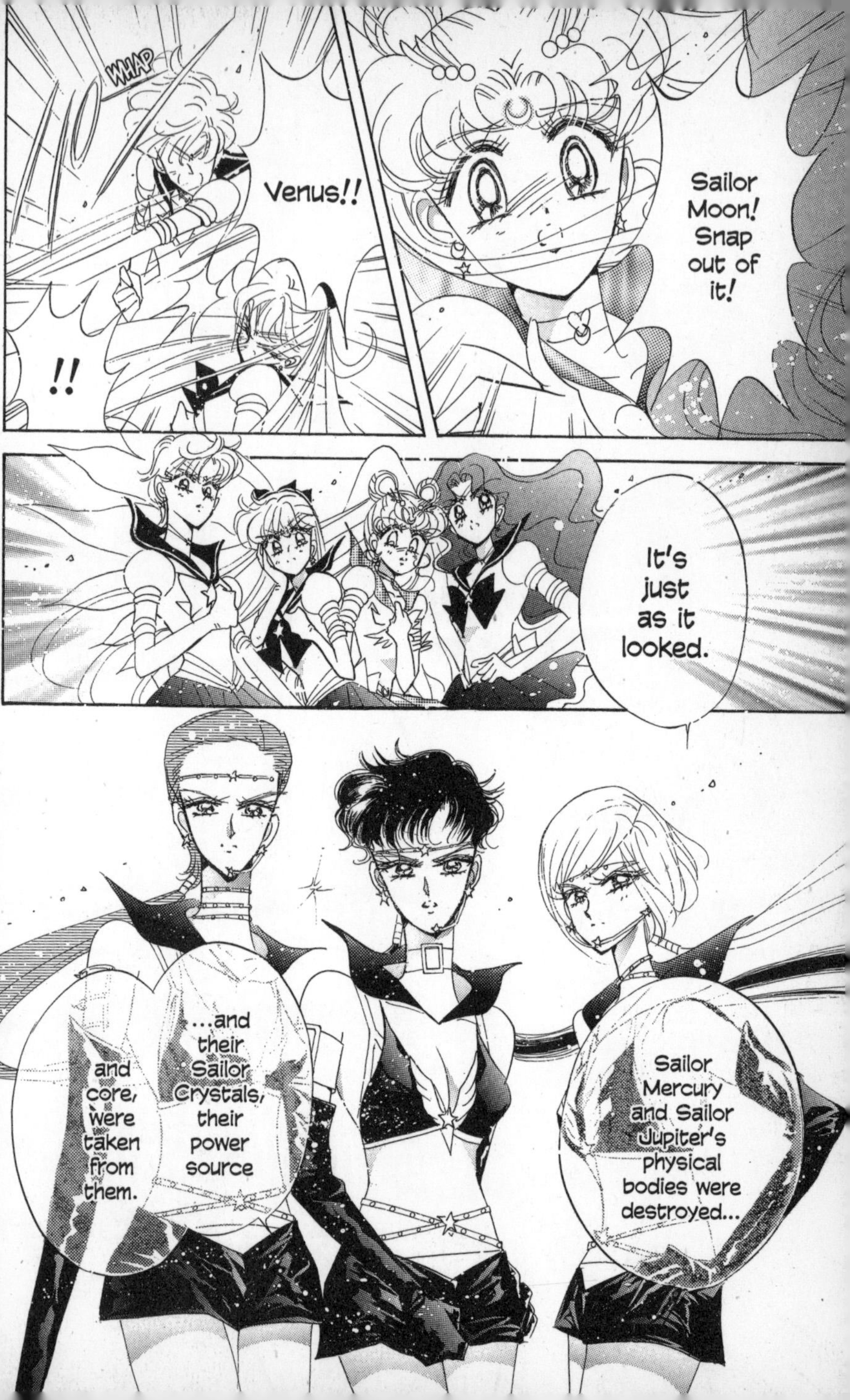
Sailor Moon! Snap out of it!
WHAP
Venus!!
!!
It's just as it looked.
Sailor Mercury and Sailor Jupiter's physical bodies were destroyed...
...and their Sailor Crystals, their power source
and core, were taken from them.

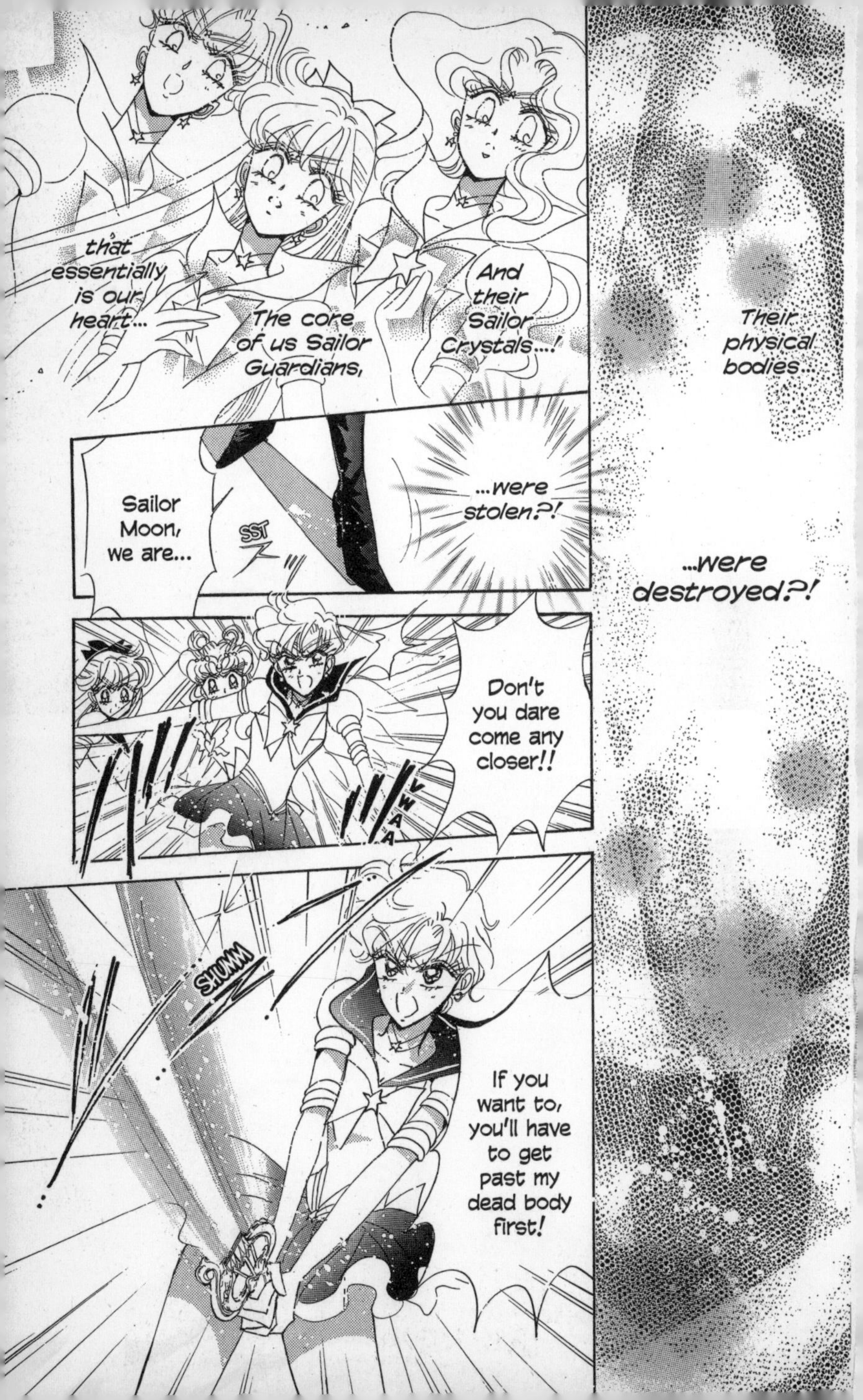
Their physical bodies...
...were destroyed?!
And their Sailor Crystals...!
The core of us Sailor Guardians,
that essentially is our heart...
...were stolen?!
SST
Sailor Moon, we are...
Don't you dare come any closer!!
VWAA
If you want to, you'll have to get past my dead body first!
SHUMM

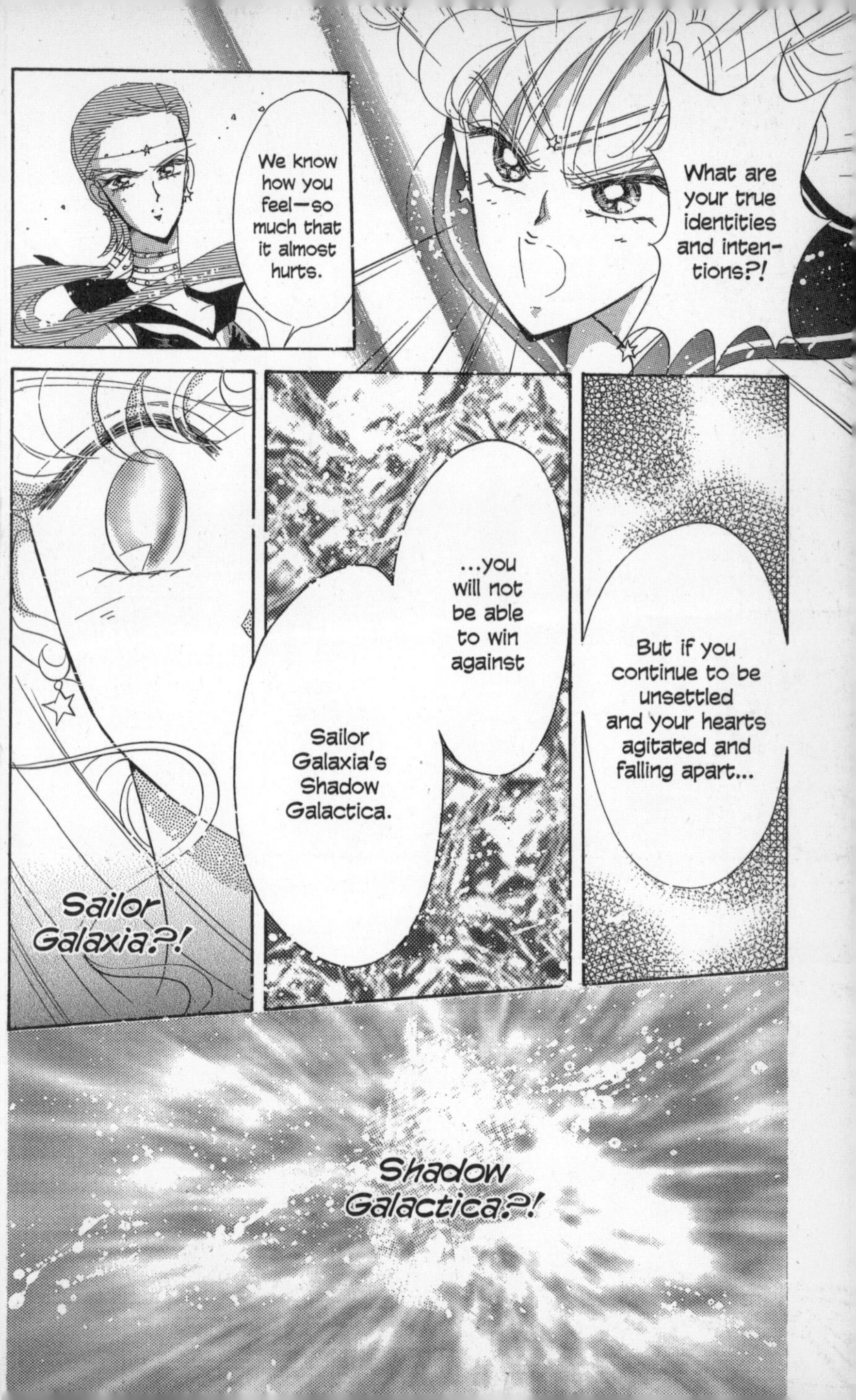
What are your true identities and intentions?!
We know how you feel—so much that it almost hurts.
But if you continue to be unsettled and your hearts agitated and falling apart...
...you will not be able to win against
Sailor Galaxia's Shadow Galactica.
Sailor Galaxia?!
Shadow Galactica?!

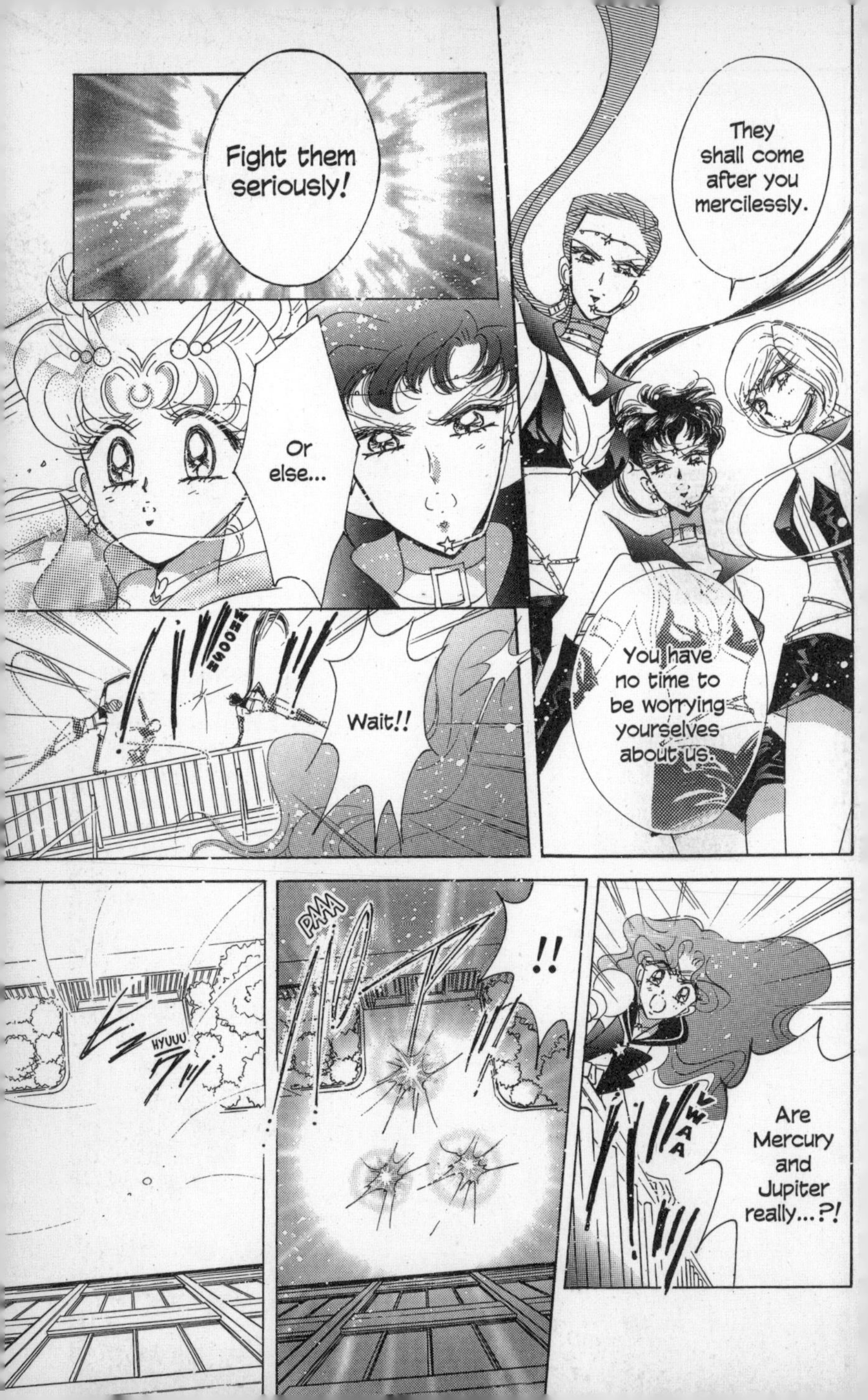
They shall come after you mercilessly.
You have no time to be worrying yourselves about us.
Fight them seriously!
Or else...
WHOOSH
Wait!!
Are Mercury and Jupiter really...?!
VWAA
PAAA
!!
HYUUU

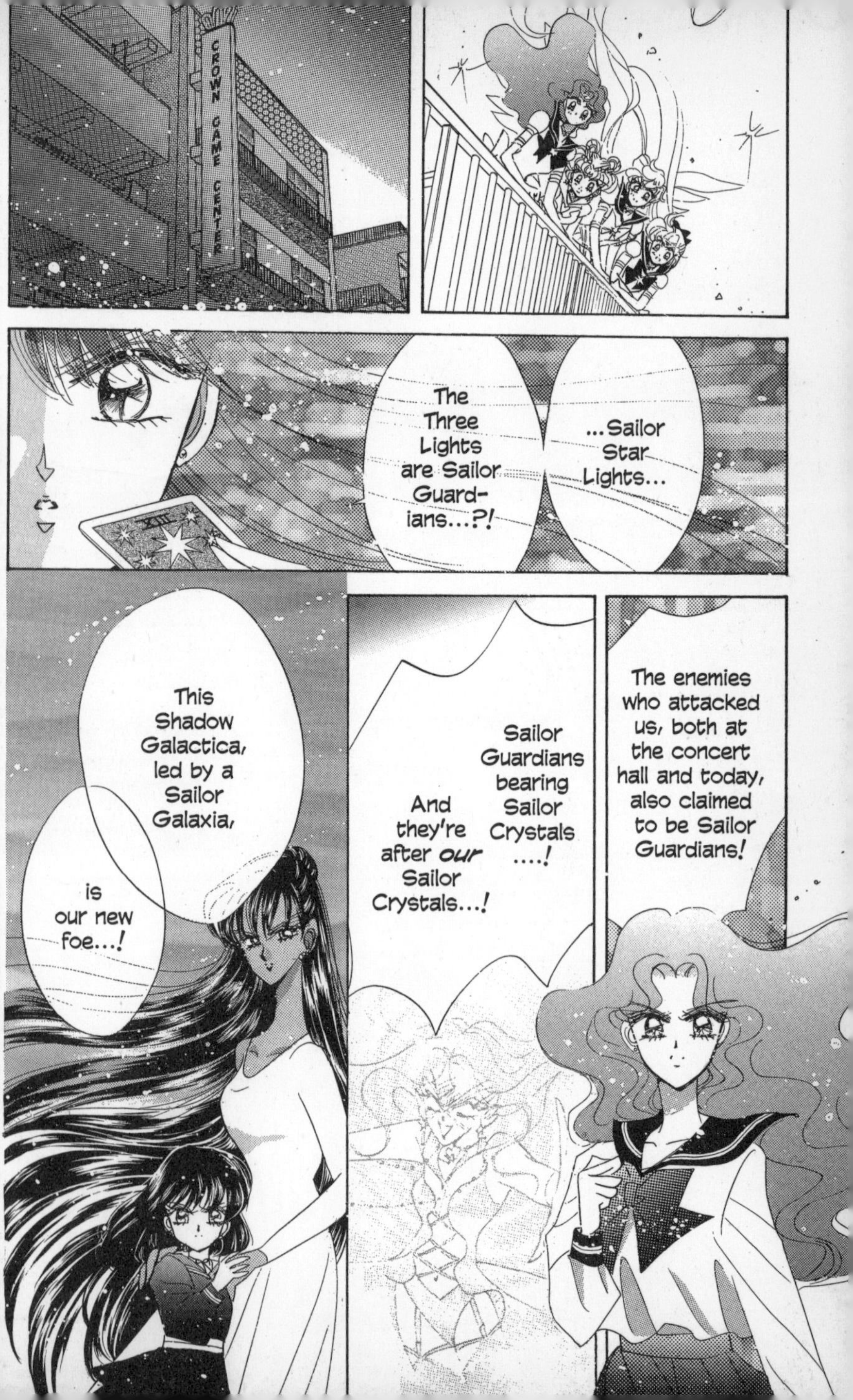
CROWN GAME CENTER
...Sailor Star Lights...
The Three Lights are Sailor Guardians...?!
The enemies who attacked us, both at the concert hall and today, also claimed to be Sailor Guardians!
Sailor Guardians bearing Sailor Crystals ....!
And they're after *our* Sailor Crystals...!
This Shadow Galactica, led by a Sailor Galaxia,
is our new foe...!

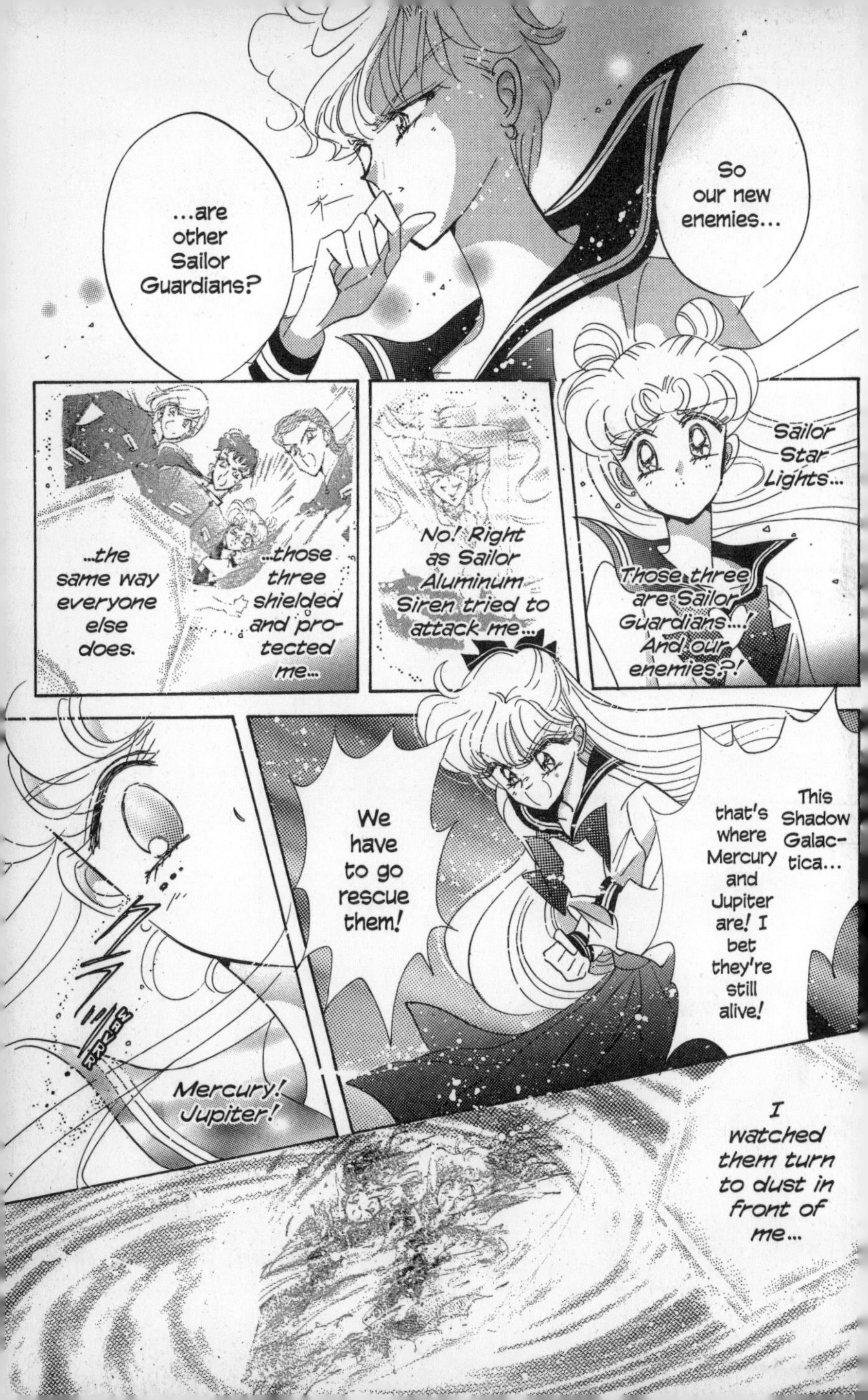
So our new enemies...
...are other Sailor Guardians?
Sailor Star Lights...
Those three are Sailor Guardians...! And our enemies?!
No! Right as Sailor Aluminum Siren tried to attack me...
...those three shielded and protected me...
...the same way everyone else does.
This Shadow Galactica...
that's where Mercury and Jupiter are! I bet they're still alive!
We have to go rescue them!
Mercury! Jupiter!
I watched them turn to dust in front of me...

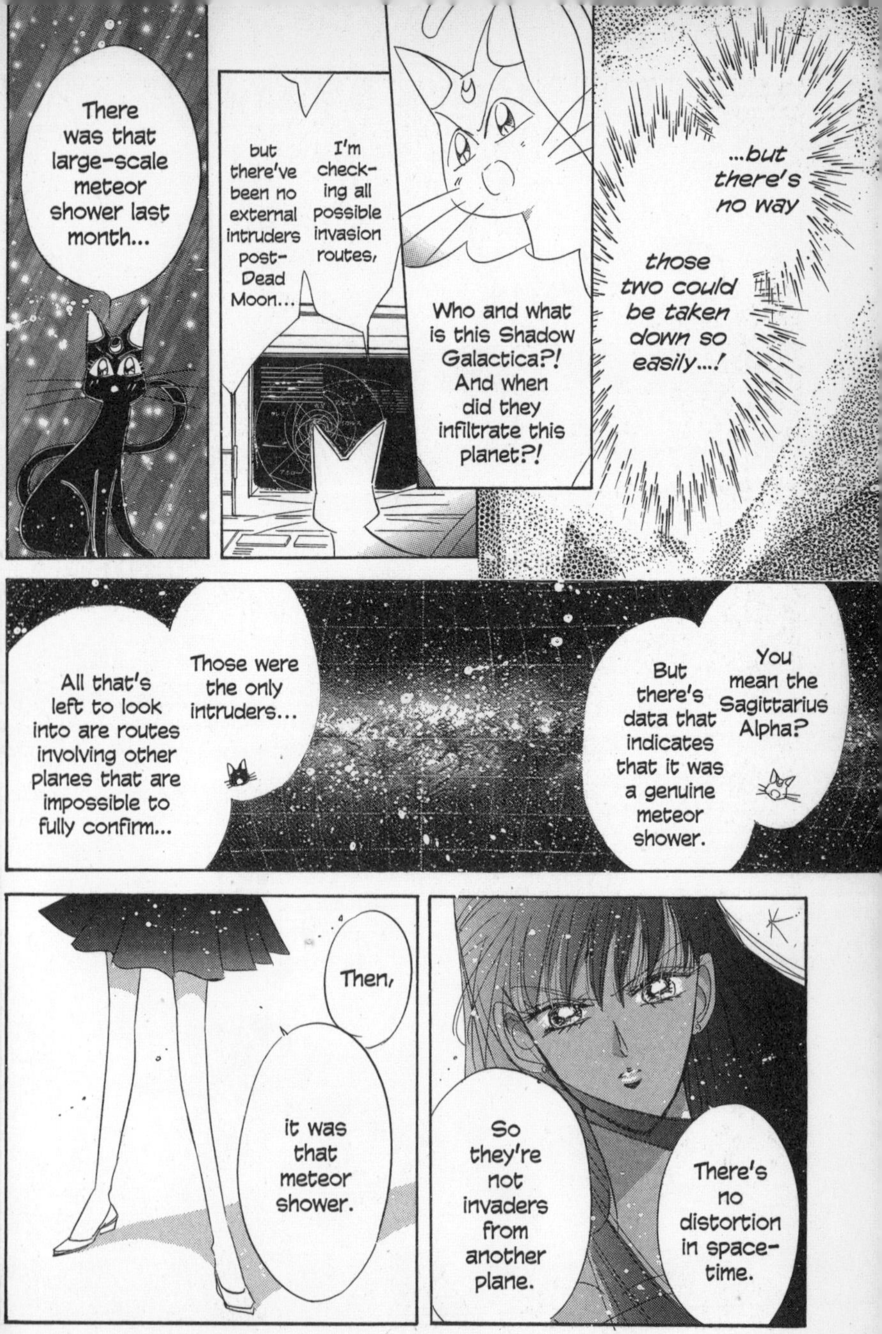
...but there's no way
those two could be taken down so easily...!
Who and what is this Shadow Galactica?! And when did they infiltrate this planet?!
I'm checking all possible invasion routes,
but there've been no external intruders post-Dead Moon...
There was that large-scale meteor shower last month...
You mean the Sagittarius Alpha?
But there's data that indicates that it was a genuine meteor shower.
Those were the only intruders...
All that's left to look into are routes involving other planes that are impossible to fully confirm...
There's no distortion in space-time.
So they're not invaders from another plane.
Then,
it was that meteor shower.

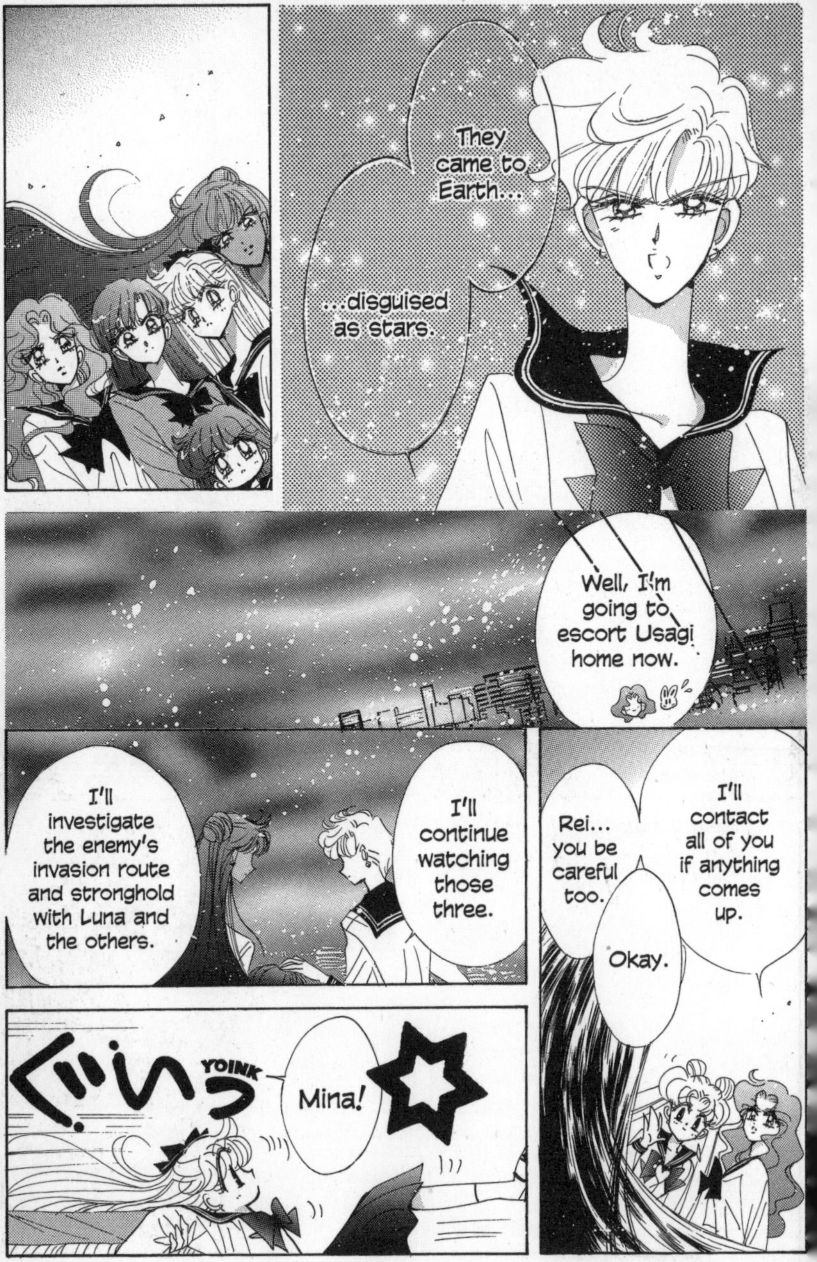
They came to Earth...
...disguised as stars.
Well, I'm going to escort Usagi home now.
I'll contact all of you if anything comes up.
Rei... you be careful too.
Okay.
I'll continue watching those three.
I'll investigate the enemy's invasion route and stronghold with Luna and the others.
くいっ
YOINK
Mina!

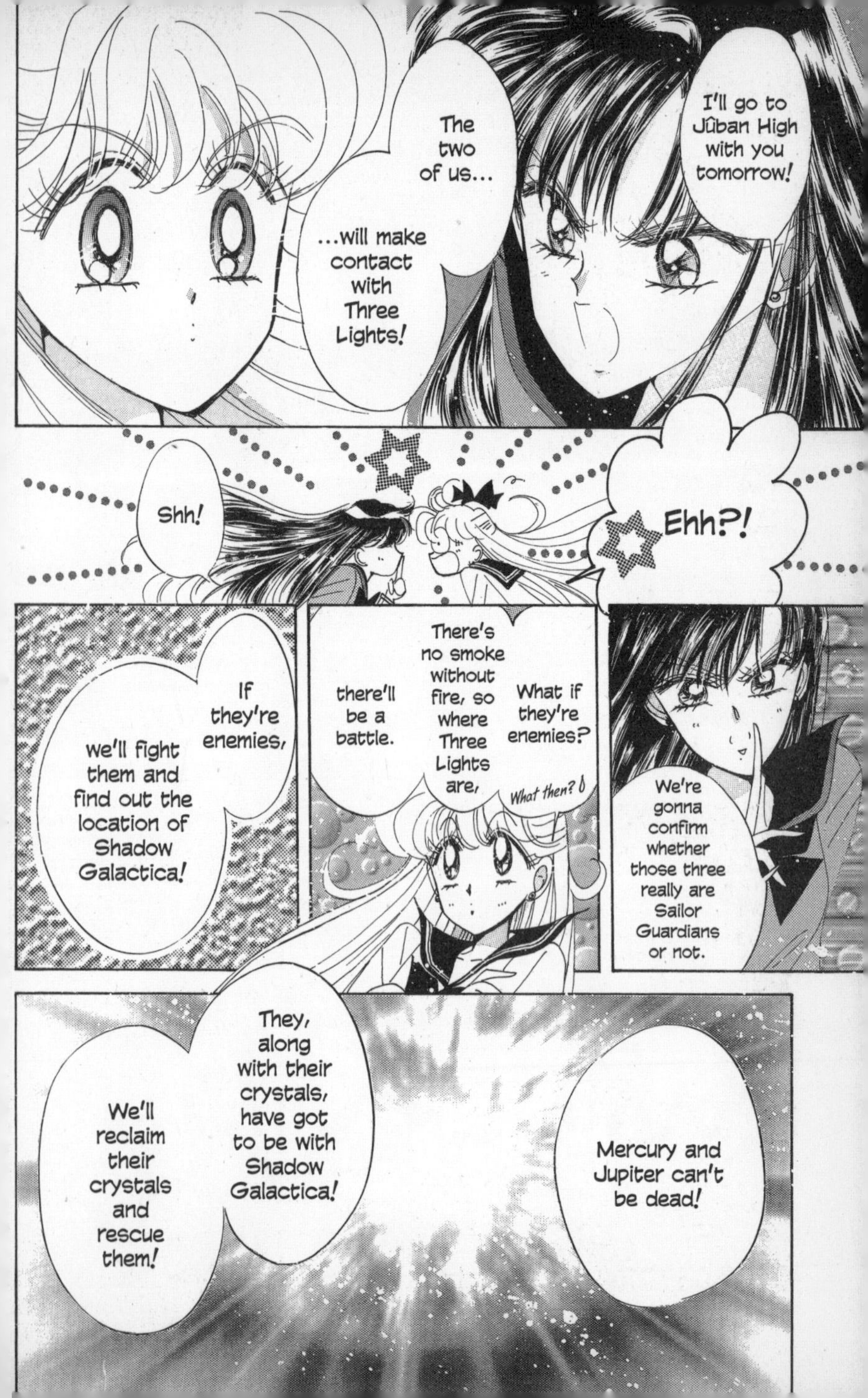
I'll go to Jûban High with you tomorrow!
The two of us...
...will make contact with Three Lights!
Ehh?!
Shh!
We're gonna confirm whether those three really are Sailor Guardians or not.
What if they're enemies?
What then?
There's no smoke without fire, so where Three Lights are,
there'll be a battle.
If they're enemies,
we'll fight them and find out the location of Shadow Galactica!
Mercury and Jupiter can't be dead!
They, along with their crystals, have got to be with Shadow Galactica!
We'll reclaim their crystals and rescue them!

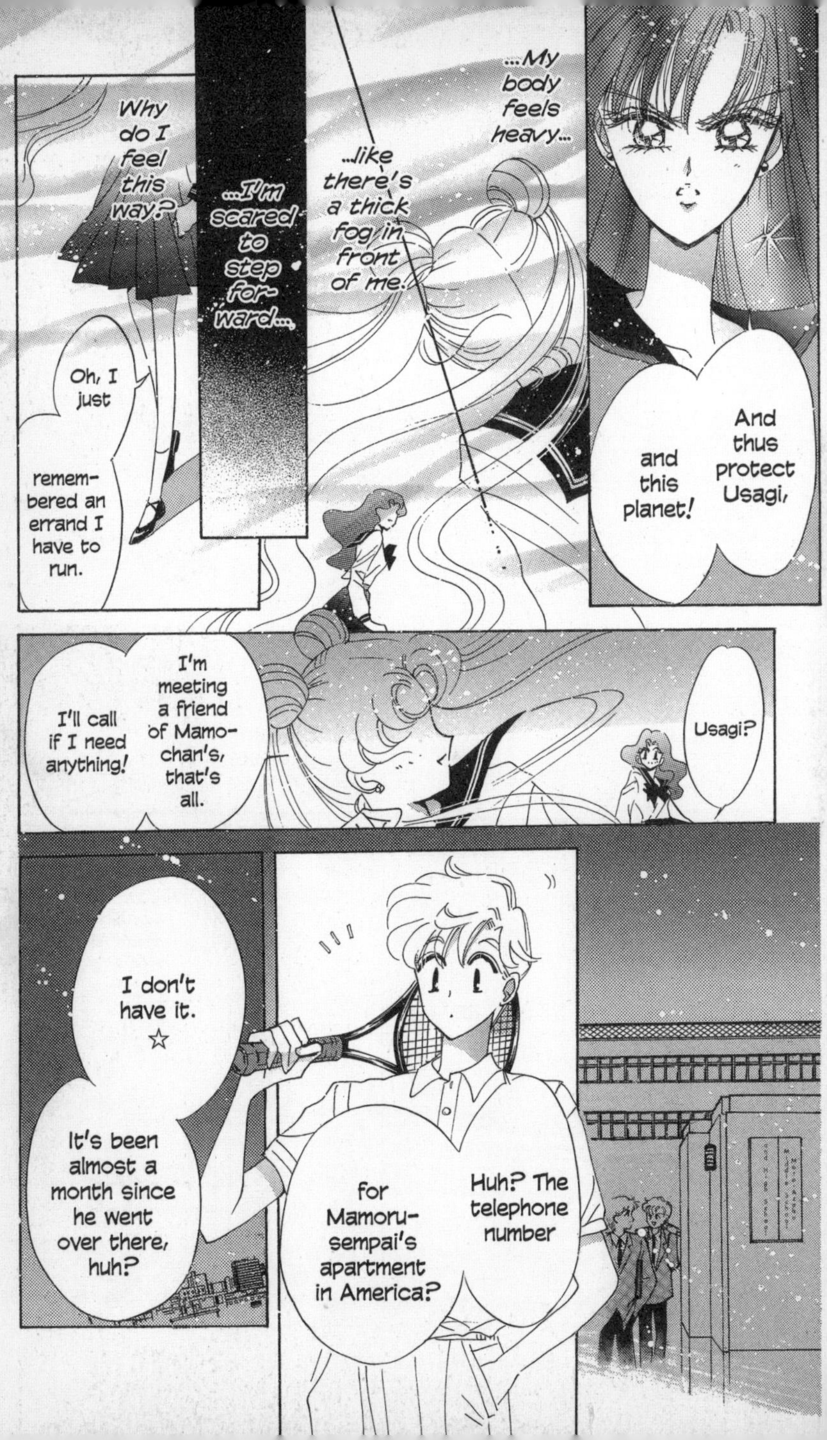
And thus protect Usagi, and this planet!
...My body feels heavy...
...like there's a thick fog in front of me.
...I'm scared to step for-ward...
Why do I feel this way?
Oh, I just remem-bered an errand I have to run.
Usagi?
I'm meeting a friend of Mamo-chan's, that's all.
I'll call if I need anything!
Huh? The telephone number for Mamoru-sempai's apartment in America?
I don't have it. ☆
It's been almost a month since he went over there, huh?

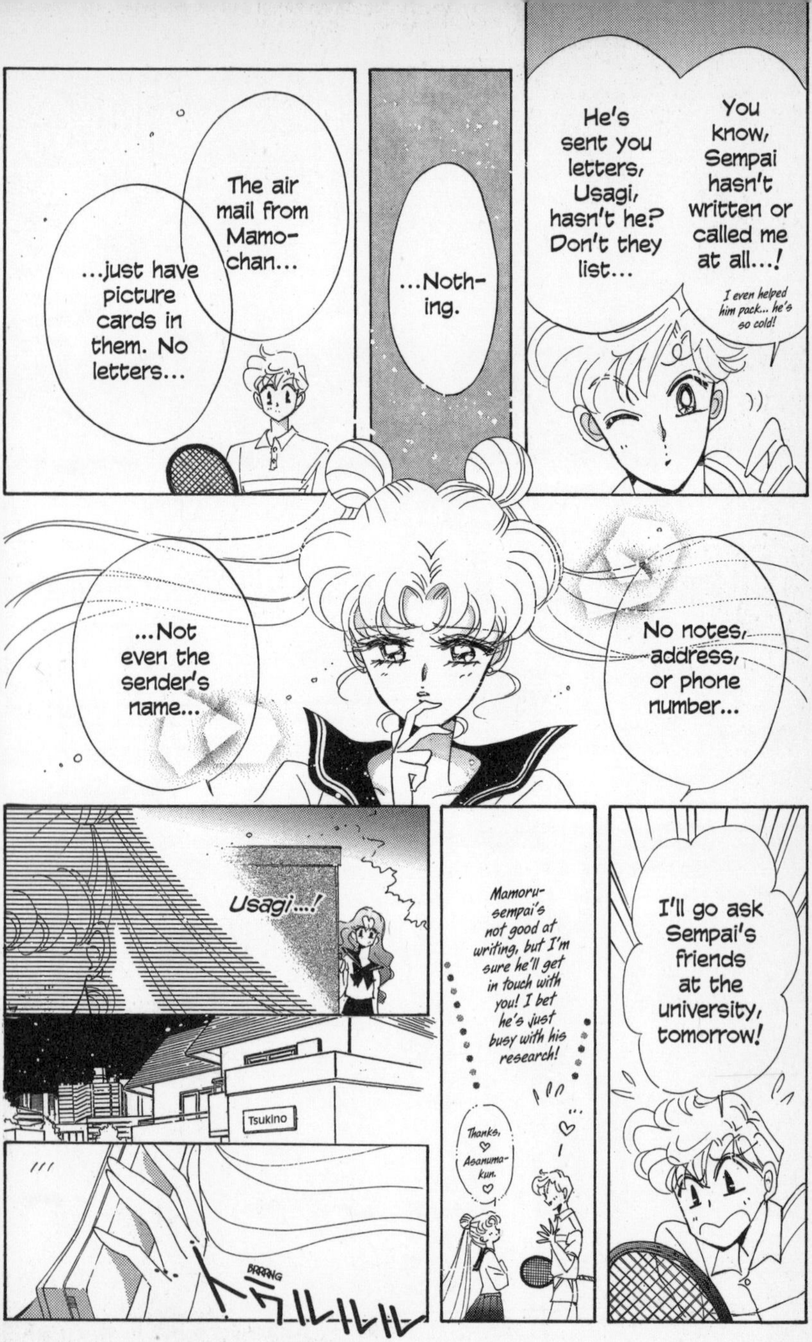
You know, Sempai hasn't written or called me at all...!
I even helped him pack... he's so cold!
He's sent you letters, Usagi, hasn't he? Don't they list...
...Nothing.
The air mail from Mamo-chan...
...just have picture cards in them. No letters...
No notes, address, or phone number...
...Not even the sender's name...
I'll go ask Sempai's friends at the university, tomorrow!
Mamoru-sempai's not good at writing, but I'm sure he'll get in touch with you! I bet he's just busy with his research!
Thanks, ♡ Asanuma-kun. ♡
Usagi...!
Tsukino
BRRRNG

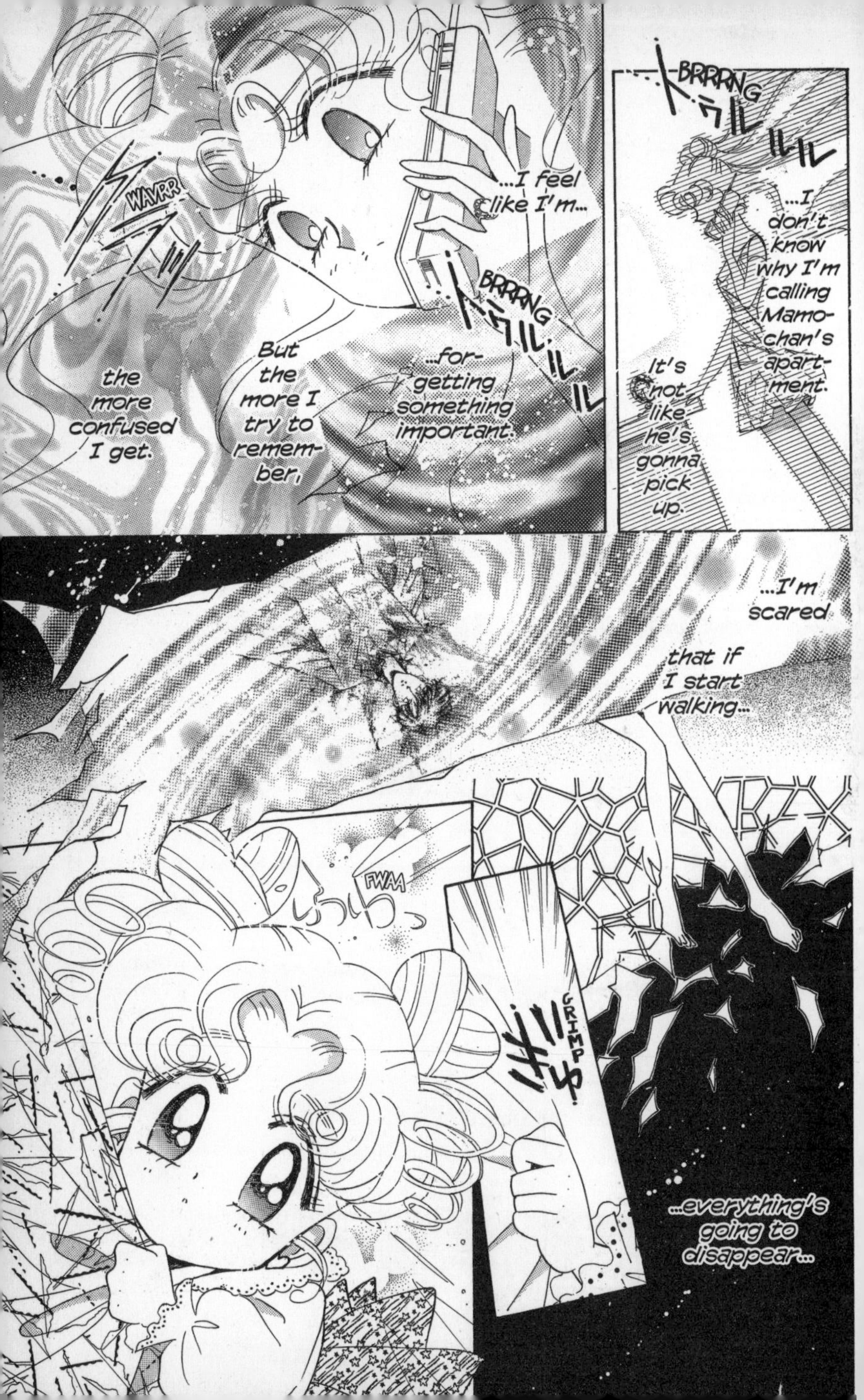
BRRRNG
...I don't know why I'm calling Mamo-chan's apartment.
It's not like he's gonna pick up.
BRRRNG
WAVRR
...I feel like I'm...
...for-getting something important.
But the more I try to remember,
the more confused I get.
...I'm scared
that if I start walking...
FWAA
GRIMP
...everything's going to disappear...

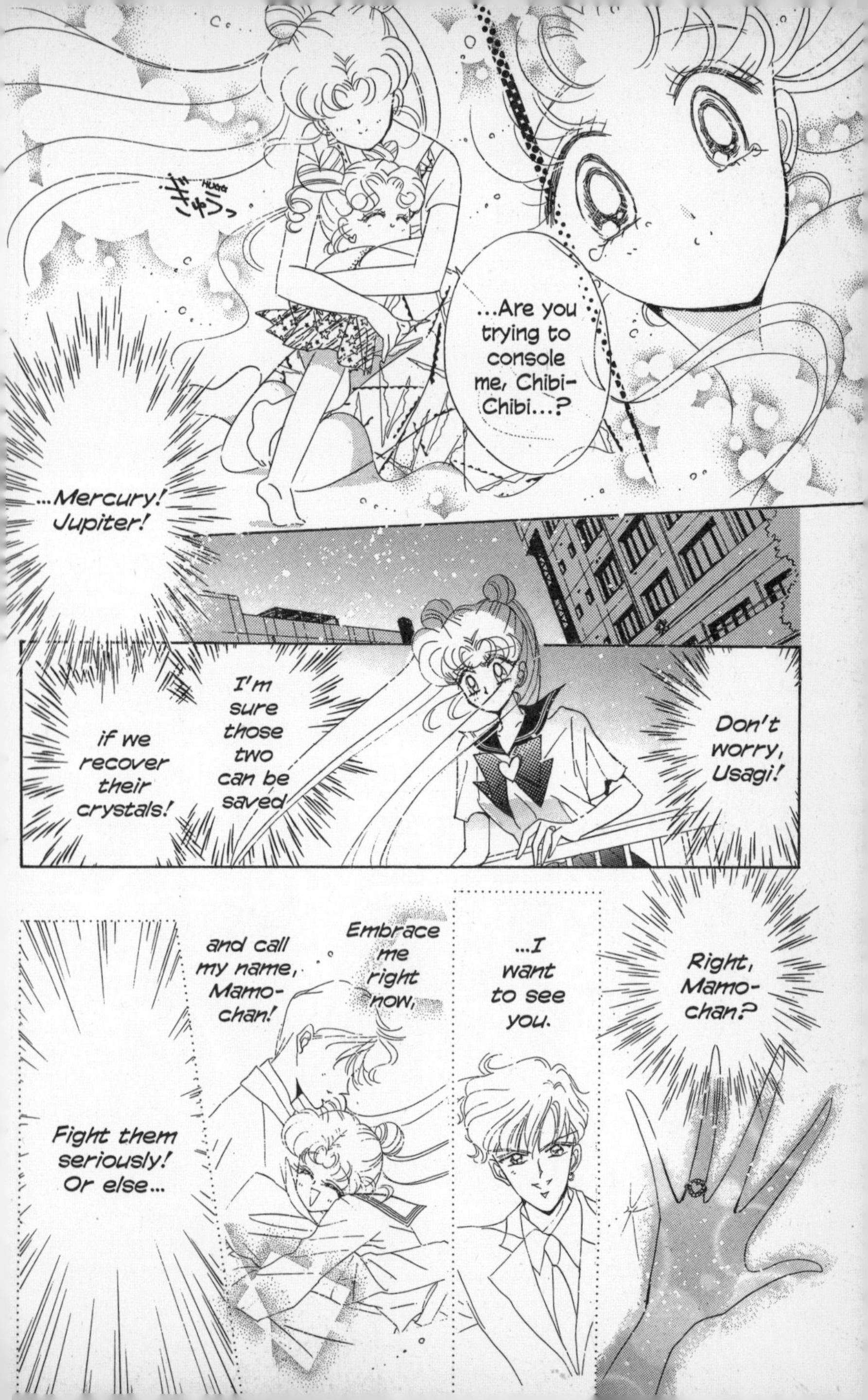
...Are you trying to console me, Chibi-Chibi...?
ぎゅうっ
HUGG
...Mercury! Jupiter!
Don't worry, Usagi!
I'm sure those two can be saved
if we recover their crystals!
Right, Mamo-chan?
...I want to see you.
Embrace me right now,
and call my name, Mamo-chan!
Fight them seriously! Or else...

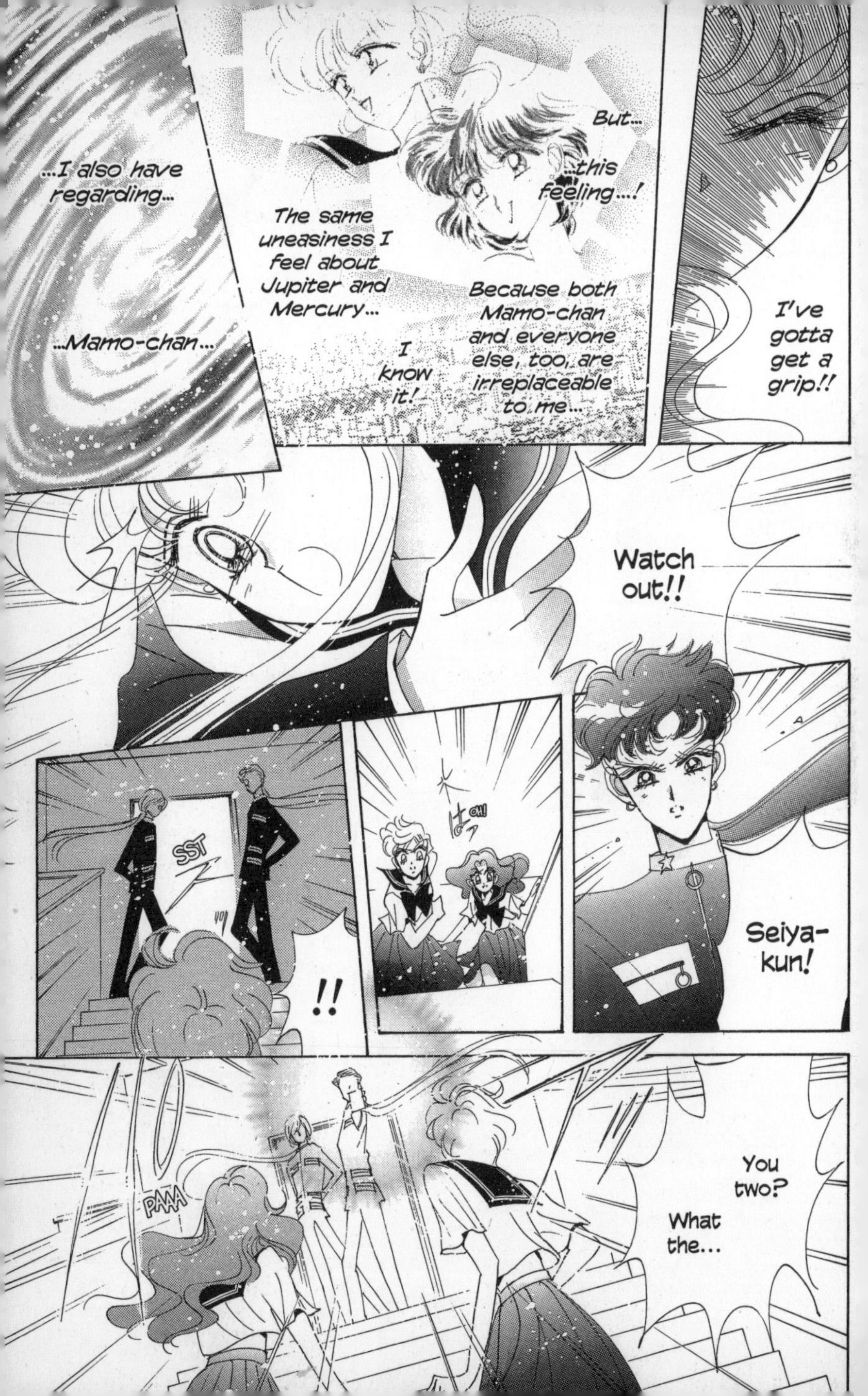
I've gotta get a grip!!
But...
...this feeling...!
Because both Mamo-chan and everyone else, too, are irreplaceable to me...
I know it!
The same uneasiness I feel about Jupiter and Mercury...
...I also have regarding...
...Mamo-chan...
Watch out!!
Seiya-kun!
OH!
SST
!!
You two?
What the...
PAAA

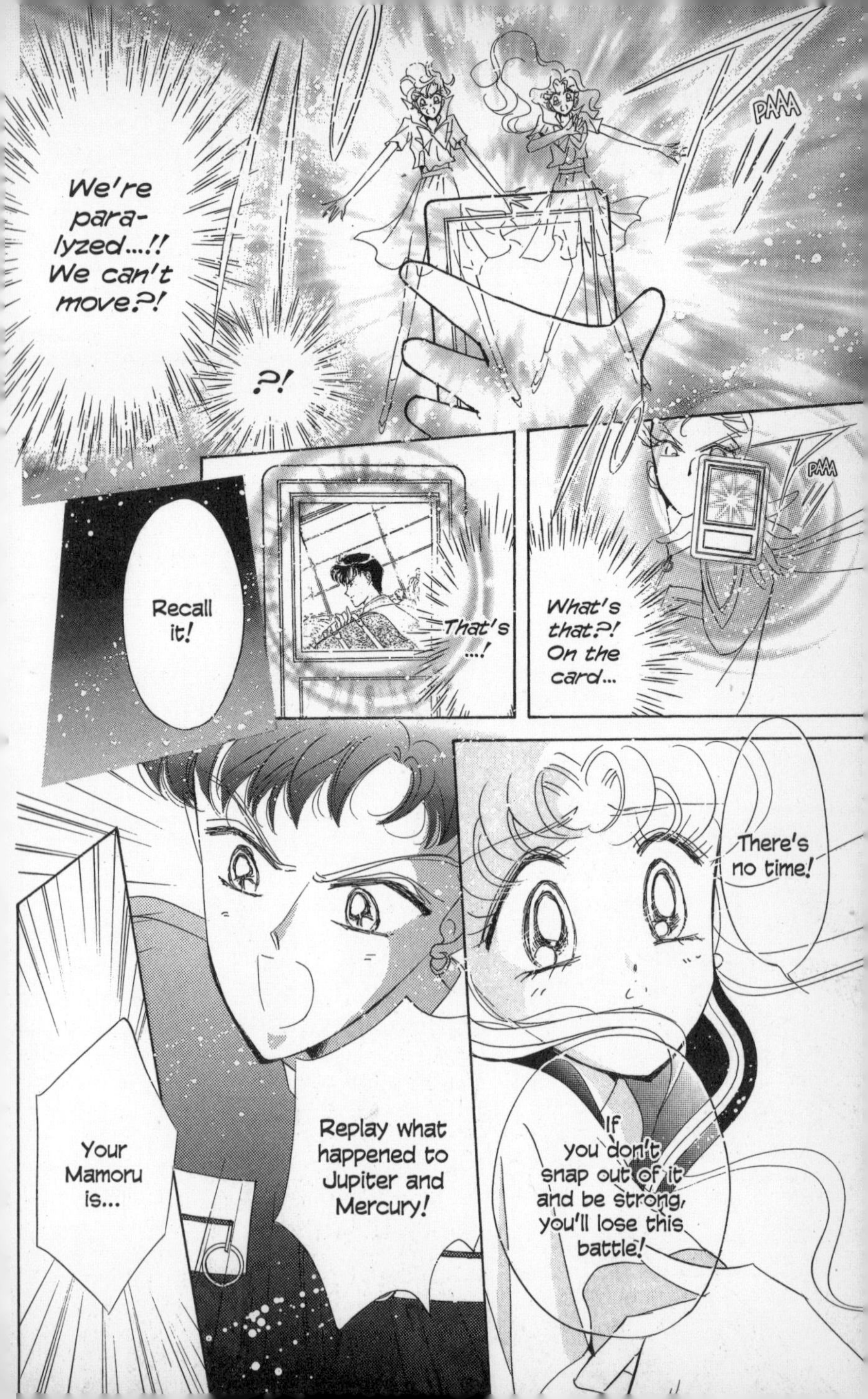
PAAA
We're para-lyzed...!! We can't move?!
?!
PAAA
What's that?! On the card...
That's ...!
Recall it!
There's no time!
If you don't snap out of it and be strong, you'll lose this battle!
Replay what happened to Jupiter and Mercury!
Your Mamoru is...

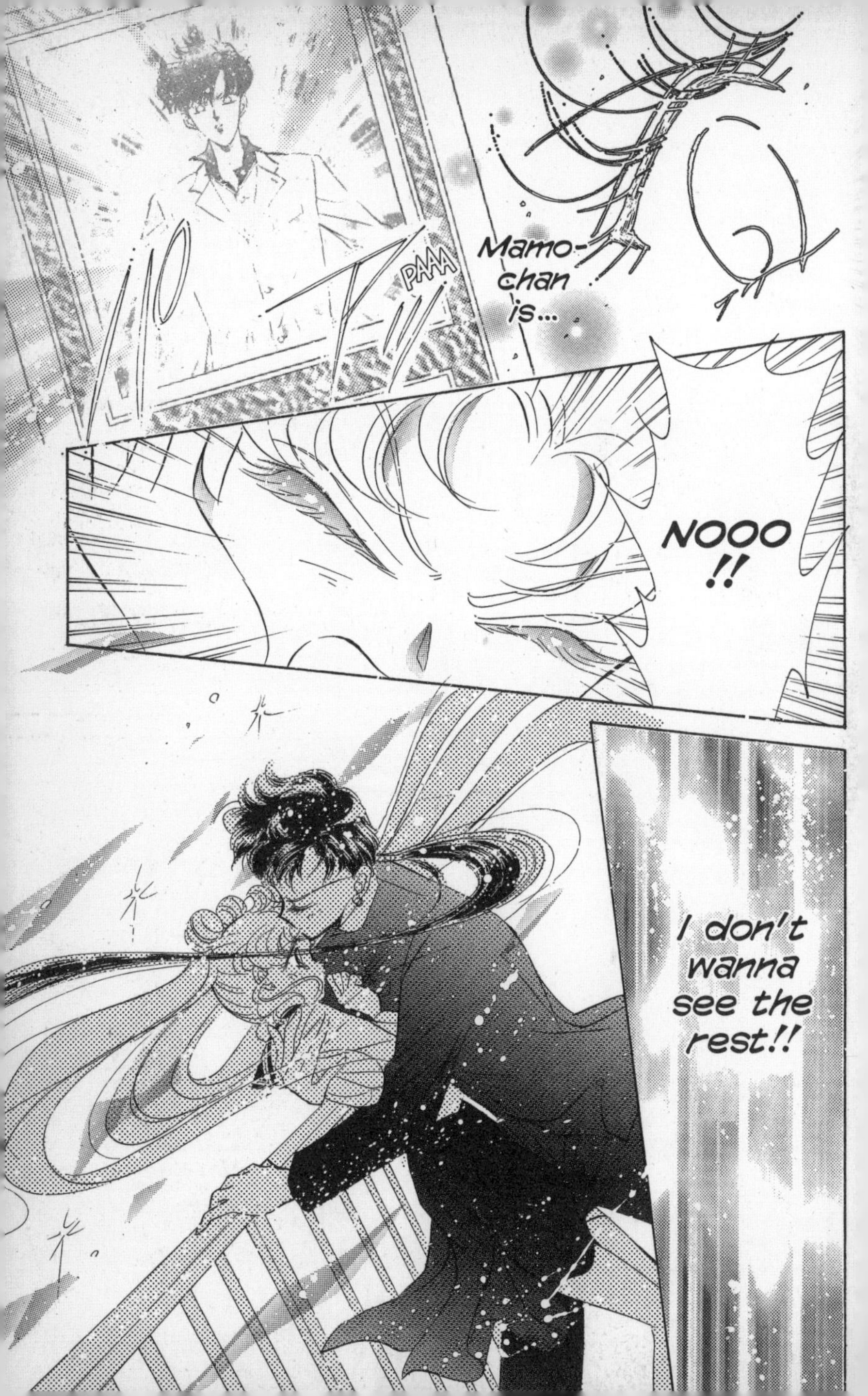
PAAA
Mamo-chan is...
NOOO!!
I don't wanna see the rest!!

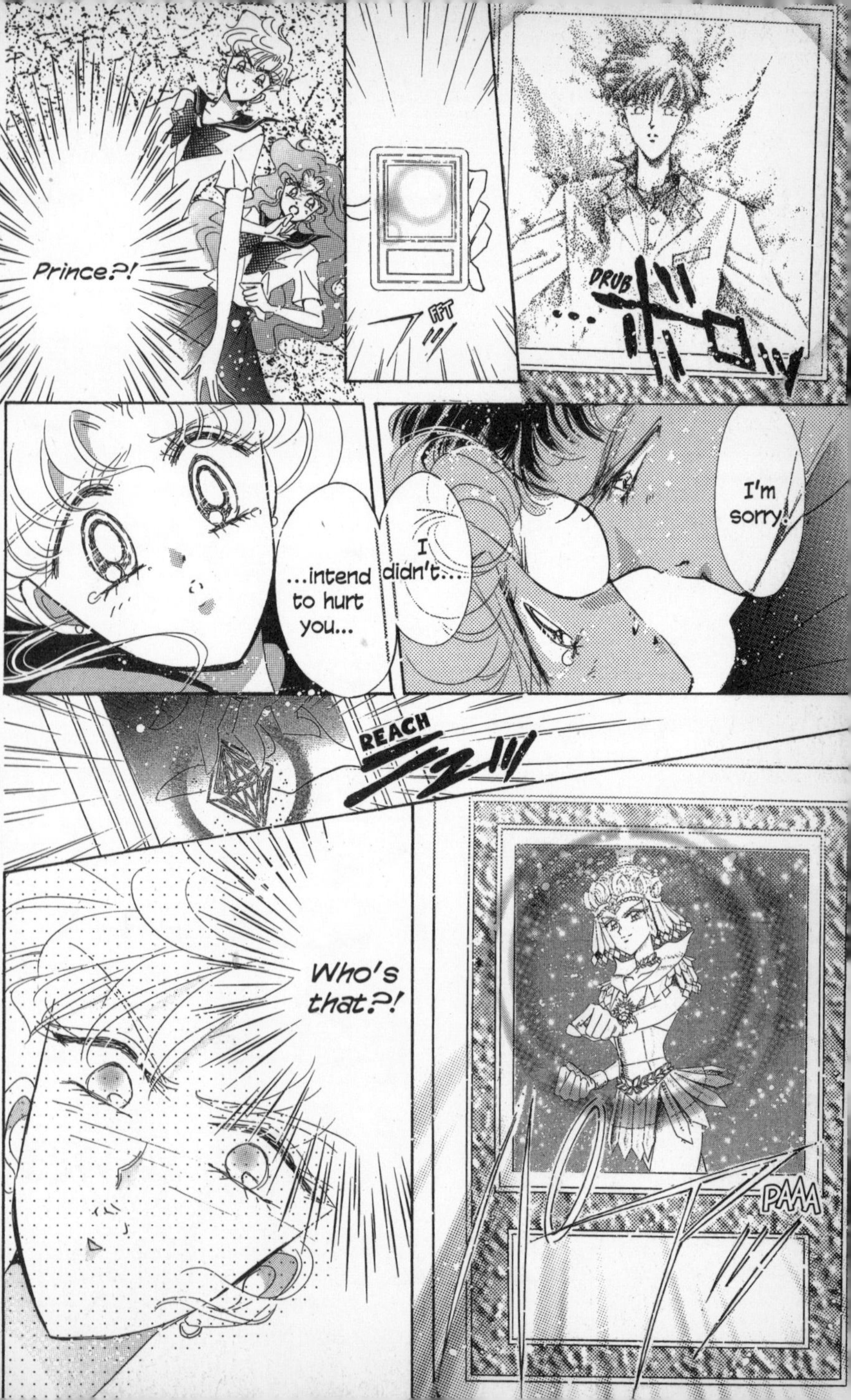
DRUB
...
FFT
Prince?!
I'm sorry.
I didn't...
...intend to hurt you...
REACH
PAAA
Who's that?!

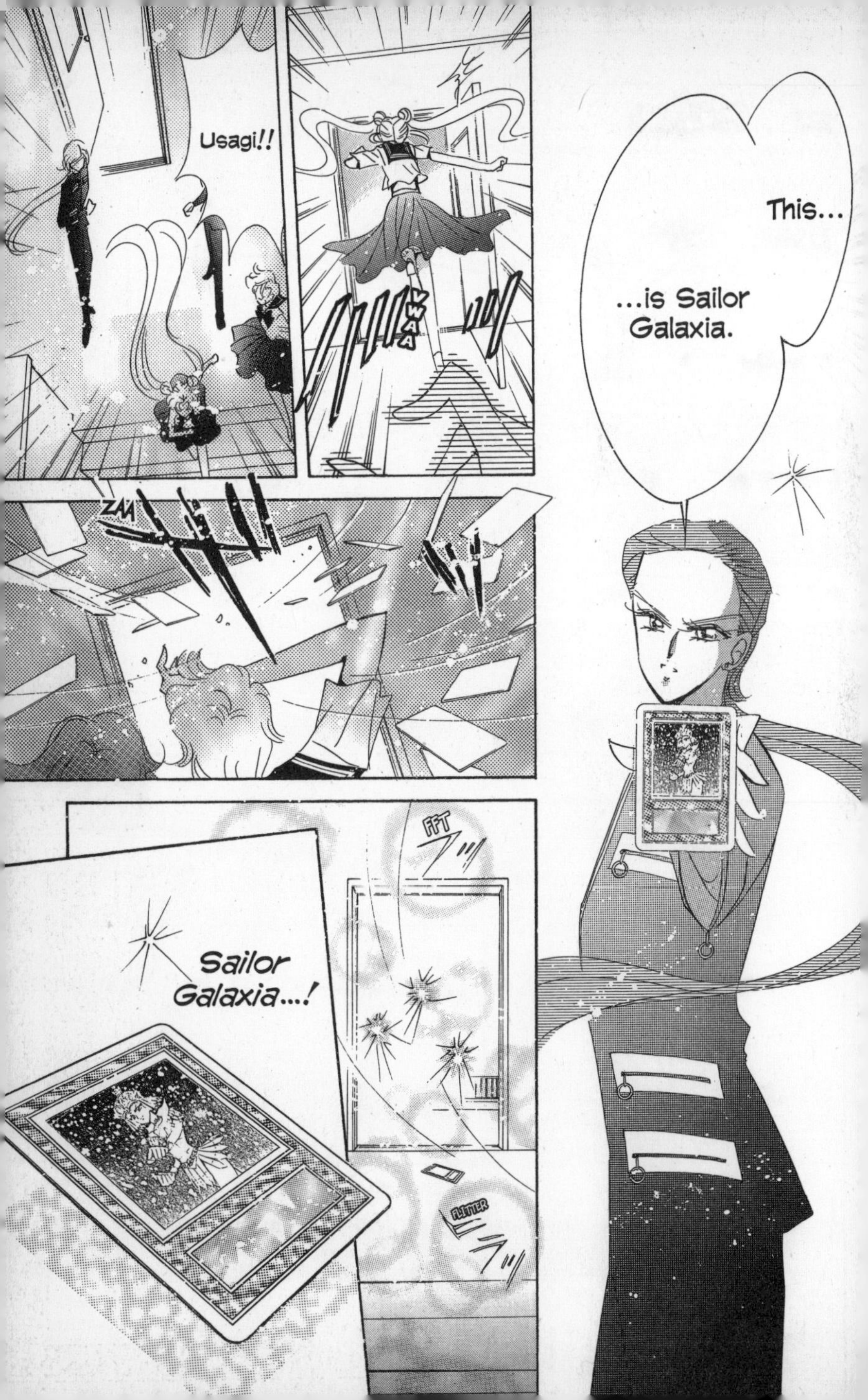
This...
...is Sailor Galaxia.
VWAA
Usagi!!
ZAA
FFT
Sailor Galaxia...!
FLUTTER

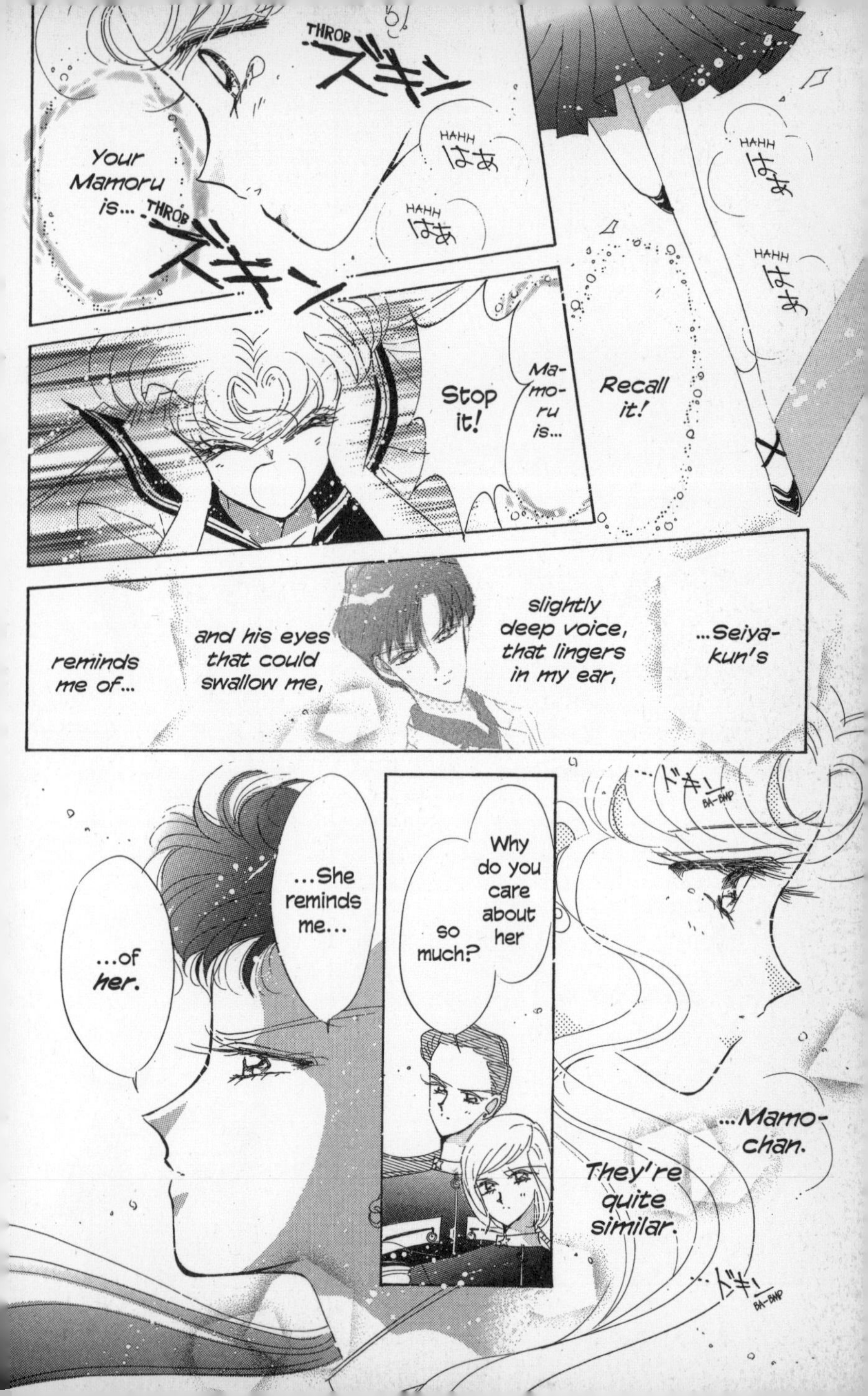
HAHH はぁ
HAHH はぁ
THROB ズキン
HAHH はぁ
HAHH はぁ
Your Mamoru is...
THROB ズキン
Recall it!
Mamoru is...
Stop it!
...Seiya-kun's
slightly deep voice, that lingers in my ear,
and his eyes that could swallow me,
reminds me of...
...ドキ! BA-BMP
...Mamo-chan.
They're quite similar.
...ドキ! BA-BMP
Why do you care about her so much?
...She reminds me...
...of her.

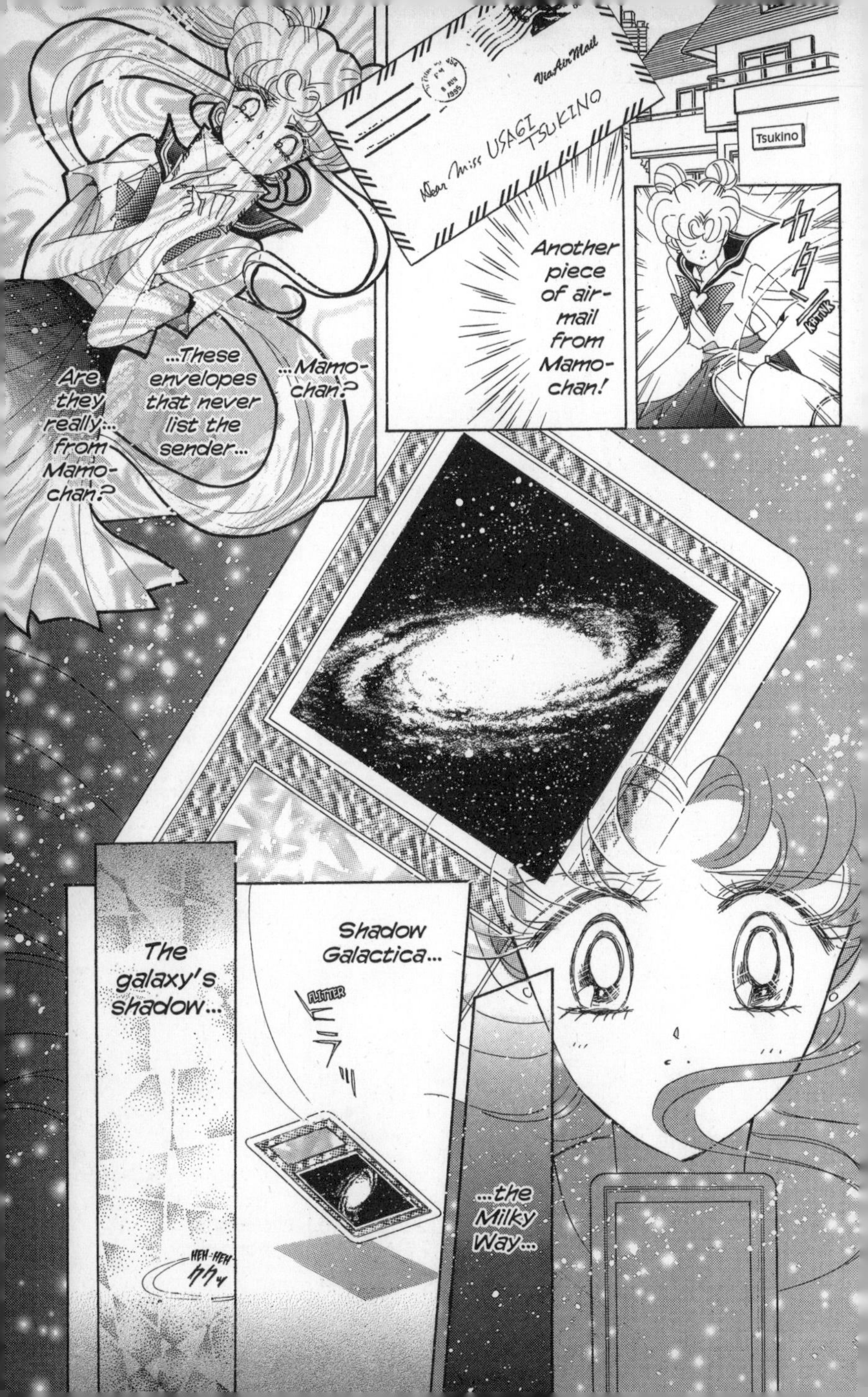
Tsukino
KA-TINK
Another piece of air-mail from Mamo-chan!
Via Air Mail
Dear Miss USAGI TSUKINO
...Mamo-chan?
...These envelopes that never list the sender...
Are they really... from Mamo-chan?
...the Milky Way...
Shadow Galactica...
FLITTER
The galaxy's shadow...
HEH HEH

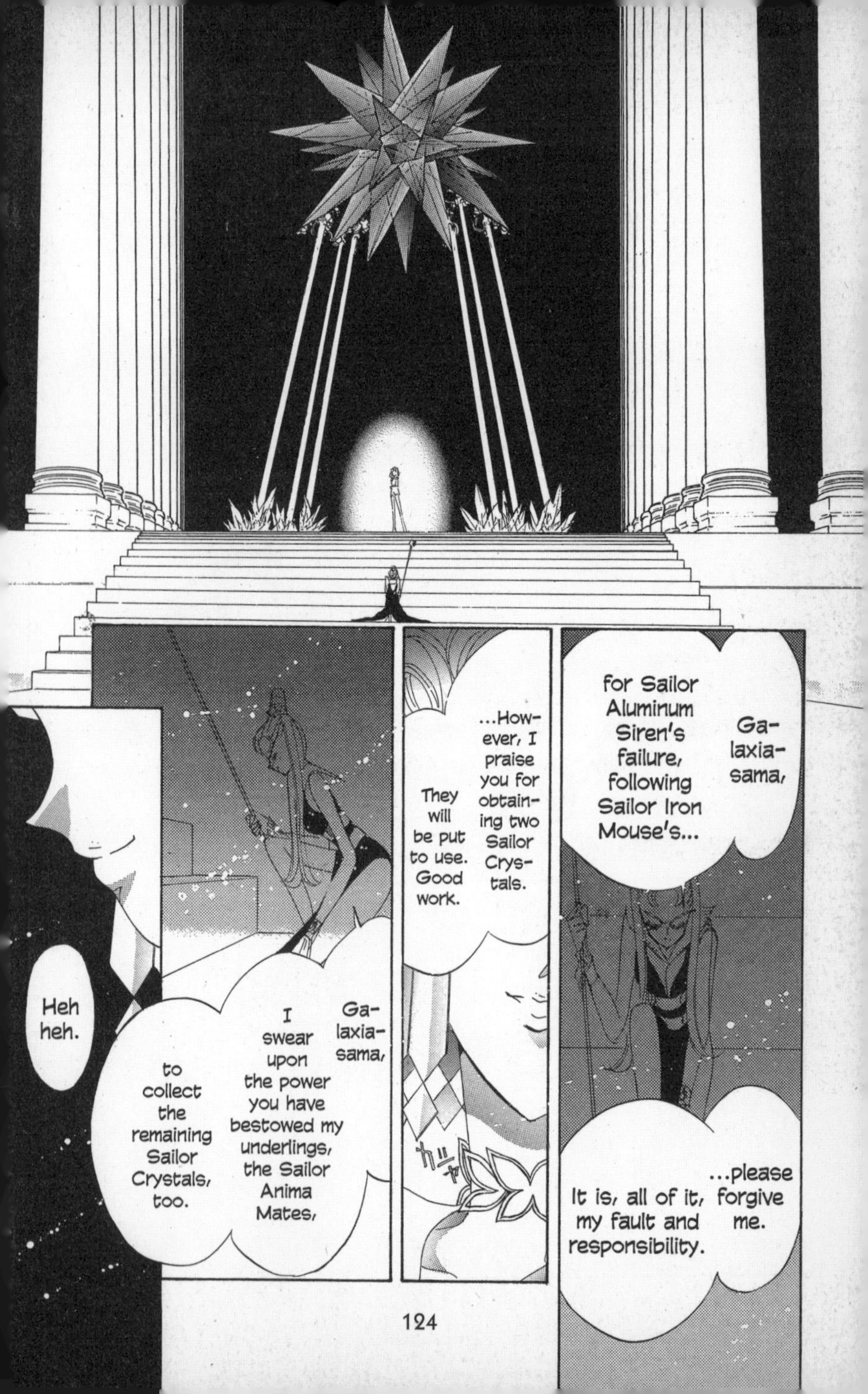
Galaxia-sama,
for Sailor Aluminum Siren's failure, following Sailor Iron Mouse's...
...please forgive me.
It is, all of it, my fault and responsibility.
...However, I praise you for obtaining two Sailor Crystals.
They will be put to use. Good work.
カシャ
Galaxia-sama,
I swear upon the power you have bestowed my underlings, the Sailor Anima Mates,
to collect the remaining Sailor Crystals, too.
Heh heh.

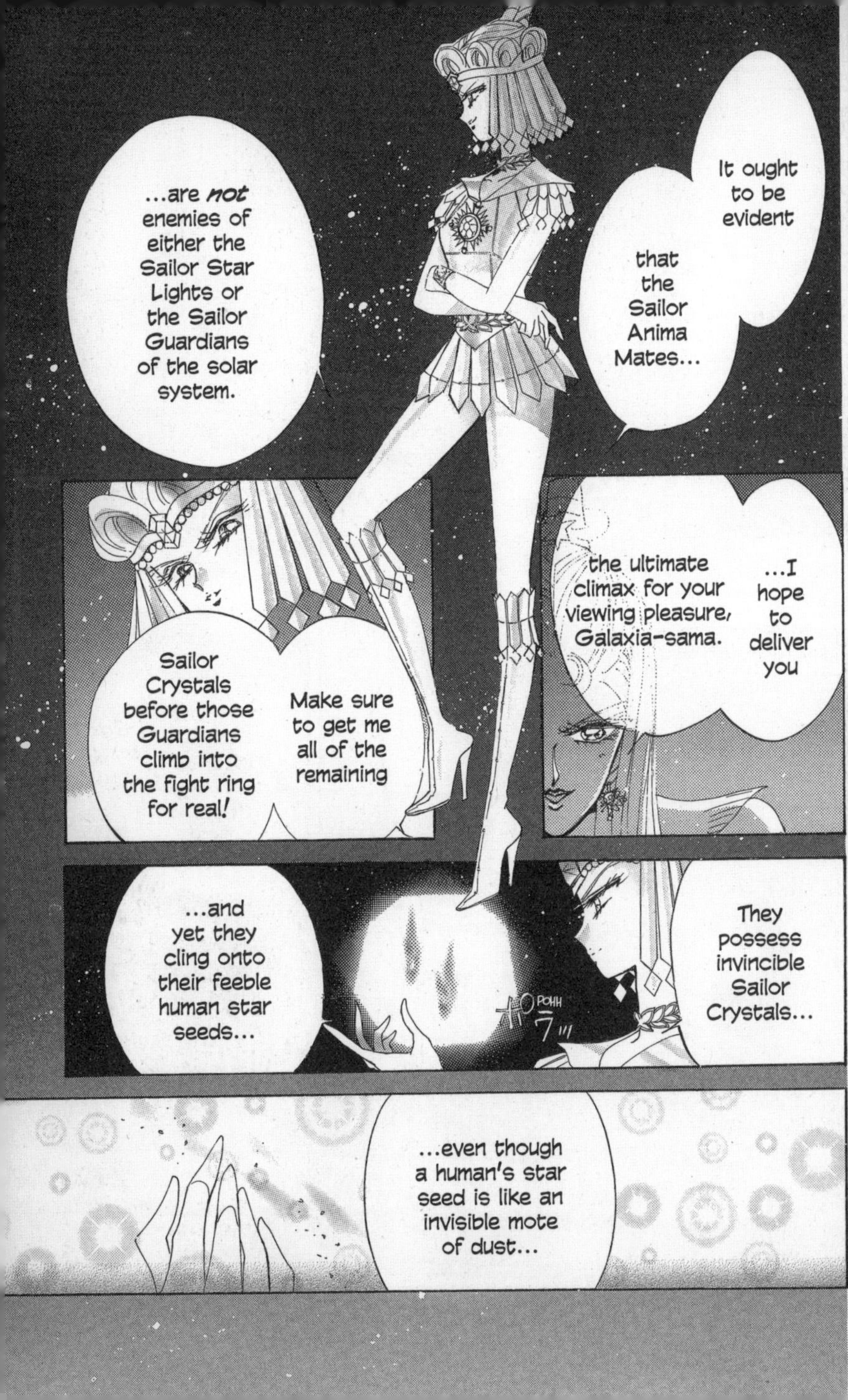

It ought to be evident
that the Sailor Anima Mates...
...are *not* enemies of either the Sailor Star Lights or the Sailor Guardians of the solar system.
...I hope to deliver you
the ultimate climax for your viewing pleasure, Galaxia-sama.
Make sure to get me all of the remaining
Sailor Crystals before those Guardians climb into the fight ring for real!
They possess invincible Sailor Crystals...
POHH
...and yet they cling onto their feeble human star seeds...
...even though a human's star seed is like an invisible mote of dust...

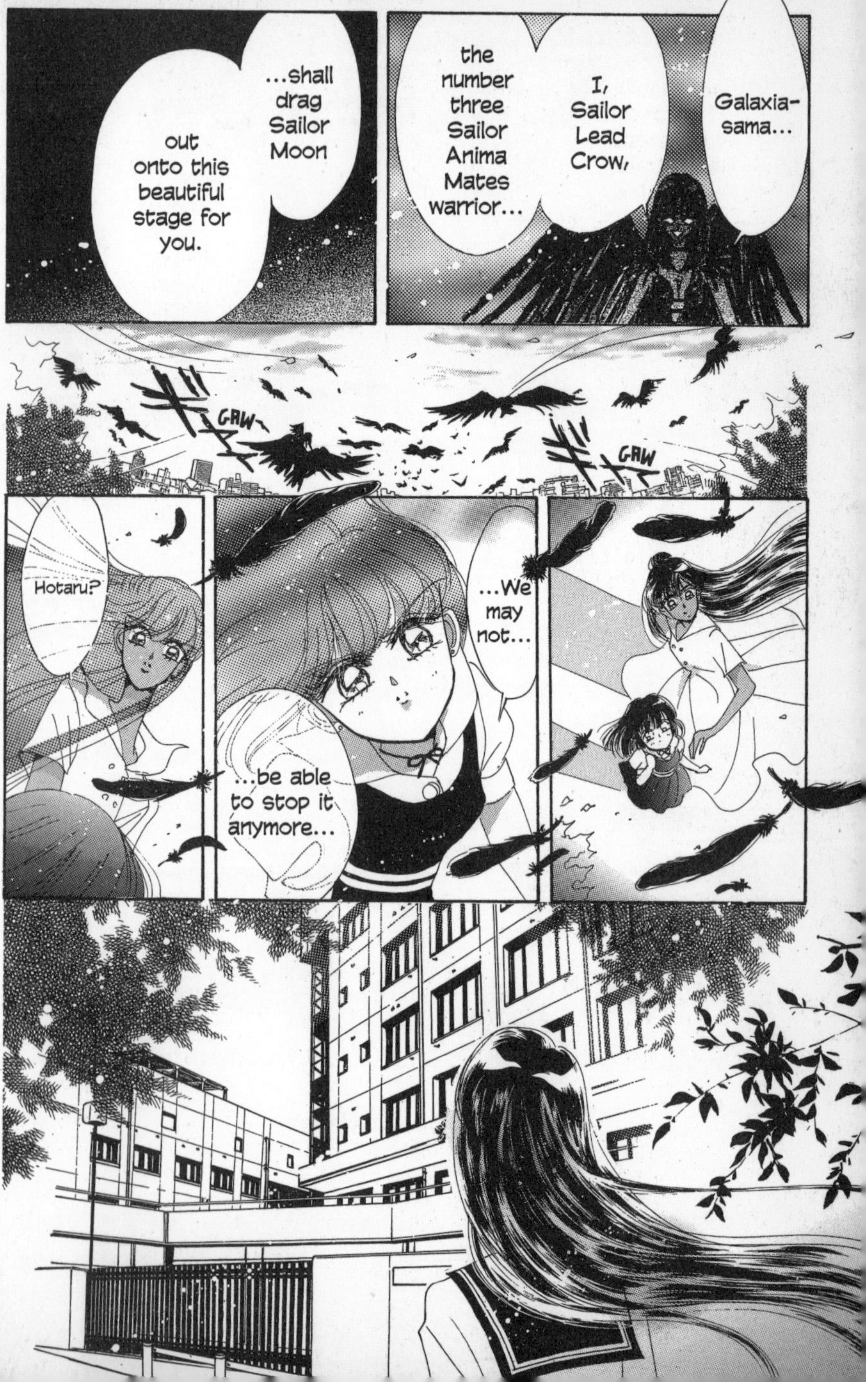
Galaxia-sama...
I, Sailor Lead Crow,
the number three Sailor Anima Mates warrior...
...shall drag Sailor Moon
out onto this beautiful stage for you.
GAW
GAW
...We may not...
...be able to stop it anymore...
Hotaru?

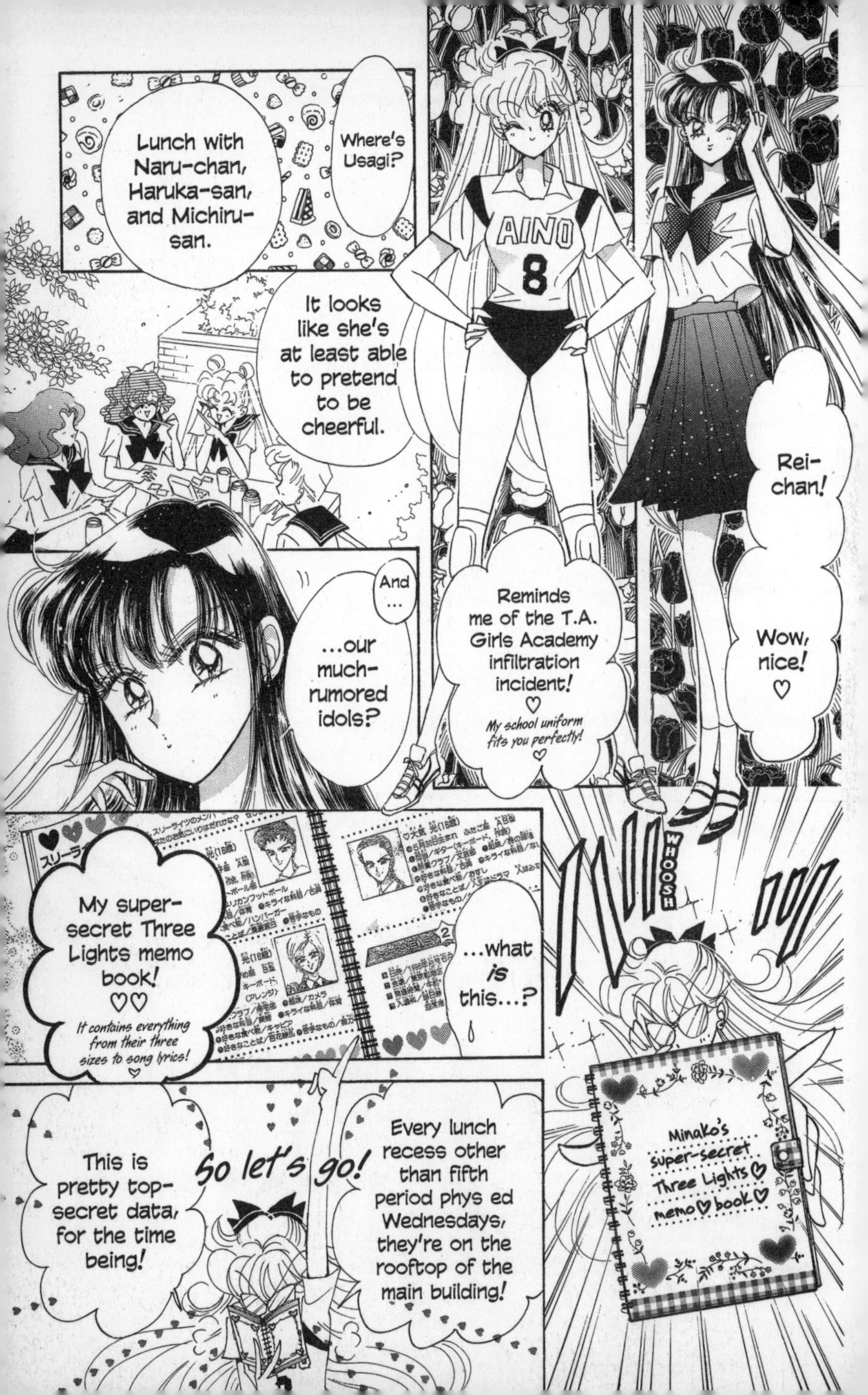

Rei-chan!
Wow, nice! ♡
Reminds me of the T.A. Girls Academy infiltration incident! ♡
My school uniform fits you perfectly! ♡
Where's Usagi?
Lunch with Naru-chan, Haruka-san, and Michiru-san.
It looks like she's at least able to pretend to be cheerful.
And ...
...our much-rumored idols?
WHOOSH
Minako's super-secret Three Lights ♡ memo ♡ book ♡
...what is this...?
My super-secret Three Lights memo book! ♡♡
It contains everything from their three sizes to song lyrics! ♡
Every lunch recess other than fifth period phys ed Wednesdays, they're on the rooftop of the main building!
So let's go!
This is pretty top-secret data, for the time being!

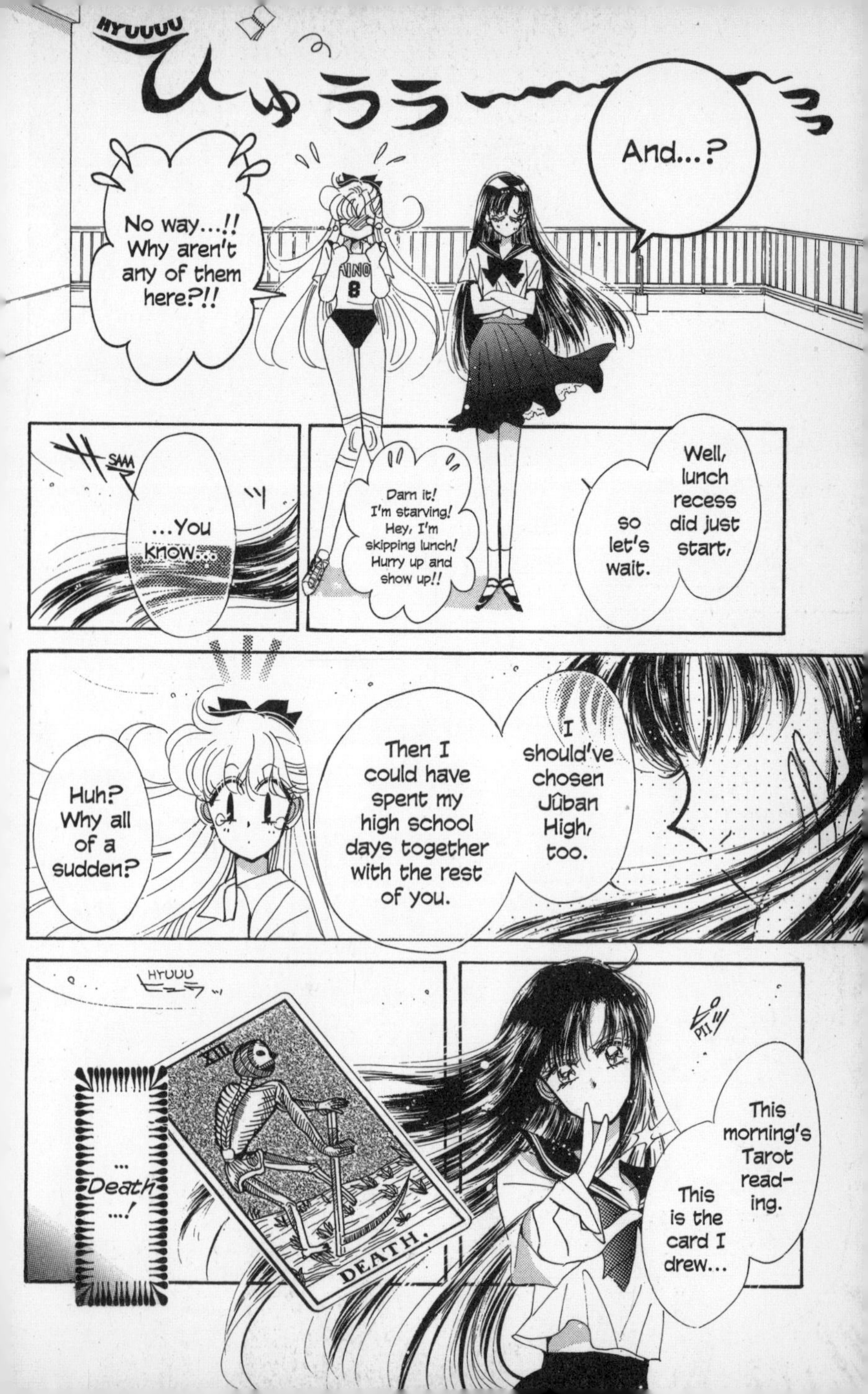
HYUUUU
ひゅラララ~
And...?
No way...!! Why aren't any of them here?!!
Well, lunch recess did just start,
so let's wait.
Darn it! I'm starving! Hey, I'm skipping lunch! Hurry up and show up!!
SAAA
...You know...
I should've chosen Jûban High, too.
Then I could have spent my high school days together with the rest of you.
Huh? Why all of a sudden?
PII
This morning's Tarot reading.
This is the card I drew...
HYUUU
XIII
DEATH.
...Death...!

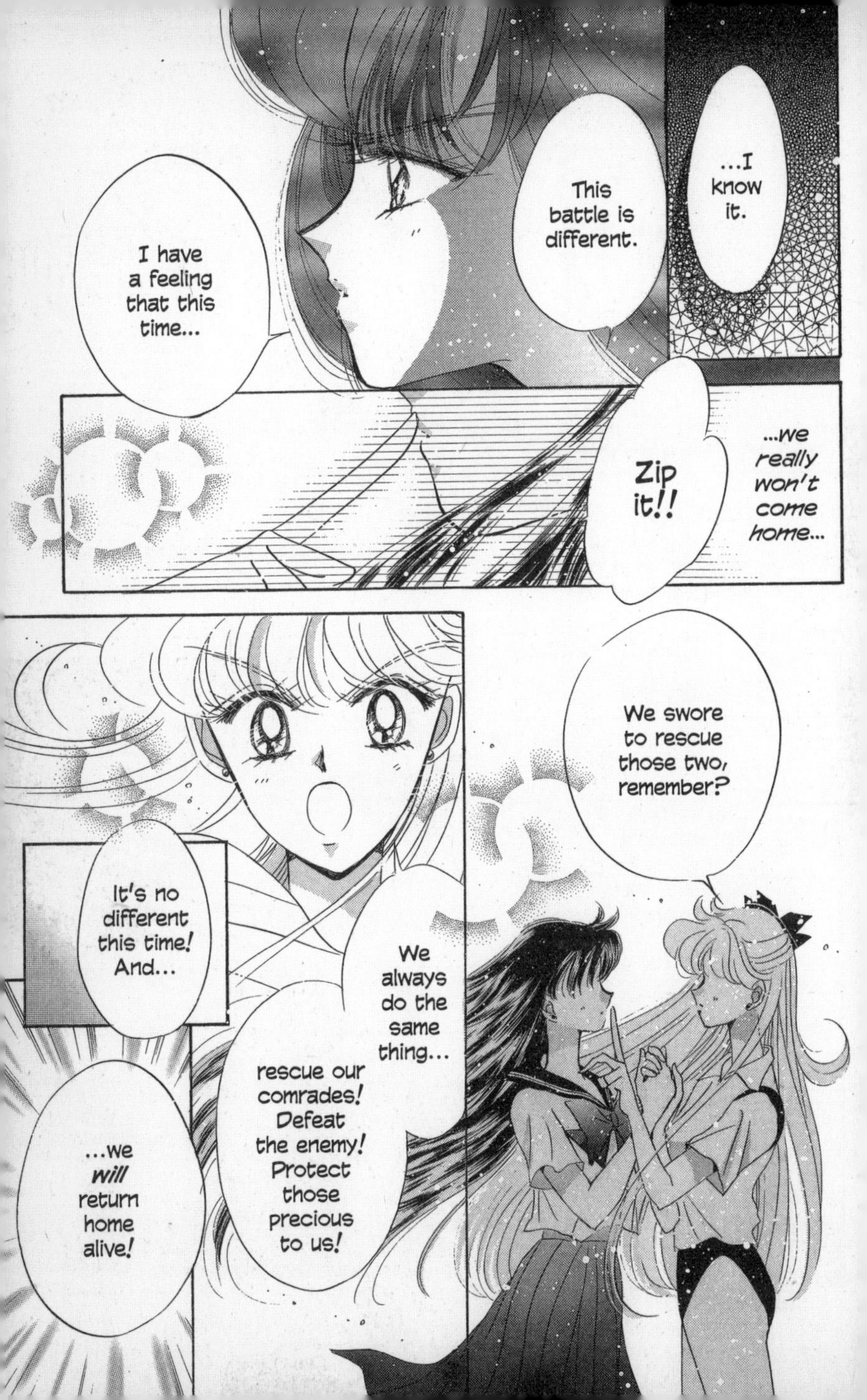
...I know it.
This battle is different.
I have a feeling that this time...
...we *really won't* come home...
Zip it!!
We swore to rescue those two, remember?
We always do the same thing...
rescue our comrades! Defeat the enemy! Protect those precious to us!
It's no different this time! And...
...we *will* return home alive!

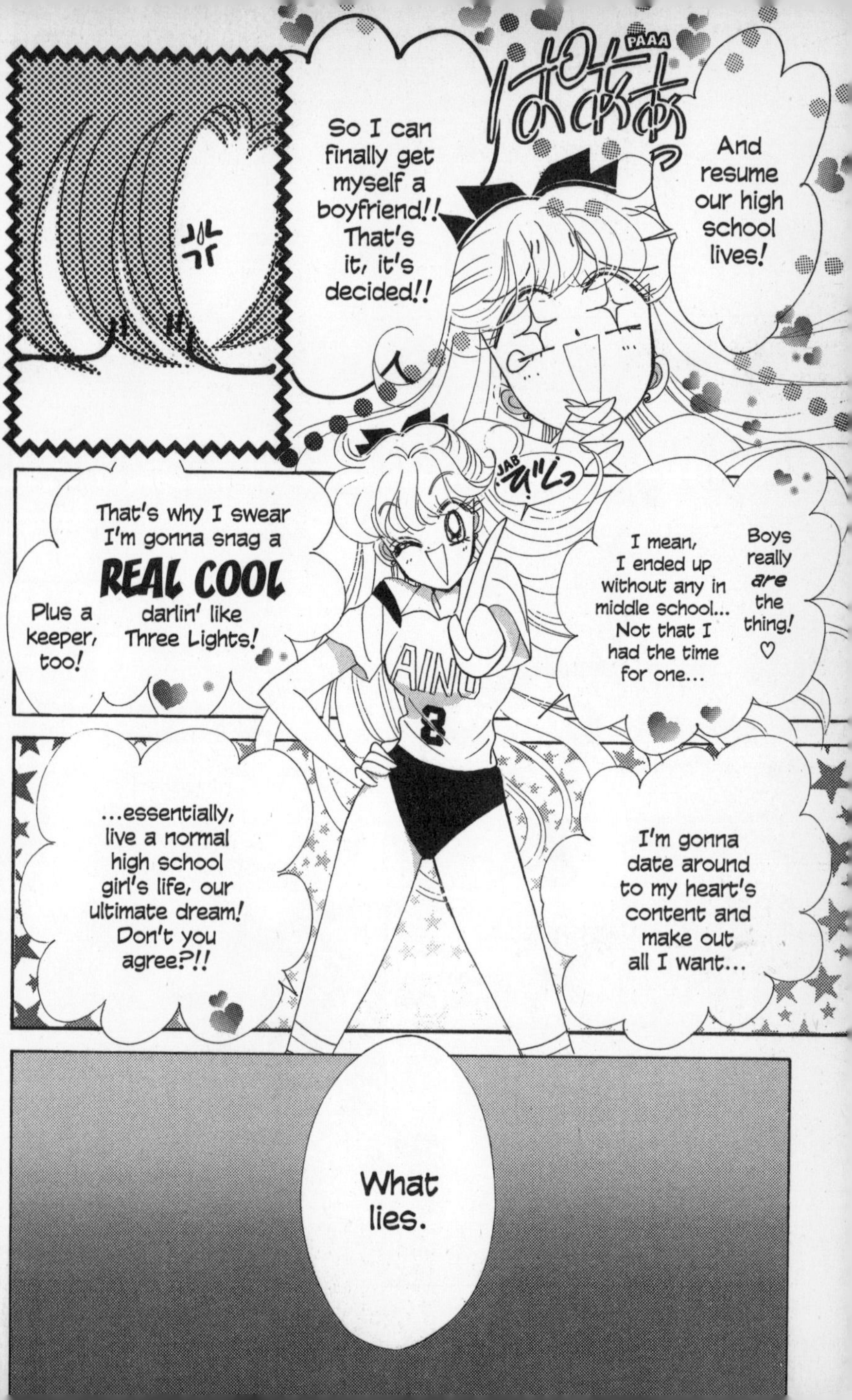
PAAA
And resume our high school lives!
So I can finally get myself a boyfriend!! That's it, it's decided!!
Boys really *are* the thing! ♡
I mean, I ended up without any in middle school... Not that I had the time for one...
JAB
That's why I swear I'm gonna snag a REAL COOL darlin' like Three Lights!
Plus a keeper, too!
I'm gonna date around to my heart's content and make out all I want...
...essentially, live a normal high school girl's life, our ultimate dream! Don't you agree?!!
What lies.

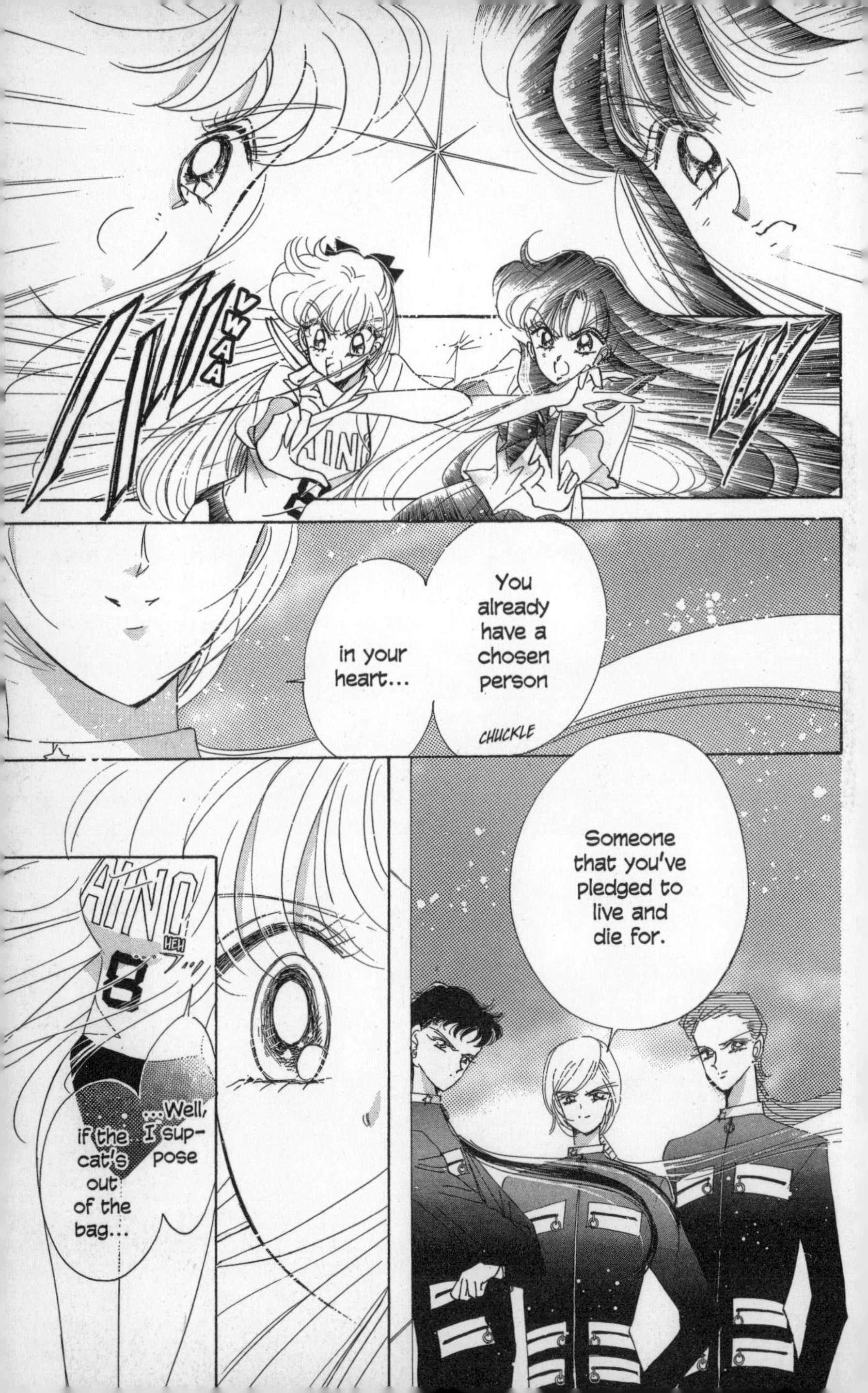
VWAA
You already have a chosen person
in your heart...
CHUCKLE
Someone that you've pledged to live and die for.
HEH
...Well, I suppose
if the cat's out of the bag...

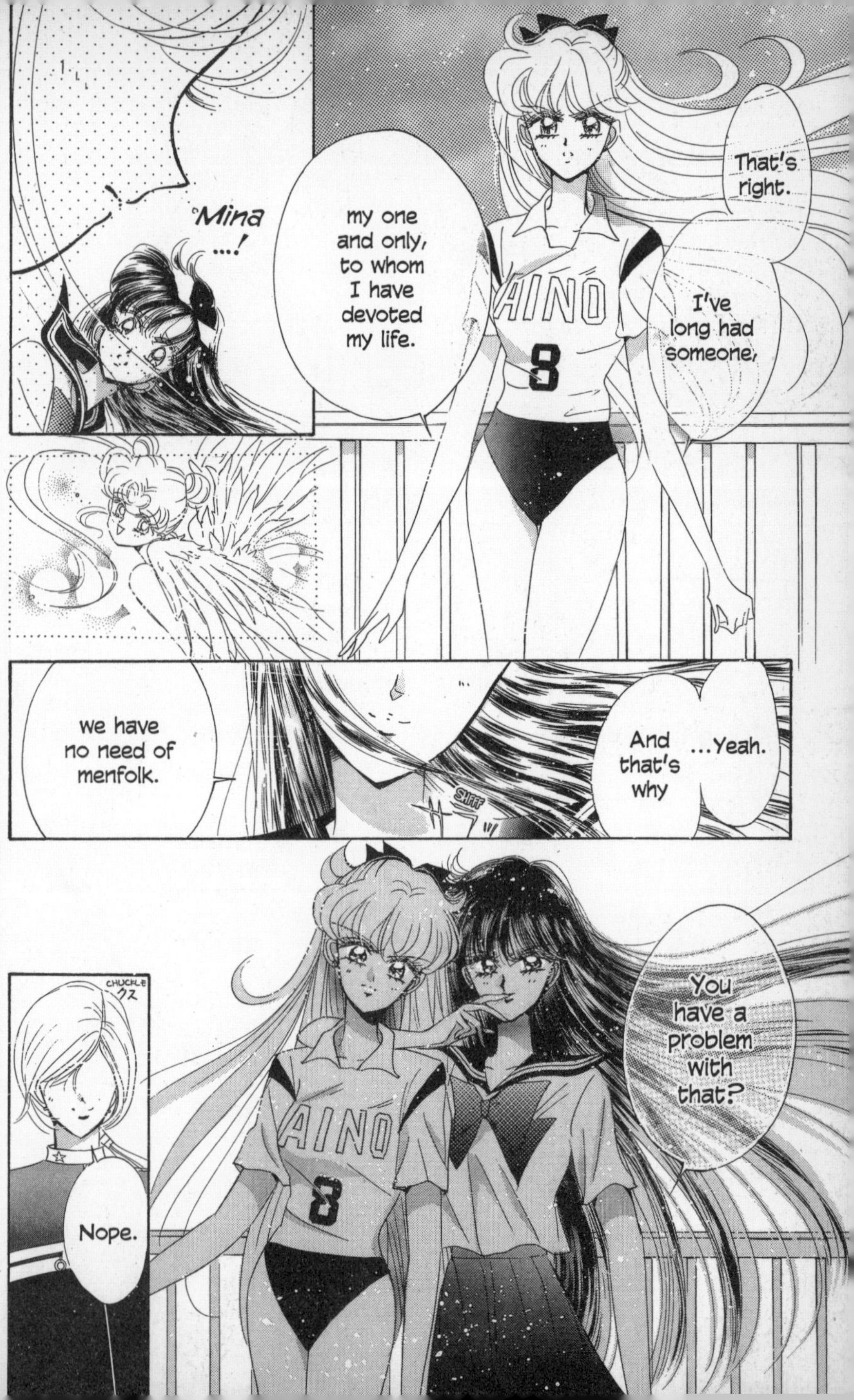
That's right.
I've long had someone,
my one and only, to whom I have devoted my life.
Mina ...!
...Yeah.
And that's why
SHFFF
we have no need of menfolk.
You have a problem with that?
CHUCKLE クス
Nope.

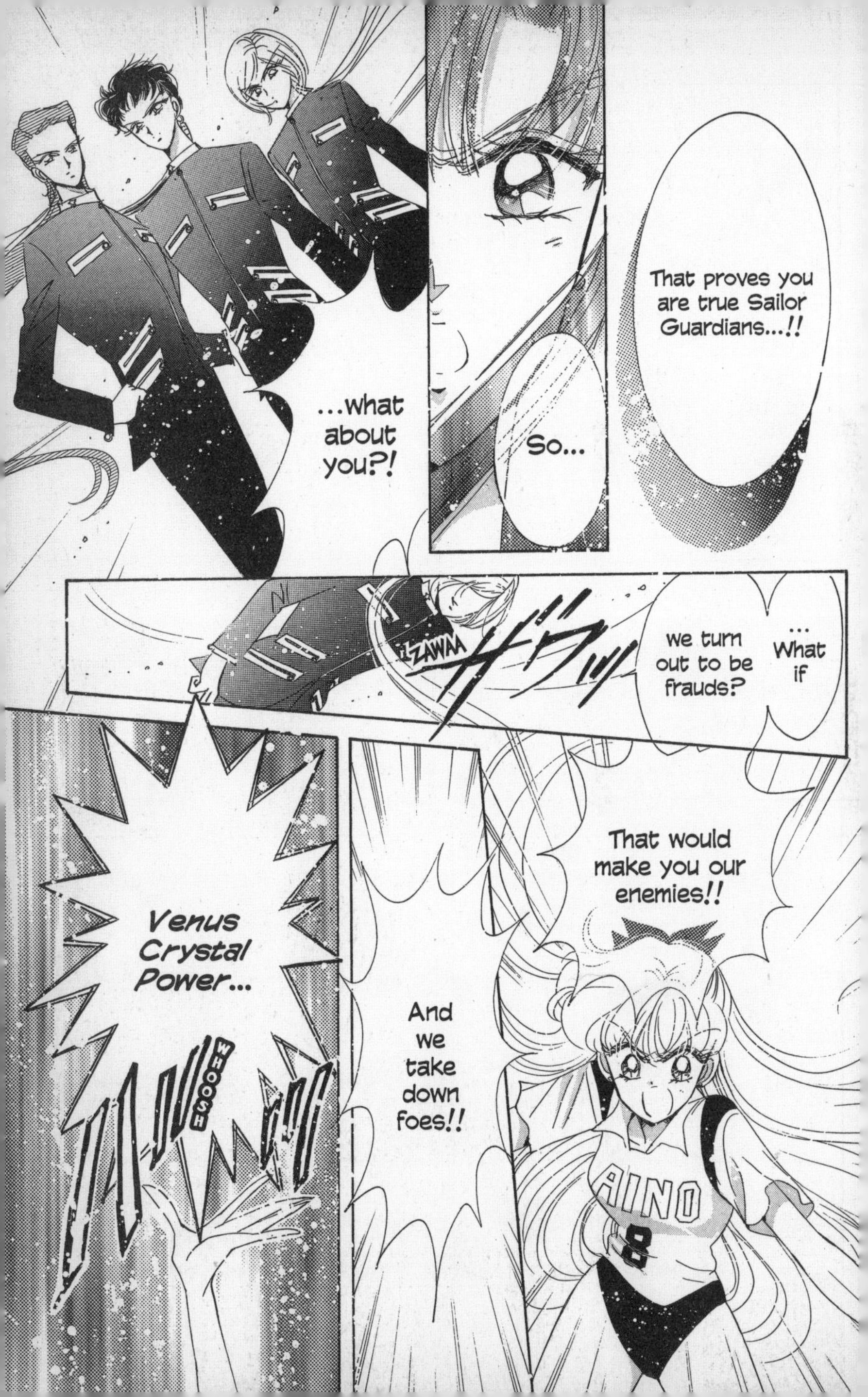
That proves you are true Sailor Guardians...!!
So...
...what about you?!
... What if
we turn out to be frauds?
ZAWAA
That would make you our enemies!!
And we take down foes!!
AINO
8
Venus Crystal Power...
WHOOSH

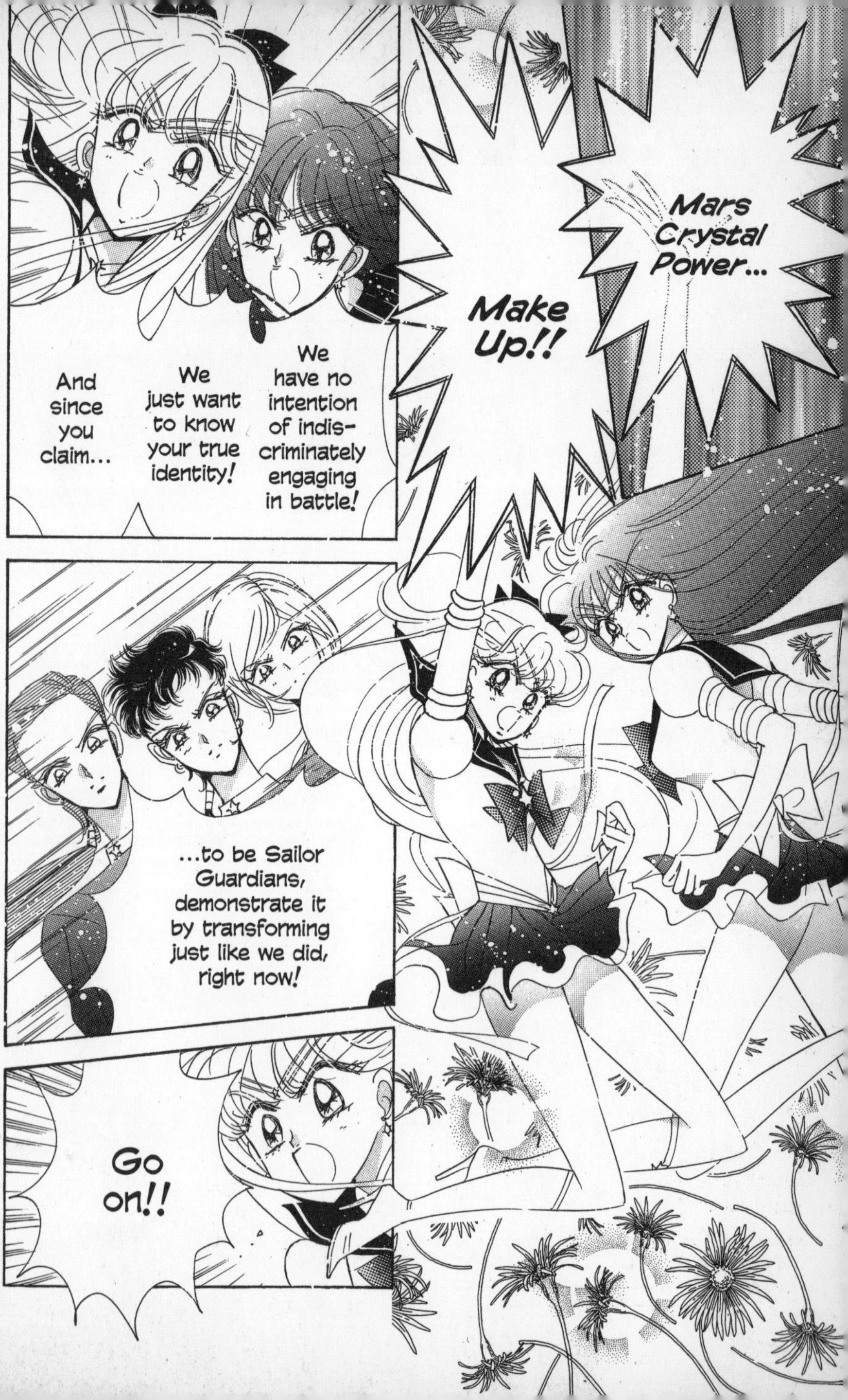

Mars Crystal Power...
Make Up!!
We have no intention of indis-criminately engaging in battle!
We just want to know your true identity!
And since you claim...
...to be Sailor Guardians, demonstrate it by transforming just like we did, right now!
Go on!!

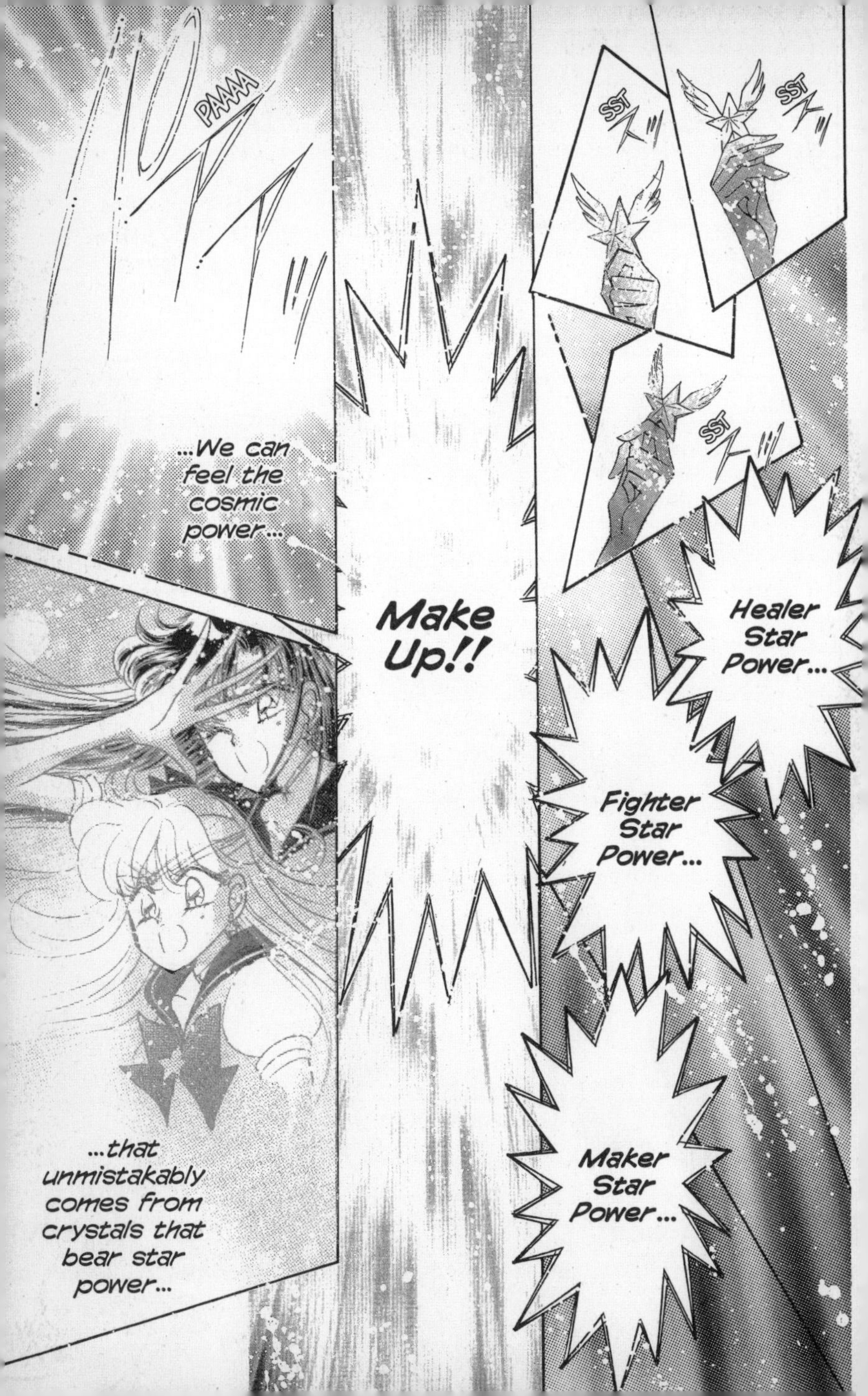
SST
SST
SST
Healer Star Power...
Fighter Star Power...
Maker Star Power...
Make Up!!
PAAAA
...We can feel the cosmic power...
...that unmistakably comes from crystals that bear star power...

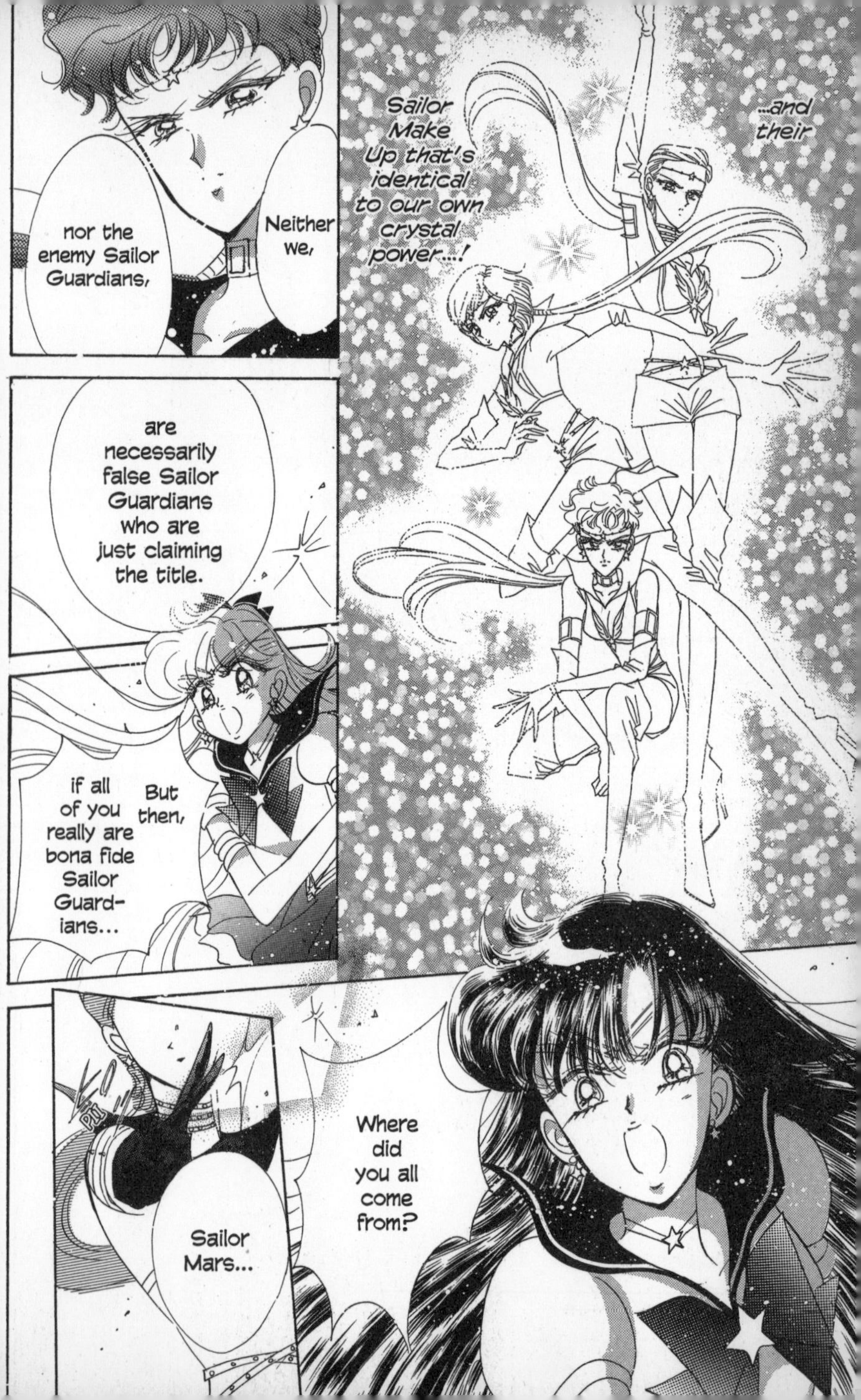
...and their
Sailor Make Up that's identical to our own crystal power...!
Neither we,
nor the enemy Sailor Guardians,
are necessarily false Sailor Guardians who are just claiming the title.
But then,
if all of you really are bona fide Sailor Guardians...
Where did you all come from?
Sailor Mars...

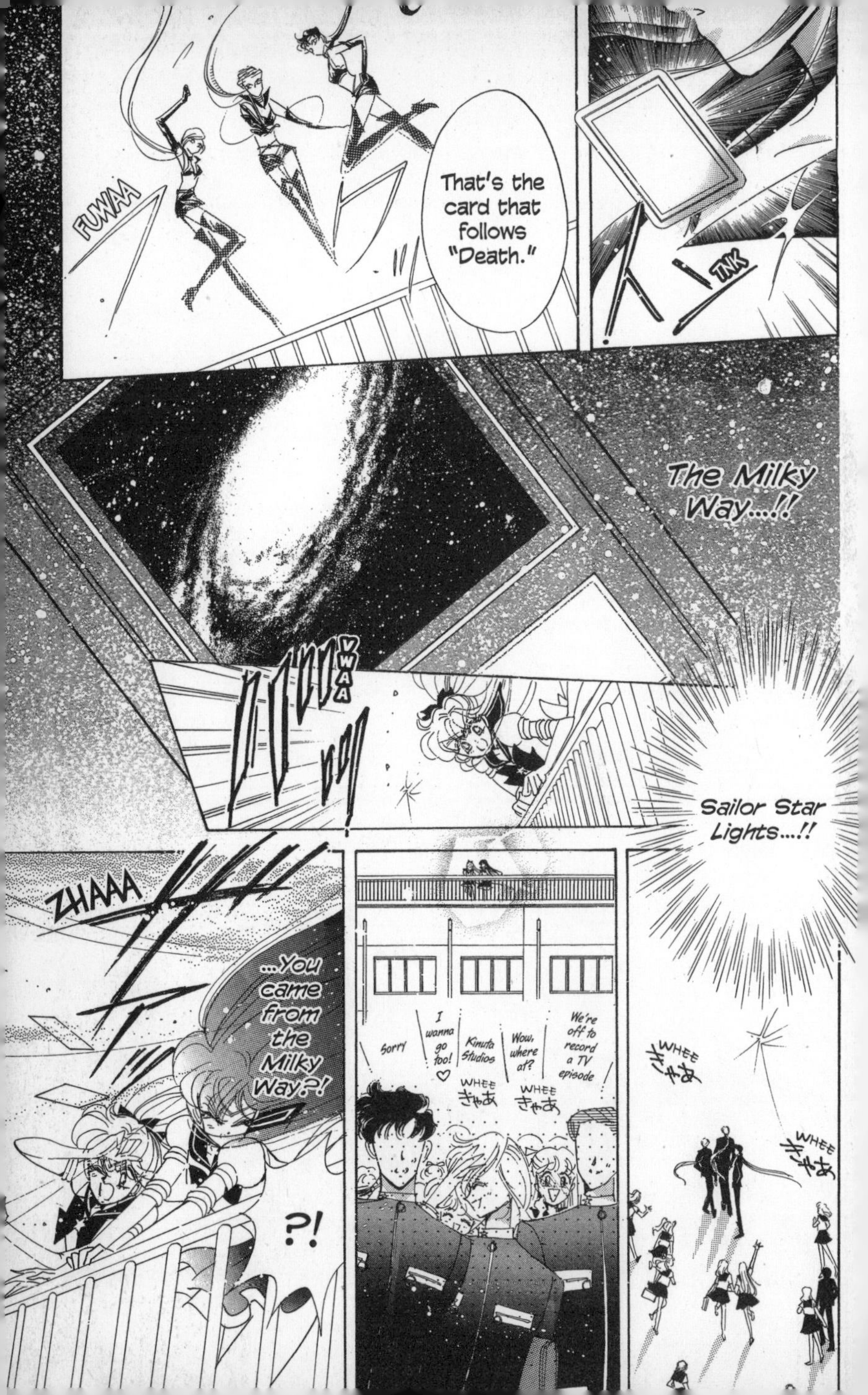
TNK
FUWAA
That's the card that follows "Death."
The Milky Way...!!
VWAA
Sailor Star Lights...!!
WHEE きゃあ
WHEE きゃあ
We're off to record a TV episode
Wow, where at?
Kinuta Studios
I wanna go too! ♡
Sorry
WHEE きゃあ
WHEE きゃあ
ZHAAA
...You came from the Milky Way?!
?!

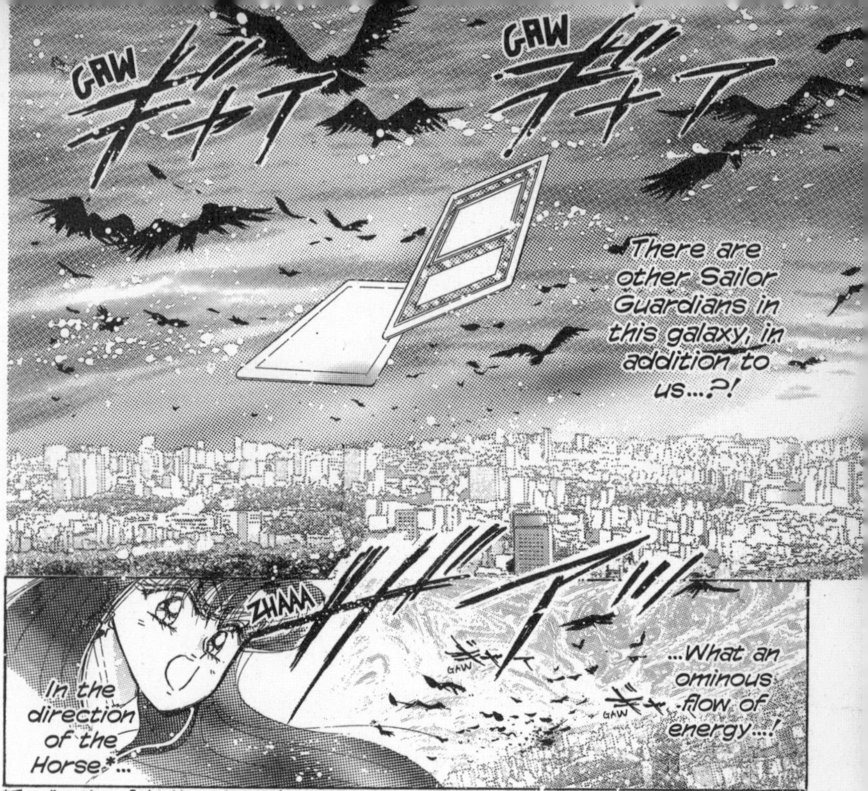
GAW
GAW
There are other Sailor Guardians in this galaxy, in addition to us...?!
...What an ominous flow of energy...!
GAW
GAW
ZHAAA
In the direction of the Horse*...

*The direction of the Horse is south.

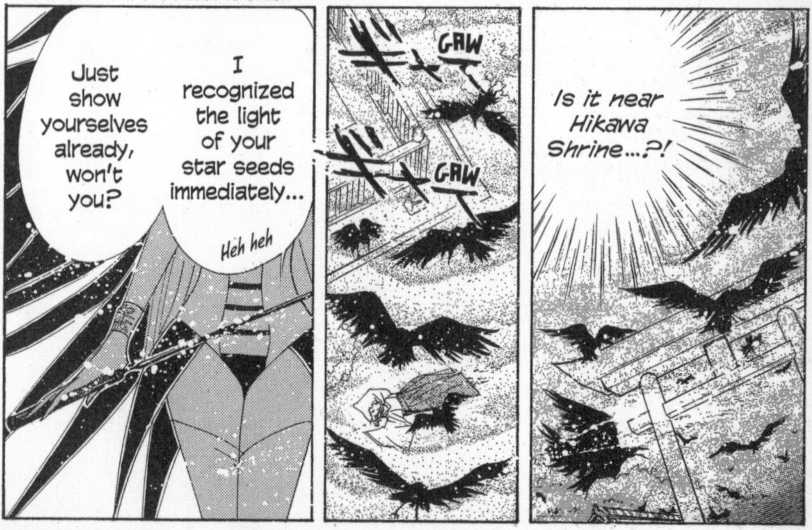
Is it near Hikawa Shrine...?!
GAW
GAW
I recognized the light of your star seeds immediately...
Just show yourselves already, won't you?
Heh heh

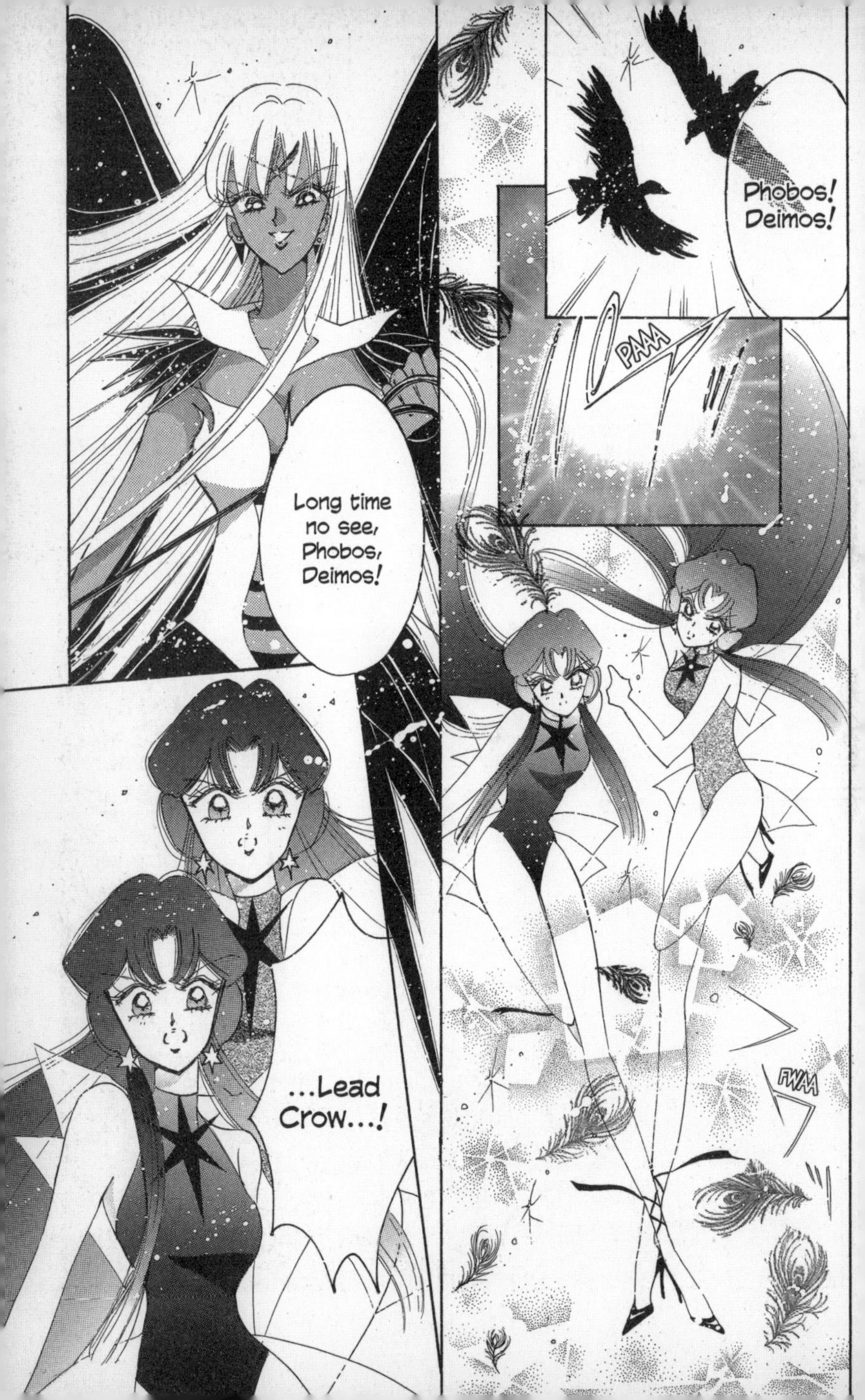
Phobos! Deimos!
PAAA
FWAA
Long time no see, Phobos, Deimos!
...Lead Crow...!

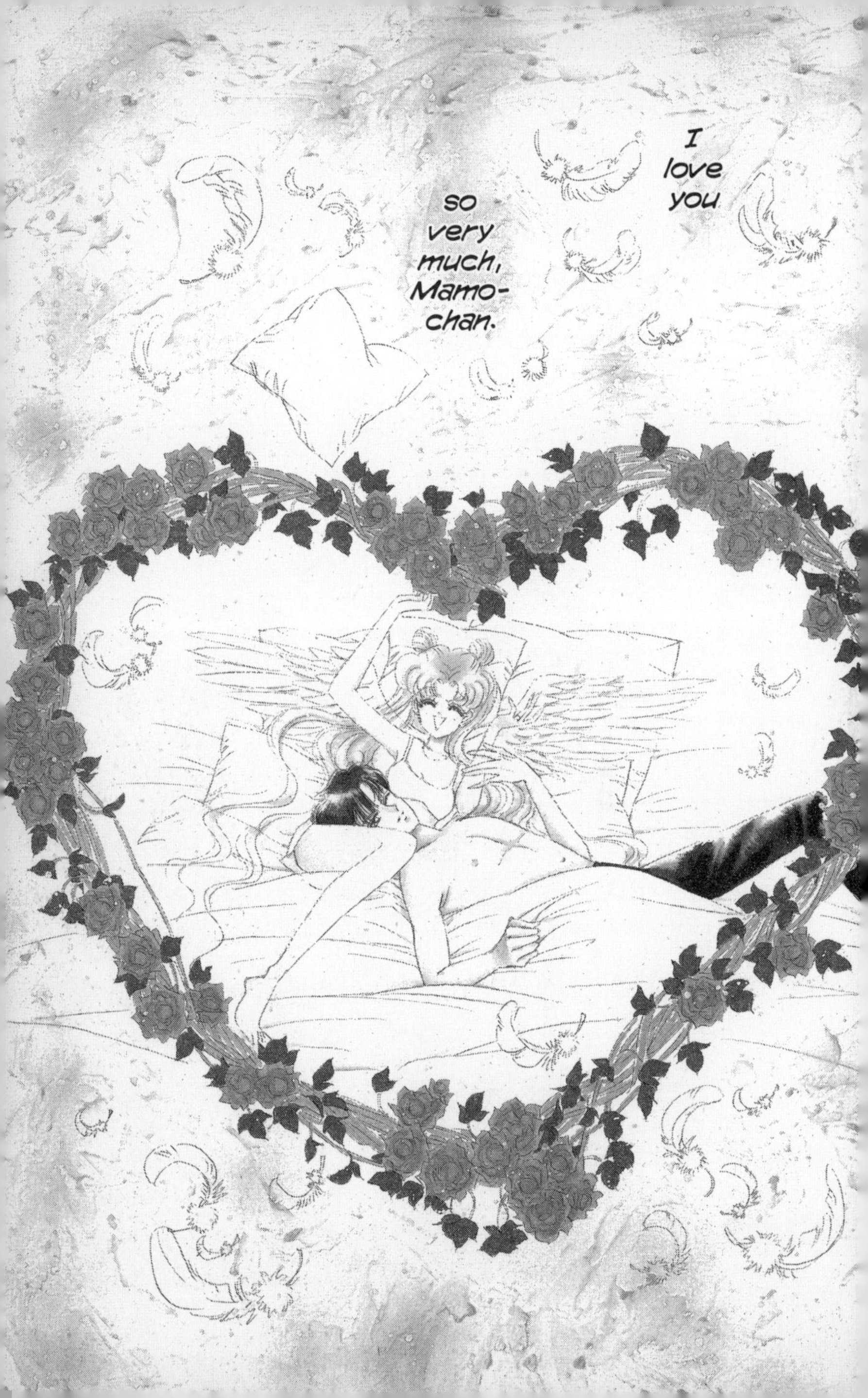
I love you
so very much, Mamo-chan.

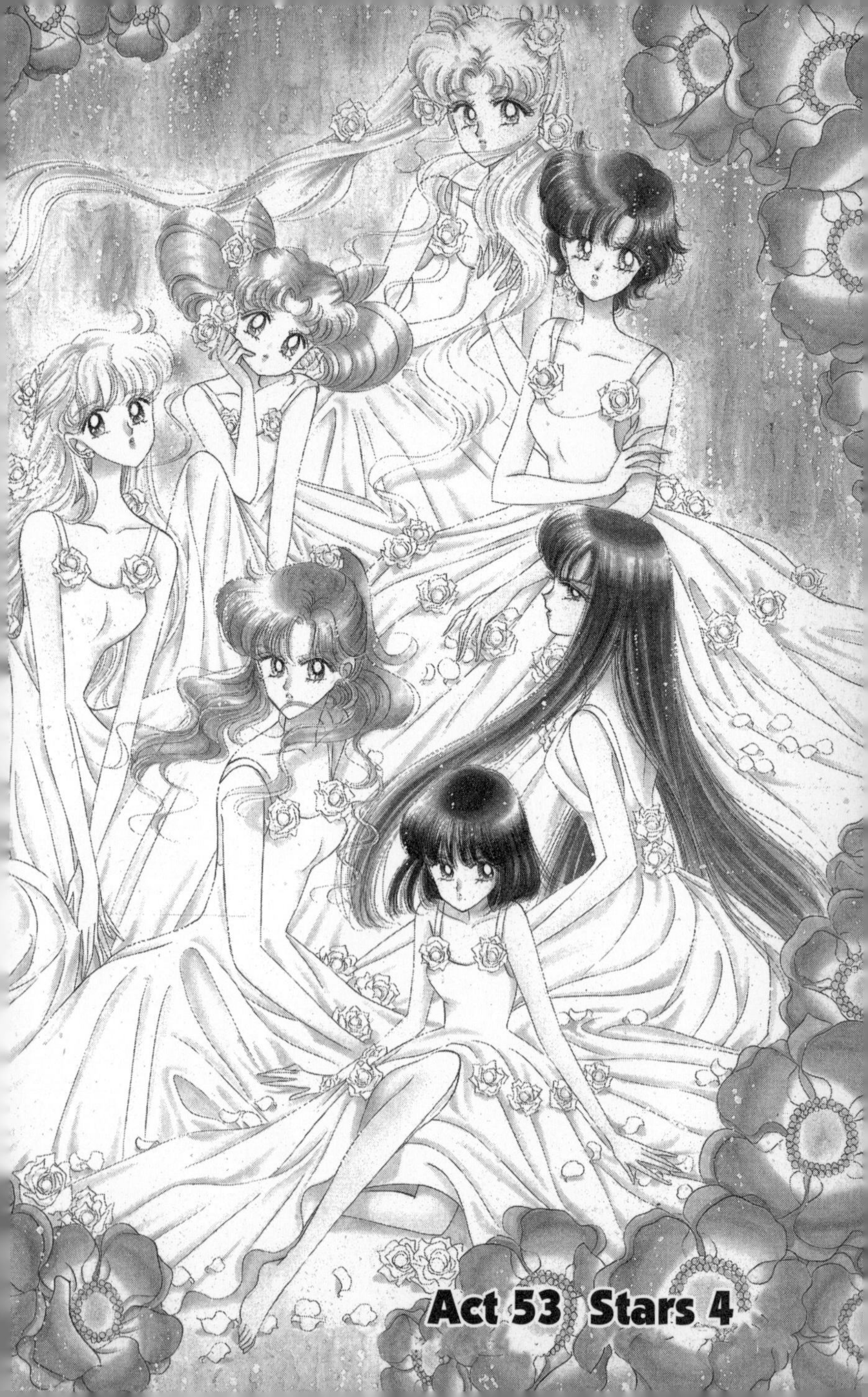

Act 53 Stars 4

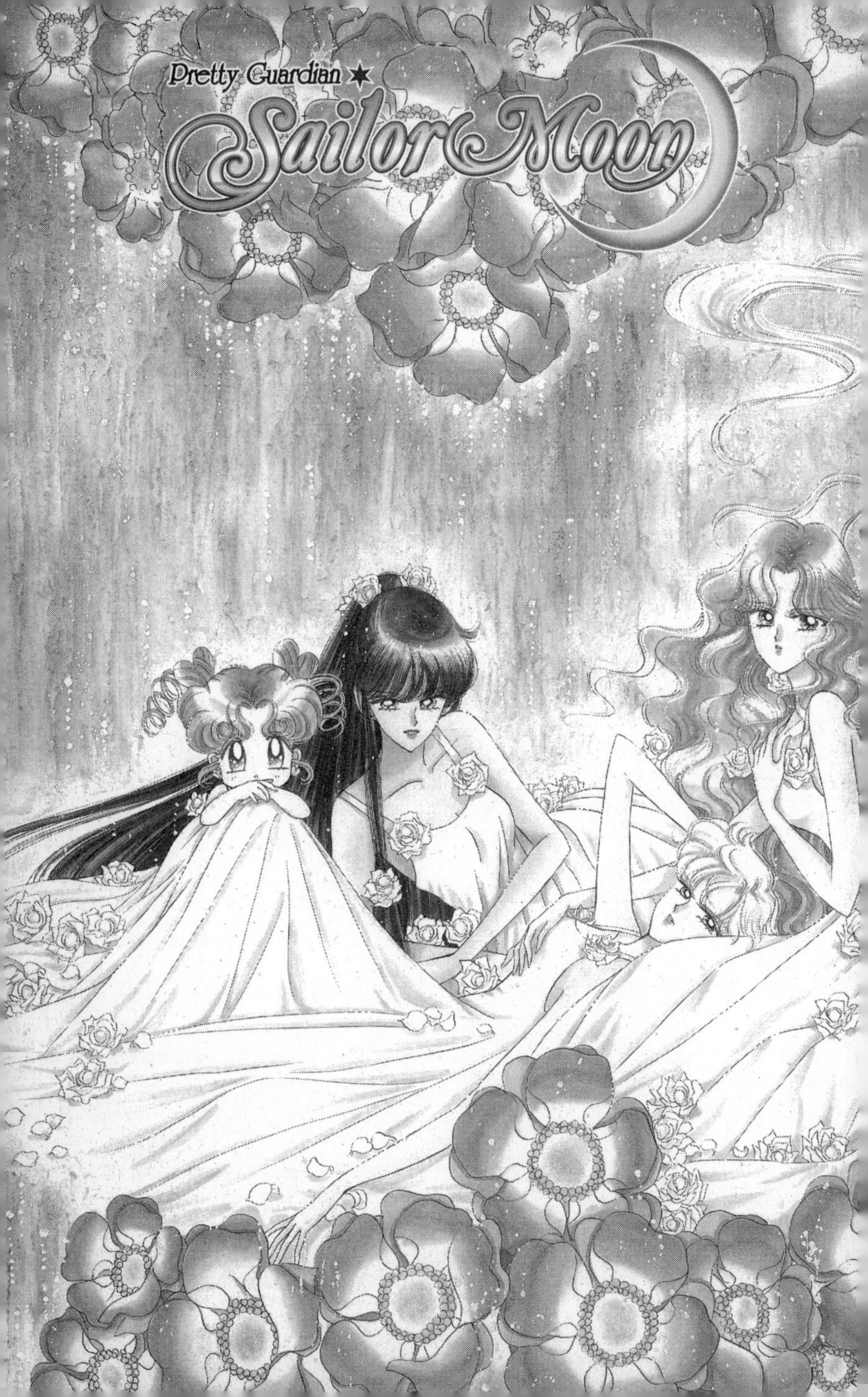
Pretty Guardian
Sailor Moon

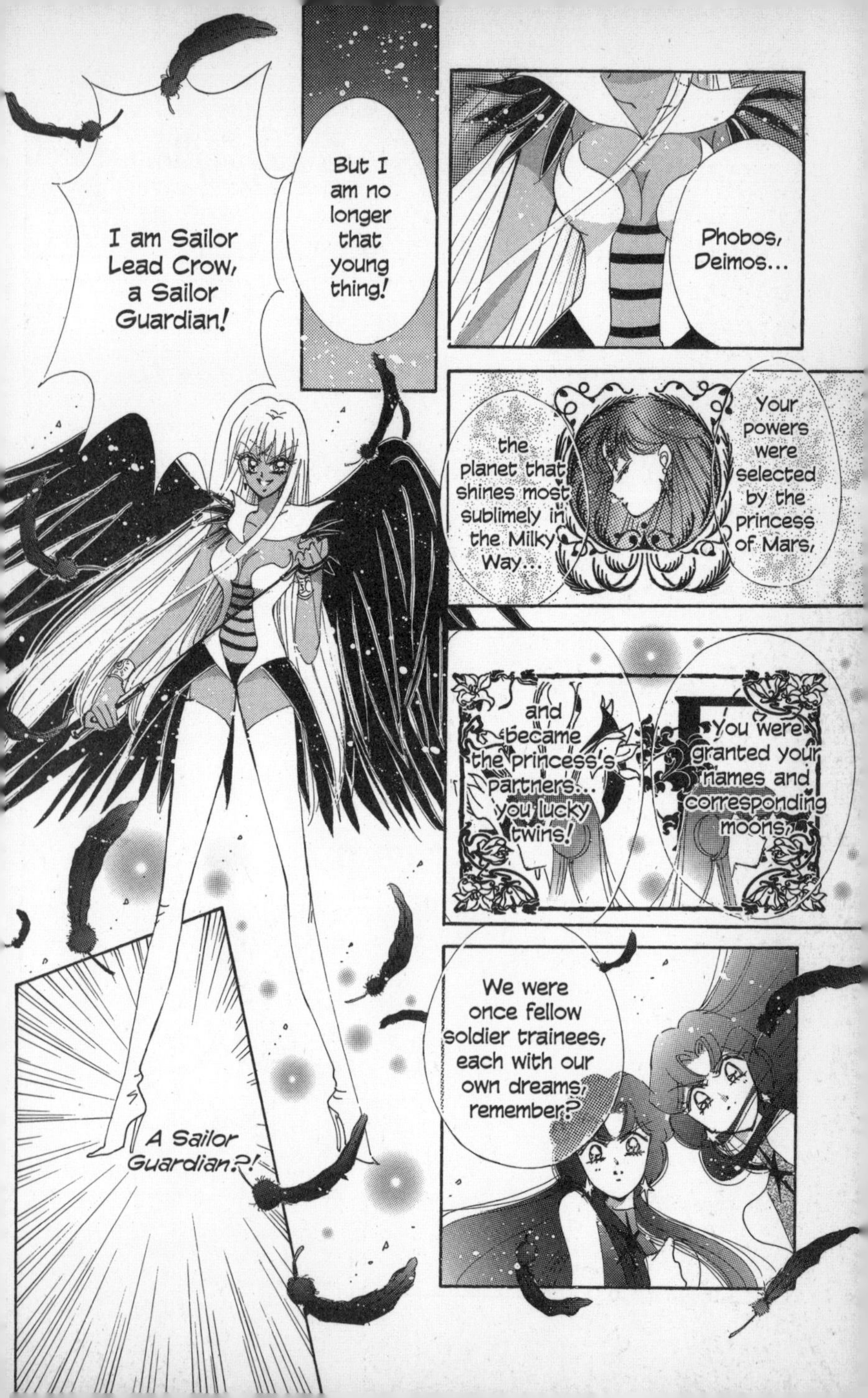
Phobos, Deimos...
Your powers were selected by the princess of Mars,
the planet that shines most sublimely in the Milky Way...
You were granted your names and corresponding moons,
and became the princess's partners... you lucky twins!
We were once fellow soldier trainees, each with our own dreams, remember?
But I am no longer that young thing!
I am Sailor Lead Crow, a Sailor Guardian!
A Sailor Guardian?!

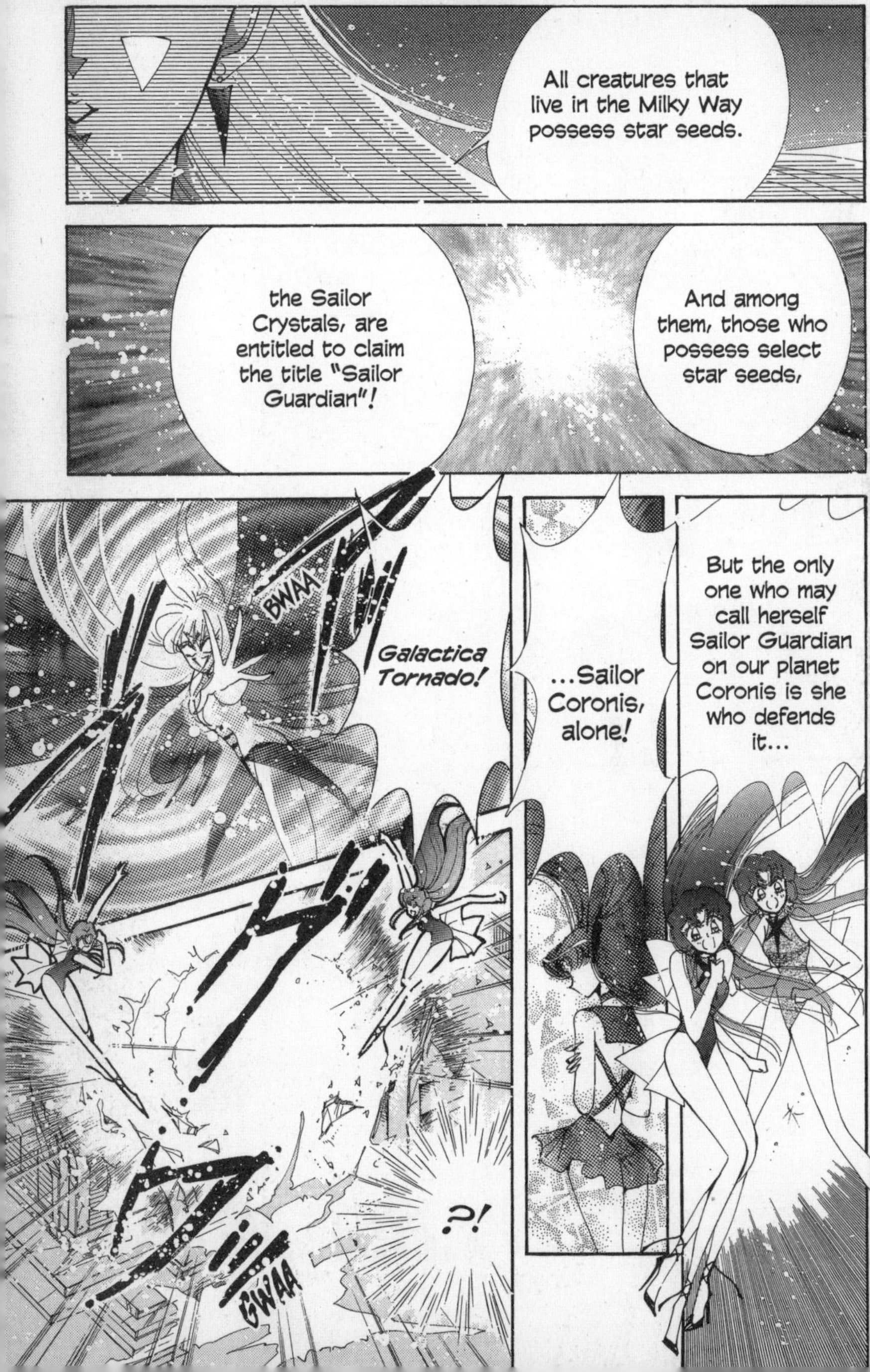
All creatures that live in the Milky Way possess star seeds.
And among them, those who possess select star seeds,
the Sailor Crystals, are entitled to claim the title "Sailor Guardian"!
But the only one who may call herself Sailor Guardian on our planet Coronis is she who defends it...
...Sailor Coronis, alone!
BWAA
Galactica Tornado!
?!
GWAA

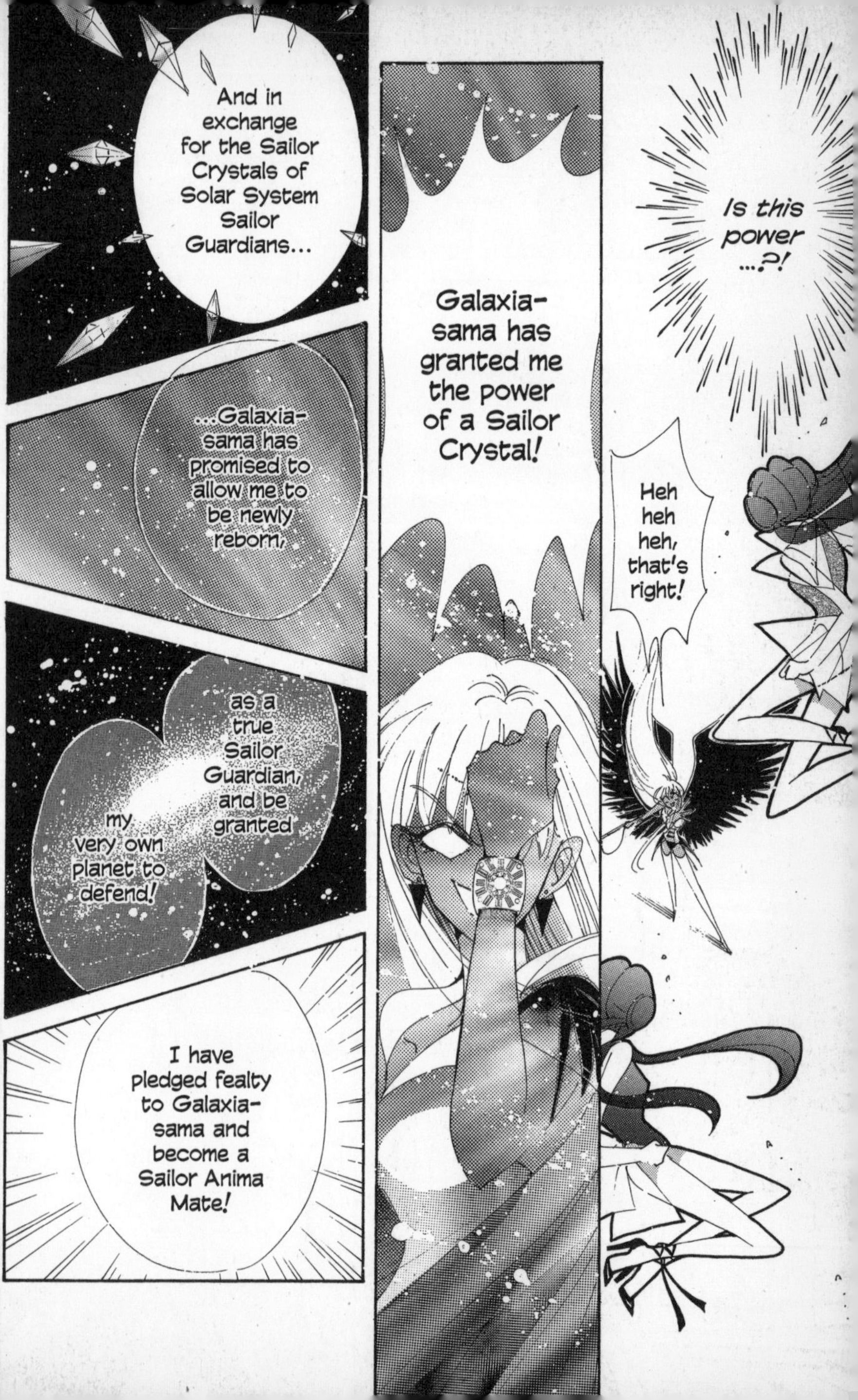
Is this power ...?!
Heh heh heh, that's right!
Galaxia-sama has granted me the power of a Sailor Crystal!
And in exchange for the Sailor Crystals of Solar System Sailor Guardians...
...Galaxia-sama has promised to allow me to be newly reborn,
as a true Sailor Guardian, and be granted
my very own planet to defend!
I have pledged fealty to Galaxia-sama and become a Sailor Anima Mate!

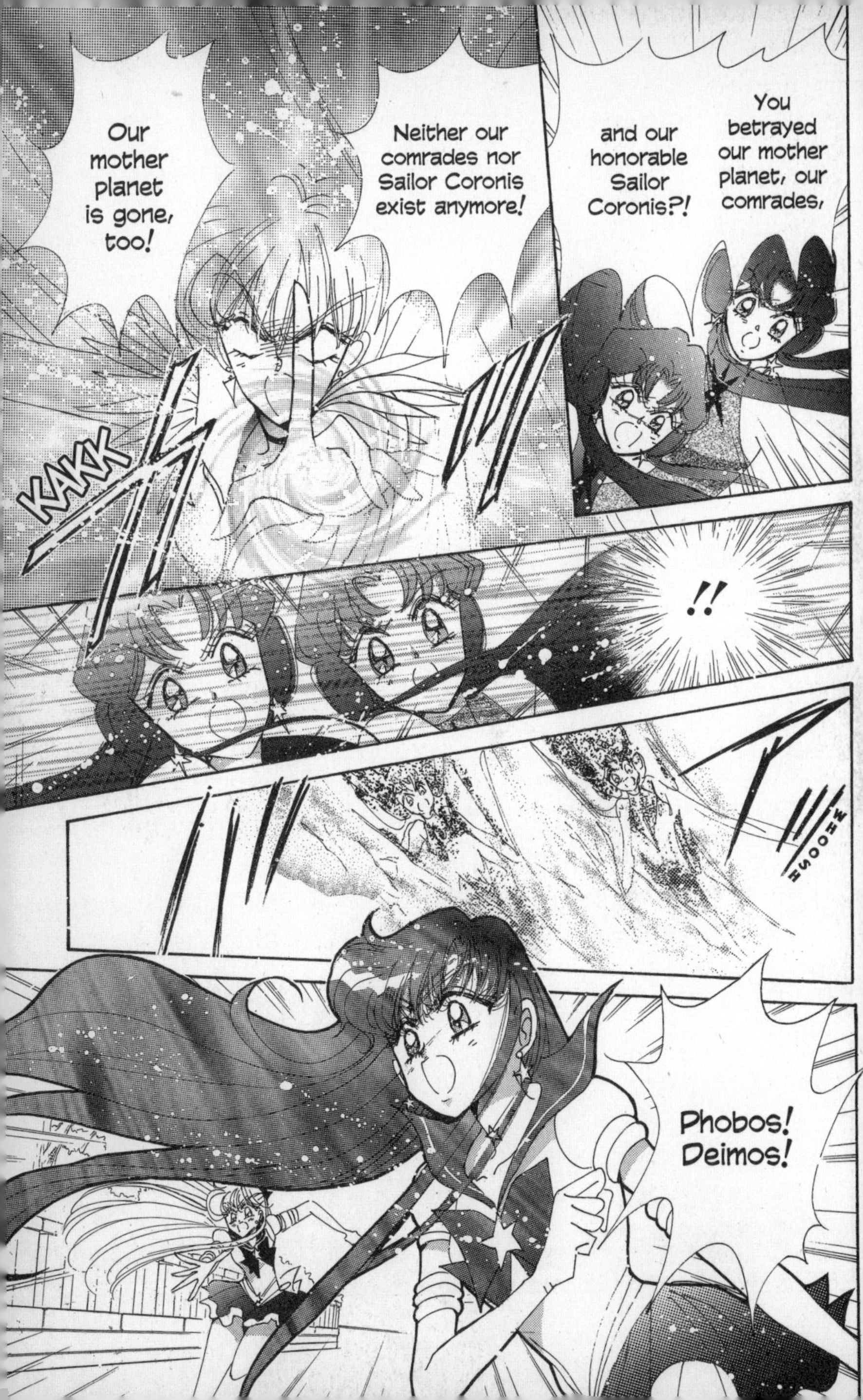

You betrayed our mother planet, our comrades,
and our honorable Sailor Coronis?!
Neither our comrades nor Sailor Coronis exist anymore!
Our mother planet is gone, too!
KAKK
!!
WHOOSH
Phobos! Deimos!

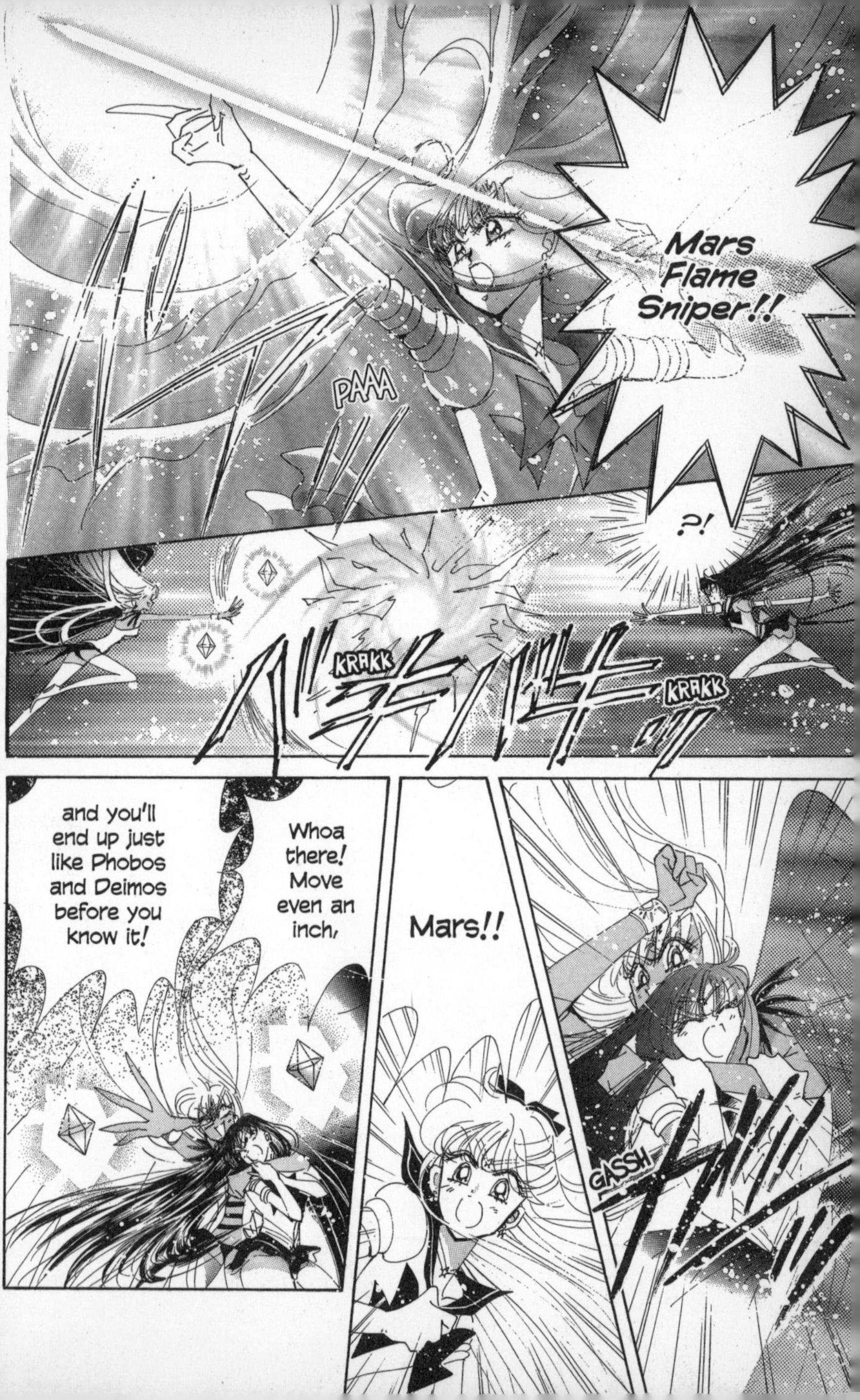

Mars Flame Sniper!!
PAAA
?!
KRAKK
KRAKK
GASSH
Mars!!
Whoa there! Move even an inch,
and you'll end up just like Phobos and Deimos before you know it!

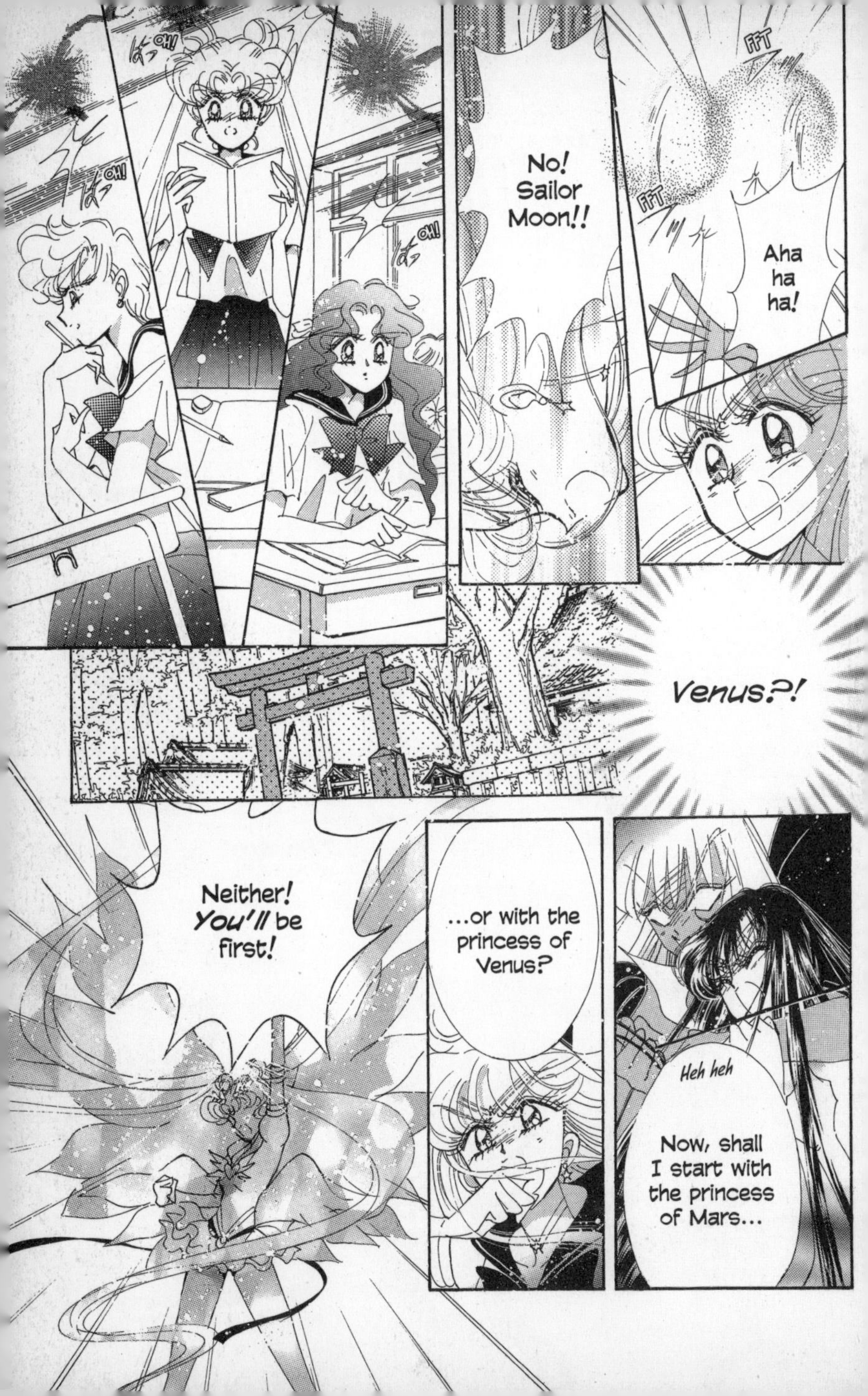
FFT
FFT
Aha ha ha!
No! Sailor Moon!!
OH!
OH!
OH!
Venus?!
Heh heh
Now, shall I start with the princess of Mars...
...or with the princess of Venus?
Neither! *You'll* be first!

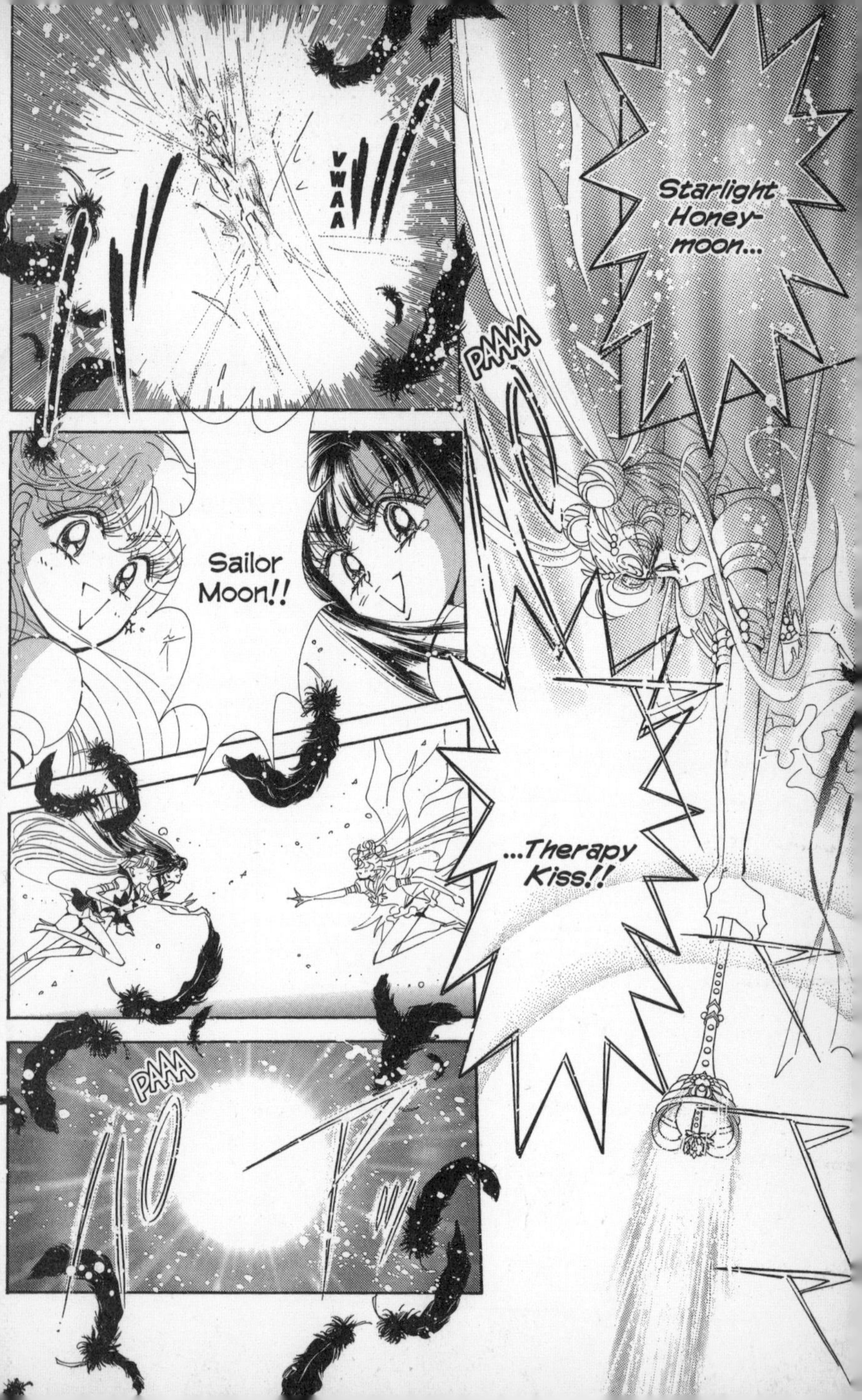
Starlight Honey-moon...
PAAAA
...Therapy Kiss!!
VWAAA
Sailor Moon!!
PAAA

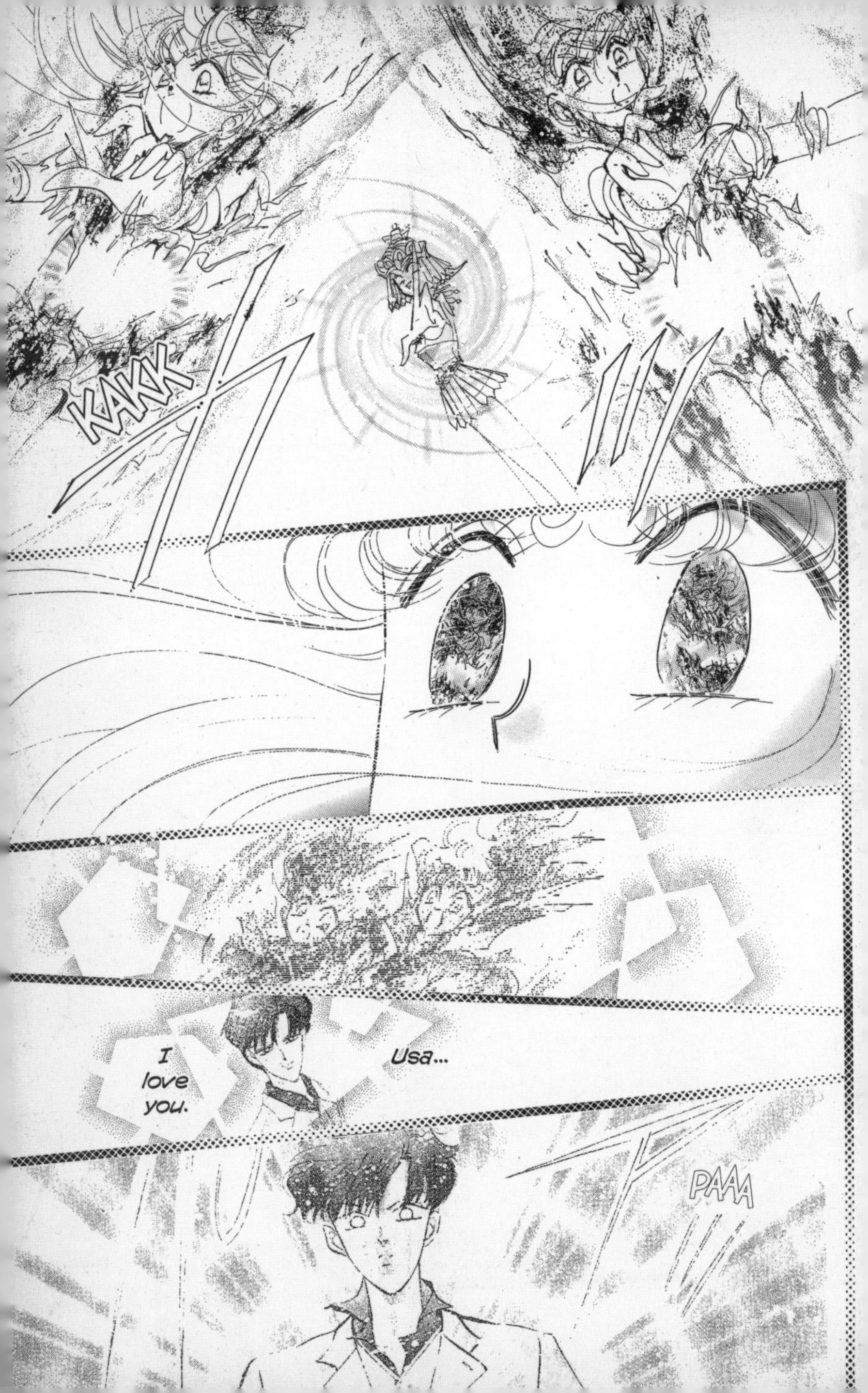
KAKK
Usa...
I love you.
PAAA

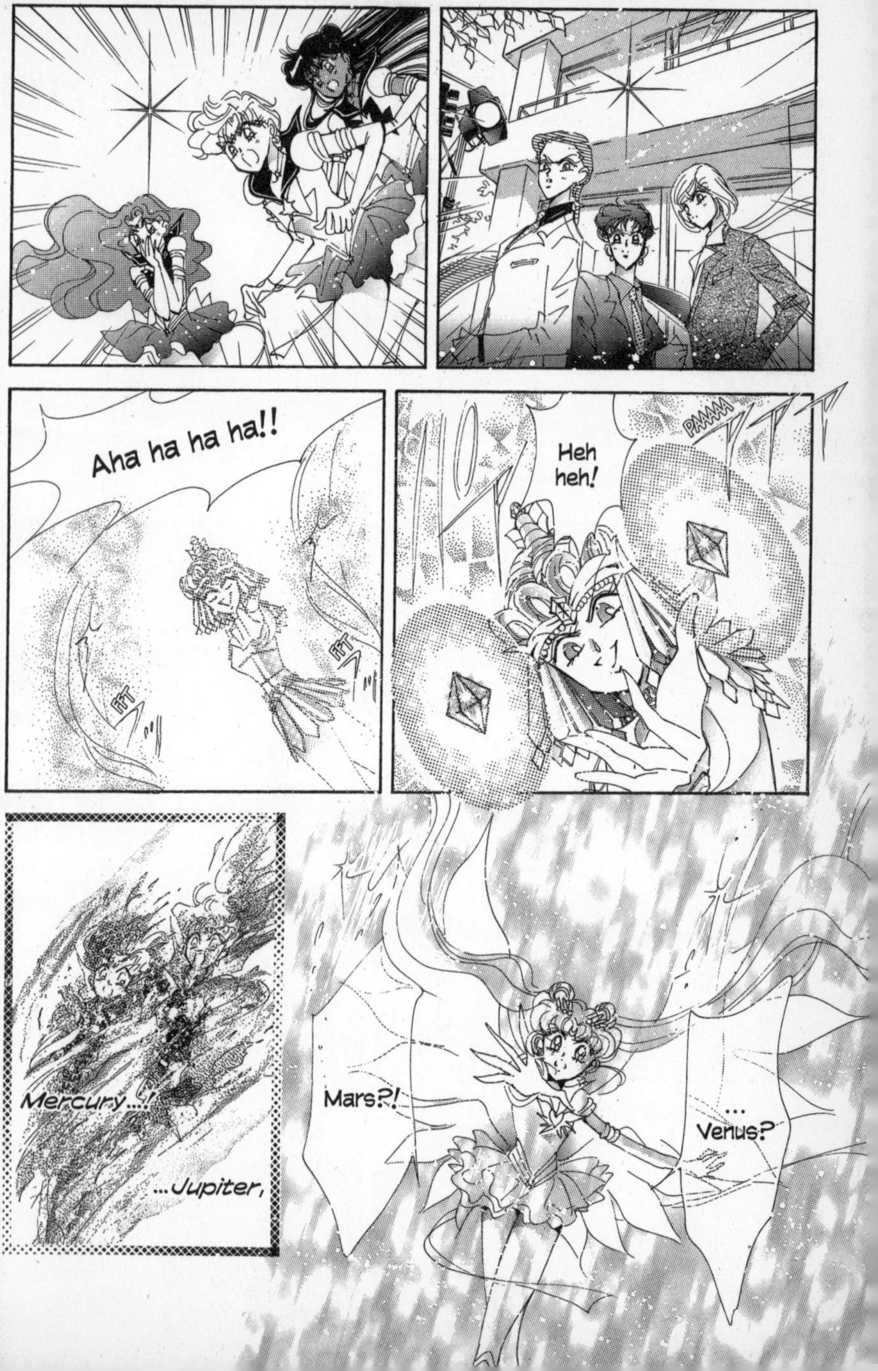
PAAAAA
Heh heh!
Aha ha ha ha!!
FFT
FFT
Mercury...!
...Jupiter,
Mars?!
...
Venus?

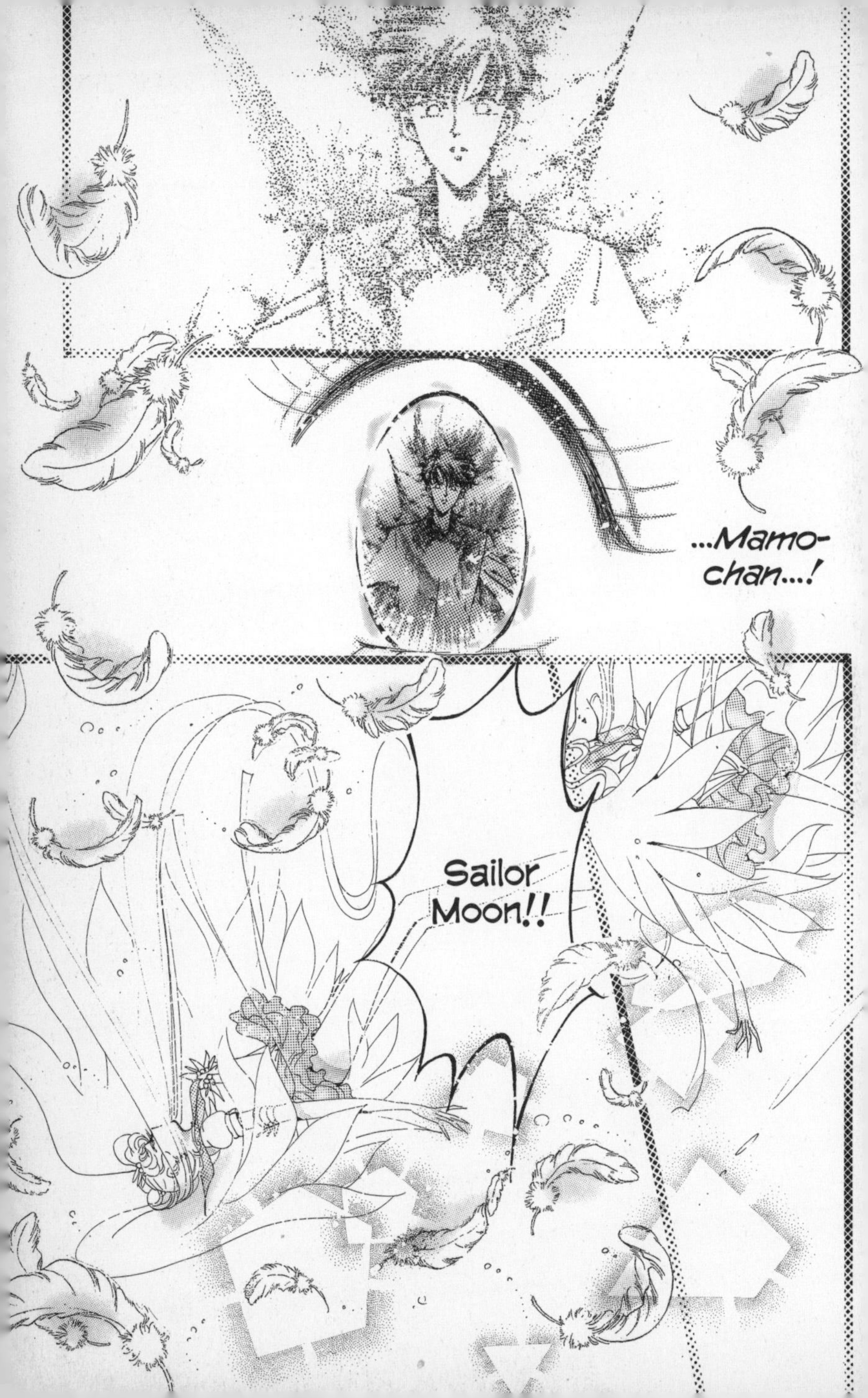
...Mamo-
chan...!
Sailor
Moon!!

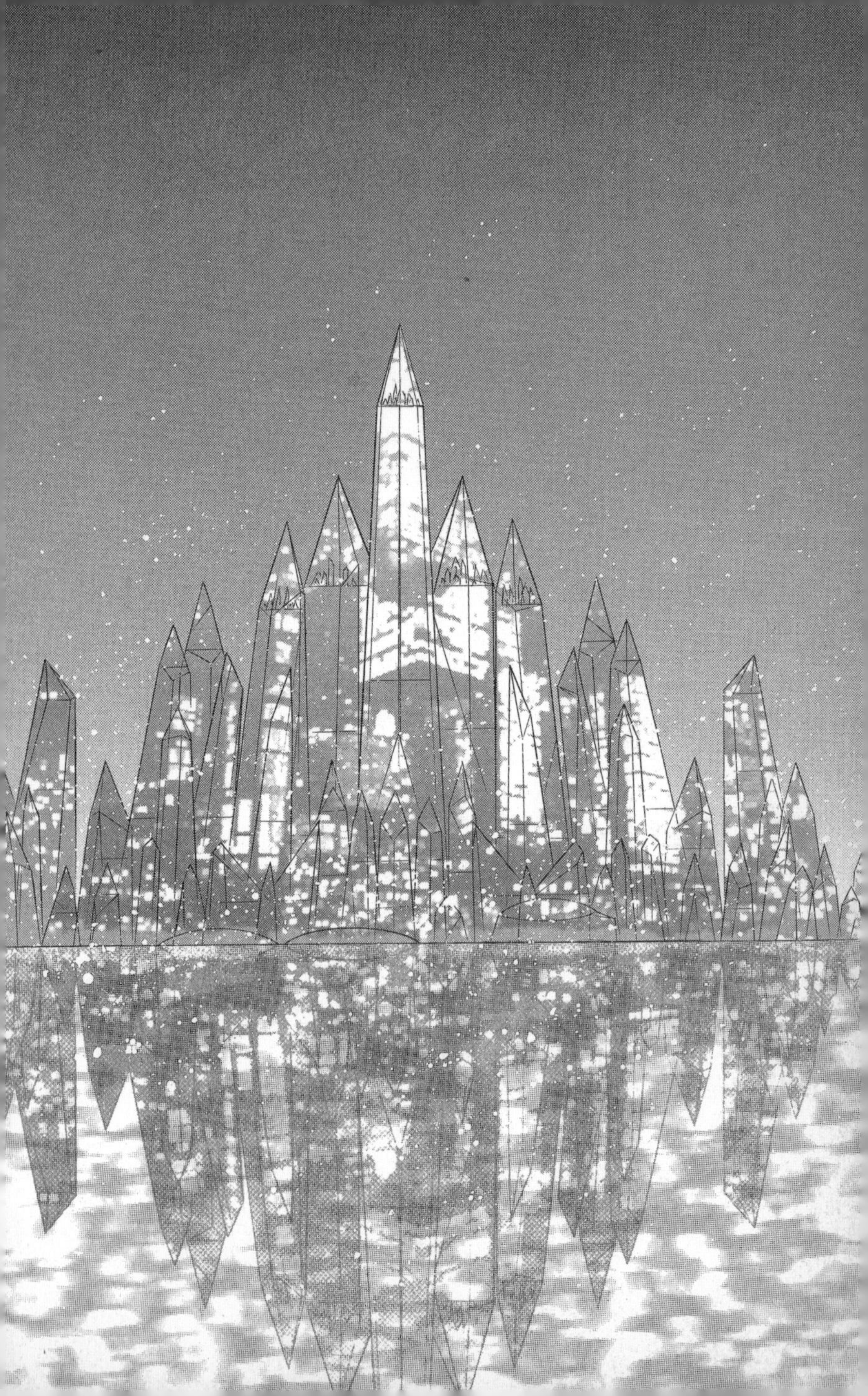

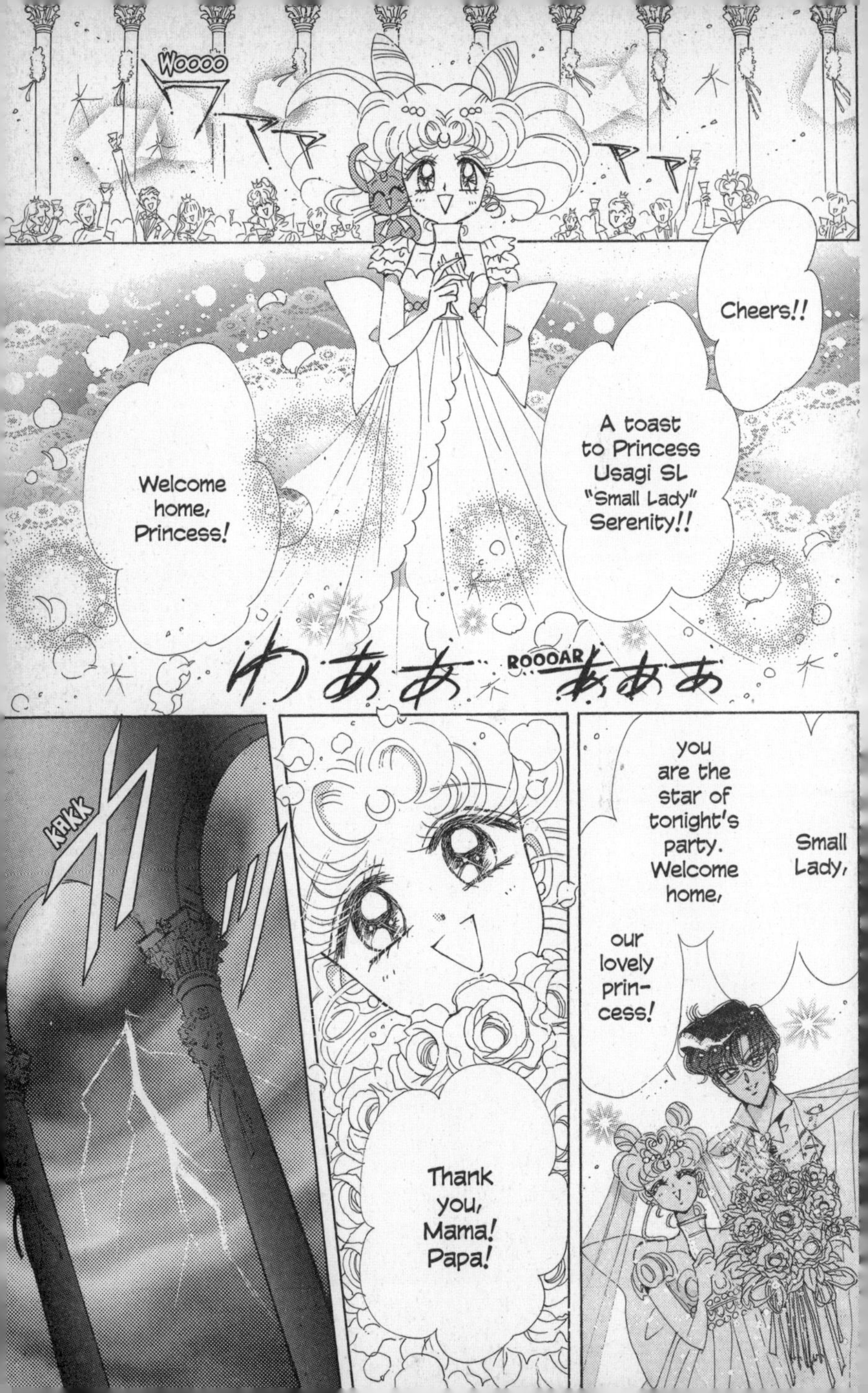
WOOOO
Cheers!!
A toast to Princess Usagi SL "Small Lady" Serenity!!
Welcome home, Princess!
ROOOAR
Small Lady,
you are the star of tonight's party. Welcome home,
our lovely princess!
Thank you, Mama! Papa!
KRKK

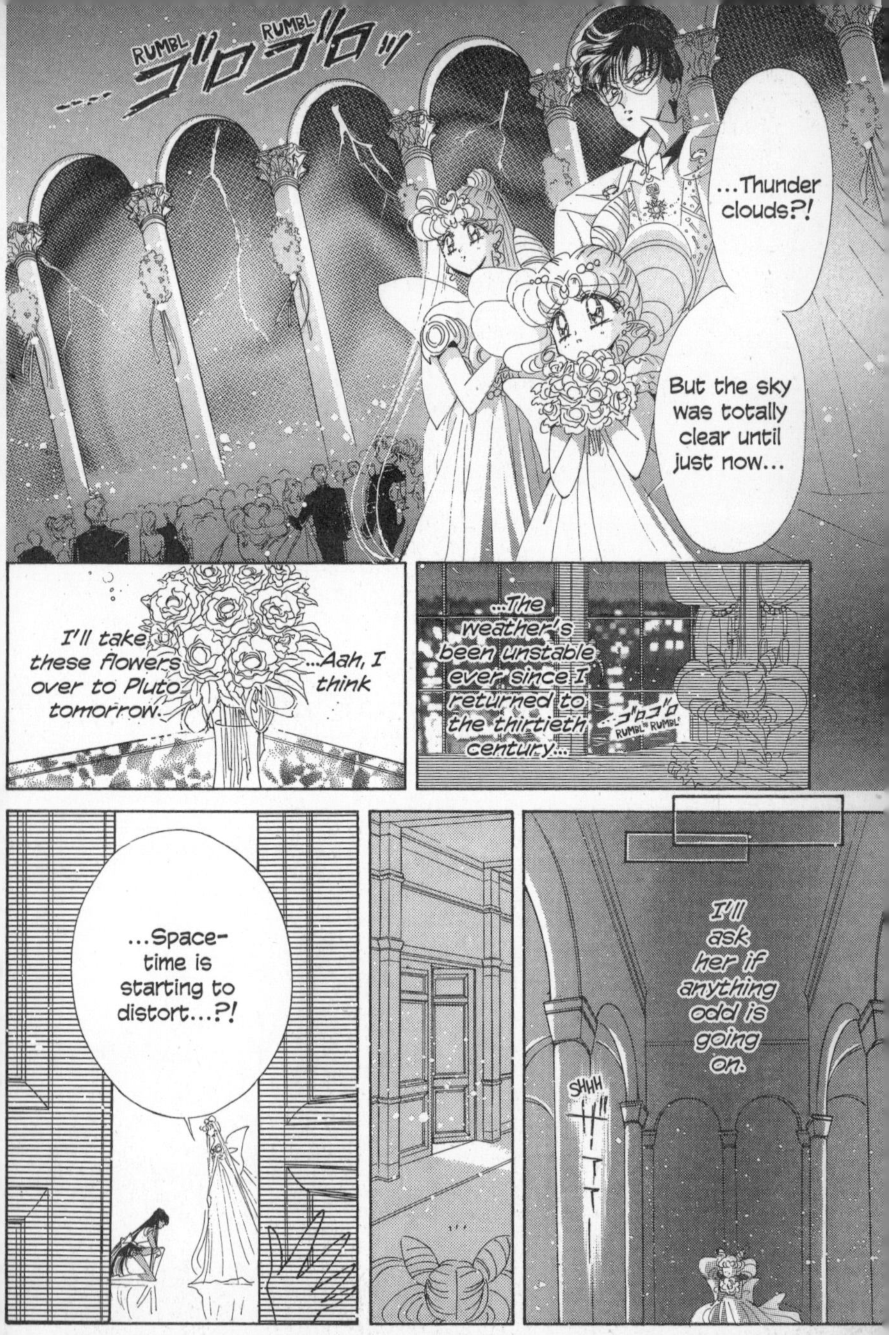
...Thunder clouds?!
But the sky was totally clear until just now...
RUMBL RUMBL
...ゴロゴロッ
...The weather's been unstable ever since I returned to the thirtieth century...
RUMBL RUMBL
...ゴロゴロ
...Aah, I think
I'll take these flowers over to Pluto tomorrow.
I'll ask her if anything odd is going on.
SHHH
...Space-time is starting to distort...?!

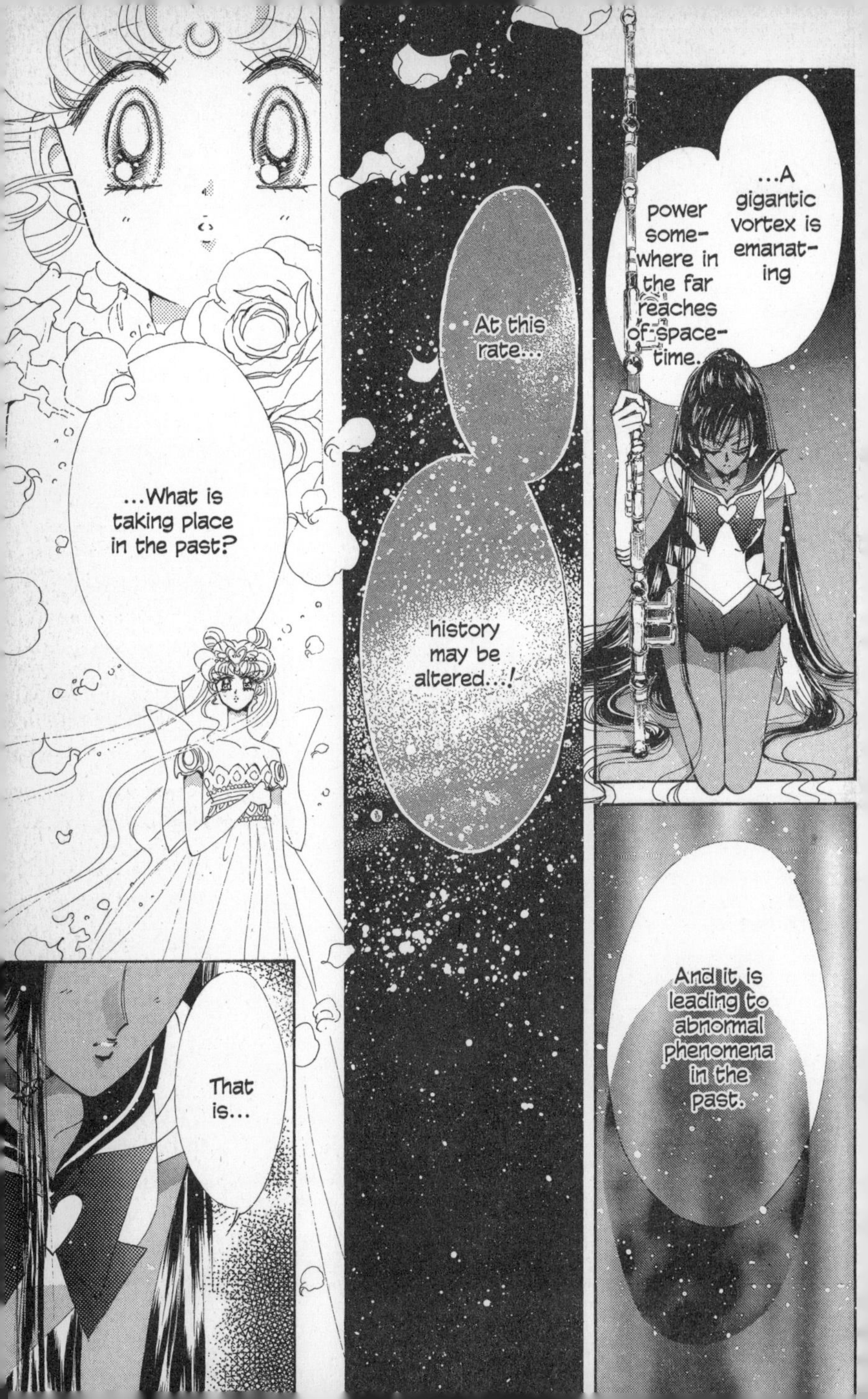

...A gigantic vortex is emanating power somewhere in the far reaches of space-time.
And it is leading to abnormal phenomena in the past.
At this rate...
history may be altered...!
...What is taking place in the past?
That is...

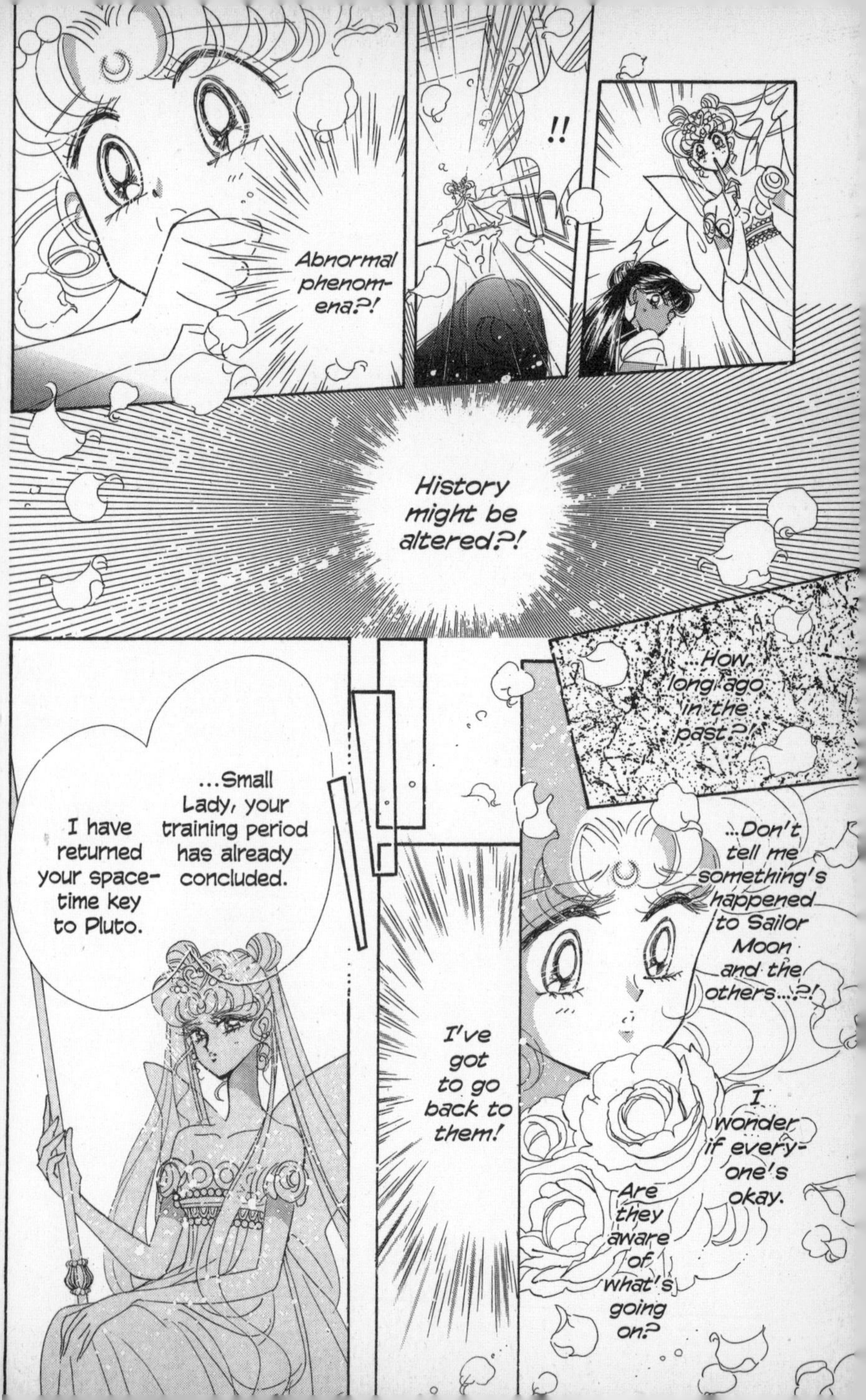
!!
Abnormal phenom-ena?!
History might be altered?!
How long ago in the past?!
...Don't tell me something's happened to Sailor Moon and the others...?!
I wonder if every-one's okay.
Are they aware of what's going on?
I've got to go back to them!
...Small Lady, your training period has already concluded.
I have returned your space-time key to Pluto.

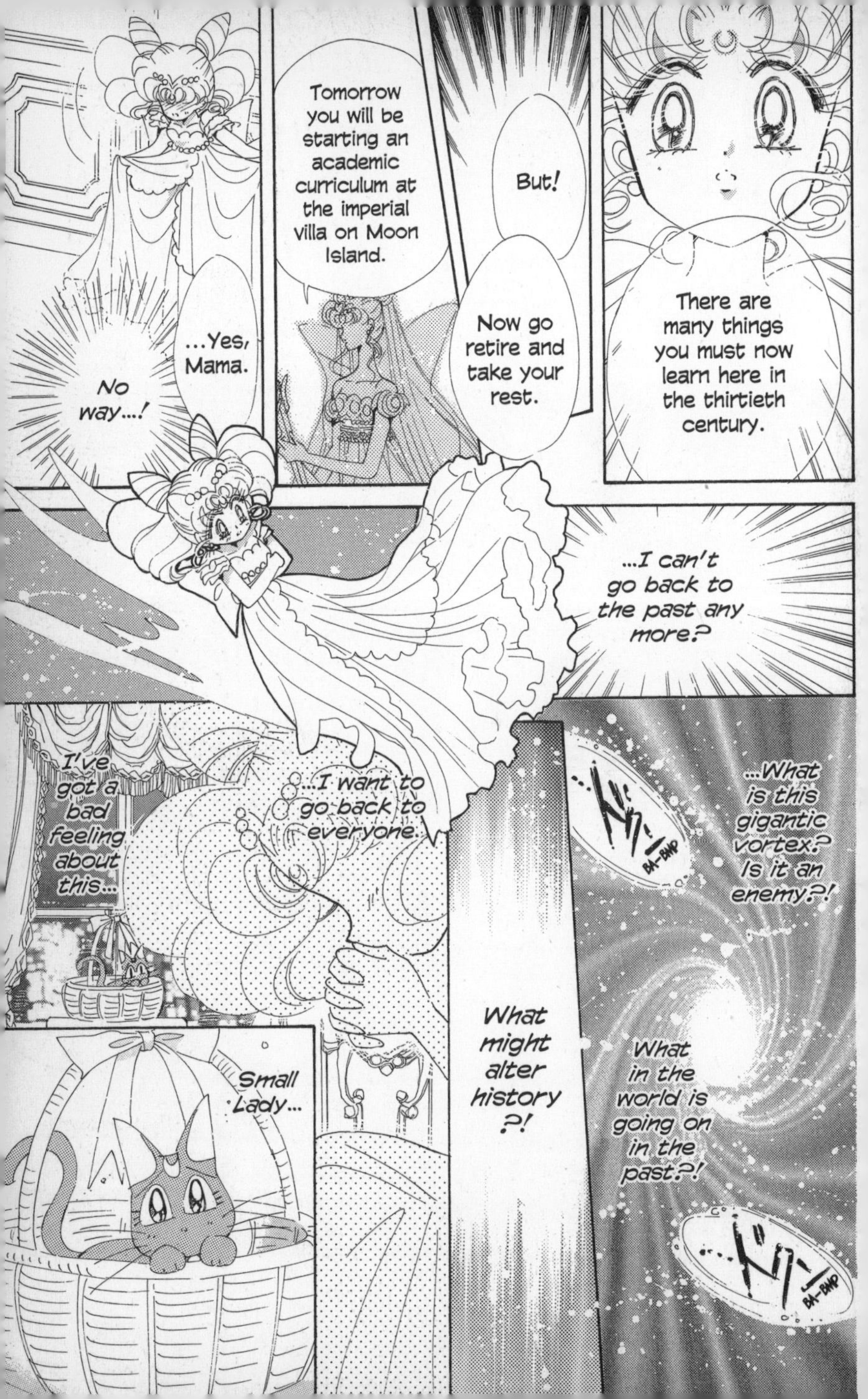
There are many things you must now learn here in the thirtieth century.
But!
Tomorrow you will be starting an academic curriculum at the imperial villa on Moon Island.
Now go retire and take your rest.
...Yes, Mama.
No way...!
...I can't go back to the past any more?
...I want to go back to everyone.
...What is this gigantic vortex? Is it an enemy?!
BA-BMP
What in the world is going on in the past?!
BA-BMP
What might alter history?!
I've got a bad feeling about this...
Small Lady...

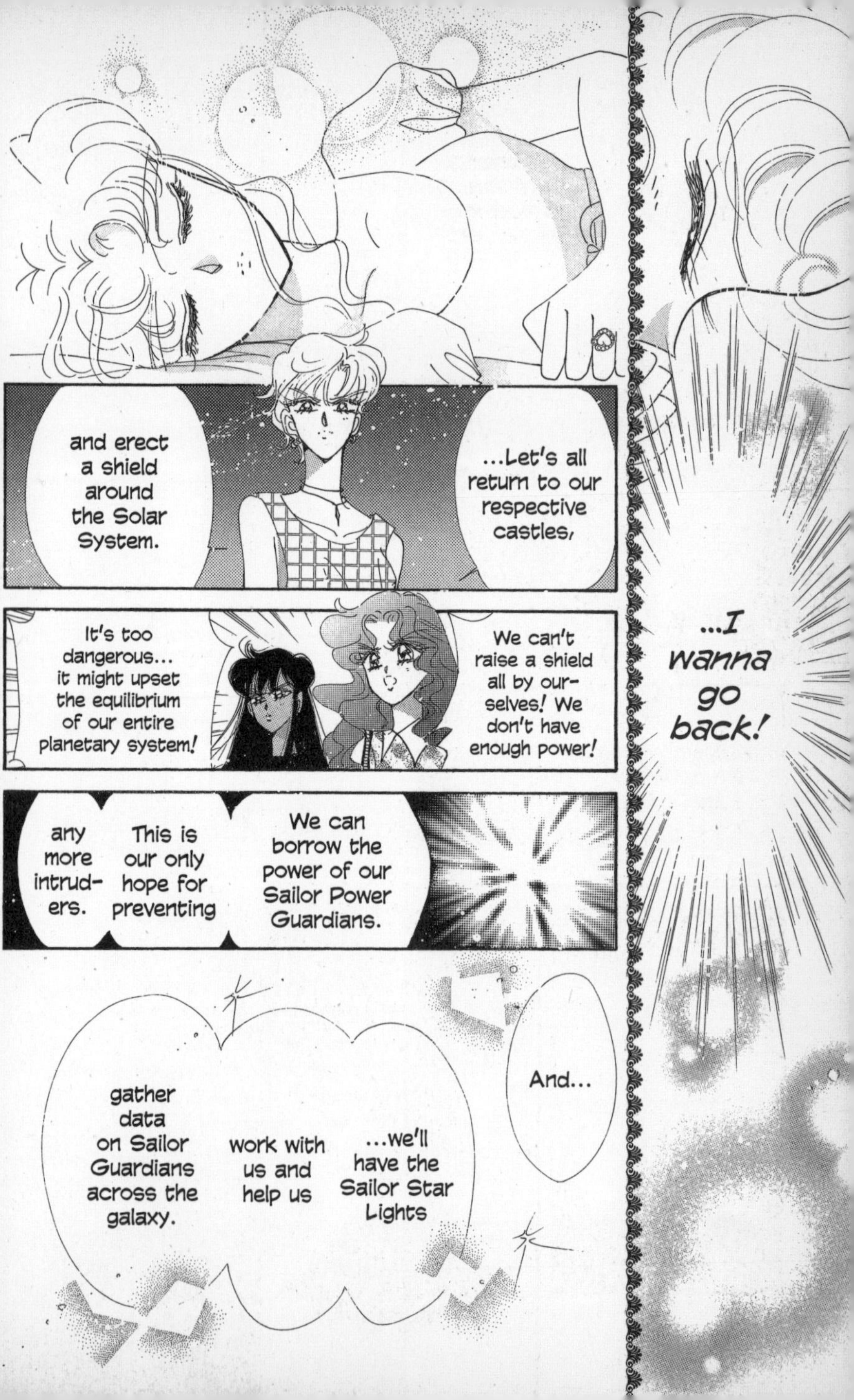
...I wanna go back!
...Let's all return to our respective castles,
and erect a shield around the Solar System.
We can't raise a shield all by our-selves! We don't have enough power!
It's too dangerous... it might upset the equilibrium of our entire planetary system!
We can borrow the power of our Sailor Power Guardians.
This is our only hope for preventing
any more intrud-ers.
And...
...we'll have the Sailor Star Lights
work with us and help us
gather data on Sailor Guardians across the galaxy.

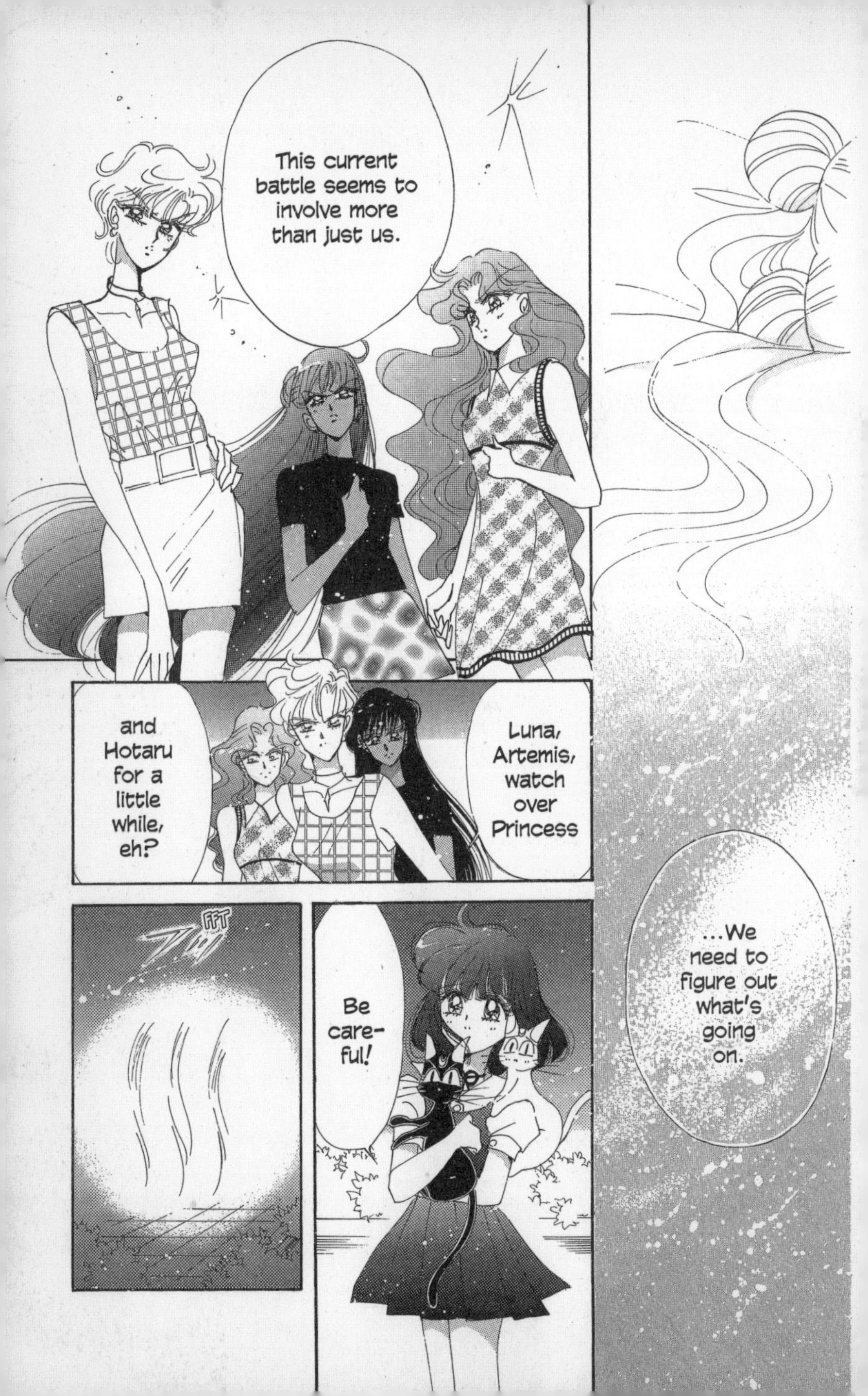
This current battle seems to involve more than just us.
...We need to figure out what's going on.
Luna, Artemis, watch over Princess
and Hotaru for a little while, eh?
Be careful!
FFT

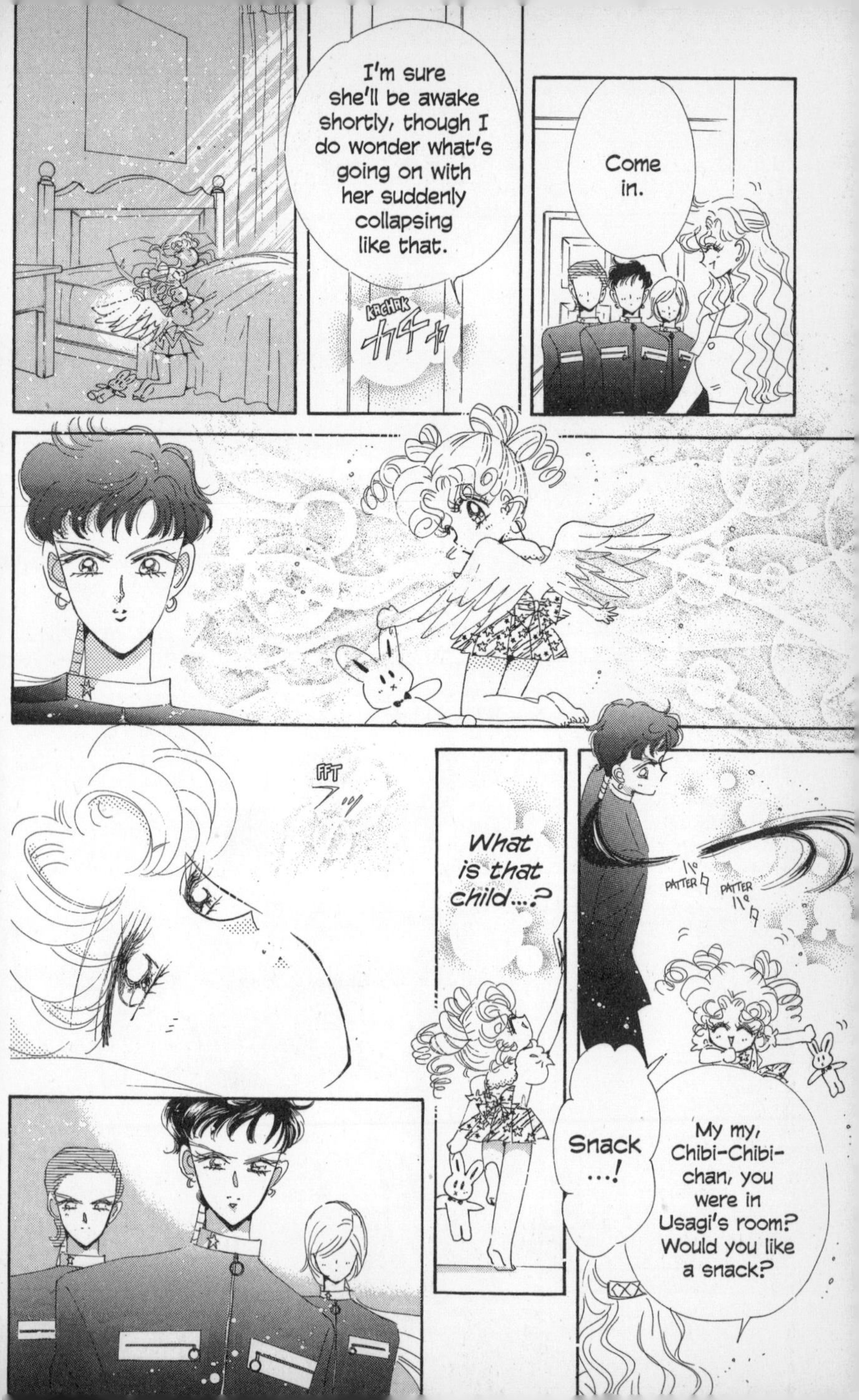
Come in.
I'm sure she'll be awake shortly, though I do wonder what's going on with her suddenly collapsing like that.
KACHAK
カチャ
PATTER パタ PATTER パタ
My my, Chibi-Chibi-chan, you were in Usagi's room? Would you like a snack?
Snack ...!
What is that child...?
FFT
フッ

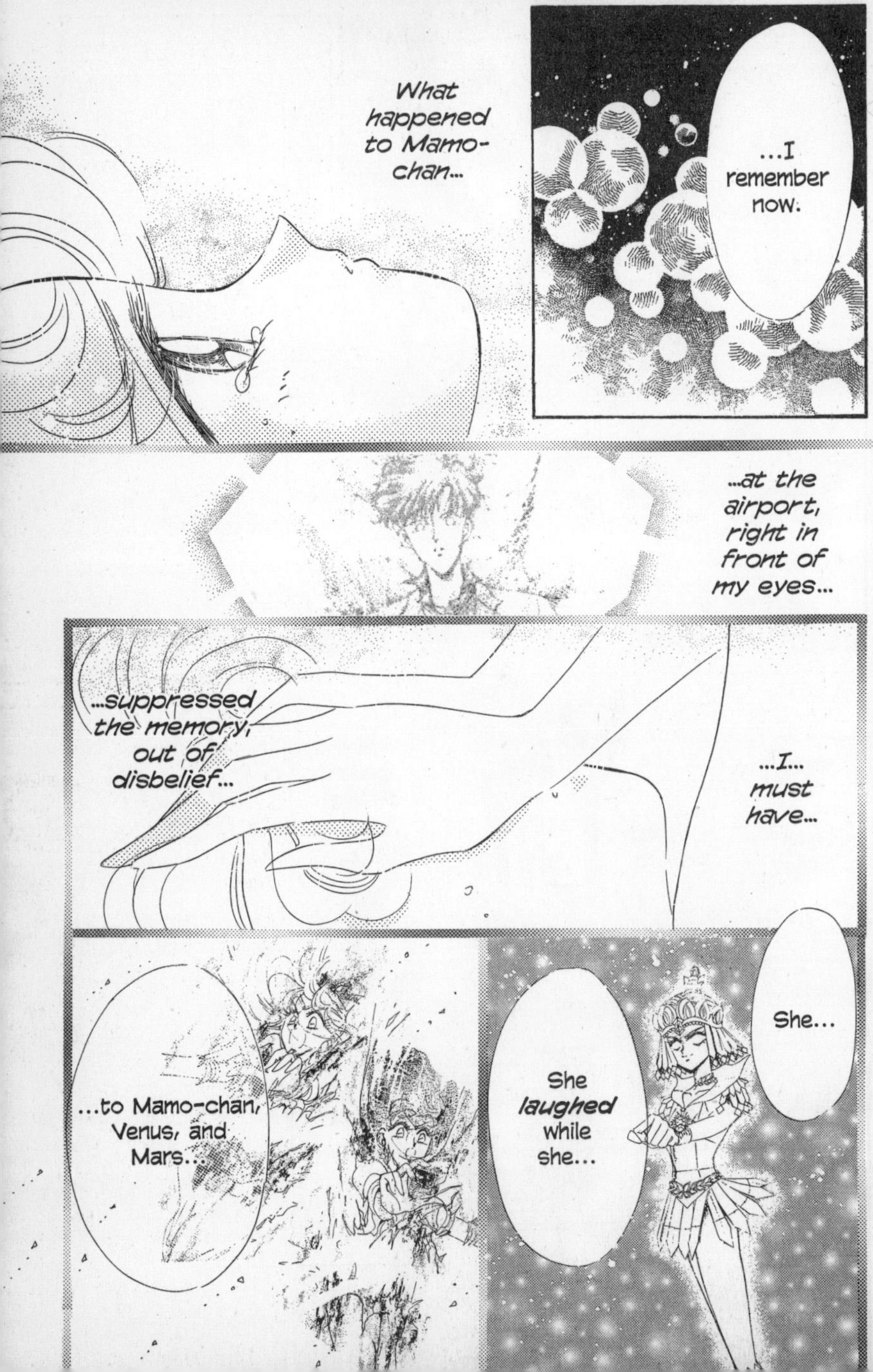
...I remember now.
What happened to Mamo-chan...
...at the airport, right in front of my eyes...
...I... must have...
...suppressed the memory, out of disbelief...
She...
She *laughed* while she...
...to Mamo-chan, Venus, and Mars...

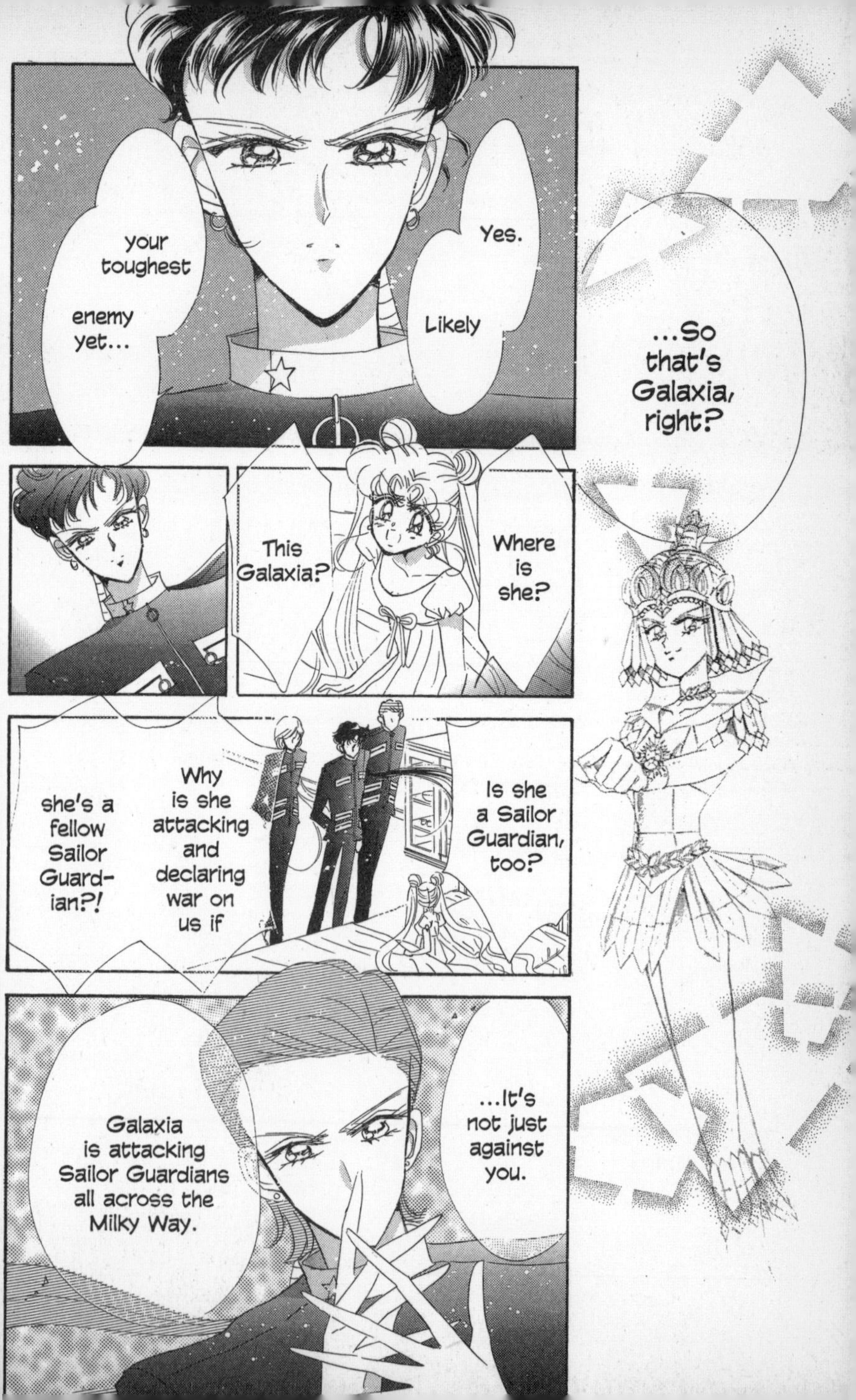
...So that's Galaxia, right?
Yes.
Likely
your toughest enemy yet...
Where is she?
This Galaxia?
Is she a Sailor Guardian, too?
Why is she attacking and declaring war on us if
she's a fellow Sailor Guardian?!
...It's not just against you.
Galaxia is attacking Sailor Guardians all across the Milky Way.

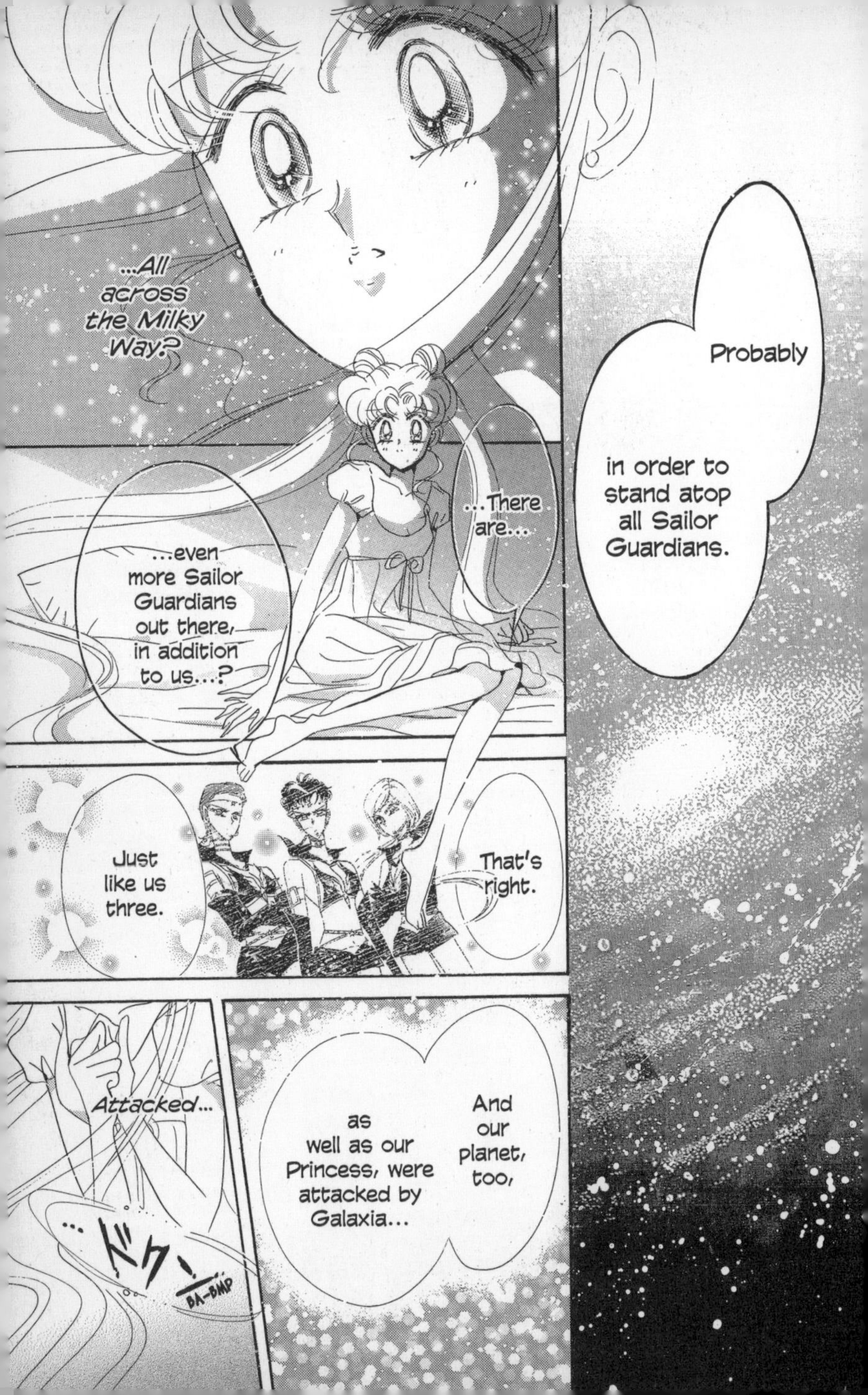
Probably
in order to stand atop all Sailor Guardians.
...All across the Milky Way?
...There are...
...even more Sailor Guardians out there, in addition to us...?
That's right.
Just like us three.
And our planet, too,
as well as our Princess, were attacked by Galaxia...
Attacked...
...
ドク
BA-BMP

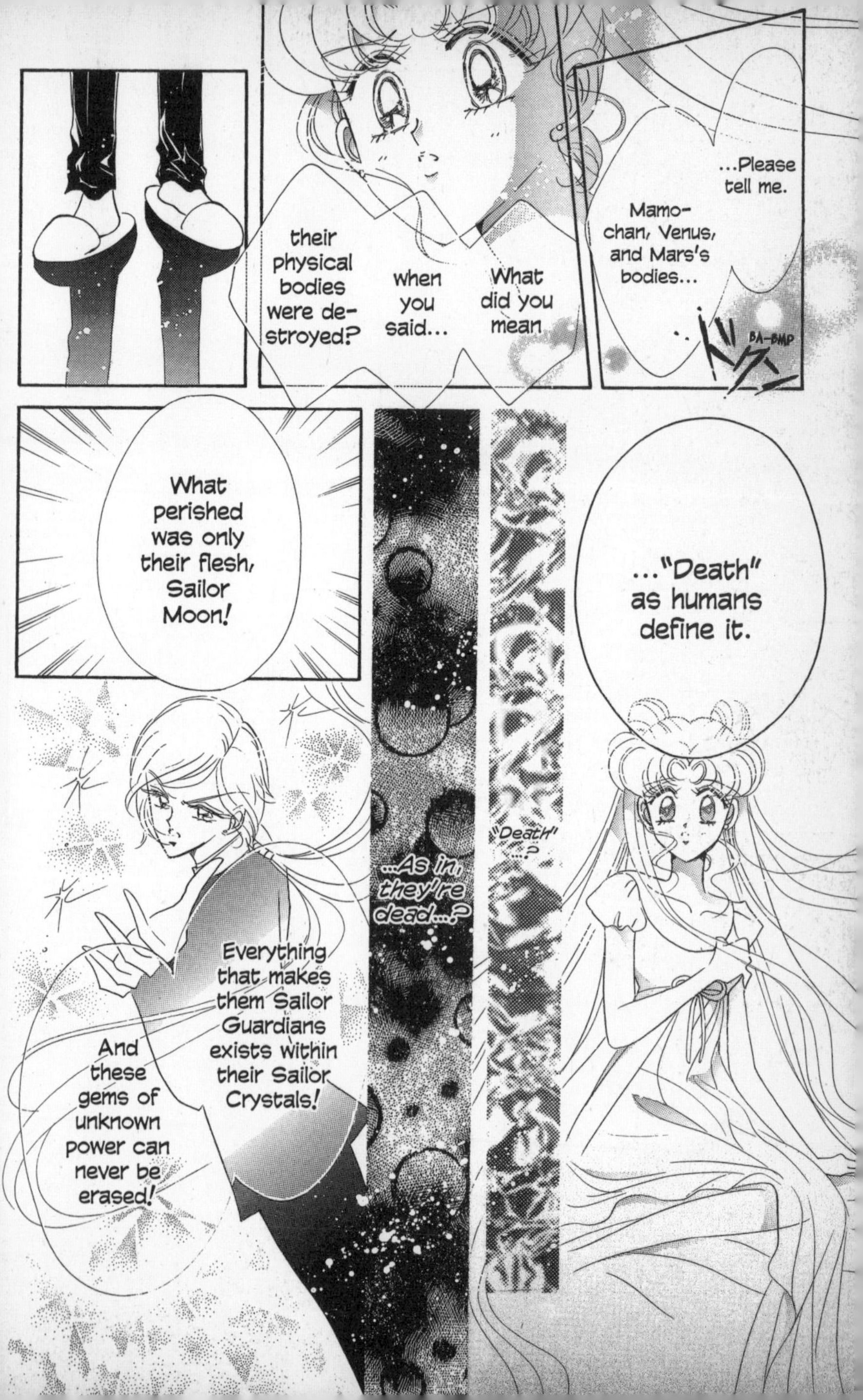
...Please tell me.
Mamo-chan, Venus, and Mars's bodies...
BA-BMP
What did you mean
when you said...
their physical bodies were de-stroyed?
..."Death" as humans define it.
"Death" ...?
...As in, they're dead...?
What perished was only their flesh, Sailor Moon!
Everything that makes them Sailor Guardians exists within their Sailor Crystals!
And these gems of unknown power can never be erased!

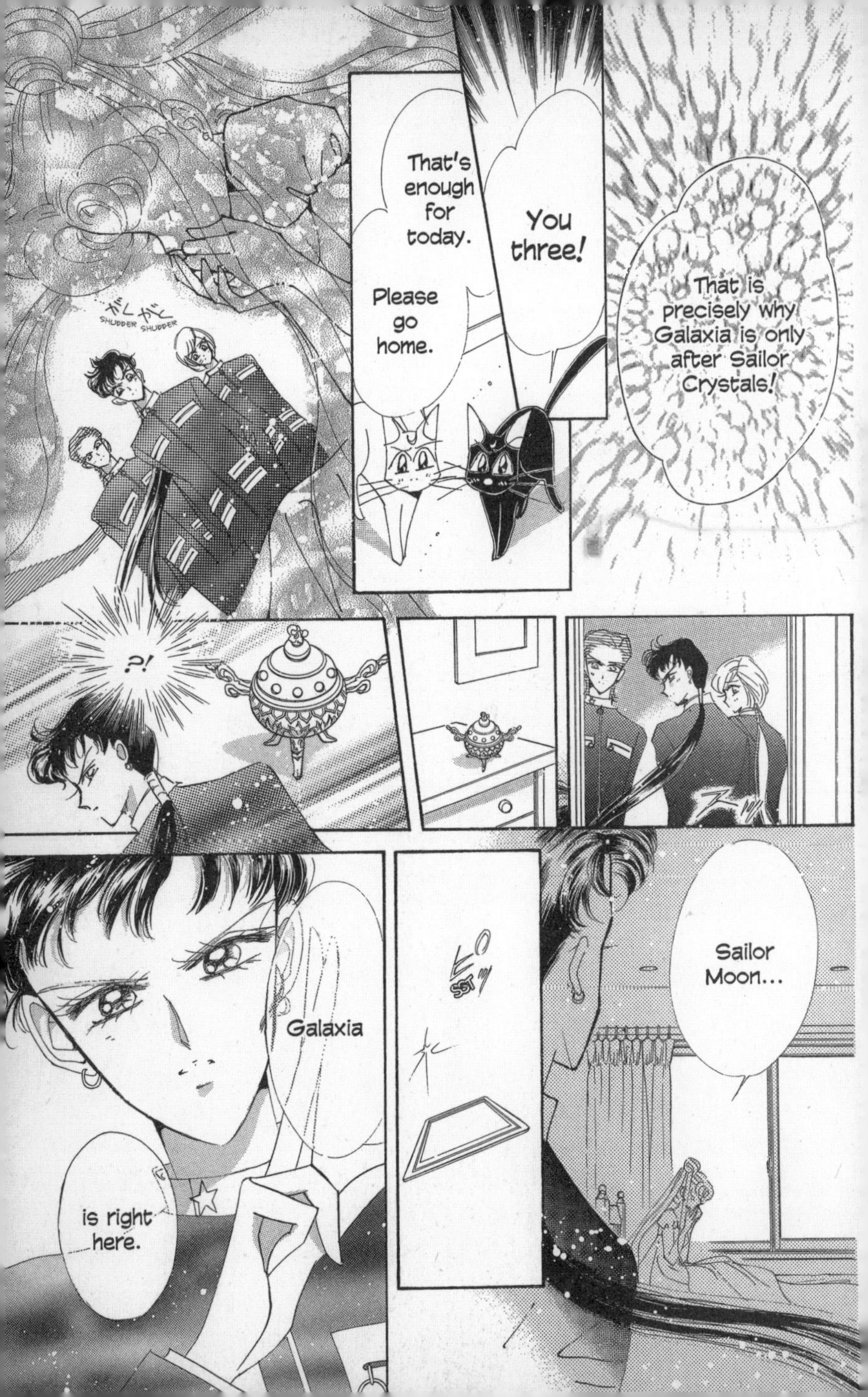
That is precisely why Galaxia is only after Sailor Crystals!
You three!
That's enough for today.
Please go home.
SHUDDER SHUDDER
?!
Sailor Moon...
SST
Galaxia
is right here.

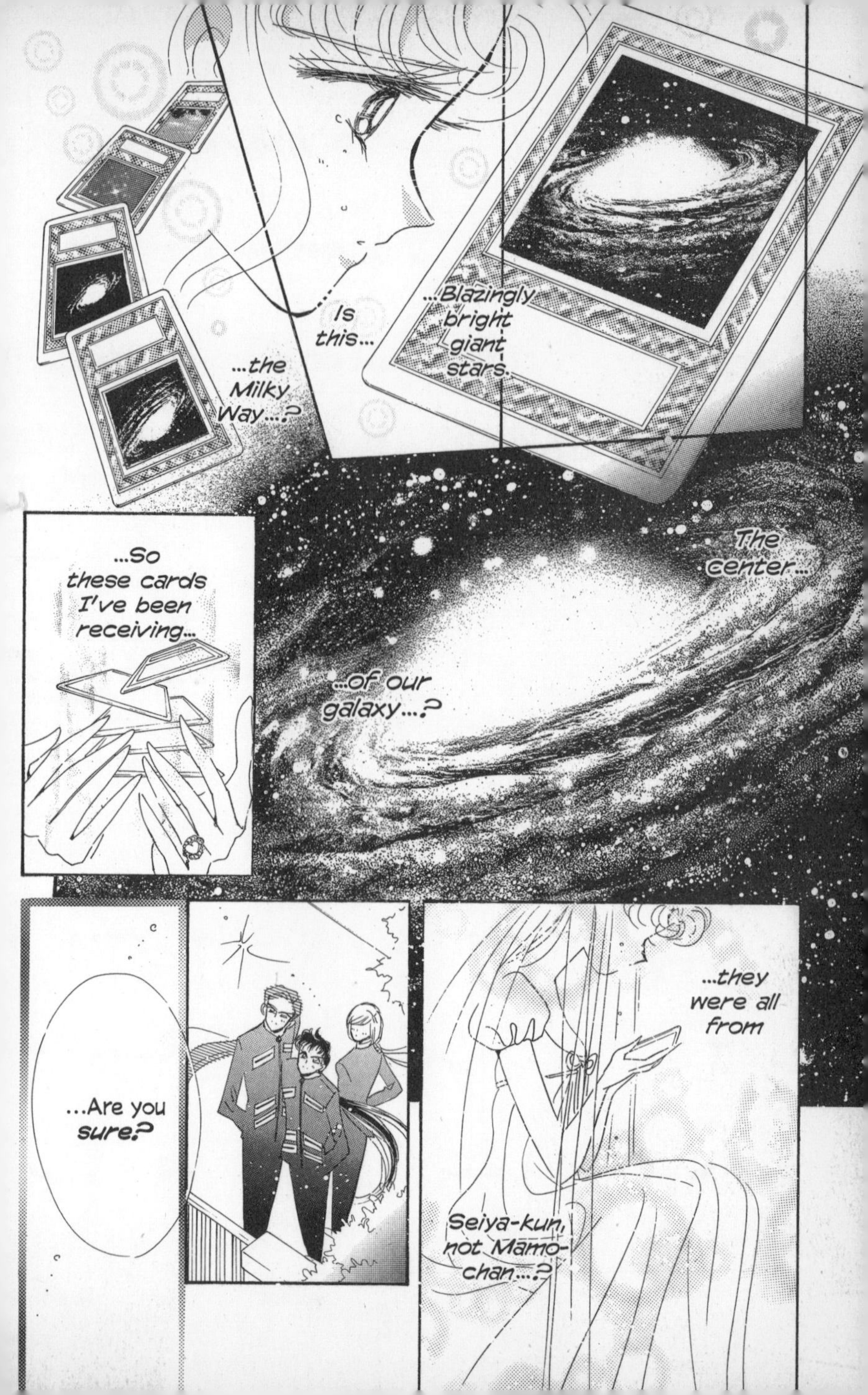
...Blazingly bright giant stars.
Is this...
...the Milky Way...?
The center...
...of our galaxy...?
...So these cards I've been receiving...
...they were all from
Seiya-kun, not Mamo-chan...?
...Are you sure?

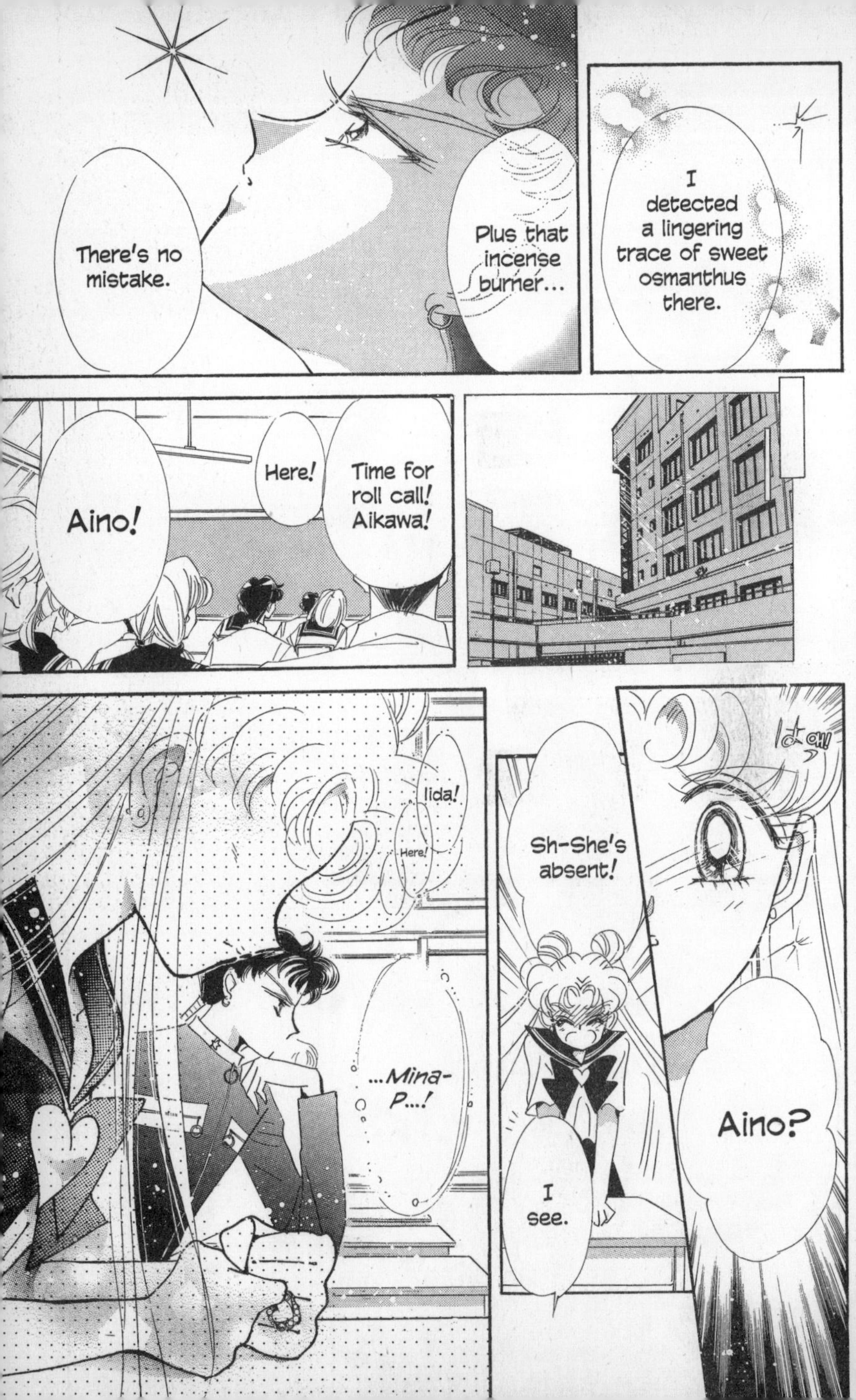
I detected a lingering trace of sweet osmanthus there.
Plus that incense burner...
There's no mistake.
Time for roll call! Aikawa!
Here!
Aino!
はっ OH!
Aino?
Sh-She's absent!
I see.
Iida!
Here!
...Mina-P...!

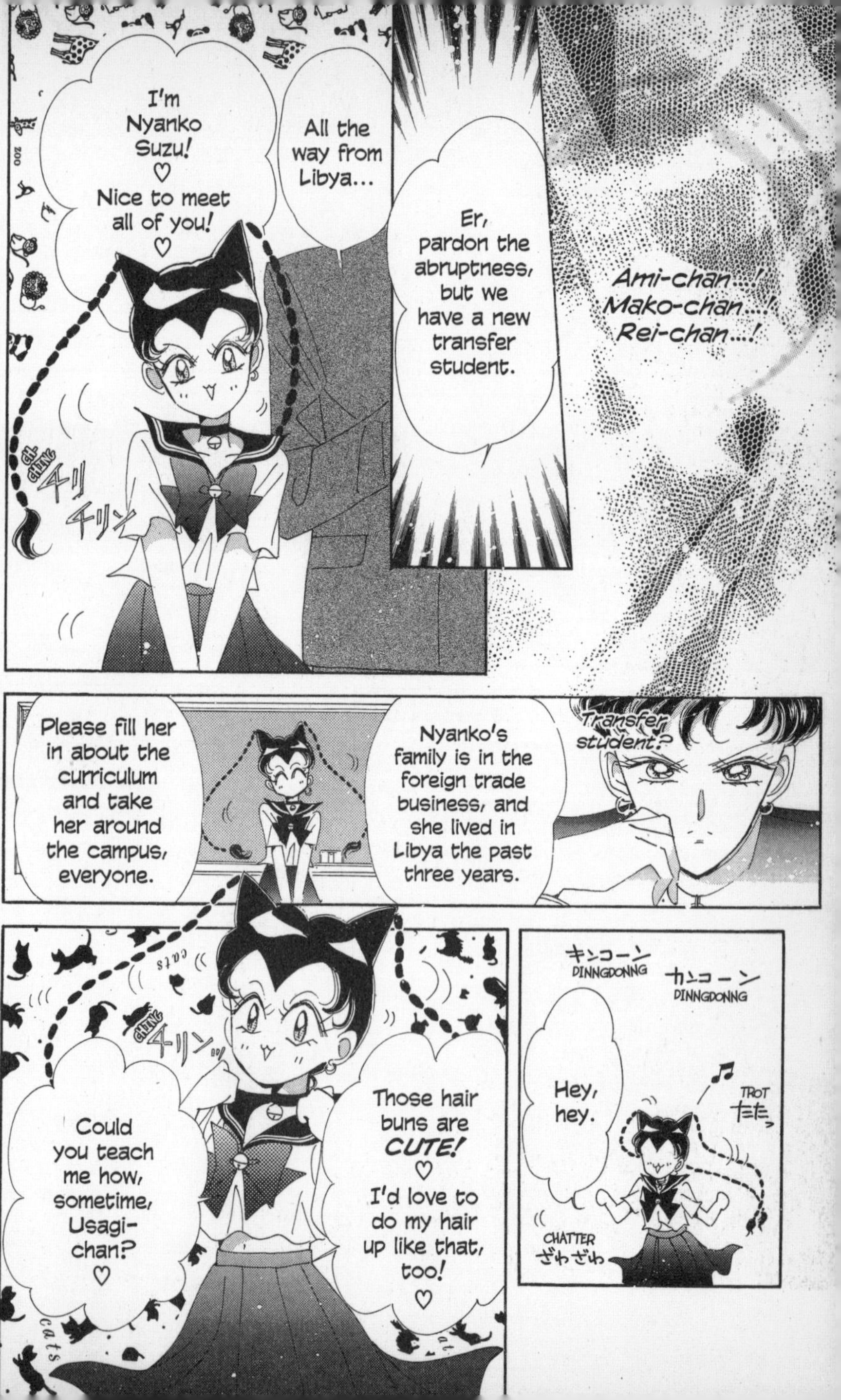
Ami-chan...! Mako-chan...! Rei-chan...!
Er, pardon the abruptness, but we have a new transfer student.
All the way from Libya...
I'm Nyanko Suzu! ♡ Nice to meet all of you! ♡
CH-CHING チリ チリン
Transfer student?
Nyanko's family is in the foreign trade business, and she lived in Libya the past three years.
Please fill her in about the curriculum and take her around the campus, everyone.
キンコーン DINNGDONNG
カンコーン DINNGDONNG
Hey, hey.
TROT たたっ
CHATTER ざわざわ
Those hair buns are CUTE! ♡ I'd love to do my hair up like that, too! ♡
Could you teach me how, sometime, Usagi-chan? ♡
CHING チリンッ

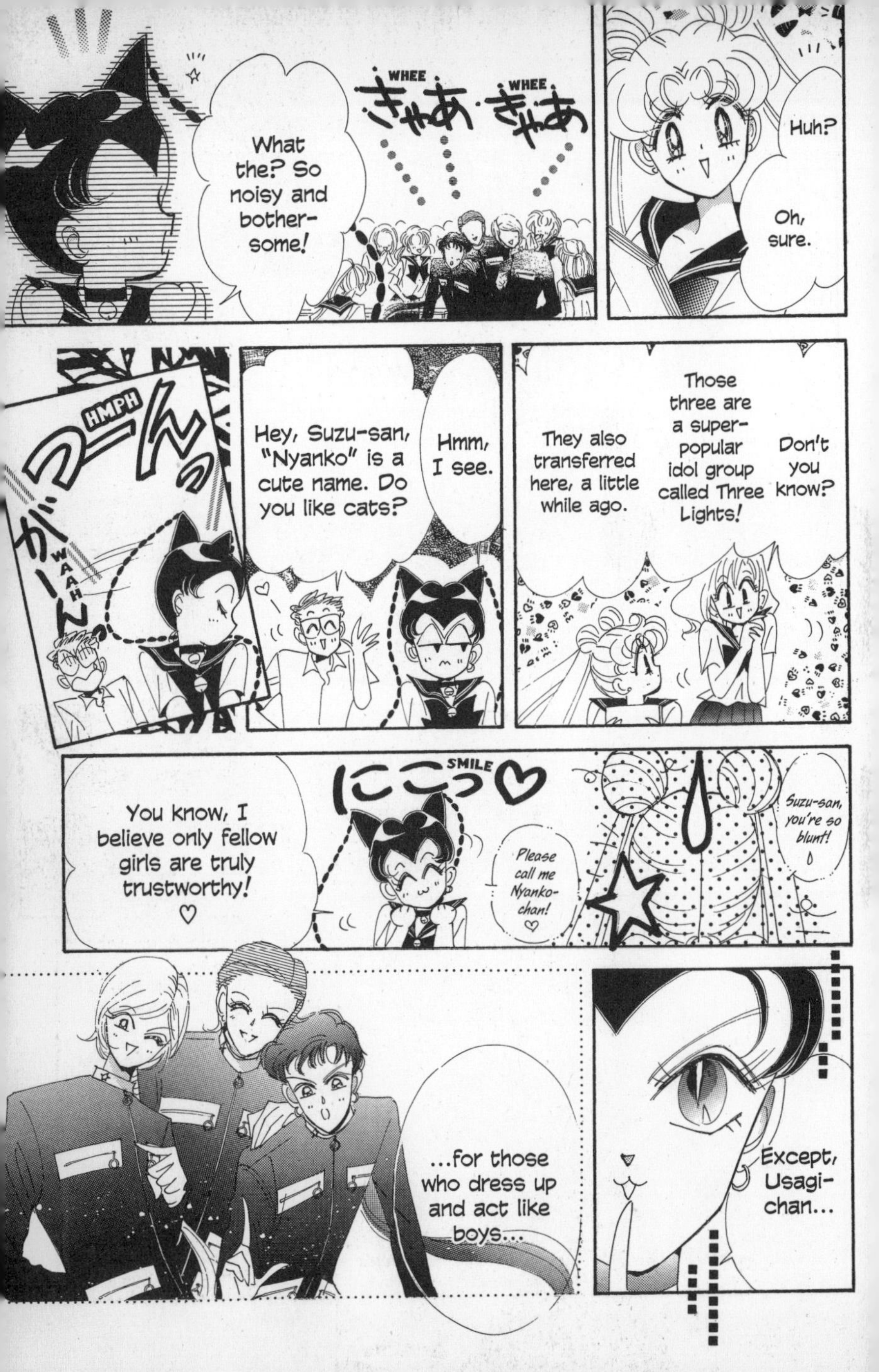
Huh?
Oh, sure.
WHEE きゃあ WHEE きゃあ
What the? So noisy and bothersome!
Don't you know?
Those three are a super-popular idol group called Three Lights!
They also transferred here, a little while ago.
Hmm, I see.
Hey, Suzu-san, "Nyanko" is a cute name. Do you like cats?
HMPH つーんっ
がーん WAAH
Suzu-san, you're so blunt!
Please call me Nyanko-chan! ♡
SMILE にこっ♡
You know, I believe only fellow girls are truly trustworthy! ♡
Except, Usagi-chan...
...for those who dress up and act like boys...

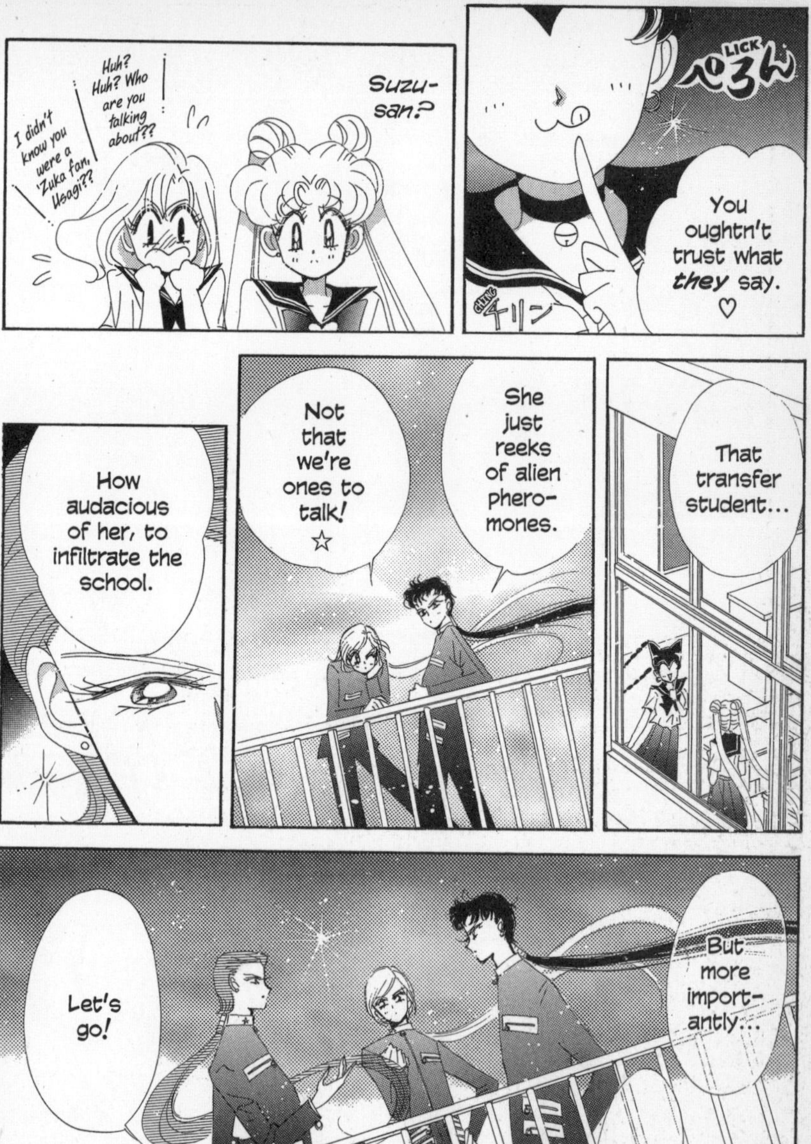
LICK
You oughtn't trust what *they* say. ♡
CHING
Suzu-san?
Huh? Huh? Who are you talking about??
I didn't know you were a 'Zuka fan, Usagi??
That transfer student...
She just reeks of alien phero-mones.
Not that we're ones to talk! ☆
How audacious of her, to infiltrate the school.
But more import-antly...
Yup!
Let's go!

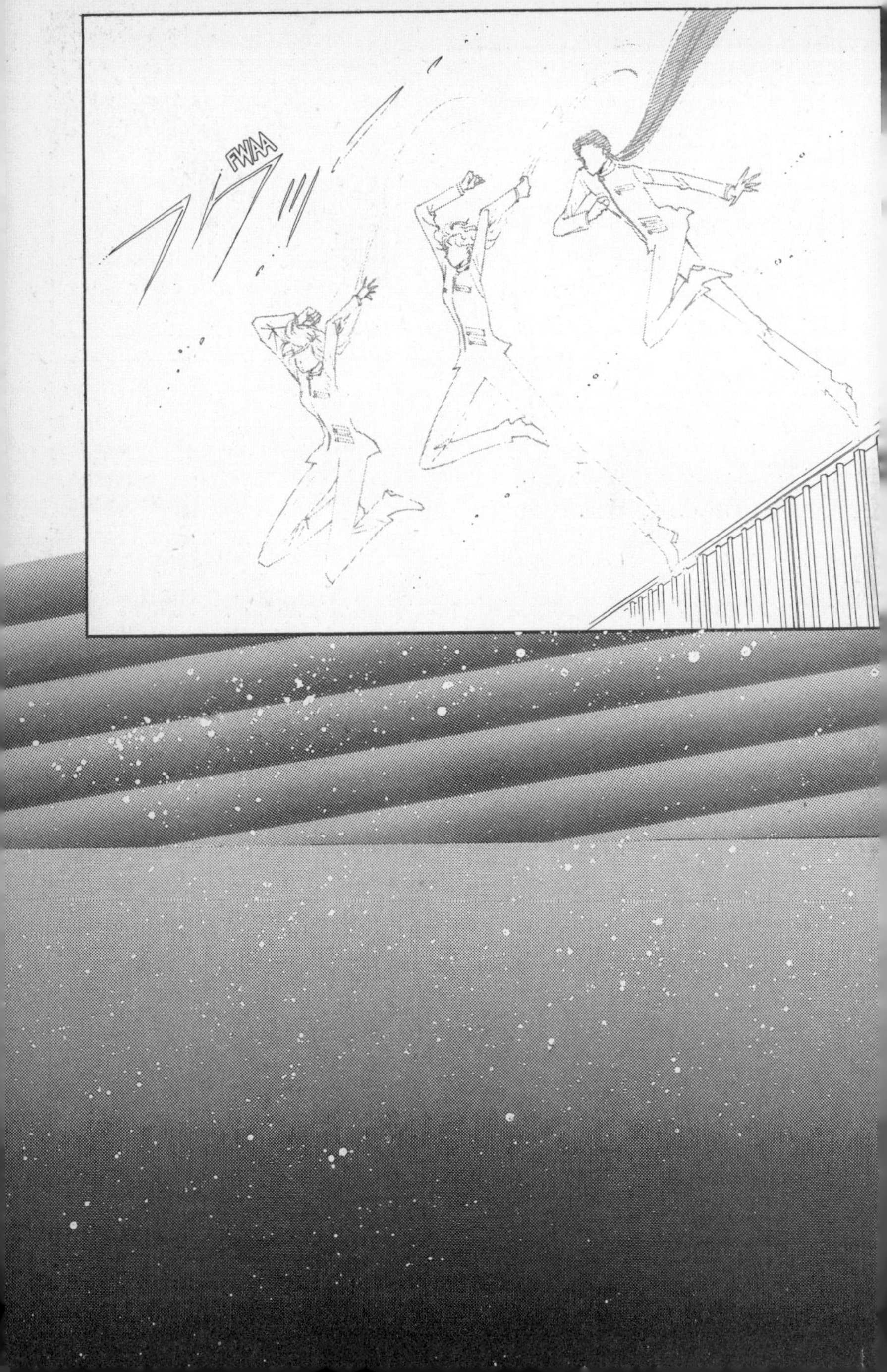
FWAA

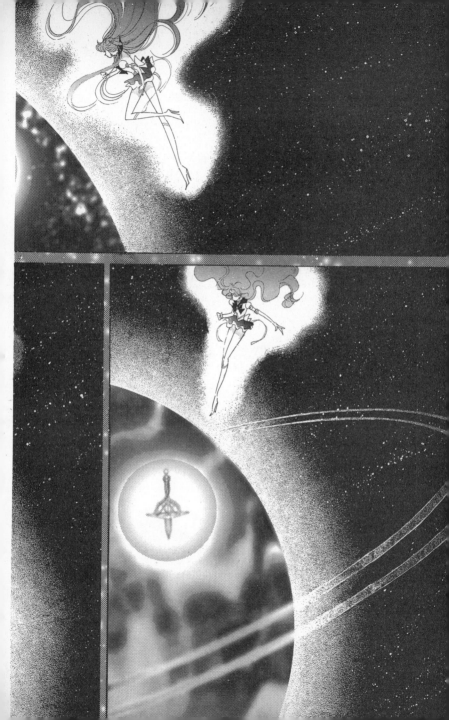

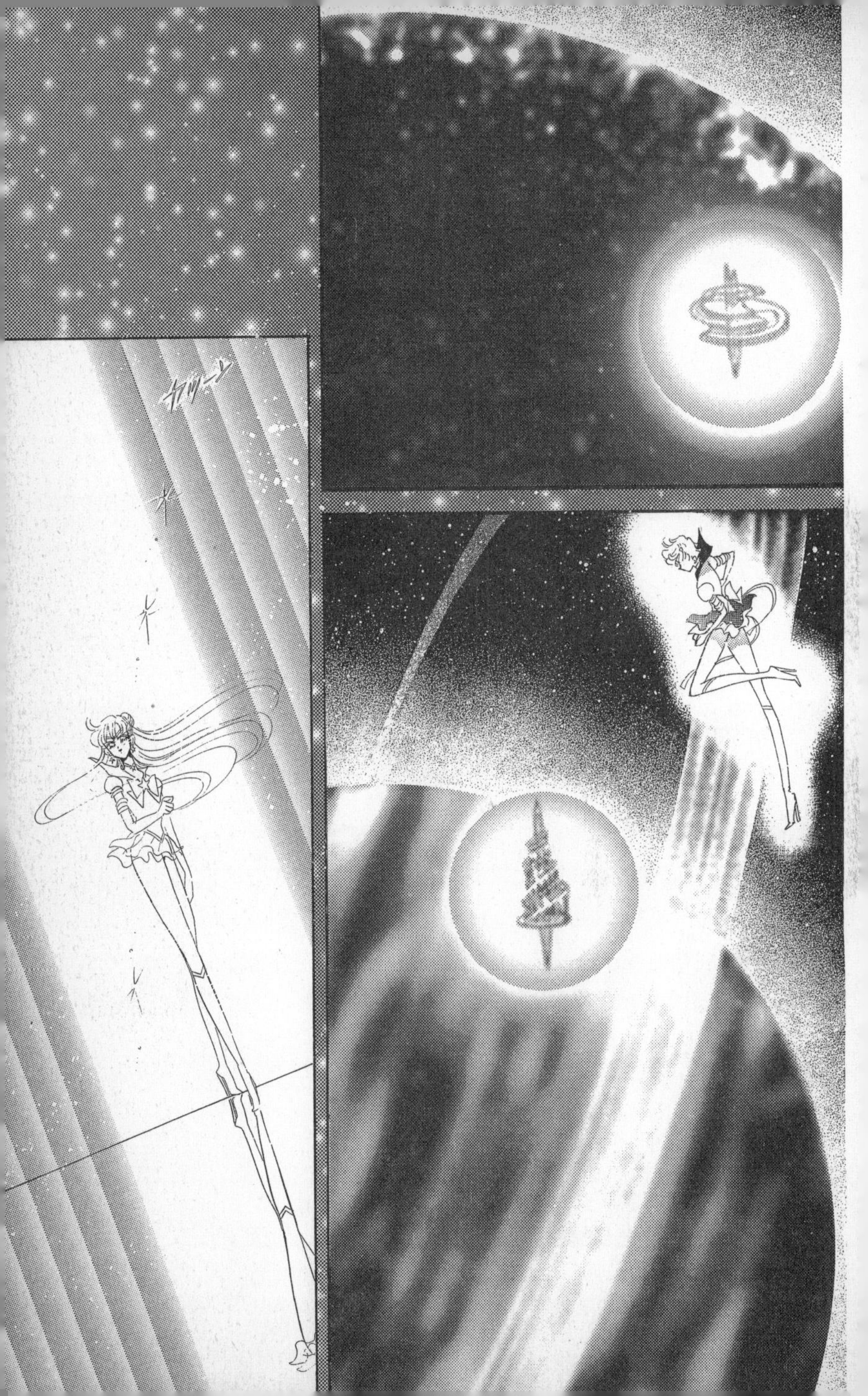
カツーン

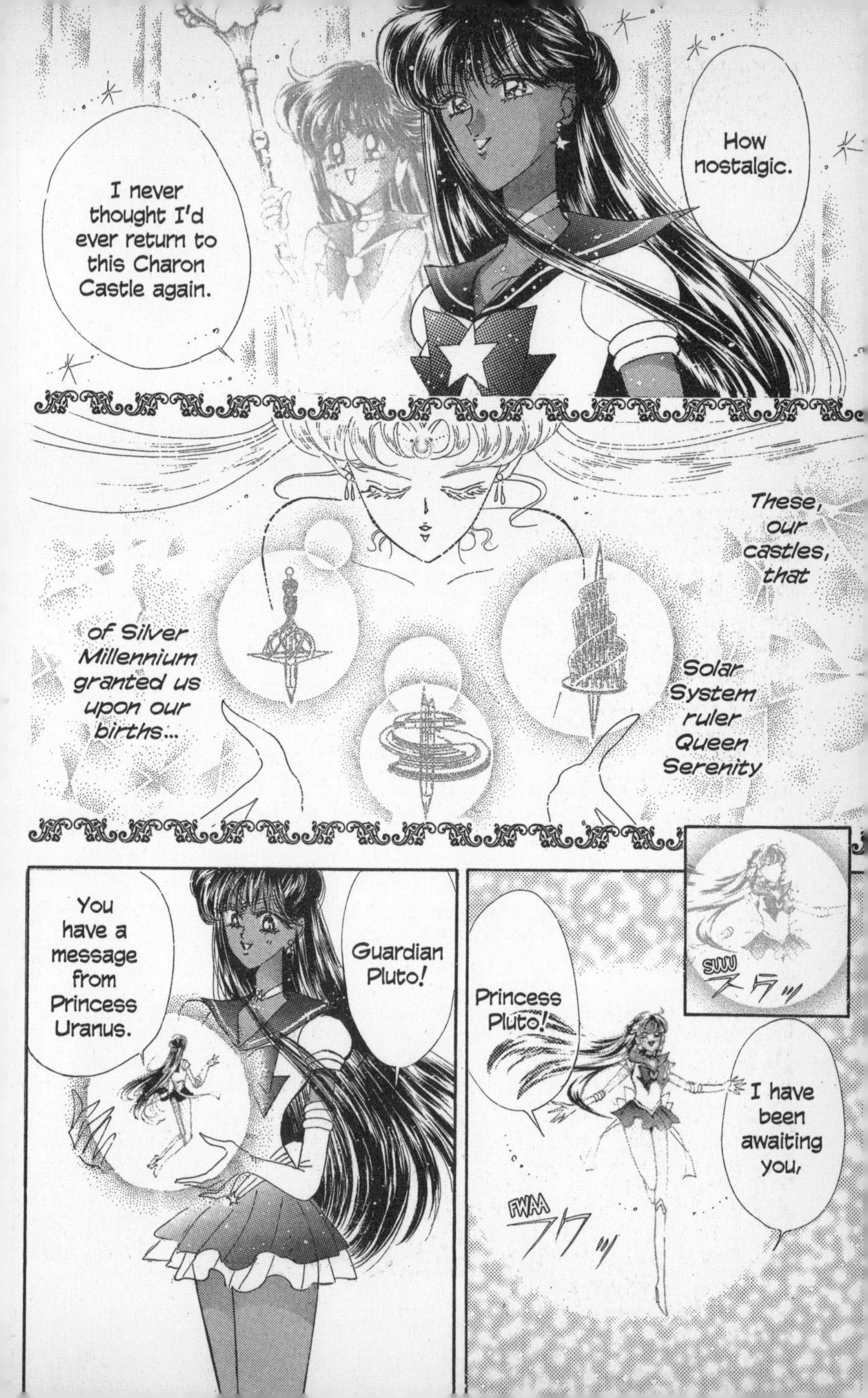
How nostalgic.
I never thought I'd ever return to this Charon Castle again.
These, our castles, that
Solar System ruler Queen Serenity
of Silver Millennium granted us upon our births...
SUU
Princess Pluto!
I have been awaiting you,
FWAA
Guardian Pluto!
You have a message from Princess Uranus.

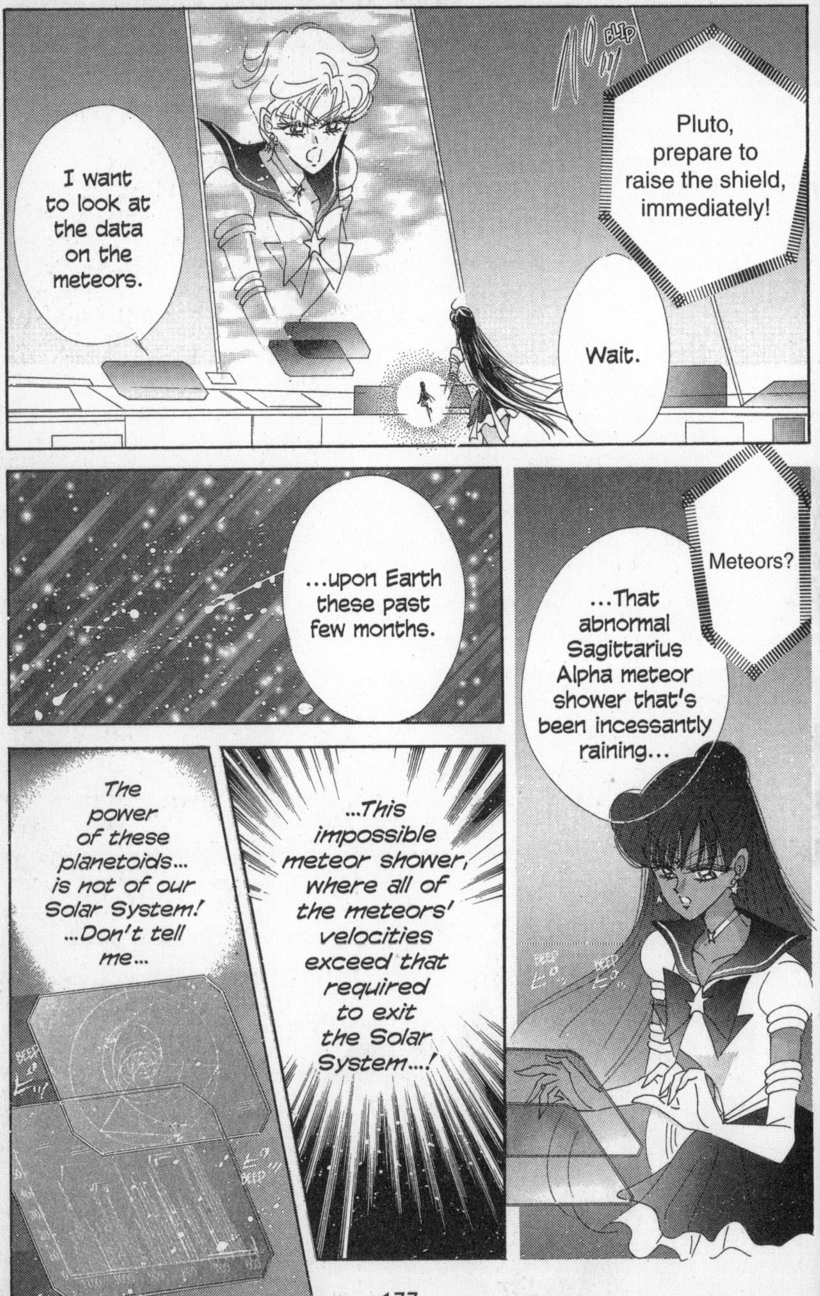
BLIP
Pluto, prepare to raise the shield, immediately!
Wait.
I want to look at the data on the meteors.
Meteors?
...That abnormal Sagittarius Alpha meteor shower that's been incessantly raining...
BEEP
BEEP
...upon Earth these past few months.
...This impossible meteor shower, where all of the meteors' velocities exceed that required to exit the Solar System...!
The power of these planetoids... is not of our Solar System! ...Don't tell me...
BEEP
BEEP

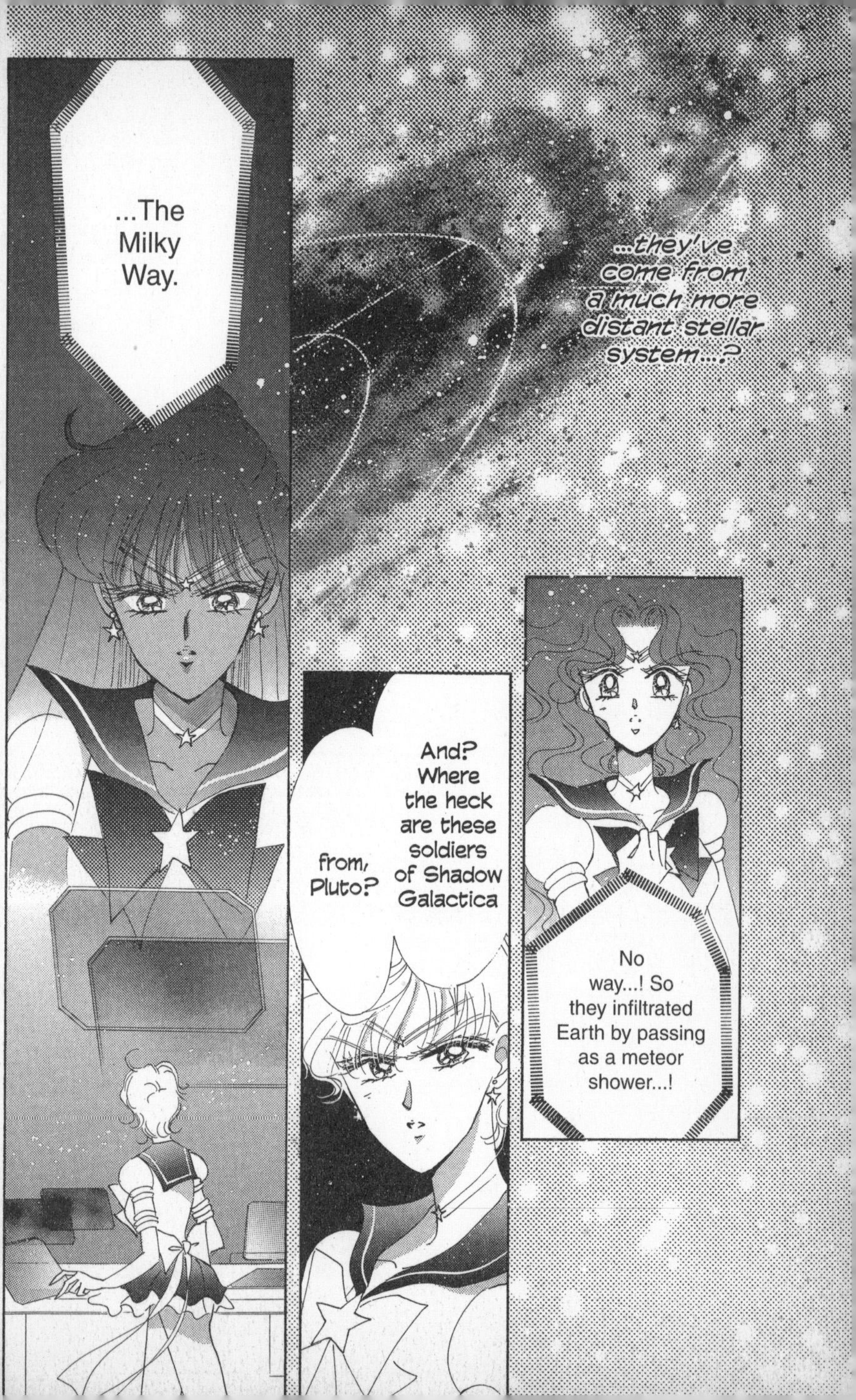
...they've come from a much more distant stellar system...?
No way...! So they infiltrated Earth by passing as a meteor shower...!
And? Where the heck are these soldiers of Shadow Galactica
from, Pluto?
...The Milky Way.

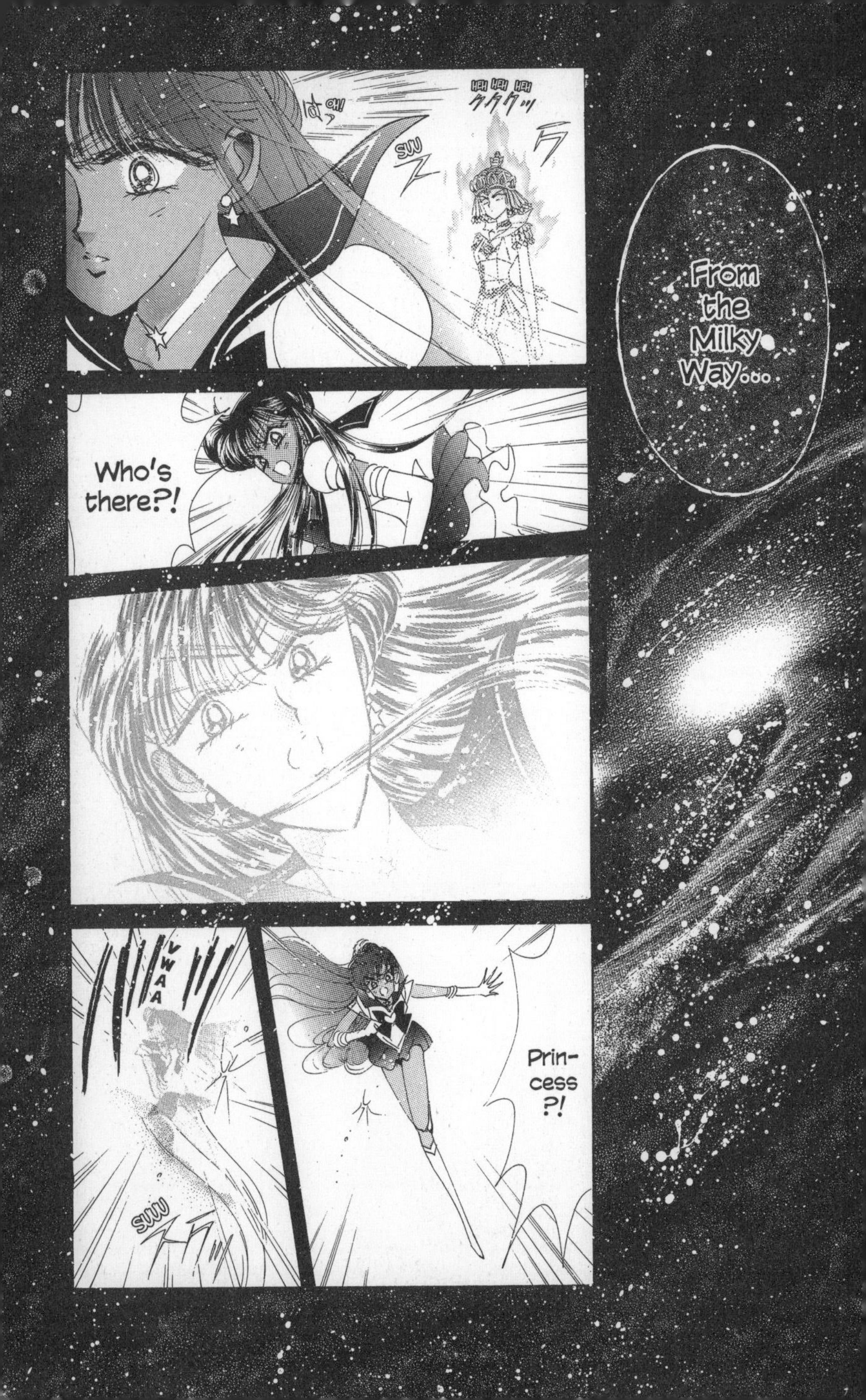
From the Milky Way...
HEH HEH HEH
OH!
SUU
Who's there?!
Prin-cess?!
VWAA
SUU

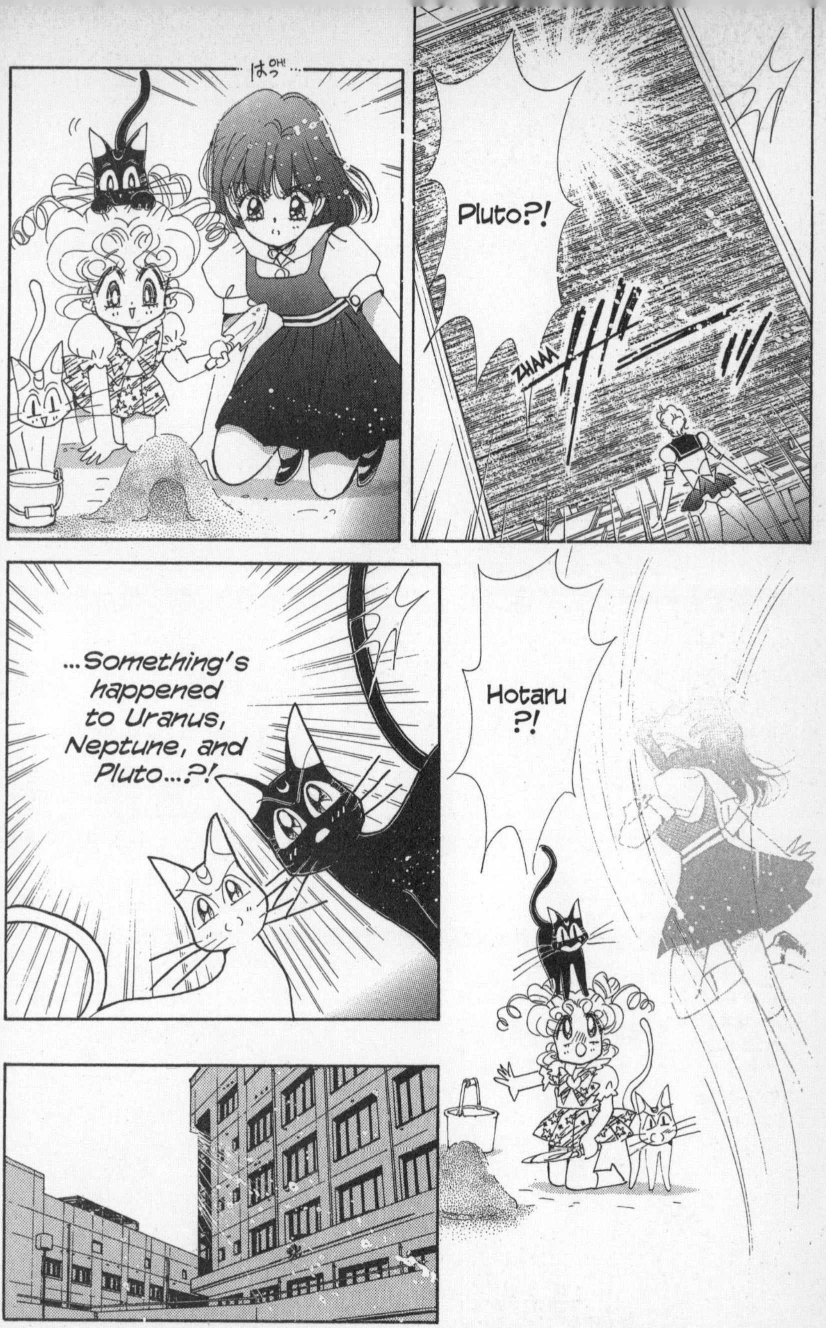
Pluto?!
ZHAAA
はっ OH!...
Hotaru ?!
...Something's happened to Uranus, Neptune, and Pluto...?!

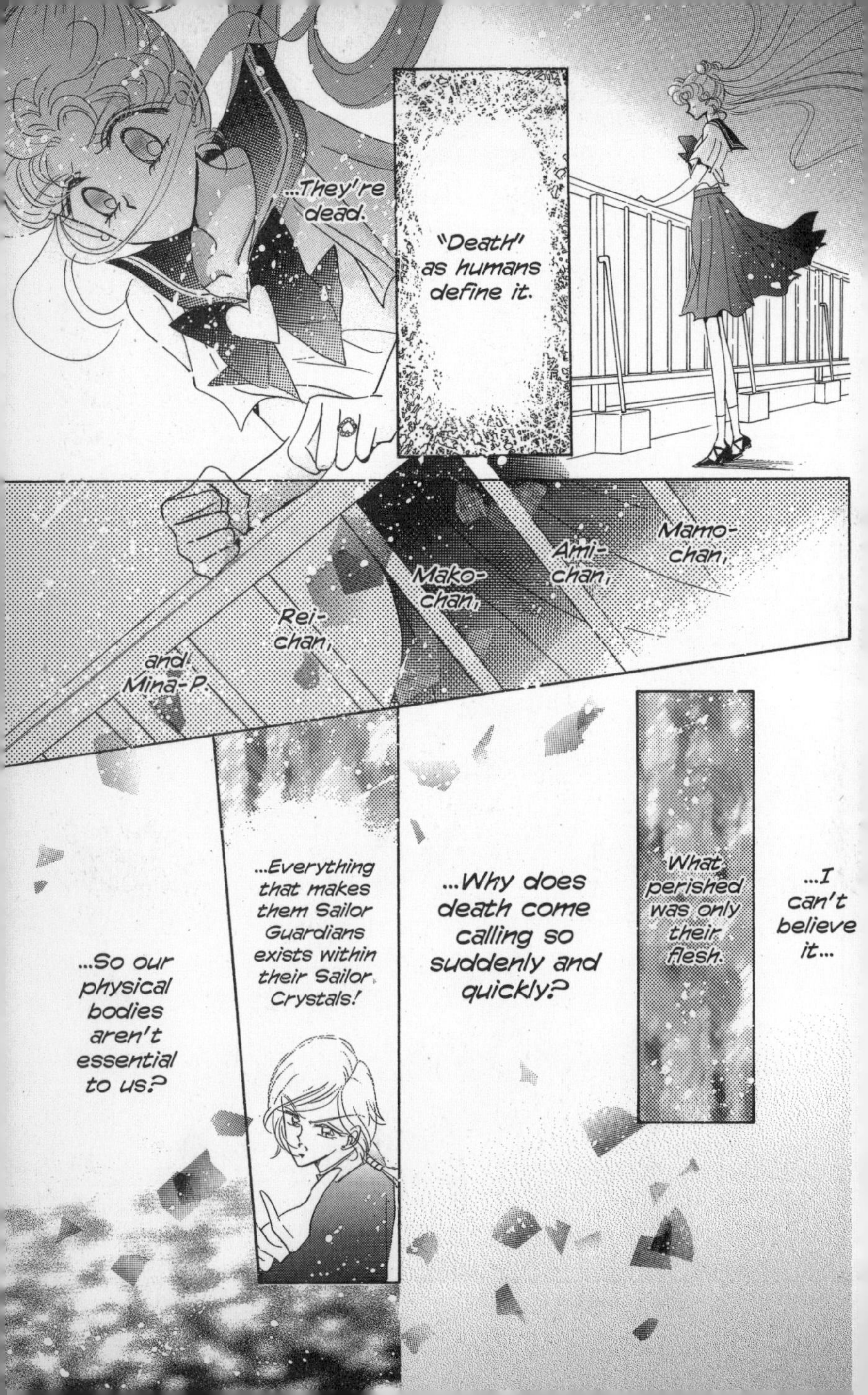
"Death" as humans define it.
...They're dead.
Mamo-chan,
Ami-chan,
Mako-chan,
Rei-chan,
and Mina-P.
...I can't believe it...
What perished was only their flesh.
...Why does death come calling so suddenly and quickly?
...Everything that makes them Sailor Guardians exists within their Sailor Crystals!
...So our physical bodies aren't essential to us?

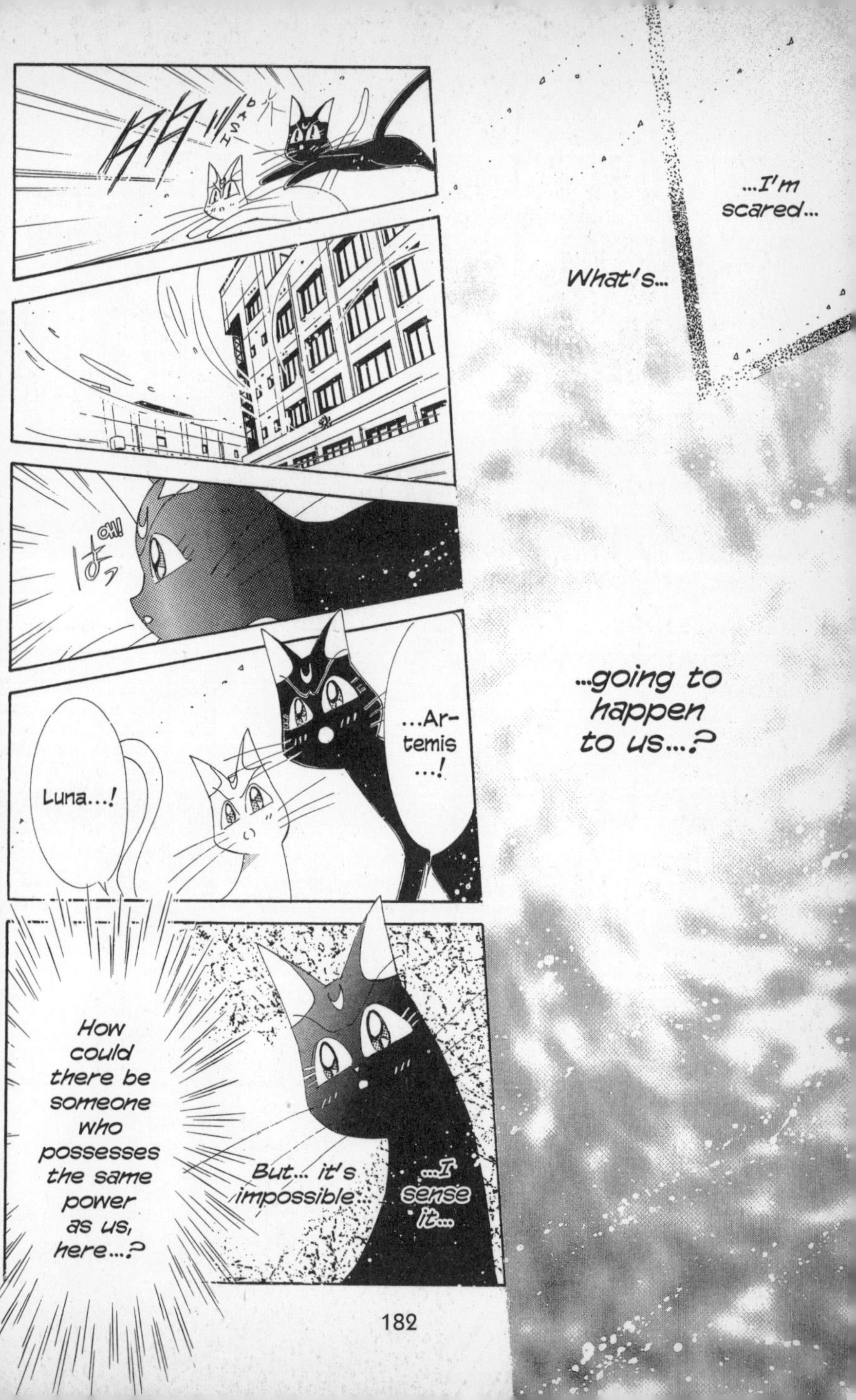
...I'm scared...
What's...
...going to happen to us...?
OH!
...Ar-temis...!
Luna...!
...I sense it...
But... it's impossible...
How could there be someone who possesses the same power as us, here...?

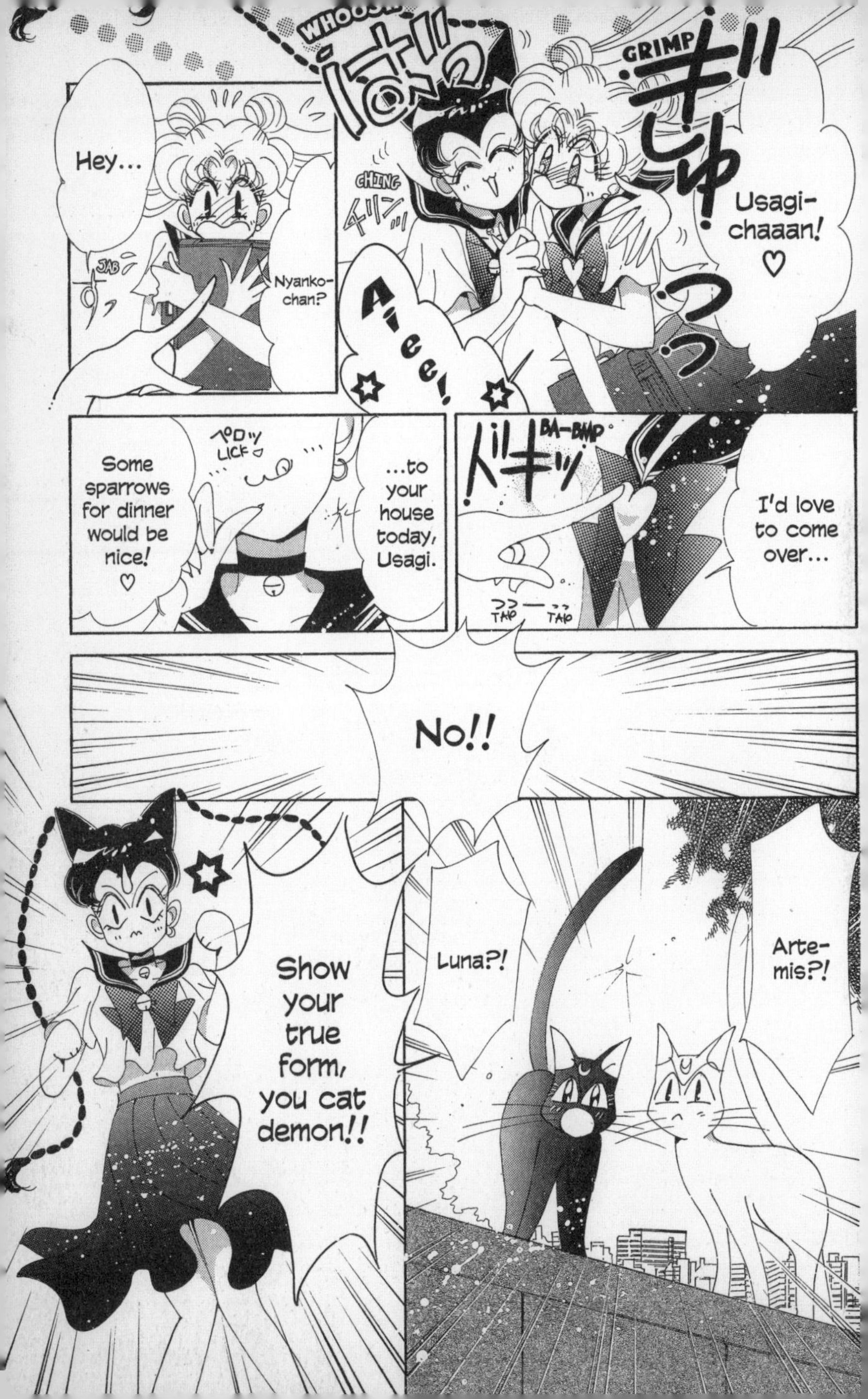
WHOOSH
GRIMP
Usagi-chaaan! ♡
CHING
Aieee!
Hey...
JAB
Nyanko-chan?
BA-BMP
I'd love to come over...
TAP TAP
...to your house today, Usagi.
LICK
Some sparrows for dinner would be nice! ♡
No!!
Arte-mis?!
Luna?!
Show your true form, you cat demon!!

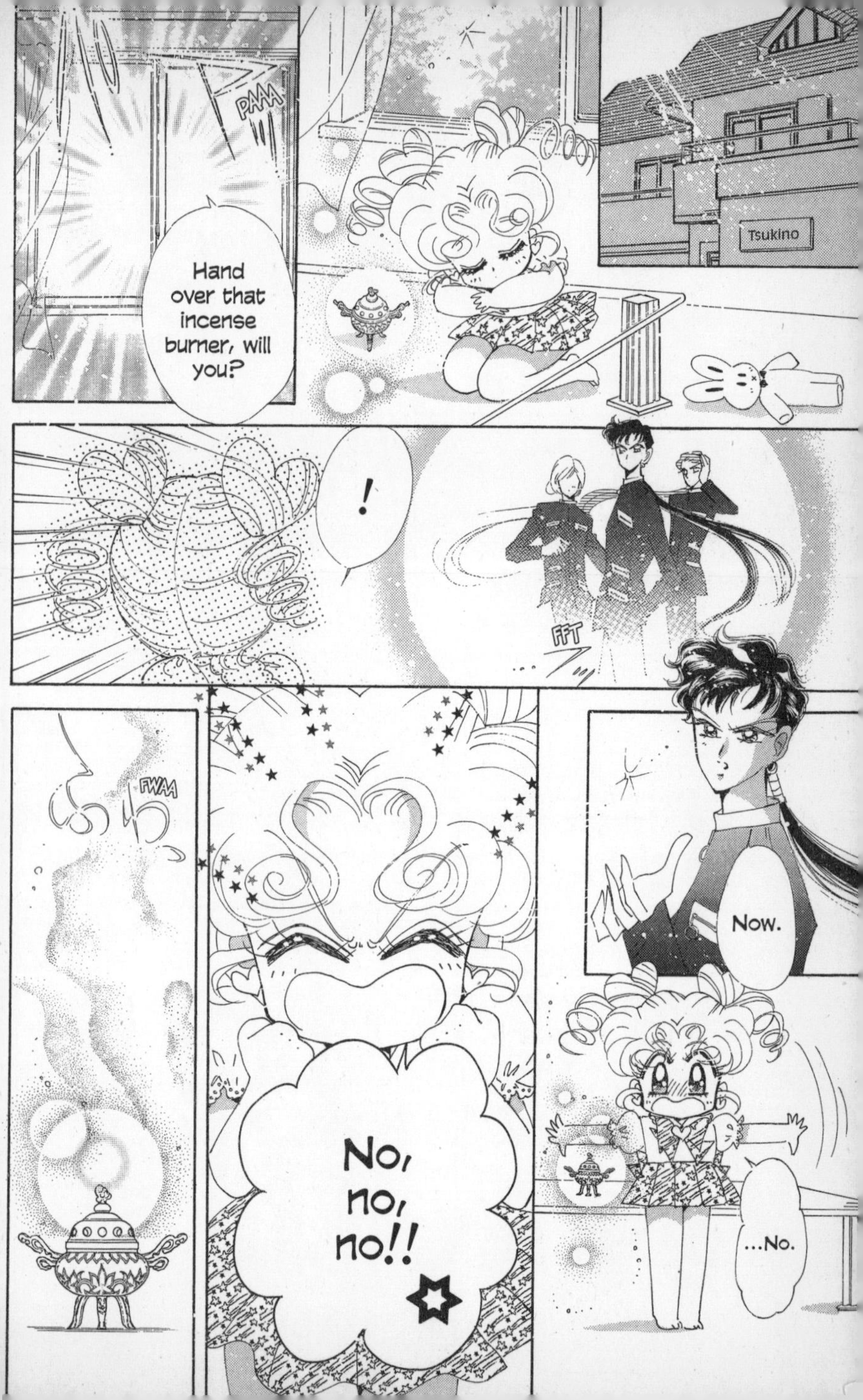
Tsukino
PAAA
Hand over that incense burner, will you?
FFT
!
Now.
...No.
No, no, no!!
FWAA

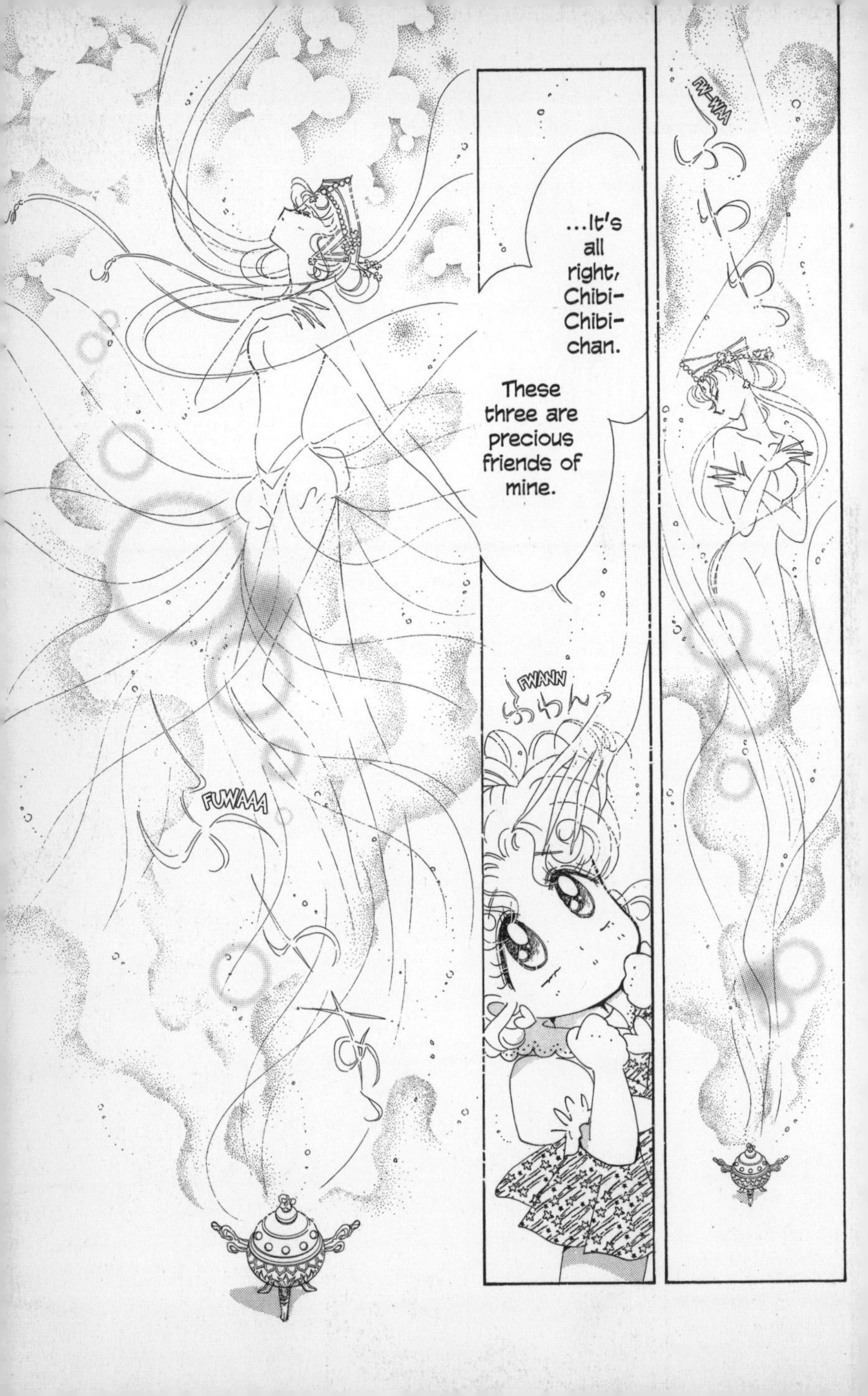
FW-WAA
...It's all right, Chibi-Chibi-chan.
These three are precious friends of mine.
FWANN
FUWAAA

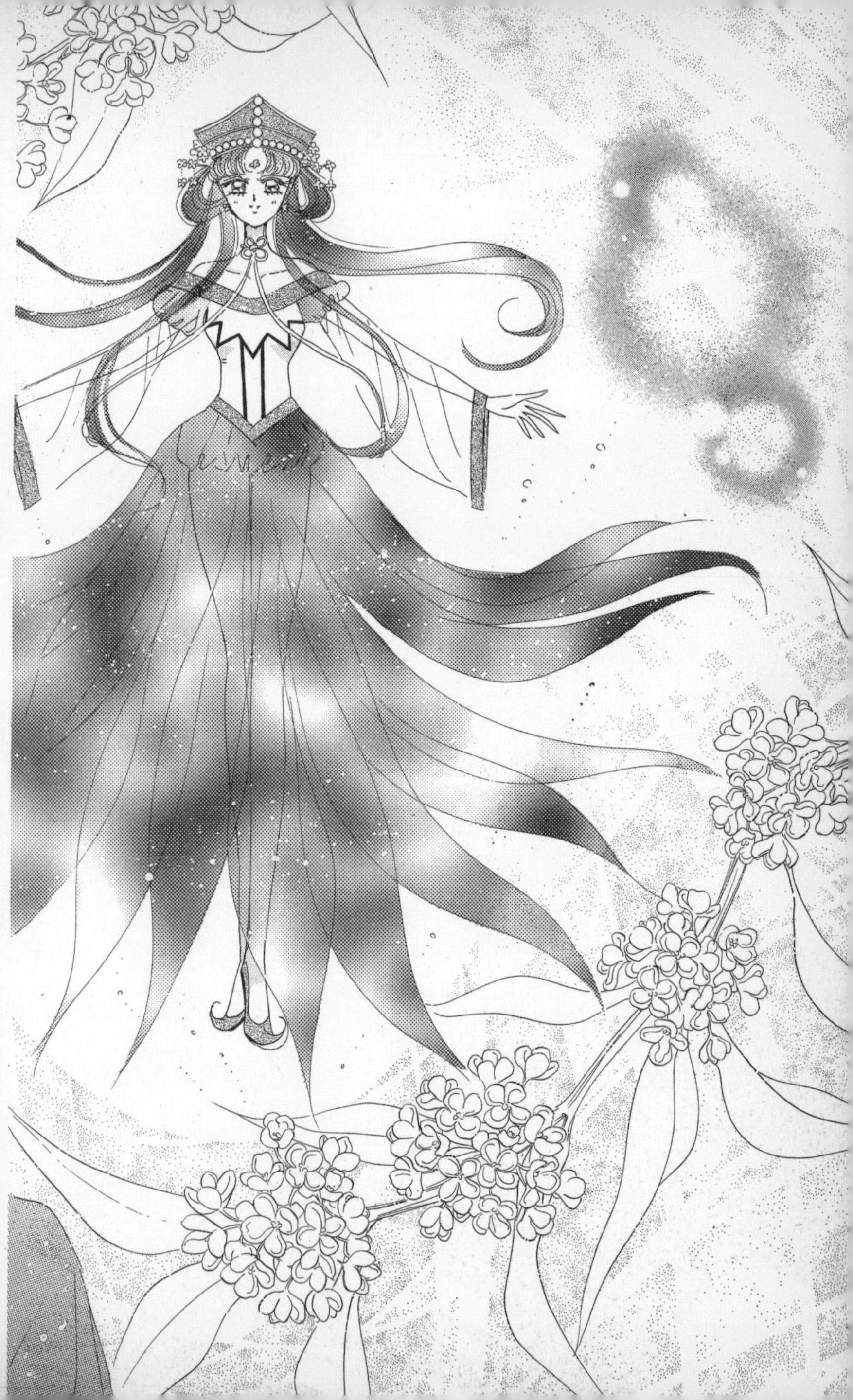

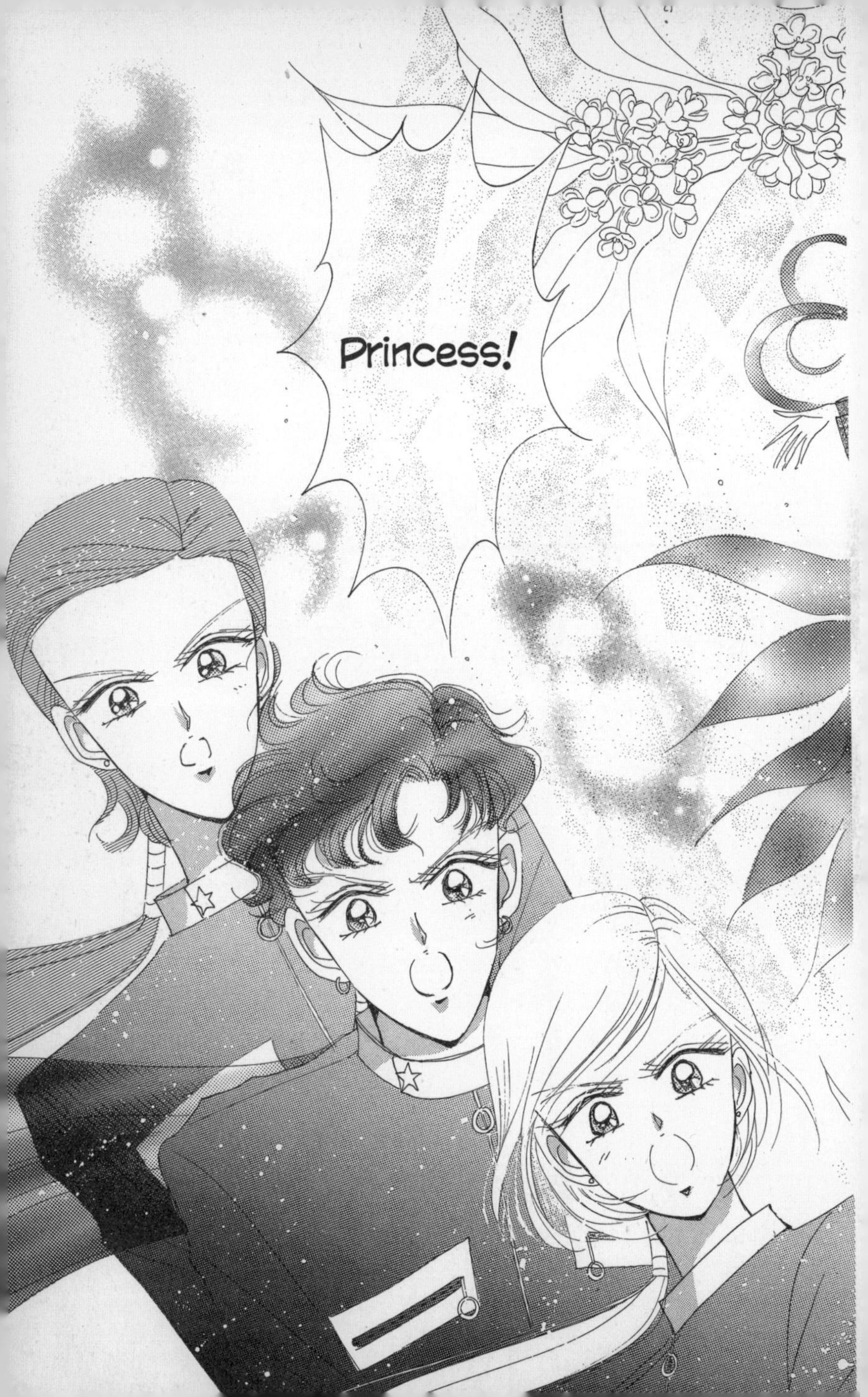
Princess!

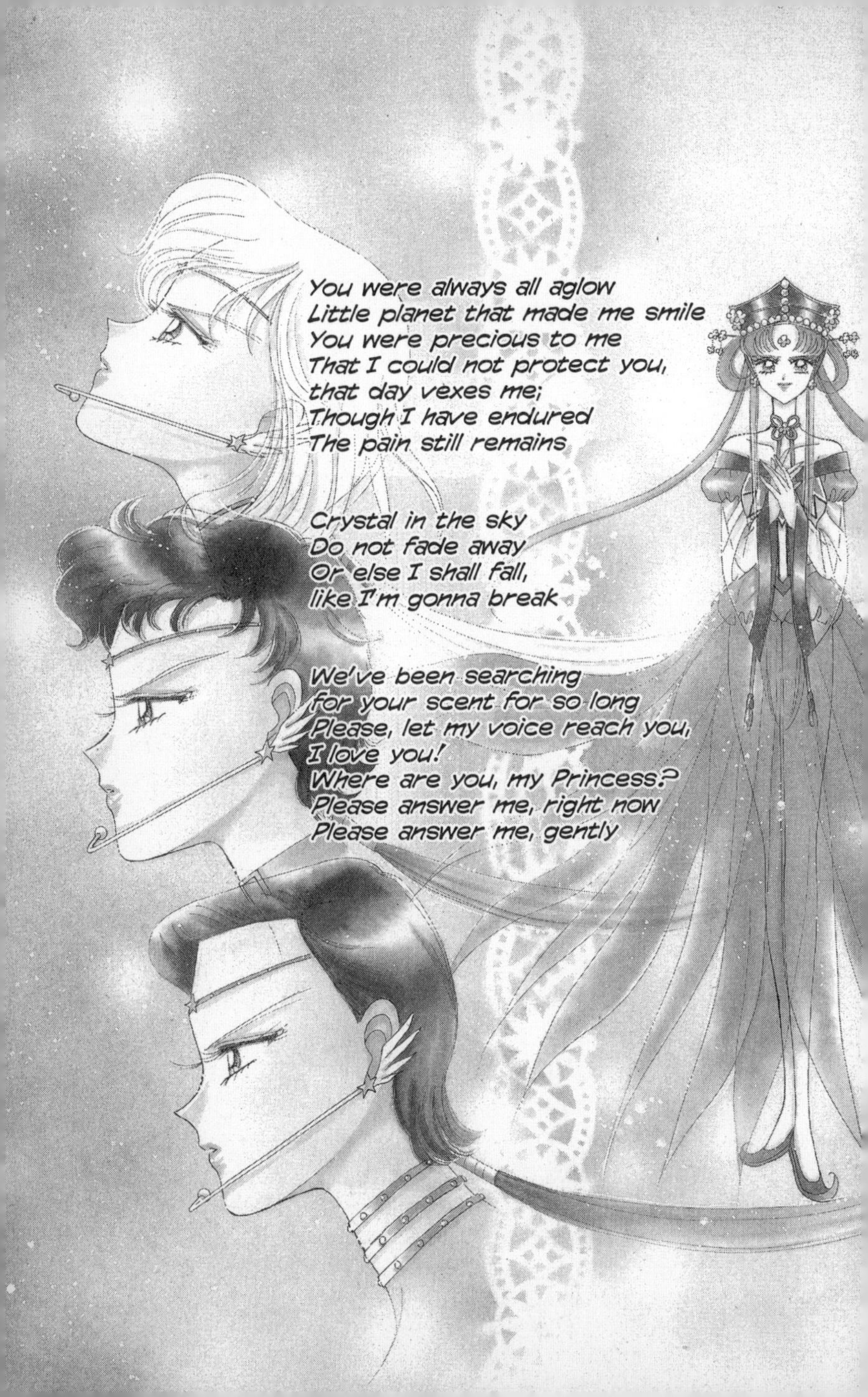
You were always all aglow
Little planet that made me smile
You were precious to me
That I could not protect you,
that day vexes me;
Though I have endured
The pain still remains

Crystal in the sky
Do not fade away
Or else I shall fall,
like I'm gonna break

We've been searching
for your scent for so long
Please, let my voice reach you,
I love you!
Where are you, my Princess?
Please answer me, right now
Please answer me, gently

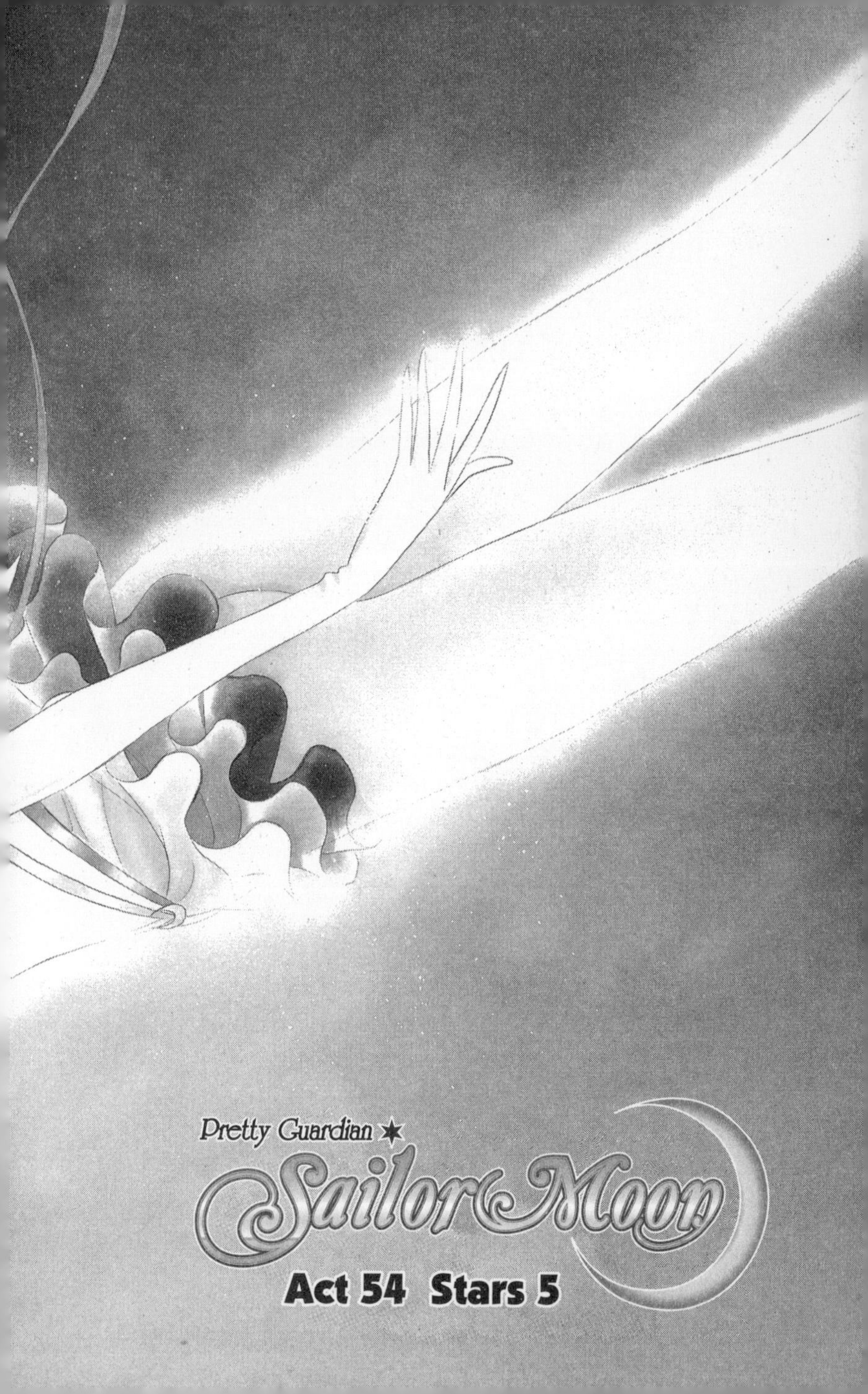
Pretty Guardian
Sailor Moon
Act 54 Stars 5

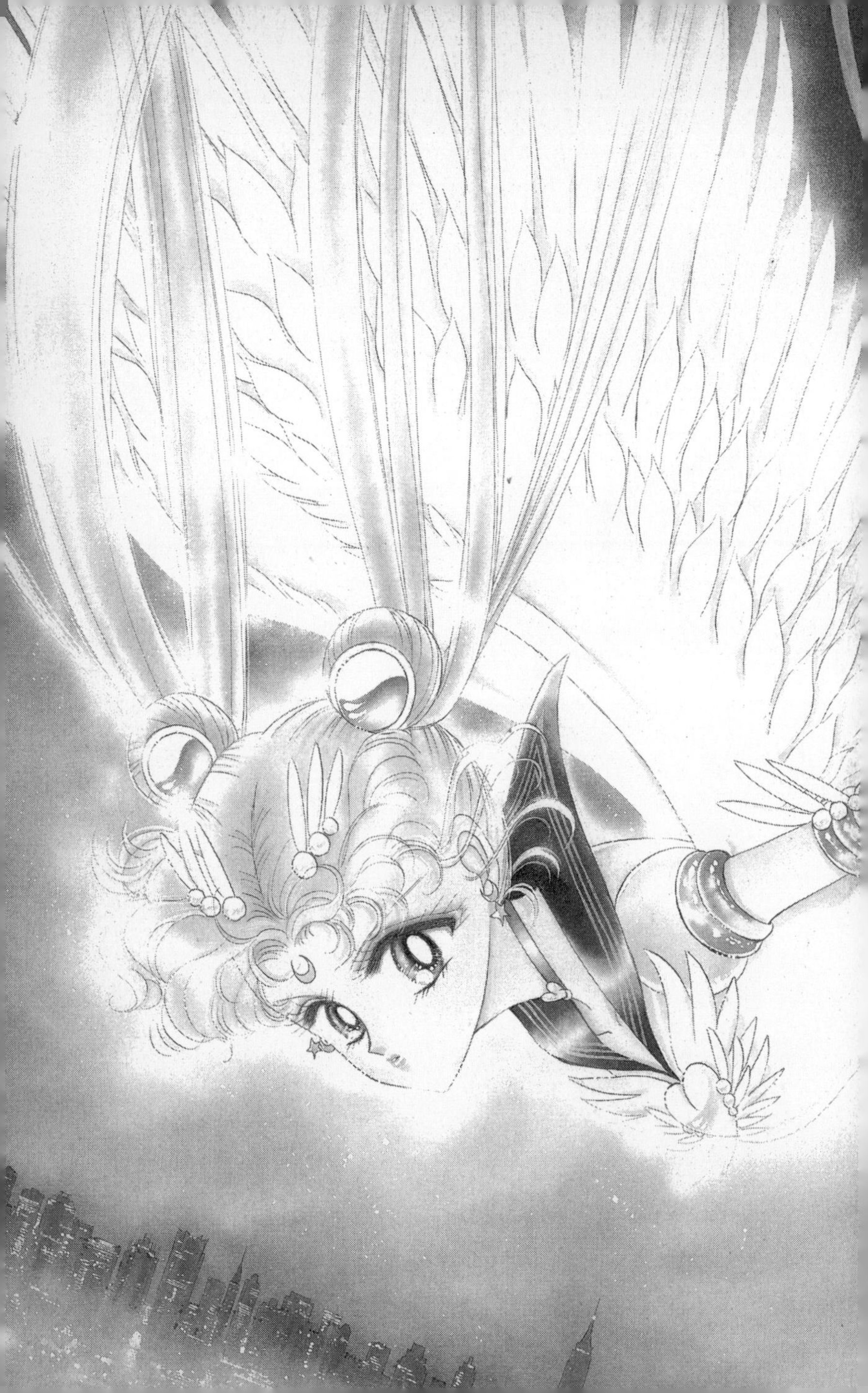

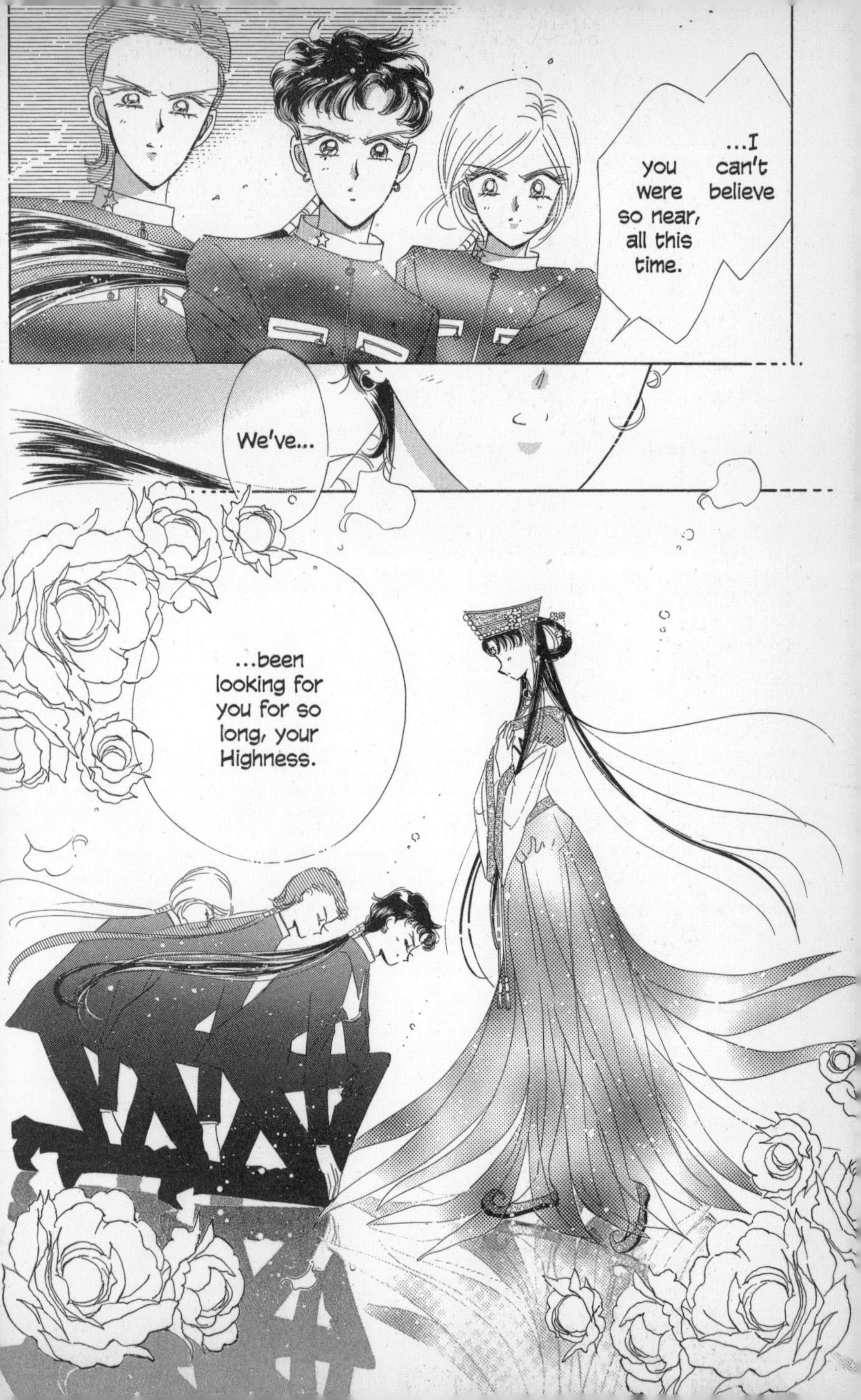
...I can't believe you were so near, all this time.
We've...
...been looking for you for so long, your Highness.

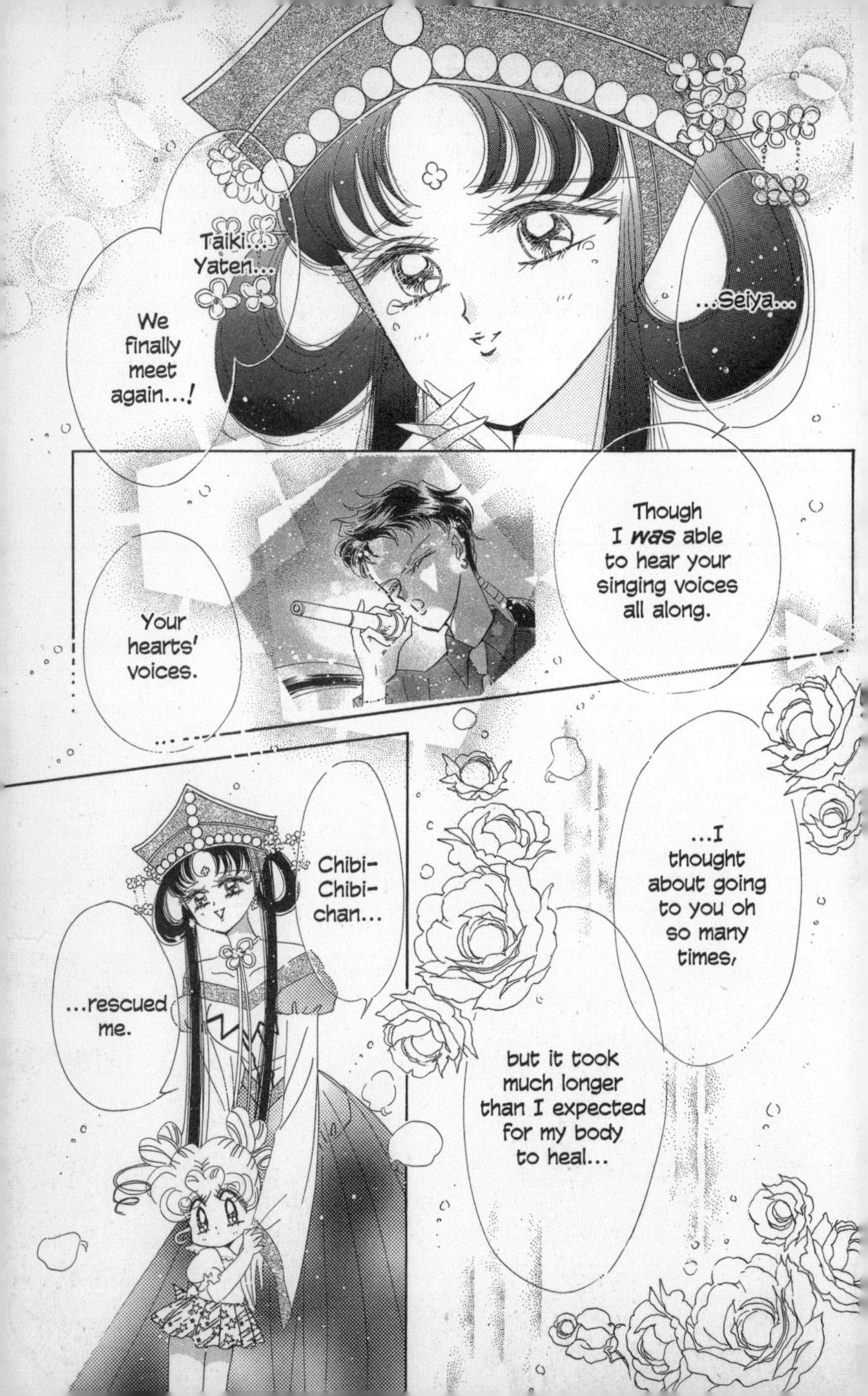
...Seiya...
Taiki... Yaten...
We finally meet again...!
Though I *was* able to hear your singing voices all along.
Your hearts' voices.
...
...I thought about going to you oh so many times,
but it took much longer than I expected for my body to heal...
Chibi-Chibi-chan...
...rescued me.

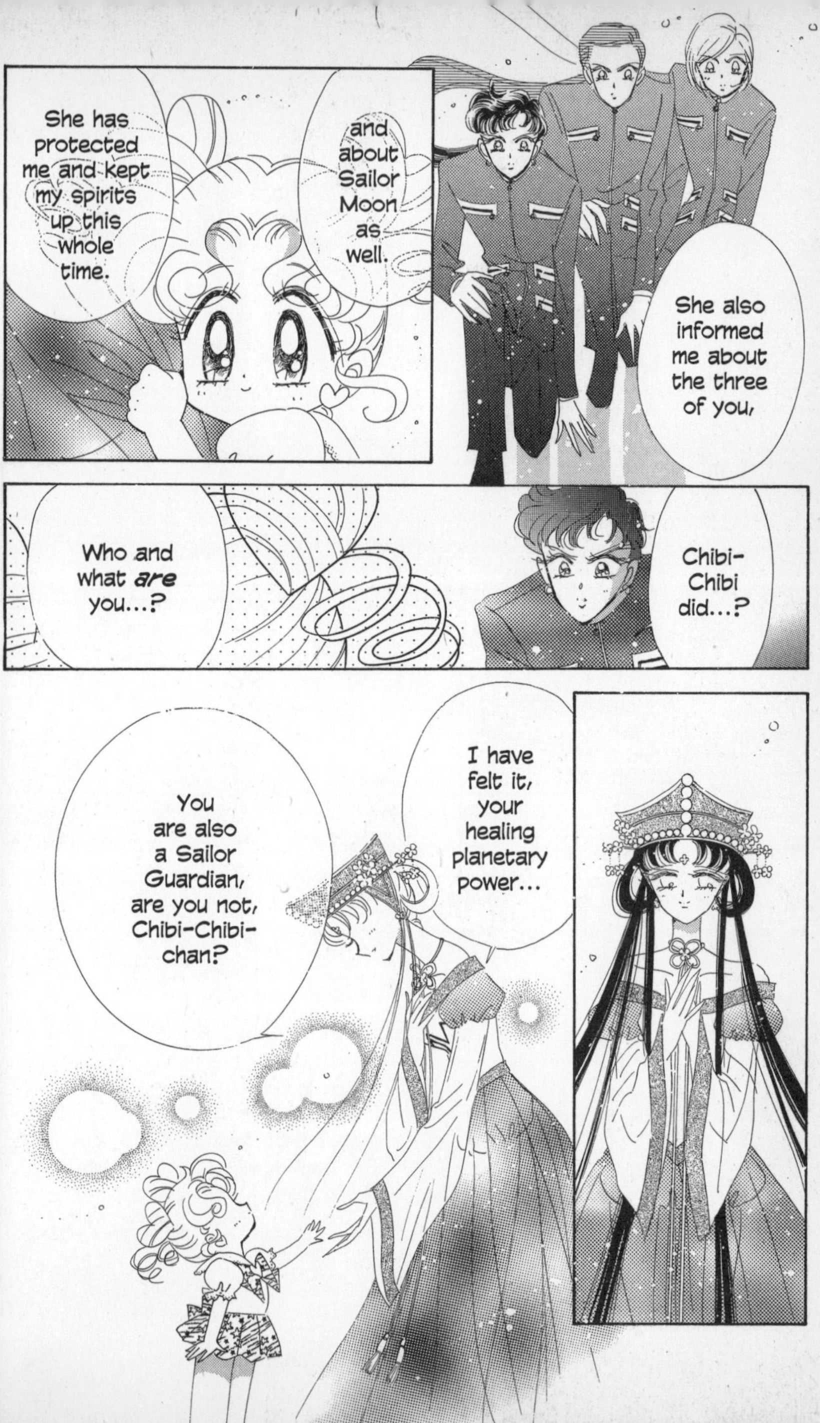

She also informed me about the three of you,
and about Sailor Moon as well.
She has protected me and kept my spirits up this whole time.
Chibi-Chibi did...?
Who and what *are* you...?
I have felt it, your healing planetary power...
You are also a Sailor Guardian, are you not, Chibi-Chibi-chan?

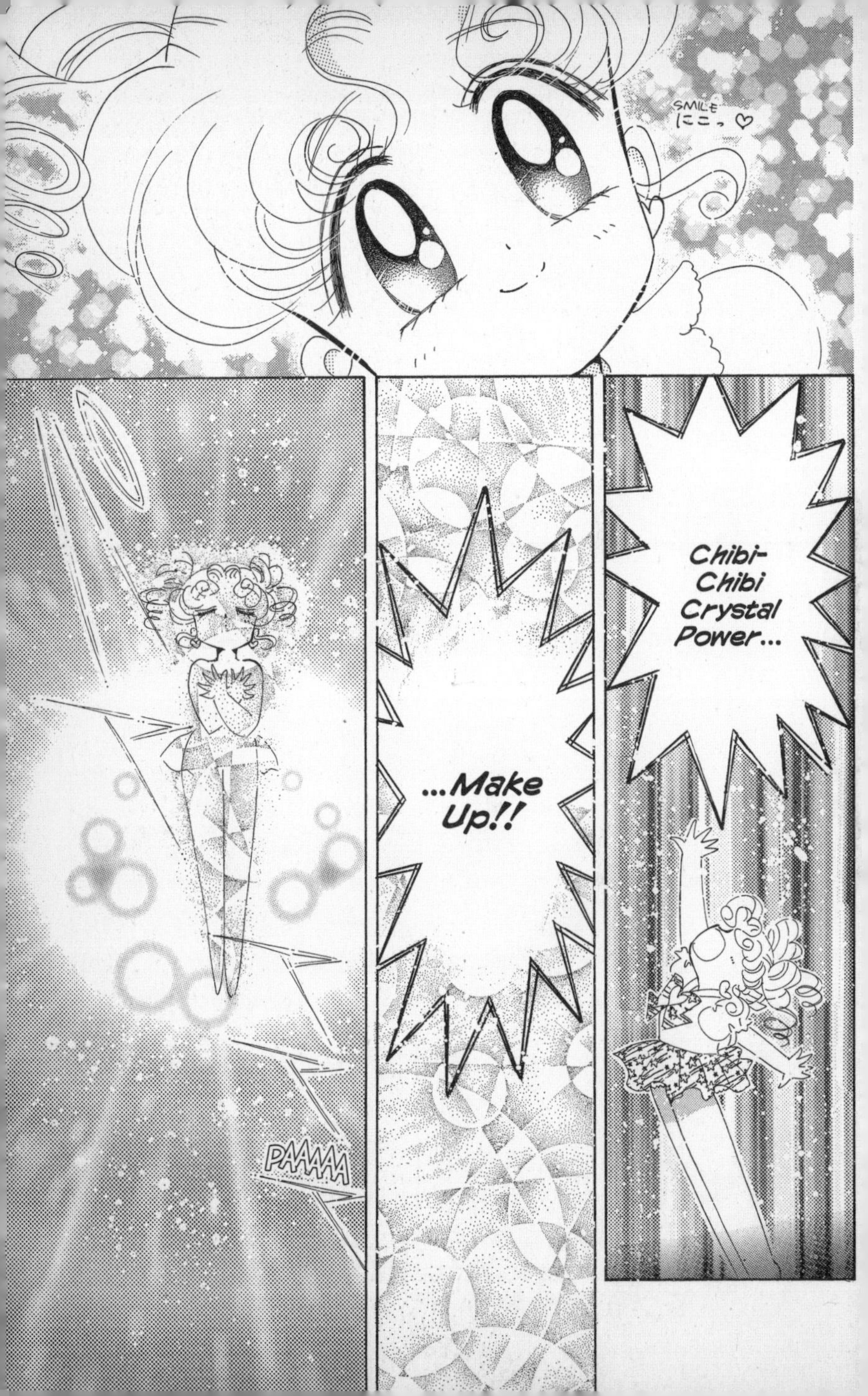
SMILE
にこっ♡
Chibi-Chibi Crystal Power...
...Make Up!!
PAAAAA

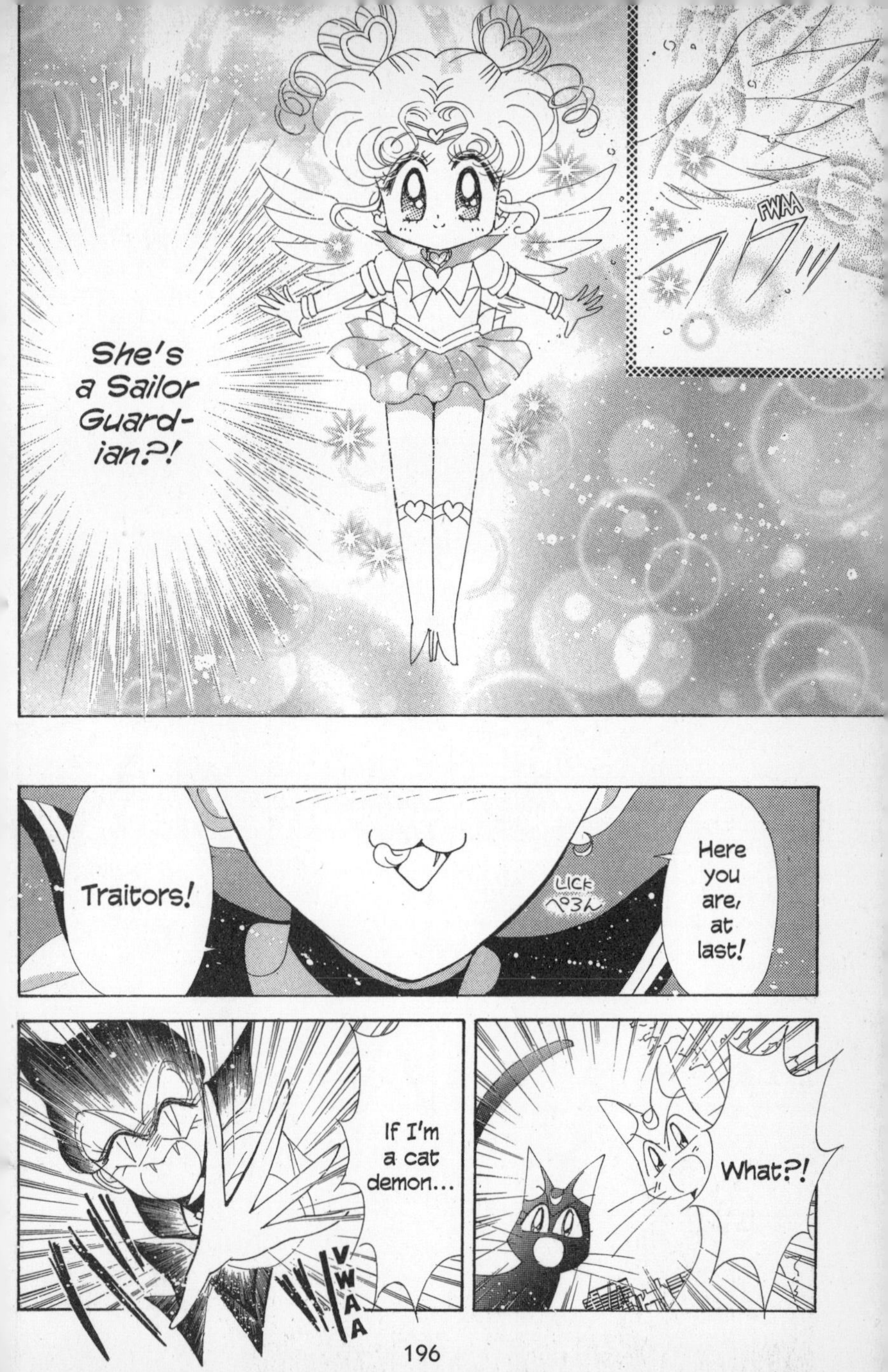
FWAA
She's a Sailor Guardian?!
Here you are, at last!
LICK
ぺろん
Traitors!
What?!
If I'm a cat demon...
VWAA

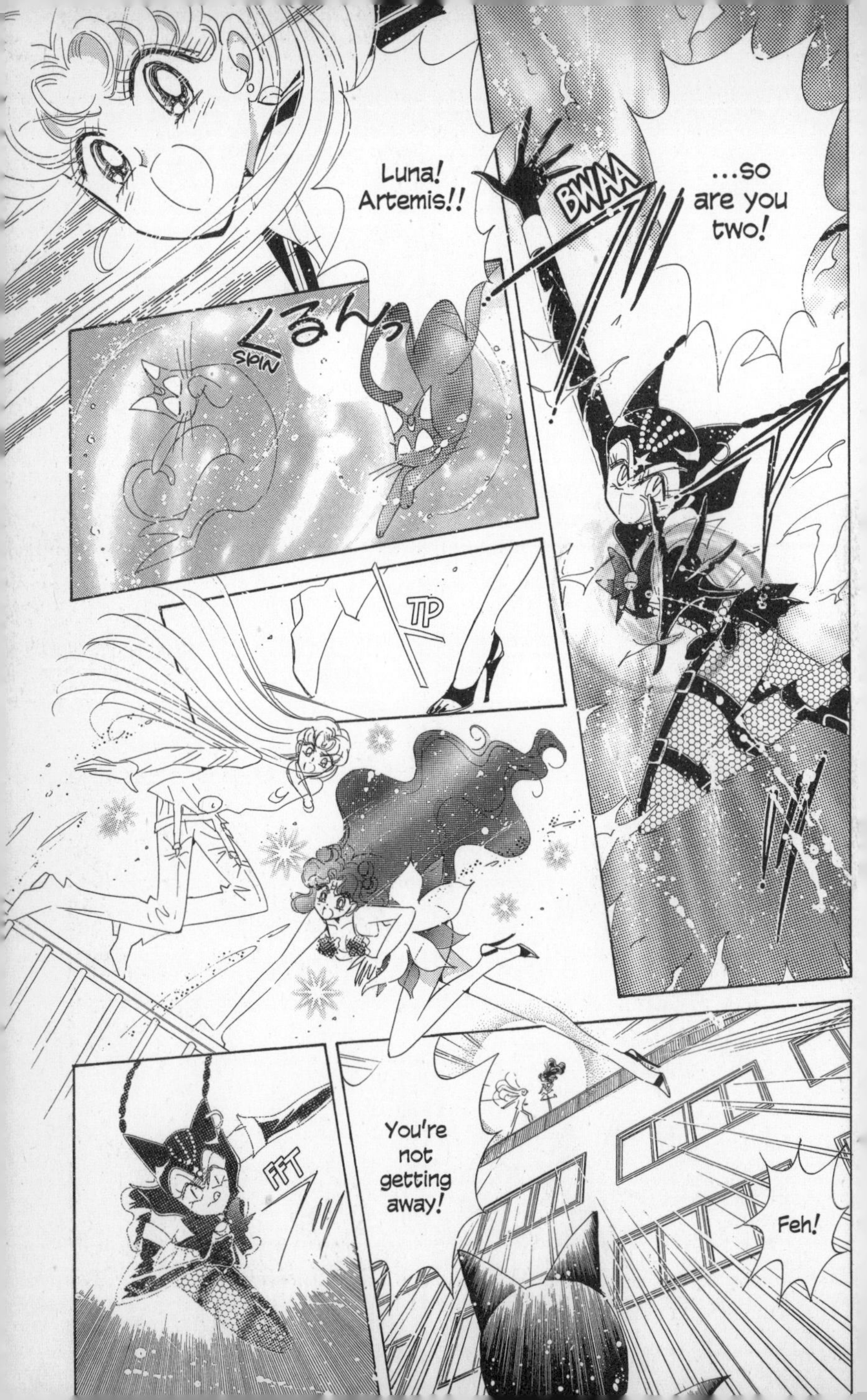
BWAA
...so are you two!
Luna! Artemis!!
くるんっ
SPIN
TP
You're not getting away!
Feh!
FFT

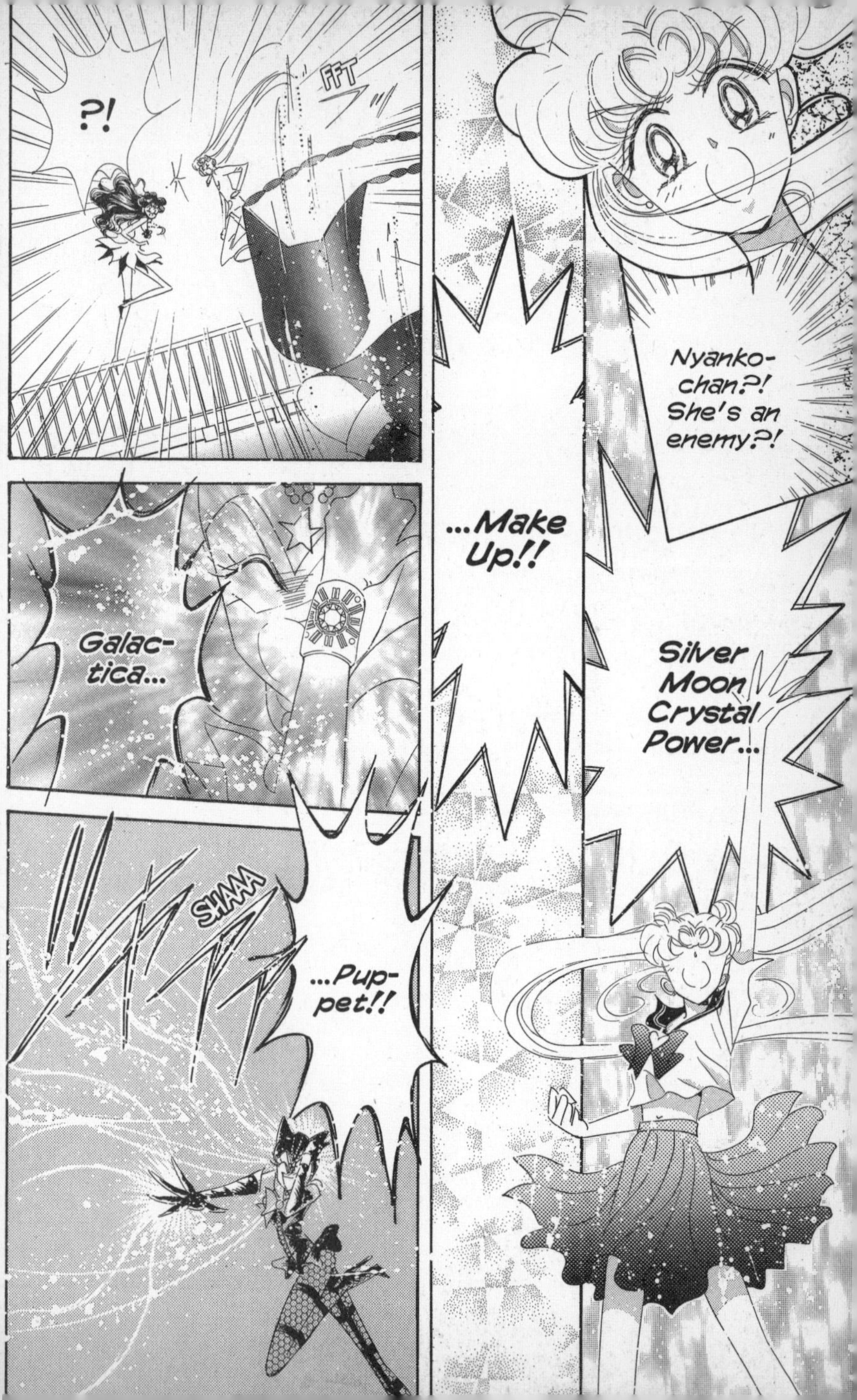
Nyanko-chan?! She's an enemy?!
Silver Moon Crystal Power...
...Make Up!!
FFT
?!
Galactica...
SHAAA
...Pup-pet!!

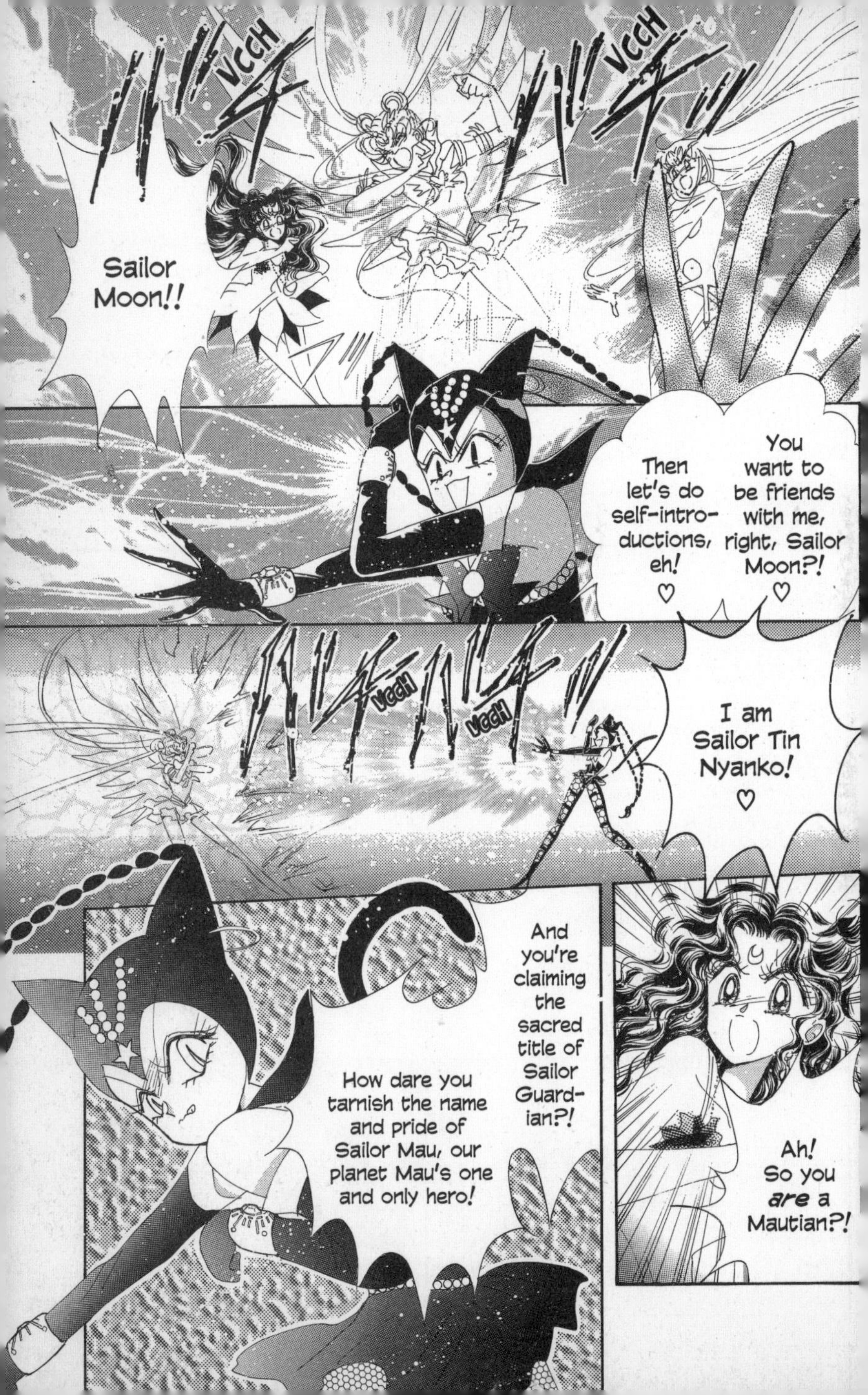
VCCH
VCCH
Sailor Moon!!
You want to be friends with me, right, Sailor Moon?! ♡
Then let's do self-introductions, eh! ♡
I am Sailor Tin Nyanko! ♡
VCCH
VCCH
Ah! So you *are* a Mautian?!
And you're claiming the sacred title of Sailor Guardian?!
How dare you tarnish the name and pride of Sailor Mau, our planet Mau's one and only hero!

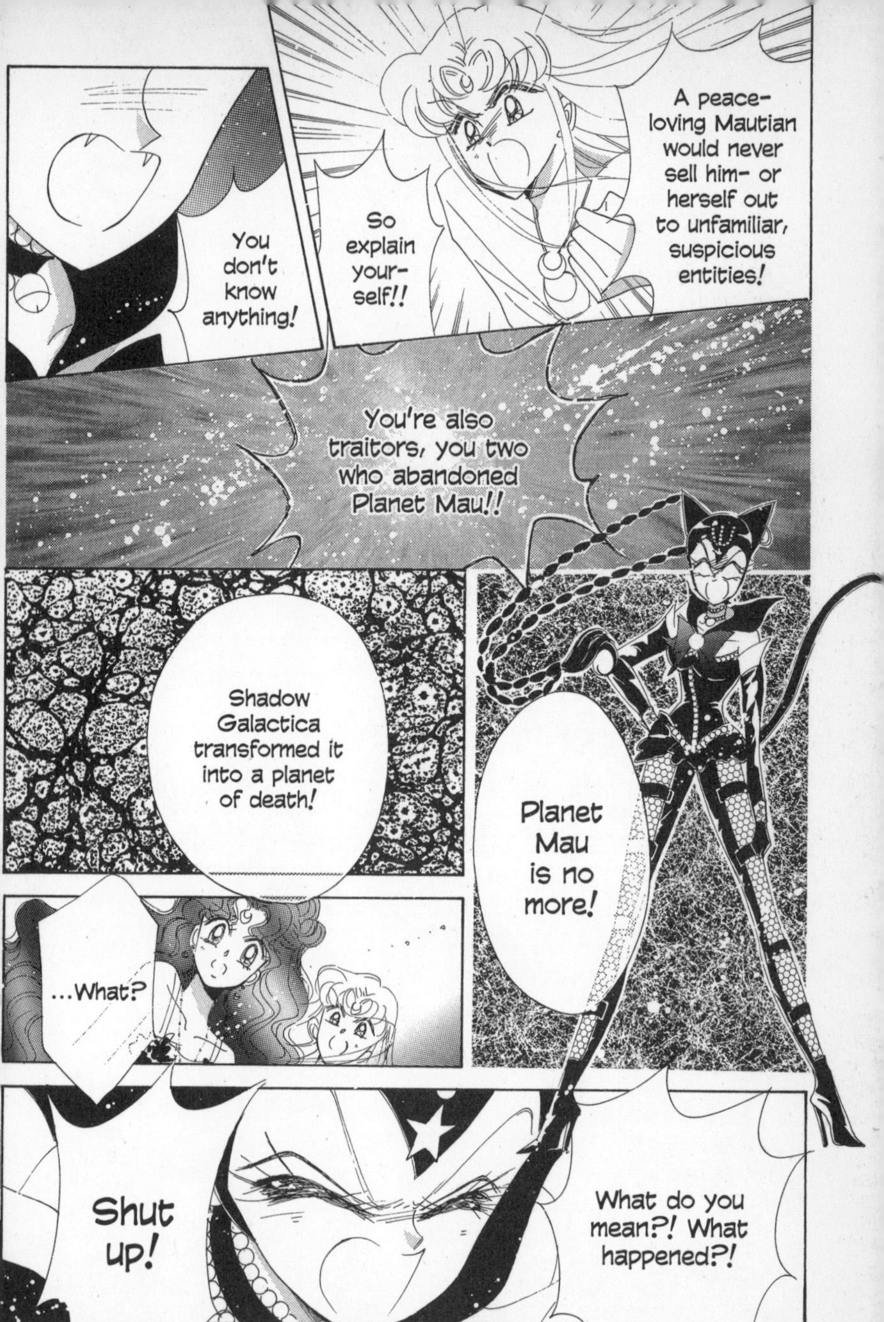
A peace-loving Mautian would never sell him- or herself out to unfamiliar, suspicious entities!
So explain your-self!!
You don't know anything!
You're also traitors, you two who abandoned Planet Mau!!
Planet Mau is no more!
Shadow Galactica transformed it into a planet of death!
...What?
What do you mean?! What happened?!
Shut up!

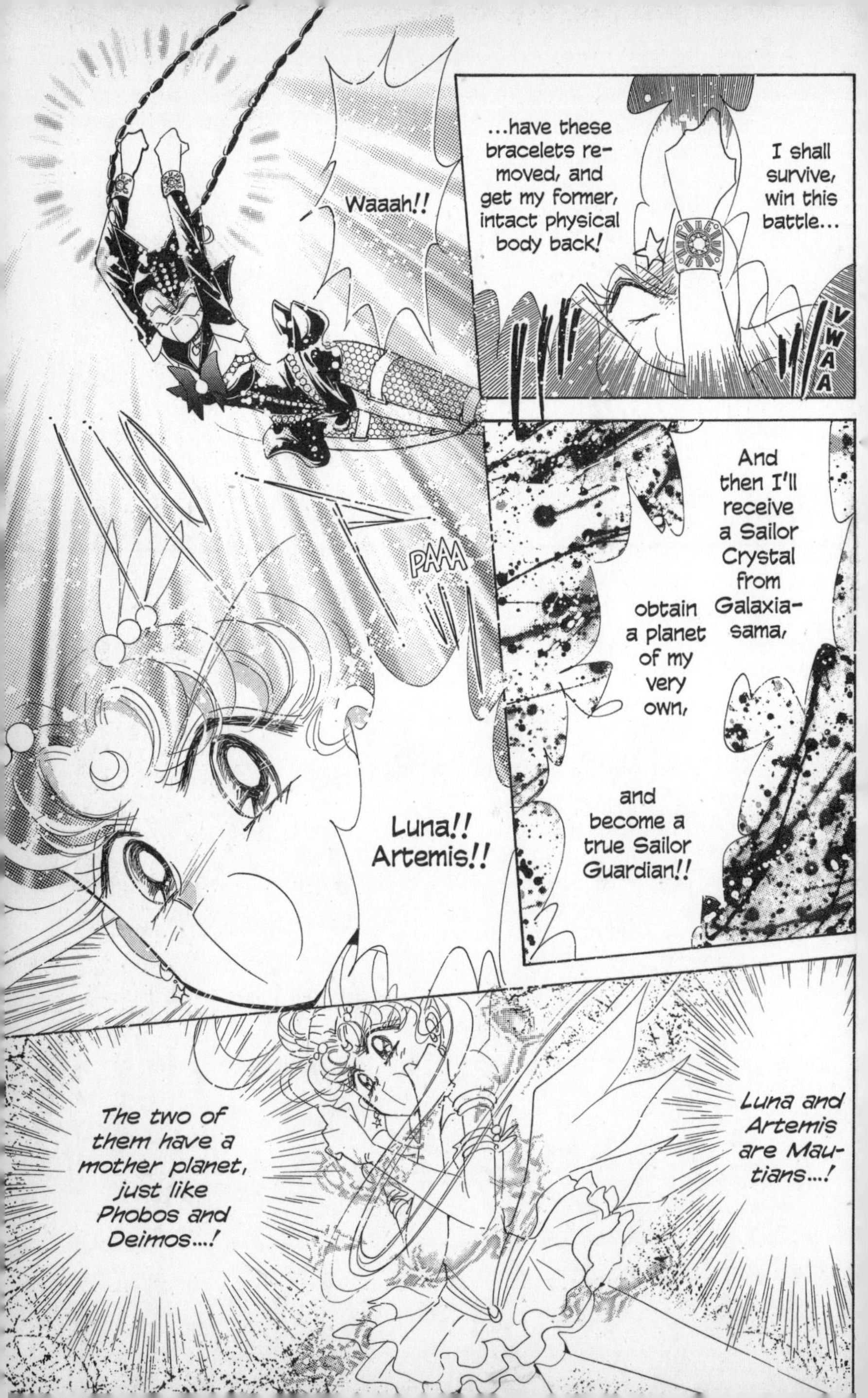
I shall survive, win this battle...
...have these bracelets re-moved, and get my former, intact physical body back!
VWAA
And then I'll receive a Sailor Crystal from Galaxia-sama,
obtain a planet of my very own,
and become a true Sailor Guardian!!
Waaah!!
PAAA
Luna!! Artemis!!
Luna and Artemis are Mau-tians...!
The two of them have a mother planet, just like Phobos and Deimos...!

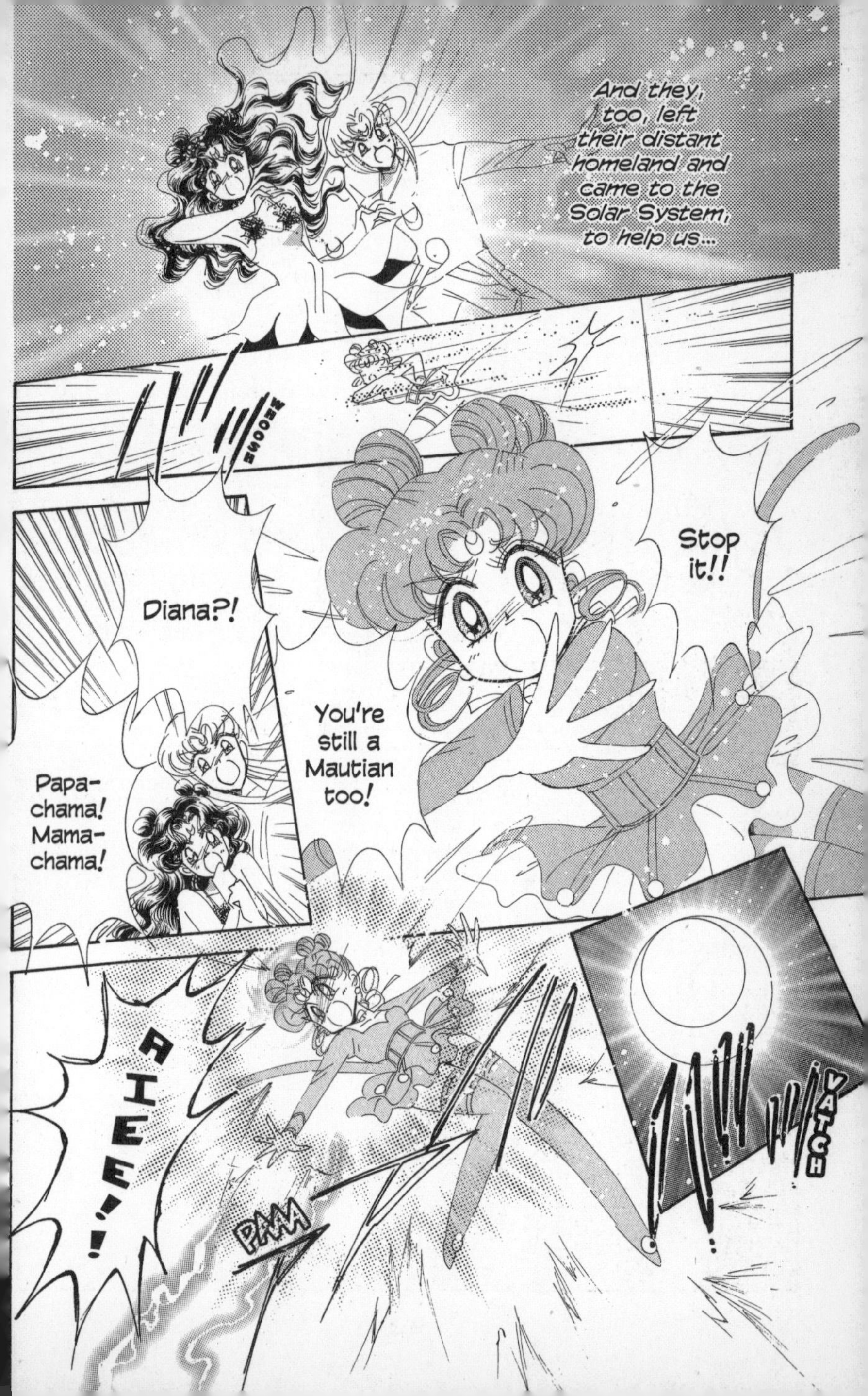
And they, too, left their distant homeland and came to the Solar System, to help us...
WHOOSH
Stop it!!
You're still a Mautian too!
Diana?!
Papa-chama! Mama-chama!
VATCH
AIEE!!!
PAAA

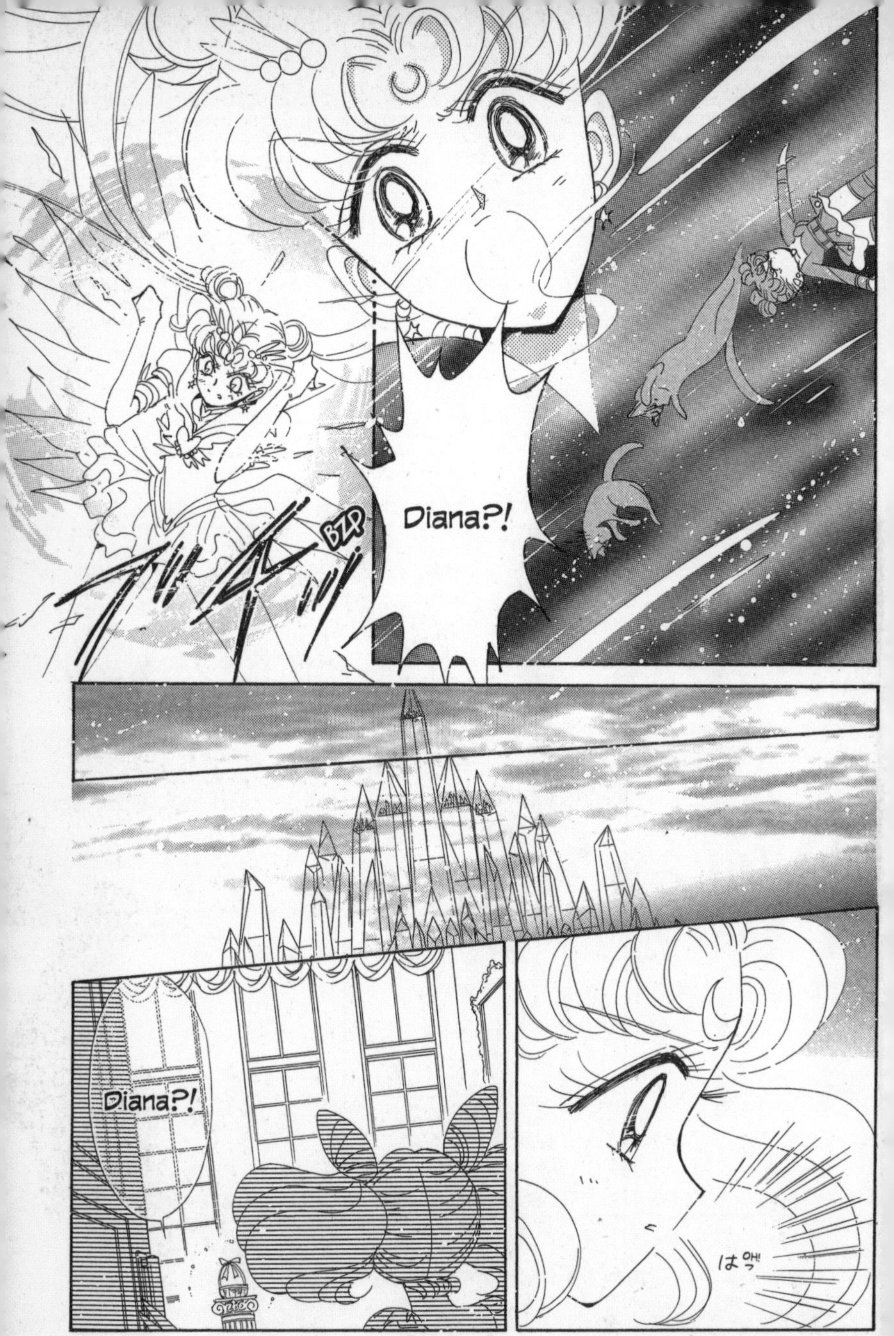
BZP
Diana?!
...
Diana?!

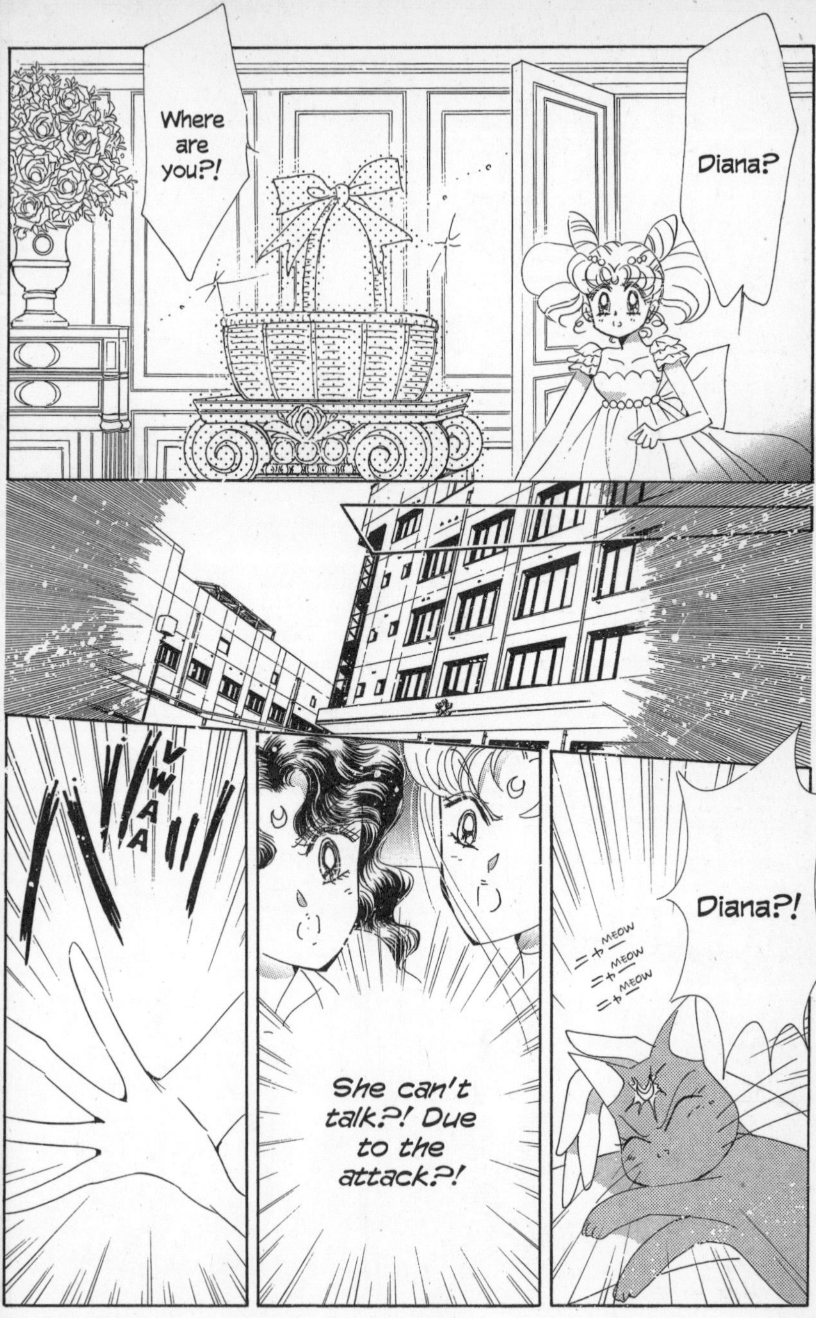
Diana?
Where are you?!
VWAAA
Diana?!
MEOW
MEOW
MEOW
She can't talk?! Due to the attack?!

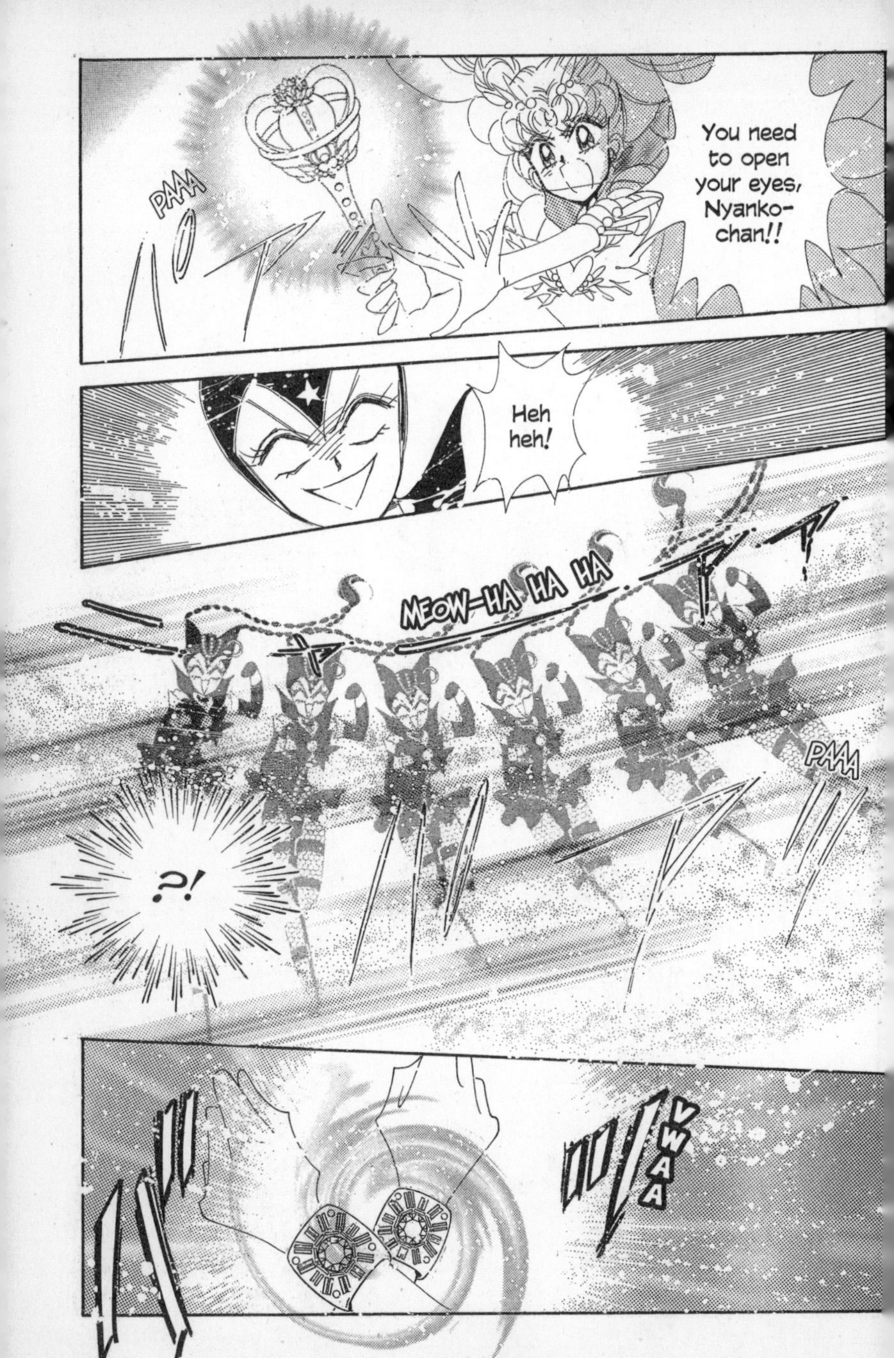
You need to open your eyes, Nyanko-chan!!
PAAA
Heh heh!
MEOW-HA HA HA
PAAA
?!
VWAA

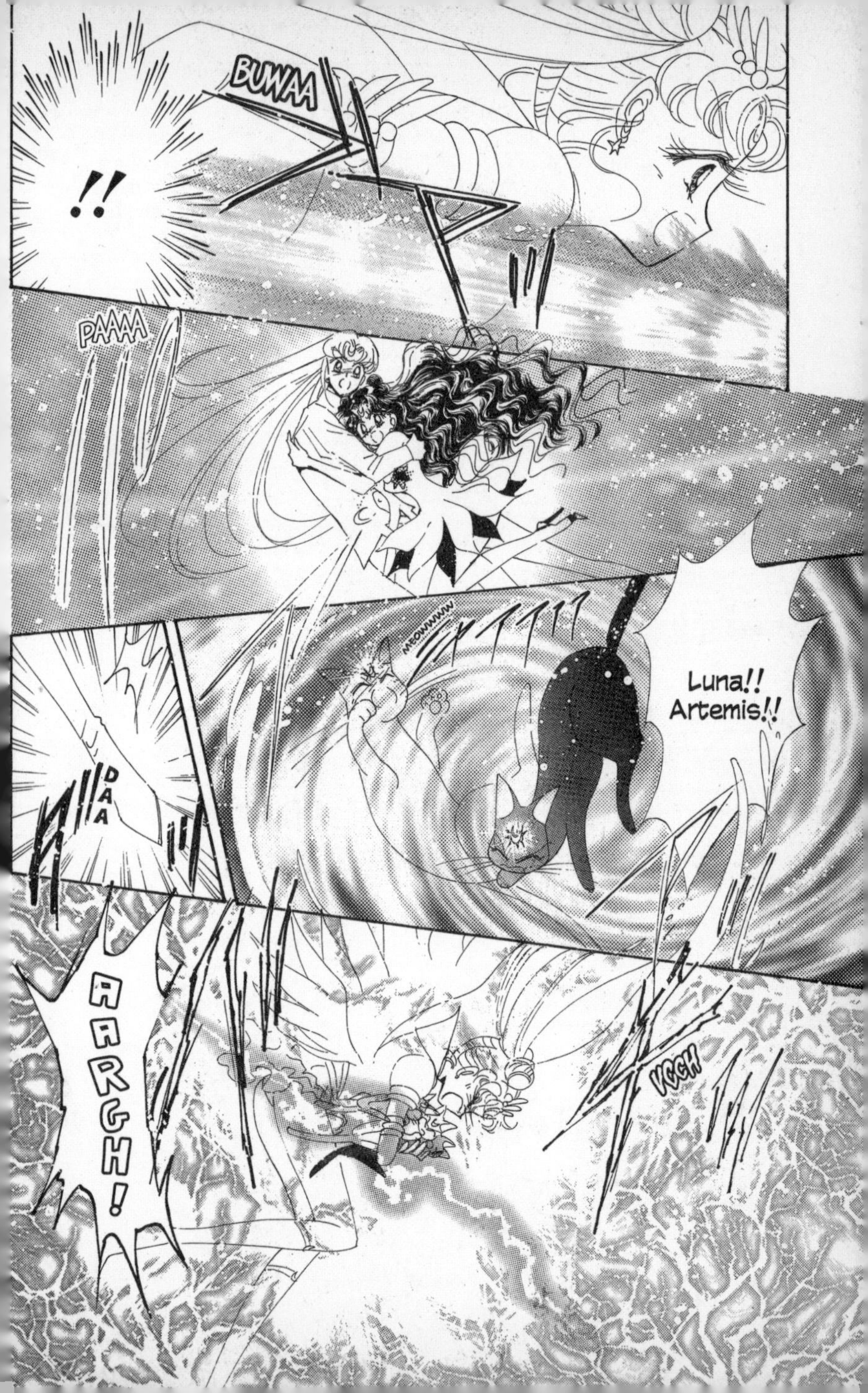
BUWAA
!!
PAAAA
Luna!!
Artemis!!
MEOWWWW
DAA
VCCH
AARGH!

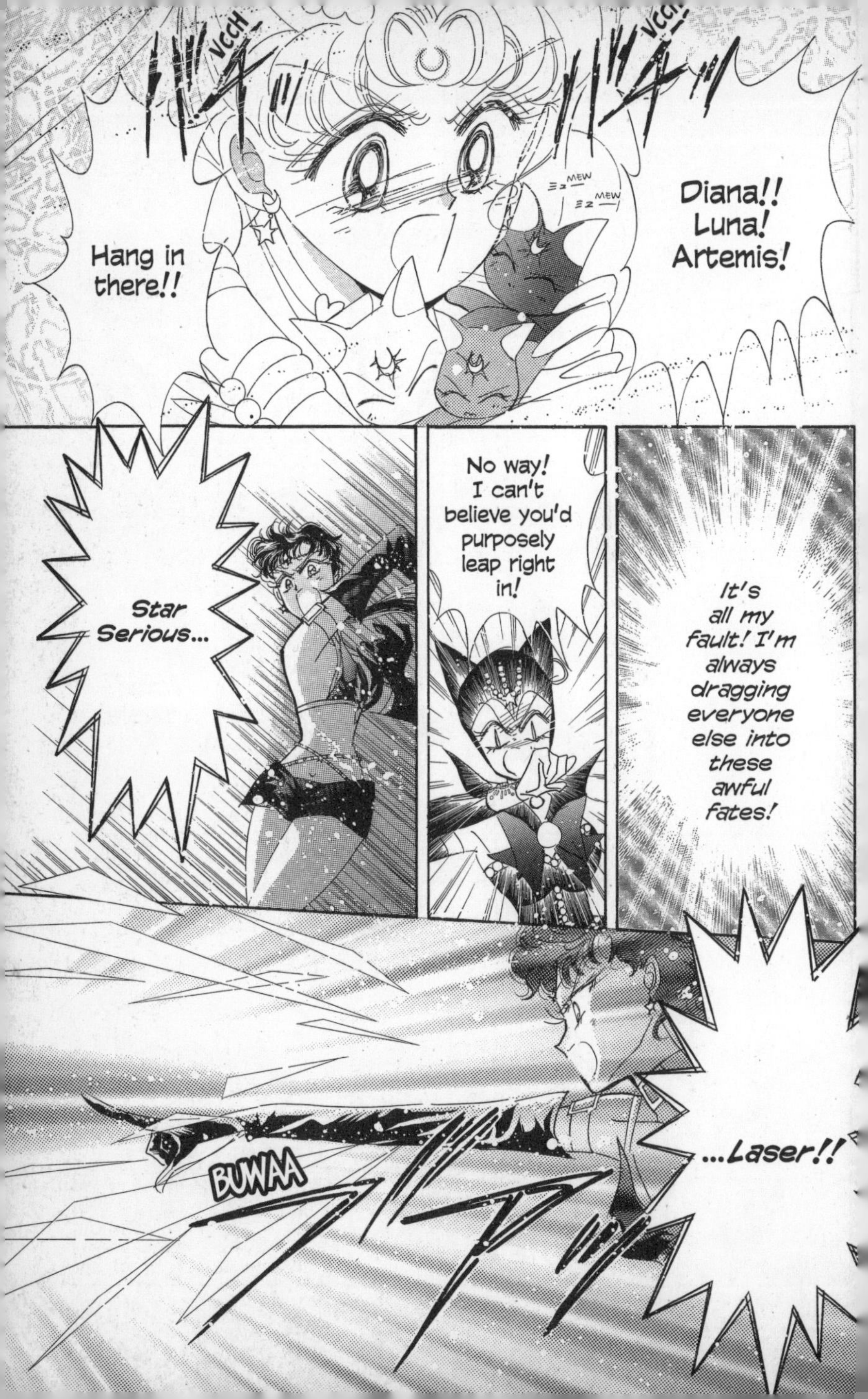
VCCH
VCCH
MEW
MEW
Diana!! Luna! Artemis!
Hang in there!!
It's all my fault! I'm always dragging everyone else into these awful fates!
No way! I can't believe you'd purposely leap right in!
Star Serious...
...Laser!!
BUWAA

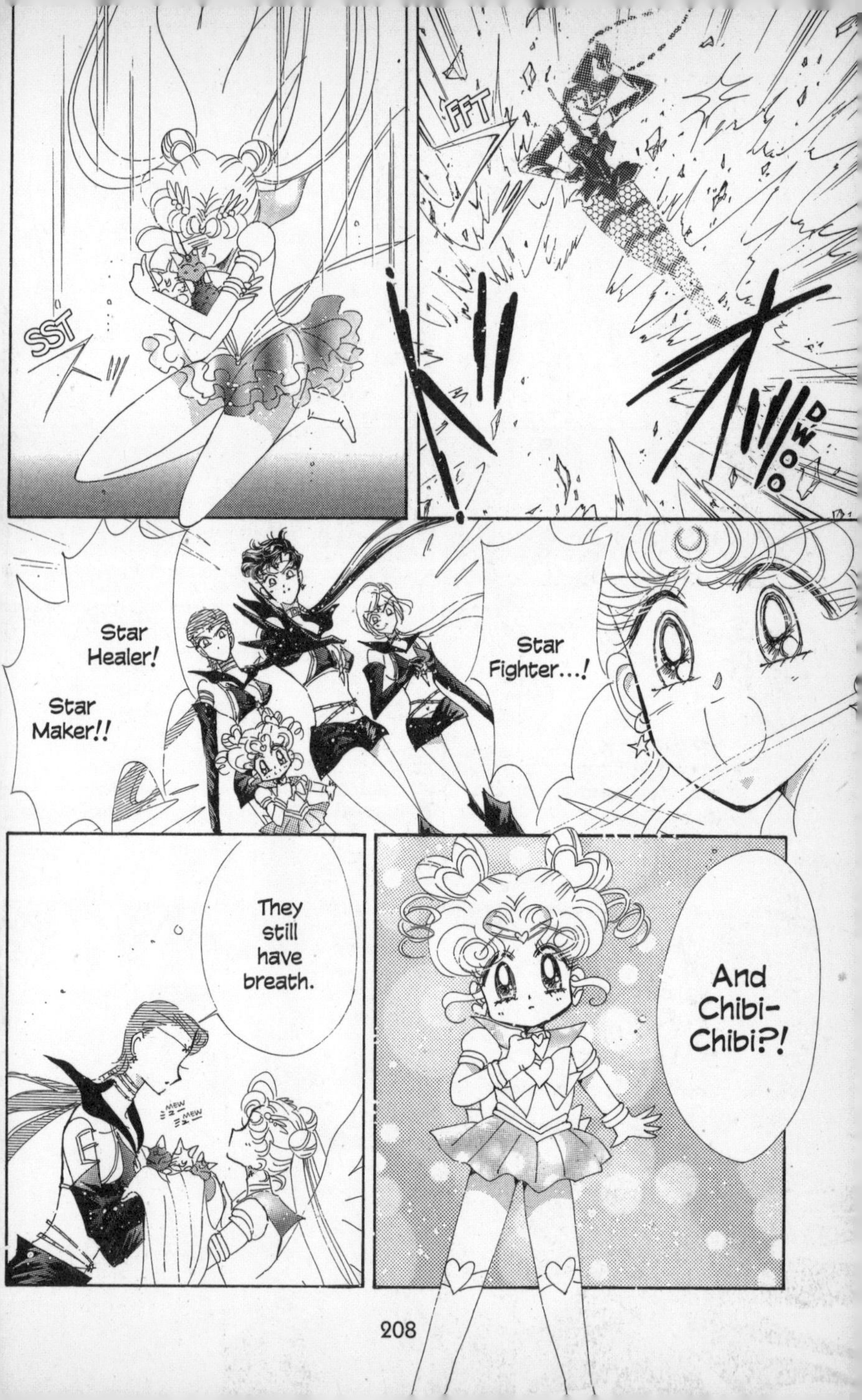
FFT
DWOOO
SST
Star Fighter...!
Star Healer!
Star Maker!!
And Chibi-Chibi?!
They still have breath.
MEW MEW

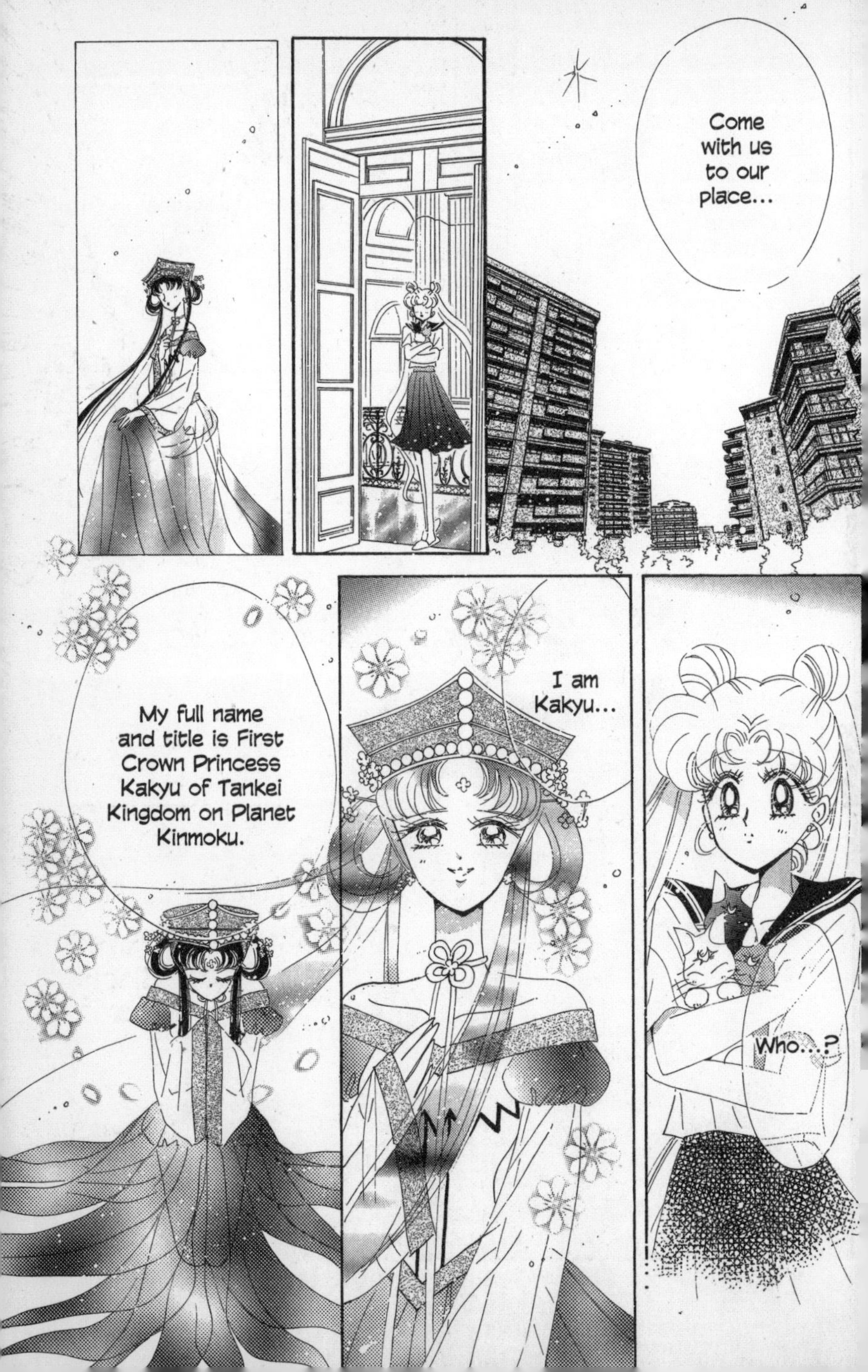
Come with us to our place...
Who...?
I am Kakyu...
My full name and title is First Crown Princess Kakyu of Tankei Kingdom on Planet Kinmoku.

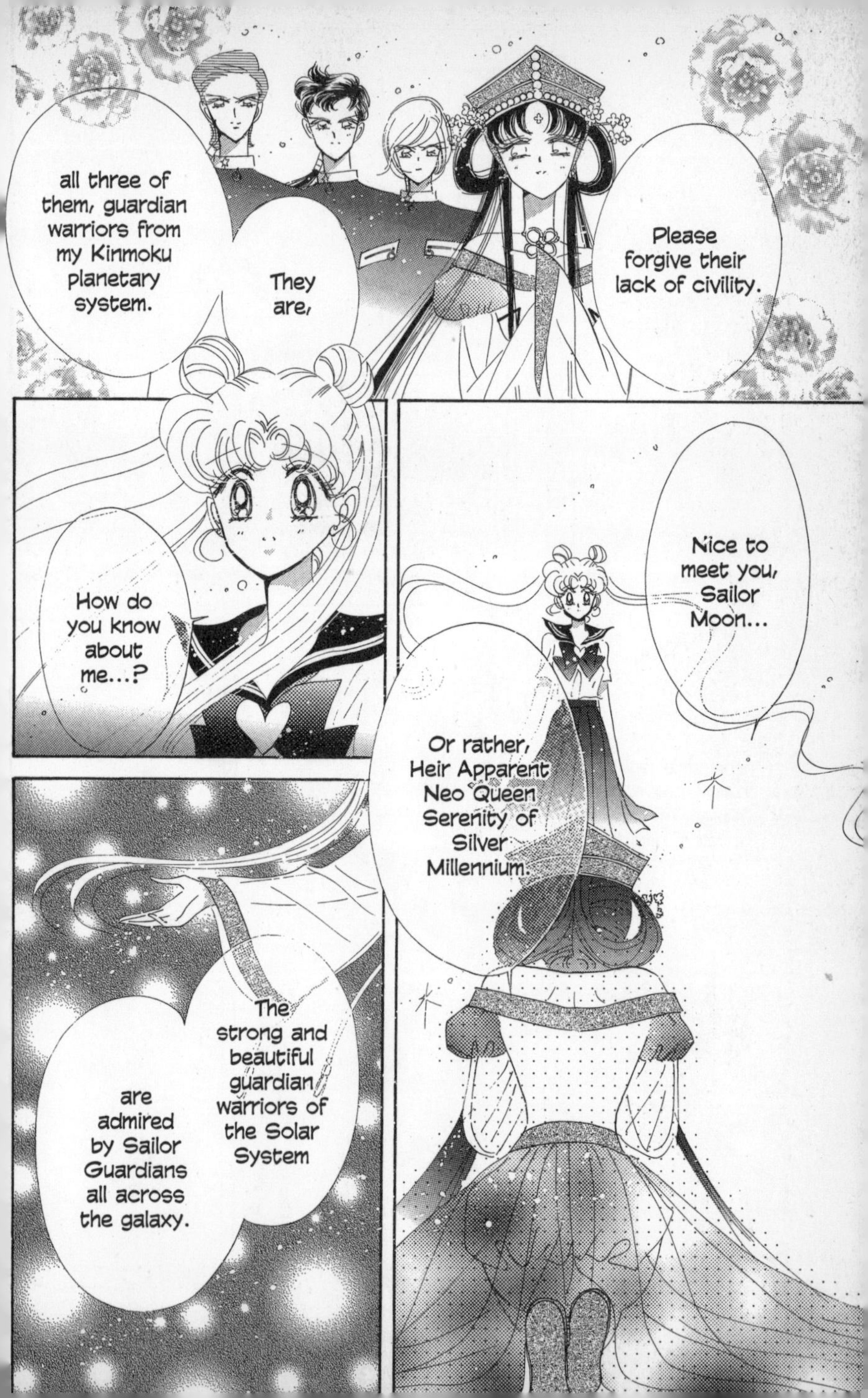
Please forgive their lack of civility.
They are,
all three of them, guardian warriors from my Kinmoku planetary system.
Nice to meet you, Sailor Moon...
Or rather, Heir Apparent Neo Queen Serenity of Silver Millennium.
How do you know about me...?
The strong and beautiful guardian warriors of the Solar System
are admired by Sailor Guardians all across the galaxy.

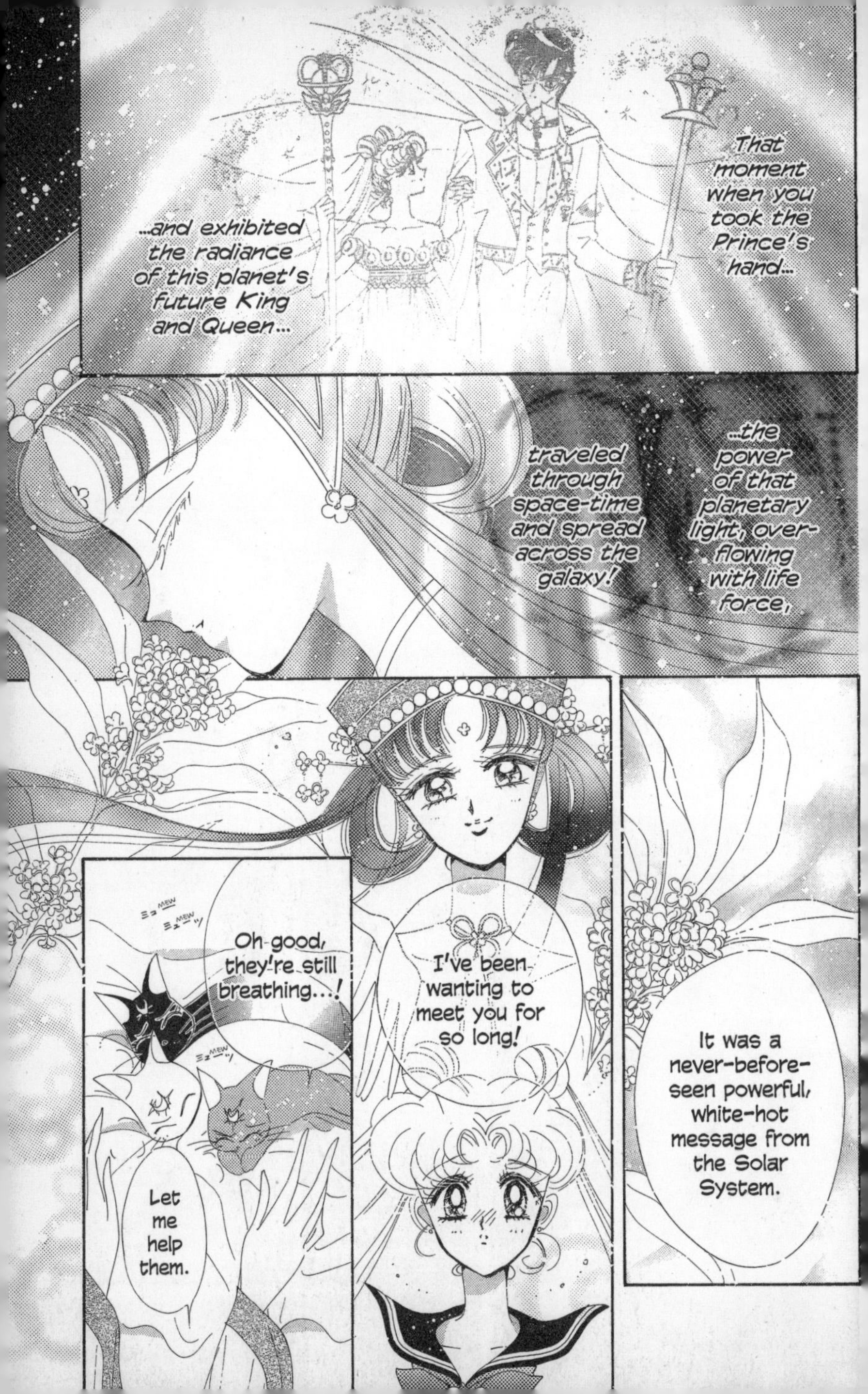

That moment when you took the Prince's hand...
...and exhibited the radiance of this planet's future King and Queen...
...the power of that planetary light, over-flowing with life force,
traveled through space-time and spread across the galaxy!
It was a never-before-seen powerful, white-hot message from the Solar System.
I've been wanting to meet you for so long!
MEW
MEW
Oh good, they're still breathing...!
MEW
Let me help them.

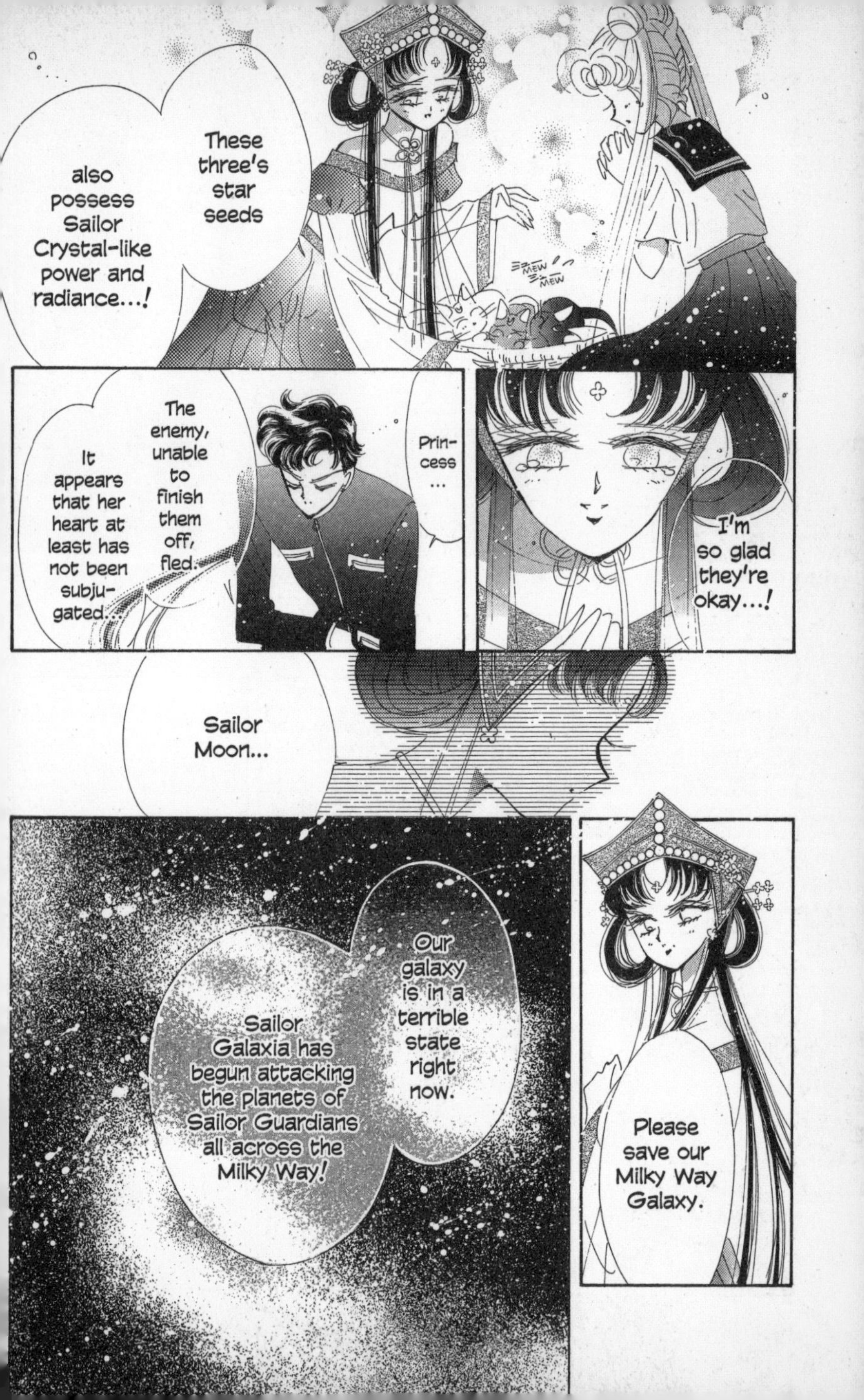
These three's star seeds
also possess Sailor Crystal-like power and radiance...!
MEW MEW
I'm so glad they're okay...!
Prin-cess...
The enemy, unable to finish them off, fled.
It appears that her heart at least has not been subjugated...
Sailor Moon...
Please save our Milky Way Galaxy.
Our galaxy is in a terrible state right now.
Sailor Galaxia has begun attacking the planets of Sailor Guardians all across the Milky Way!

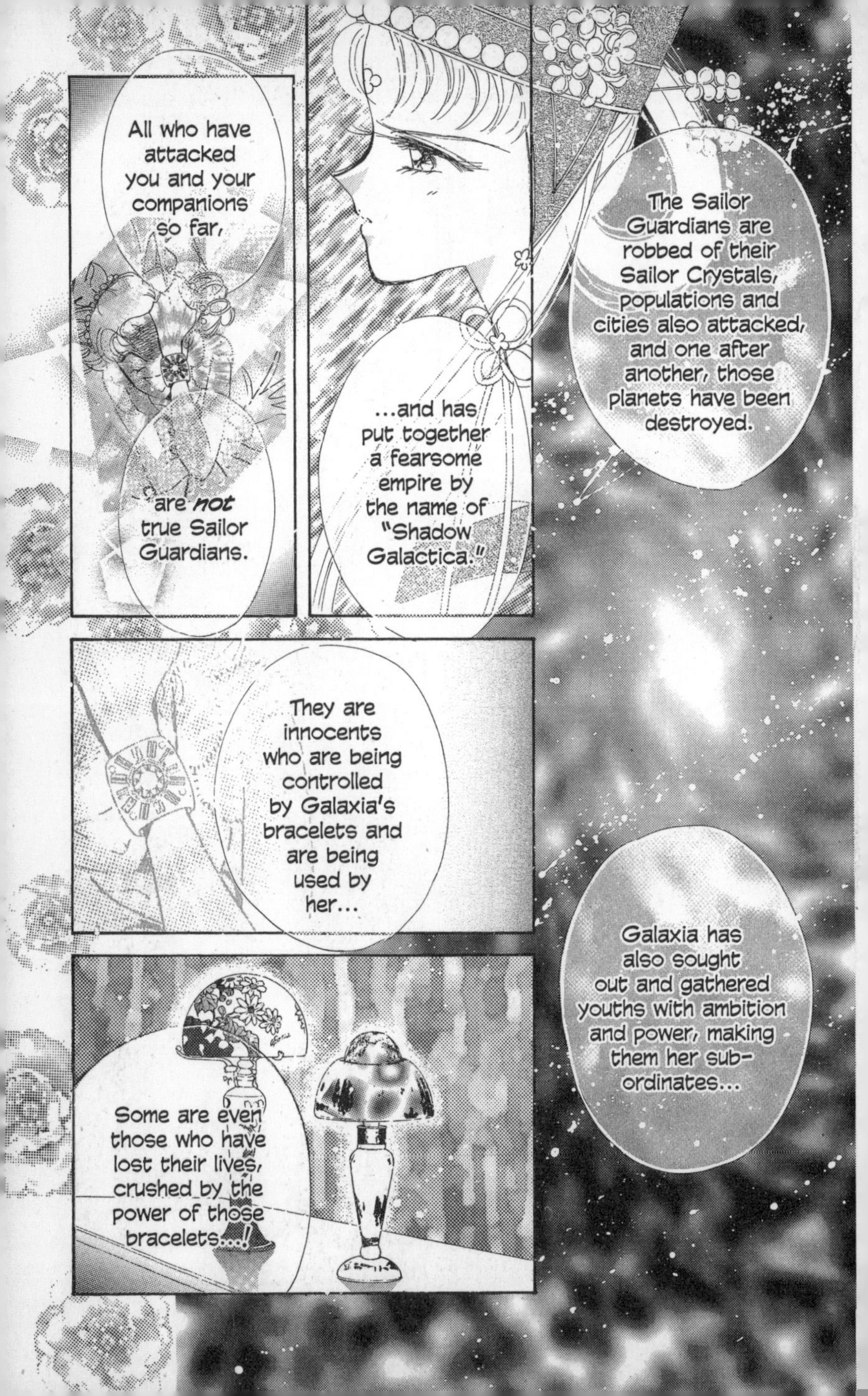
The Sailor Guardians are robbed of their Sailor Crystals, populations and cities also attacked, and one after another, those planets have been destroyed.
Galaxia has also sought out and gathered youths with ambition and power, making them her sub-ordinates...
...and has put together a fearsome empire by the name of "Shadow Galactica."
All who have attacked you and your companions so far,
are *not* true Sailor Guardians.
They are innocents who are being controlled by Galaxia's bracelets and are being used by her...
Some are even those who have lost their lives, crushed by the power of those bracelets...!

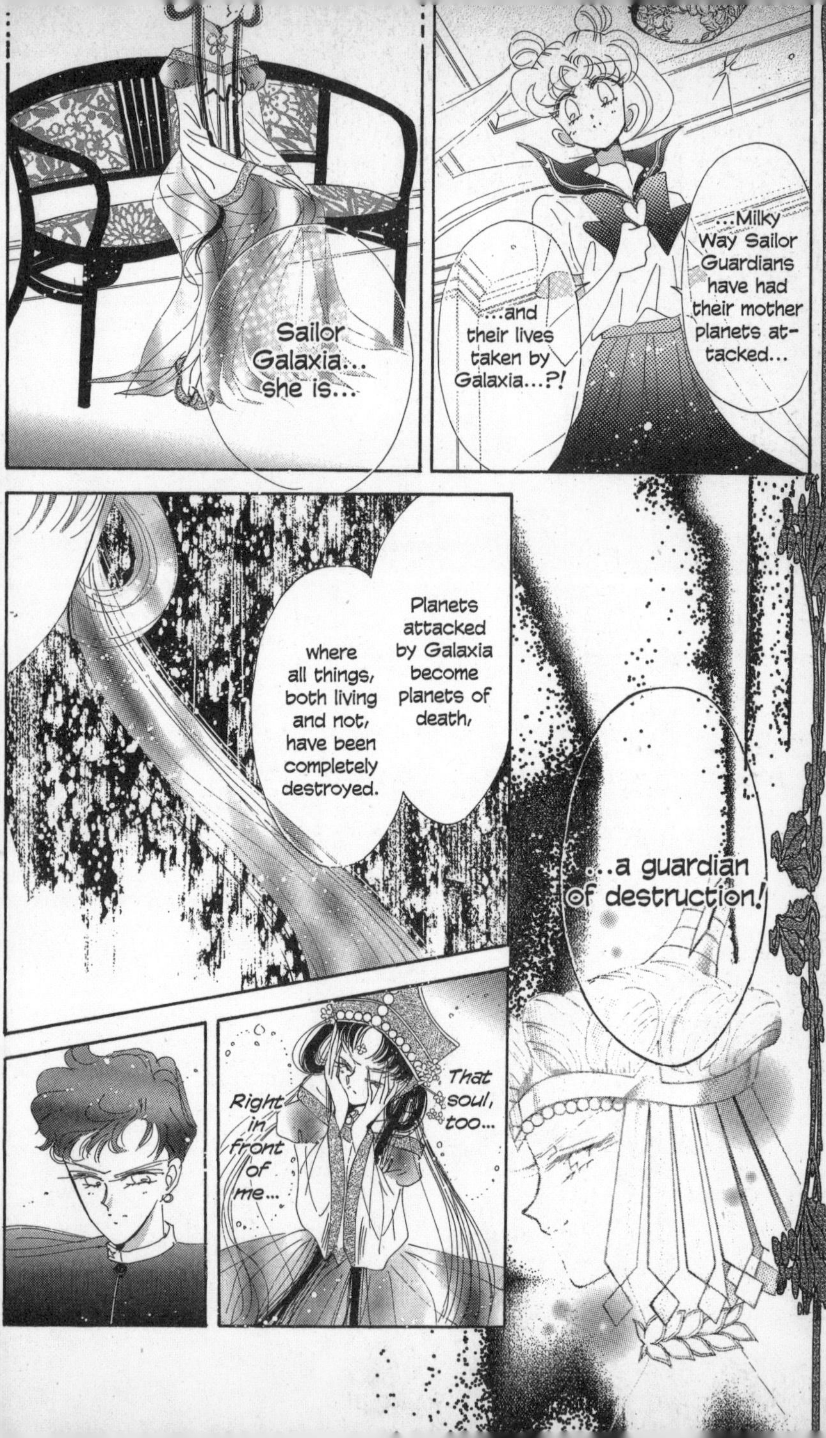
...Milky Way Sailor Guardians have had their mother planets at-tacked...
...and their lives taken by Galaxia...?!
Sailor Galaxia... she is...
...a guardian of destruction!
Planets attacked by Galaxia become planets of death,
where all things, both living and not, have been completely destroyed.
That soul, too...
Right in front of me...

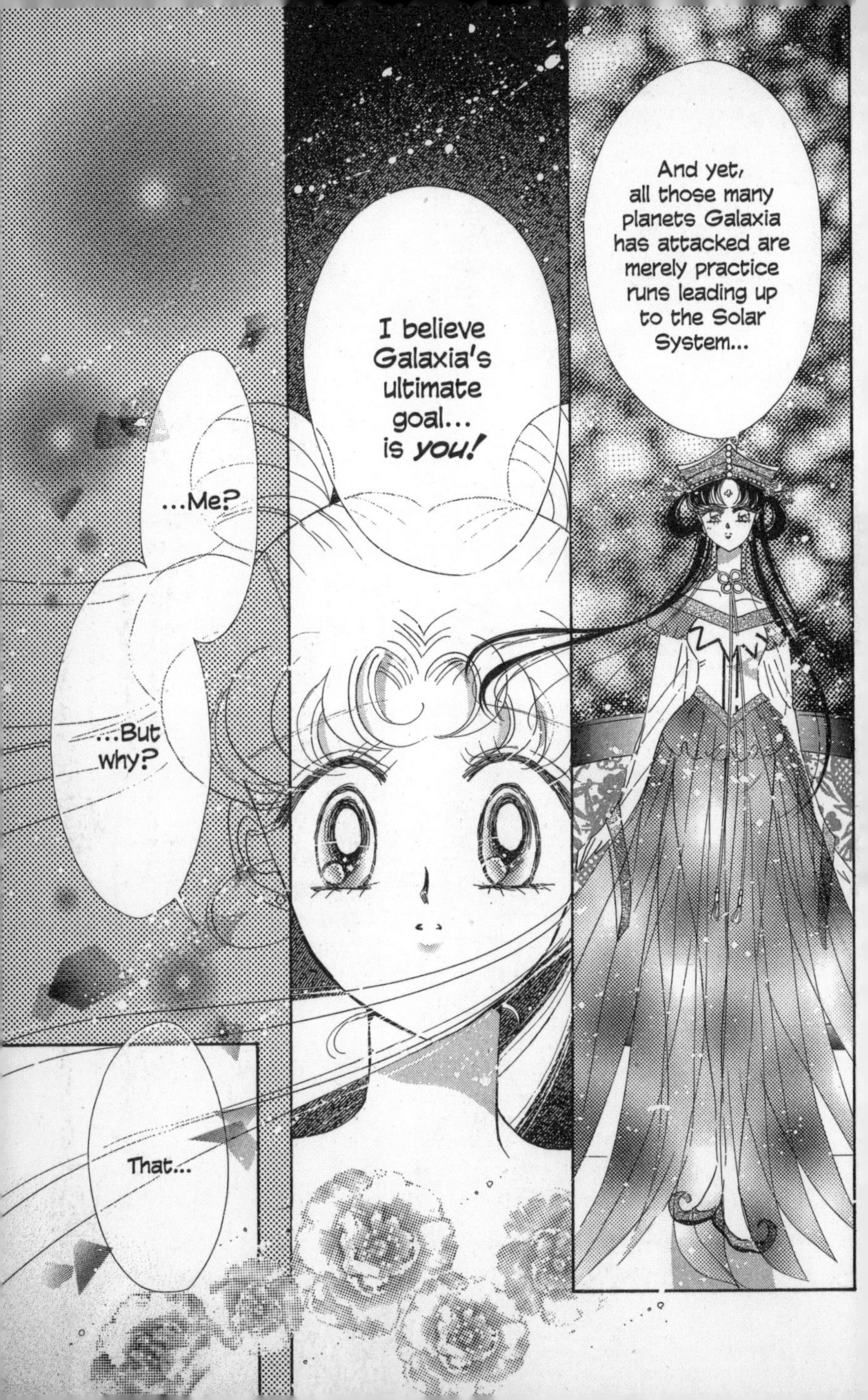
And yet, all those many planets Galaxia has attacked are merely practice runs leading up to the Solar System...
I believe Galaxia's ultimate goal... is *you!*
...Me?
...But why?
That...

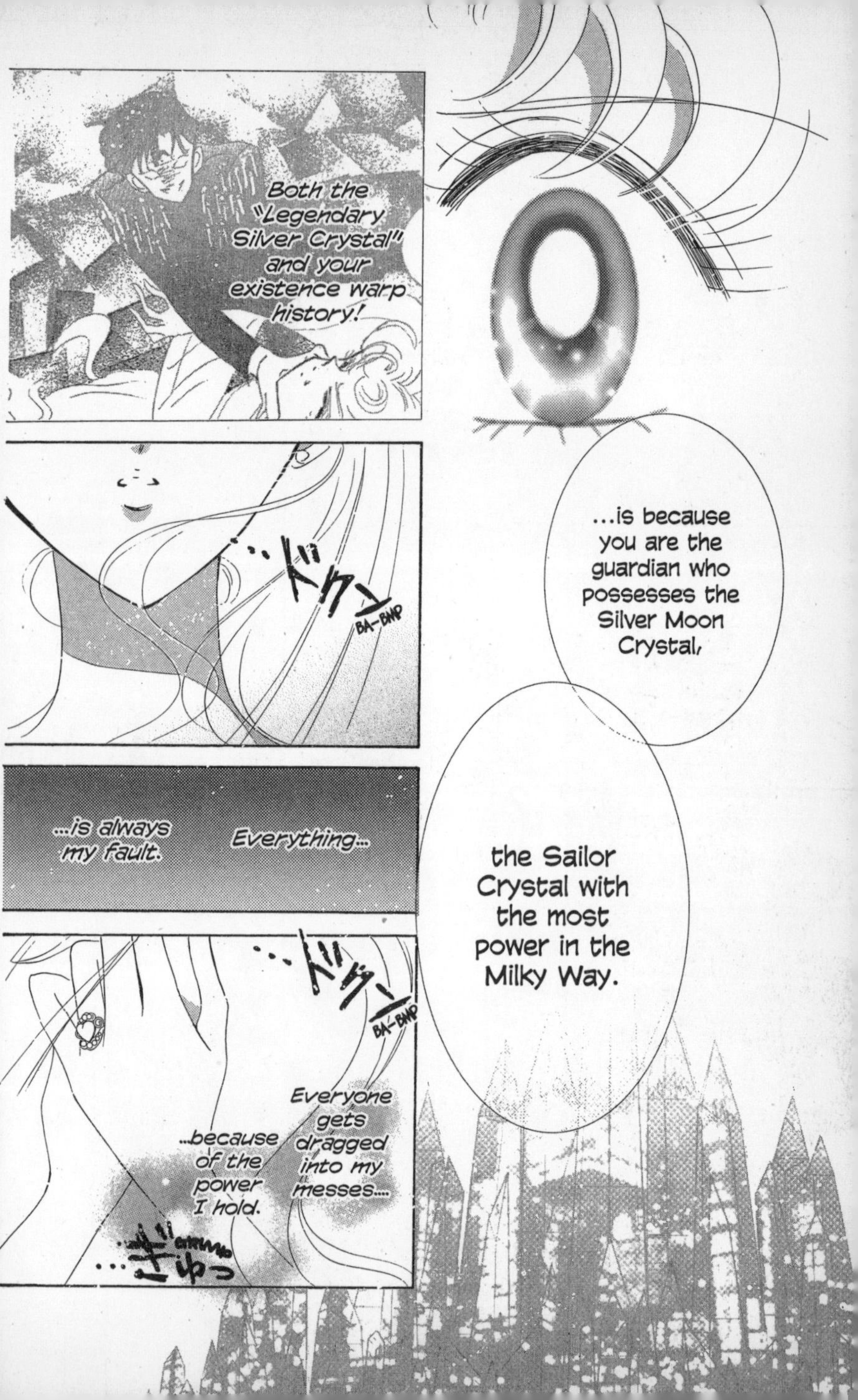
...is because you are the guardian who possesses the Silver Moon Crystal,
the Sailor Crystal with the most power in the Milky Way.
Both the "Legendary Silver Crystal" and your existence warp history!
BA-BMP
Everything...
...is always my fault.
BA-BMP
Everyone gets dragged into my messes....
...because of the power I hold.

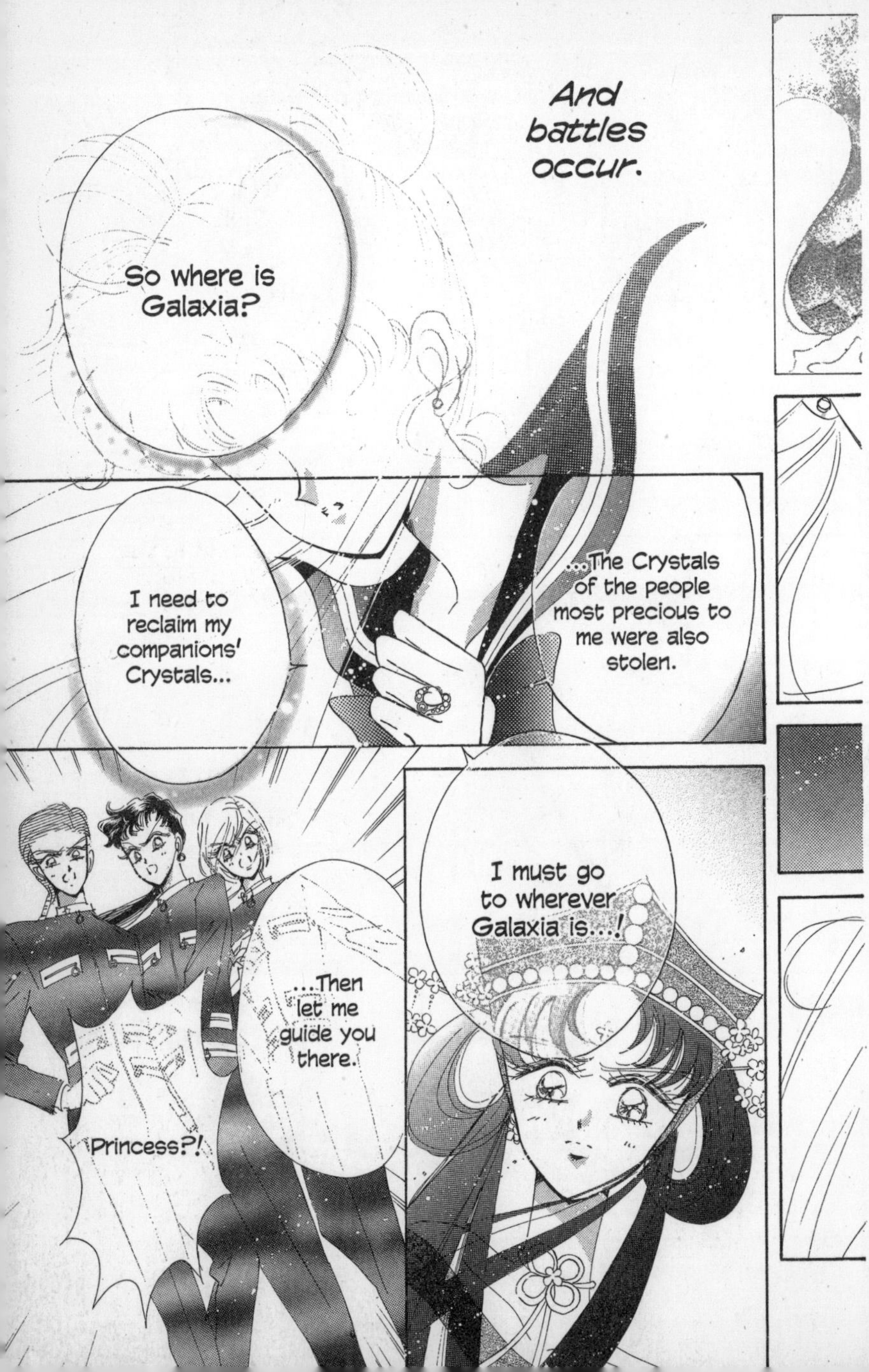
And battles occur.
So where is Galaxia?
...The Crystals of the people most precious to me were also stolen.
I need to reclaim my companions' Crystals...
I must go to wherever Galaxia is...!
...Then let me guide you there.
Princess?!

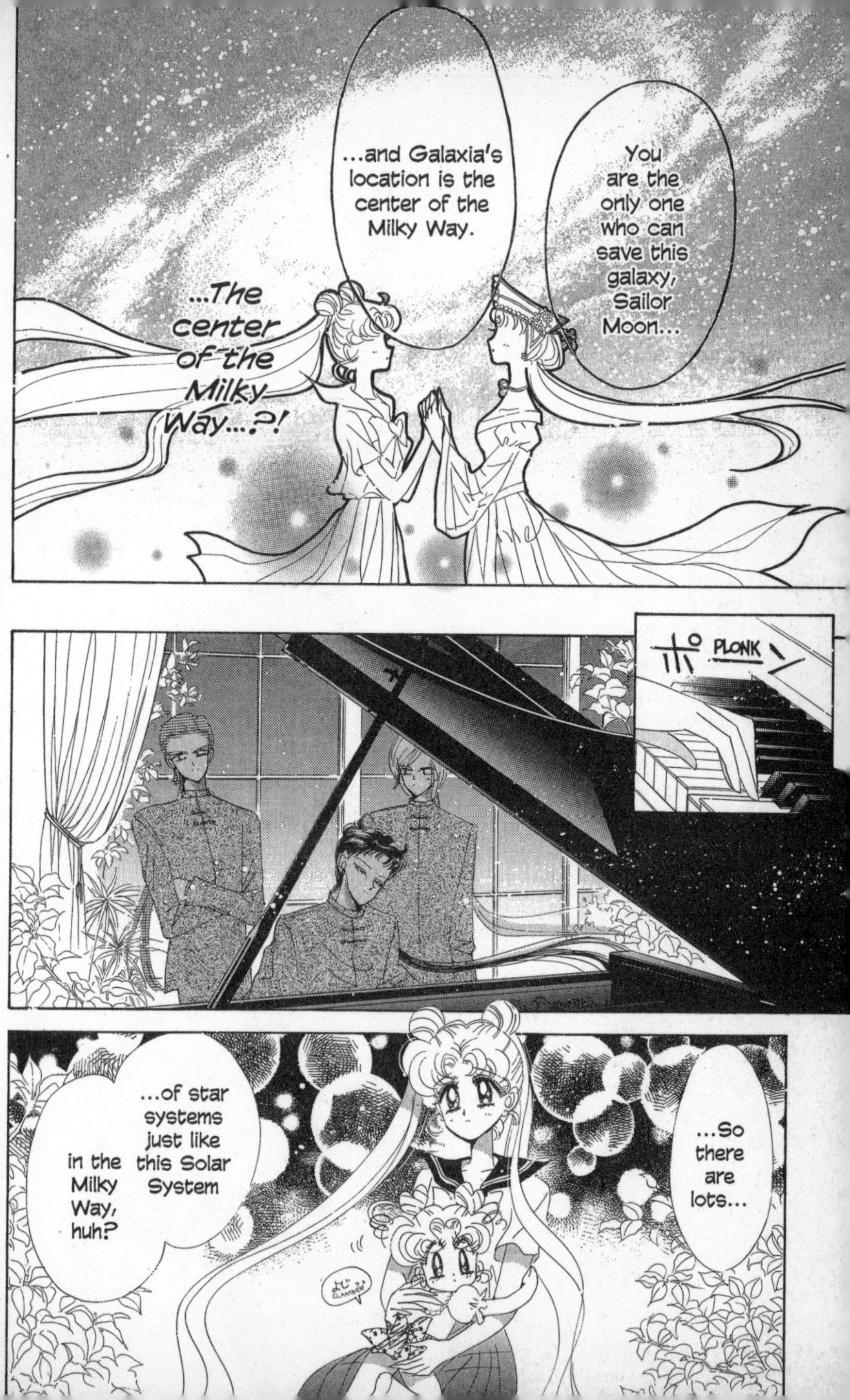
You are the only one who can save this galaxy, Sailor Moon...
...and Galaxia's location is the center of the Milky Way.
...The center of the Milky Way...?!
ポ PLONK
...So there are lots...
...of star systems just like this Solar System
in the Milky Way, huh?
CLAMBER

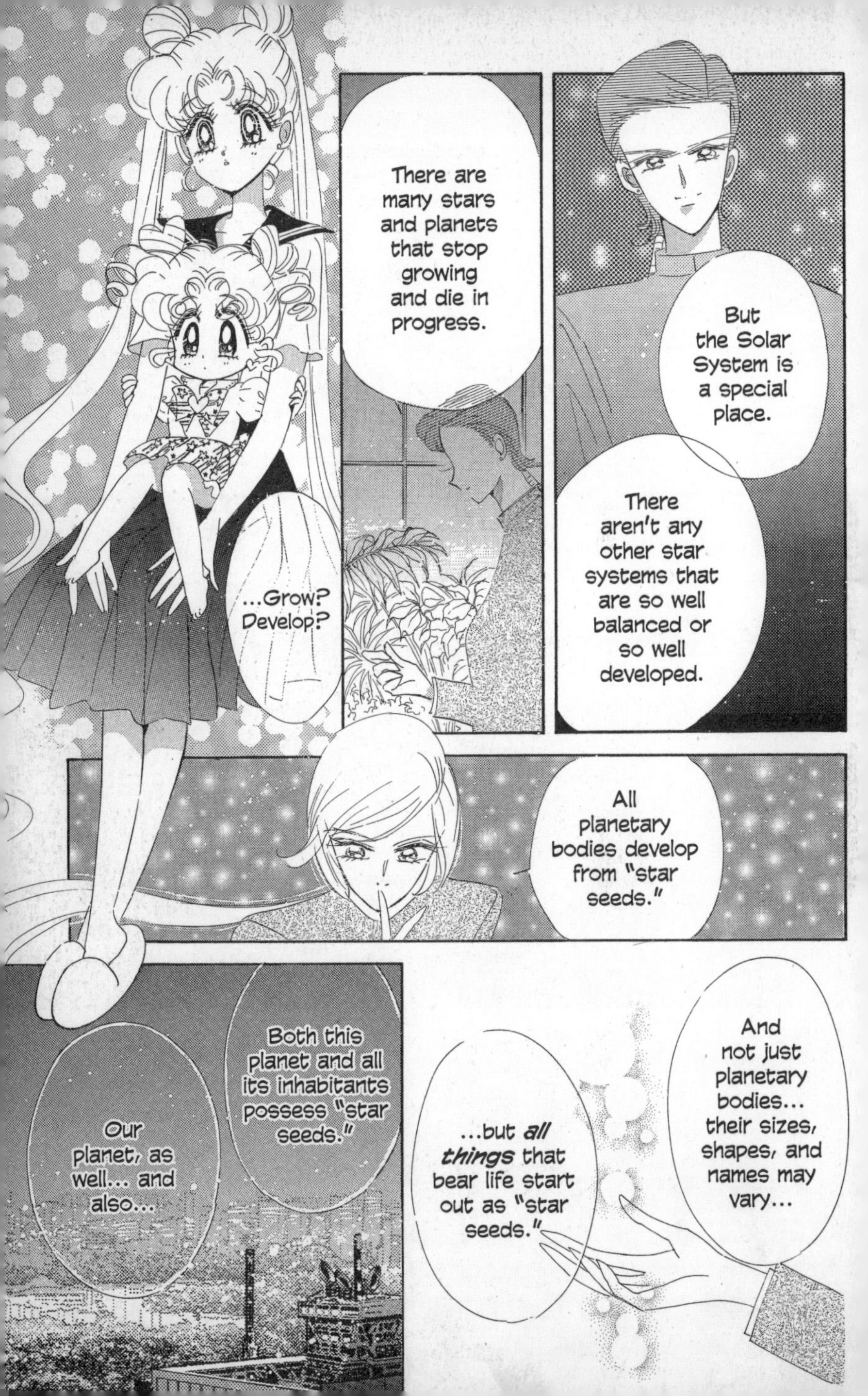
But the Solar System is a special place.
There aren't any other star systems that are so well balanced or so well developed.
There are many stars and planets that stop growing and die in progress.
...Grow? Develop?
All planetary bodies develop from "star seeds."
And not just planetary bodies... their sizes, shapes, and names may vary...
...but *all things* that bear life start out as "star seeds."
Both this planet and all its inhabitants possess "star seeds."
Our planet, as well... and also...

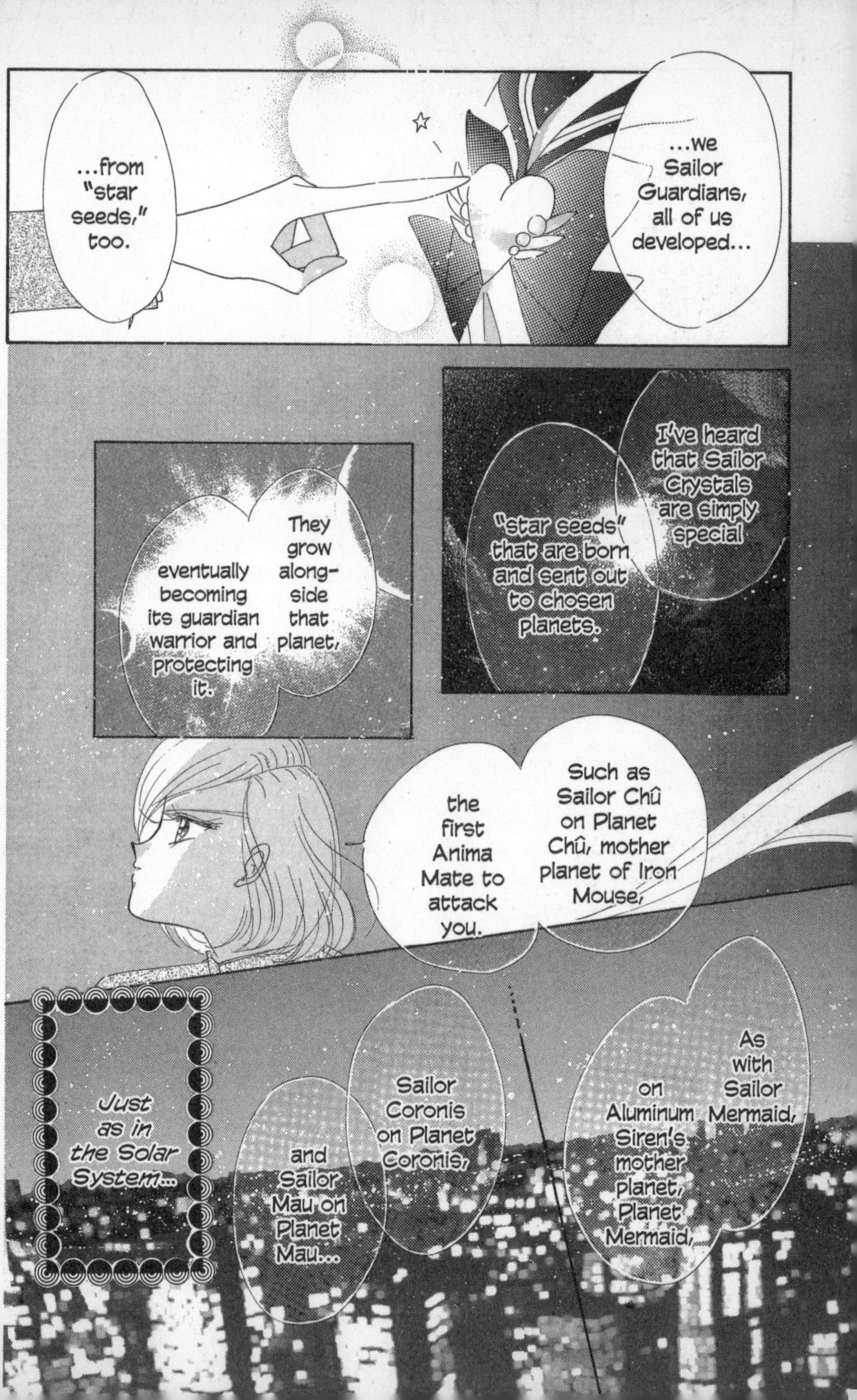
...we Sailor Guardians, all of us developed...
...from "star seeds," too.
I've heard that Sailor Crystals are simply special
"star seeds" that are born and sent out to chosen planets.
They grow alongside that planet,
eventually becoming its guardian warrior and protecting it.
Such as Sailor Chû on Planet Chû, mother planet of Iron Mouse,
the first Anima Mate to attack you.
As with Sailor Mermaid,
on Aluminum Siren's mother planet, Planet Mermaid,
Sailor Coronis on Planet Coronis,
and Sailor Mau on Planet Mau...
Just as in the Solar System...

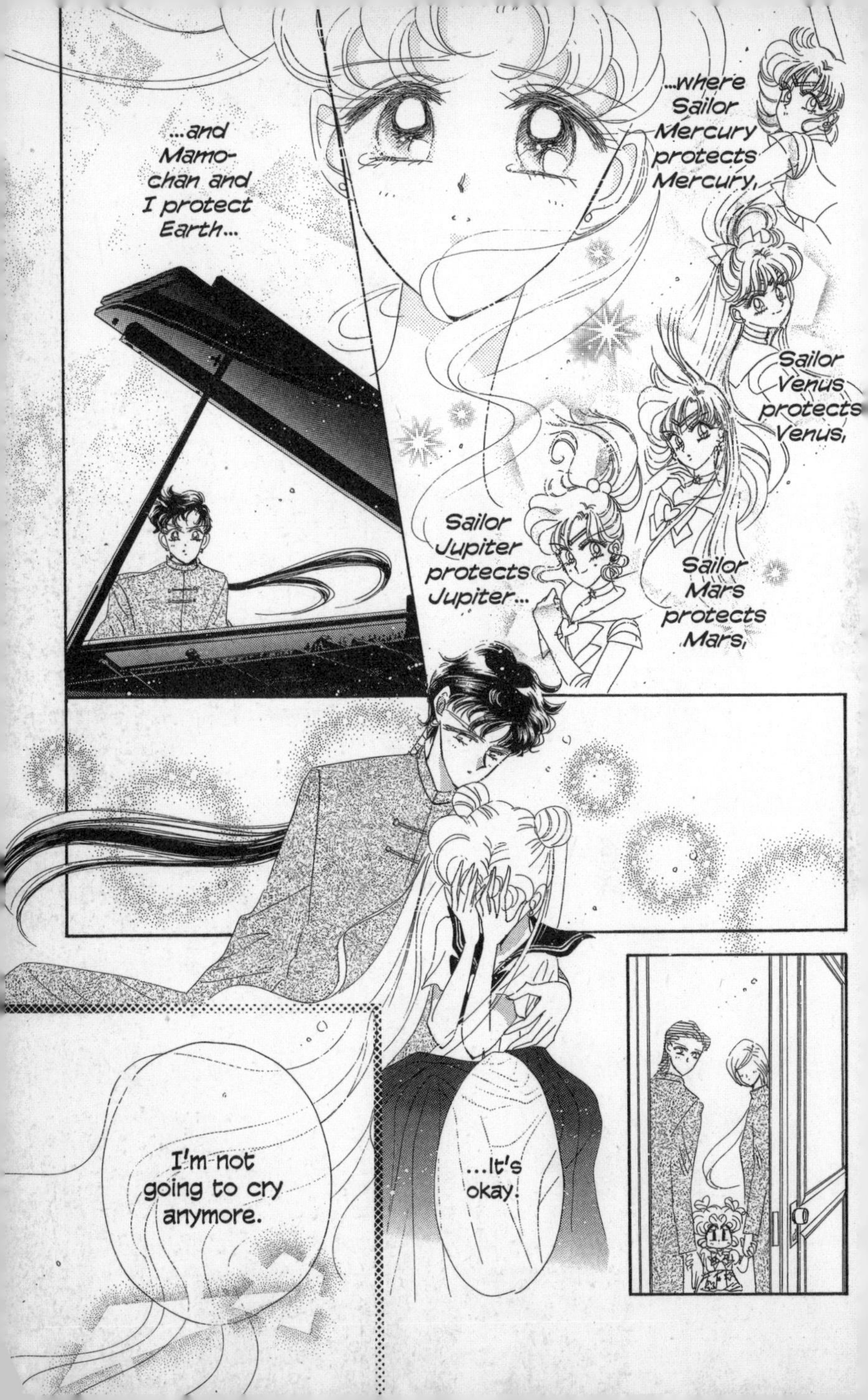
...where Sailor Mercury protects Mercury,
Sailor Venus protects Venus,
Sailor Mars protects Mars,
Sailor Jupiter protects Jupiter...
...and Mamo-chan and I protect Earth...
...It's okay.
I'm not going to cry anymore.

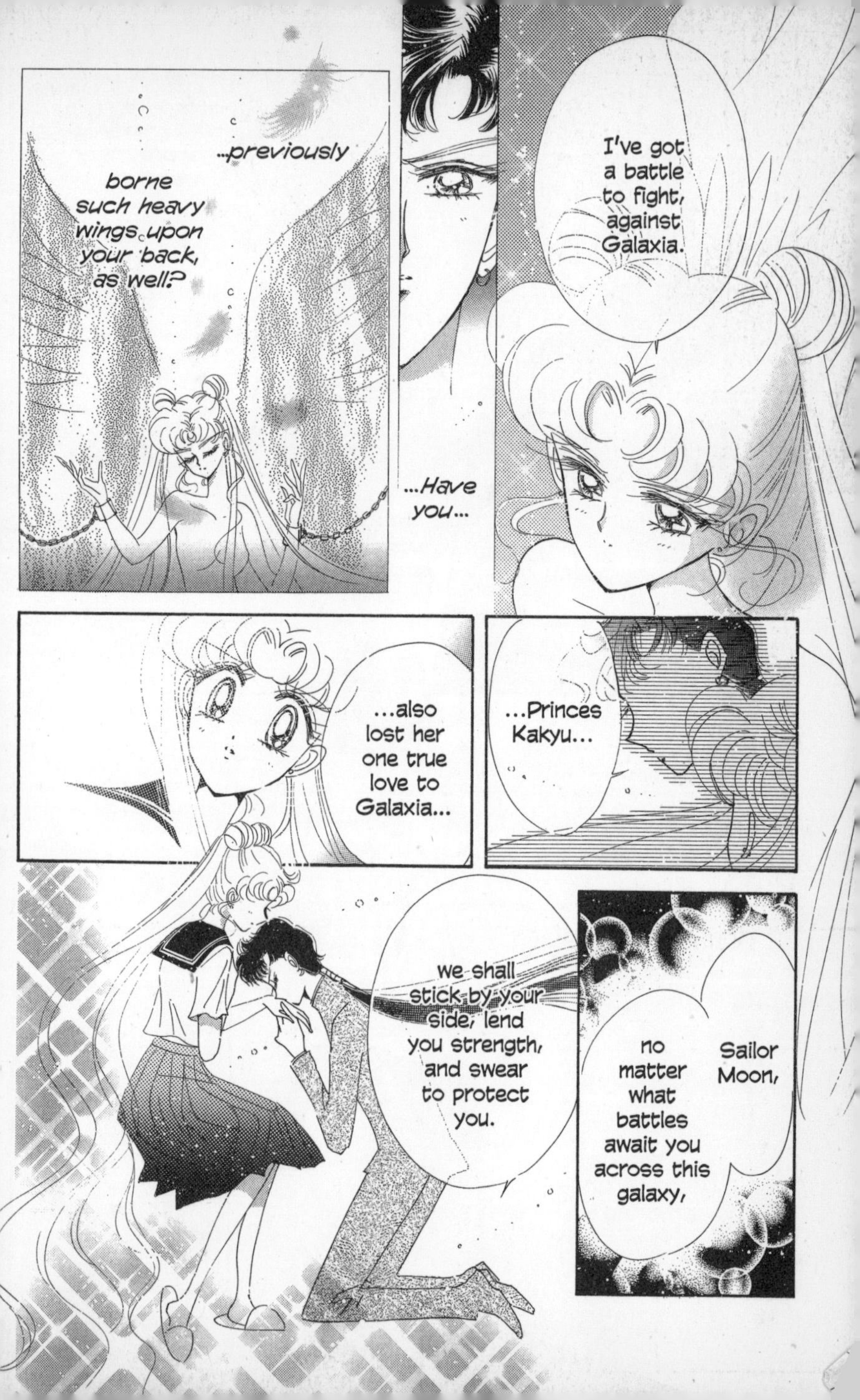
I've got a battle to fight, against Galaxia.
...Have you...
...previously
borne such heavy wings upon your back, as well?
...Princes Kakyu...
...also lost her one true love to Galaxia...
Sailor Moon,
no matter what battles await you across this galaxy,
we shall stick by your side, lend you strength, and swear to protect you.

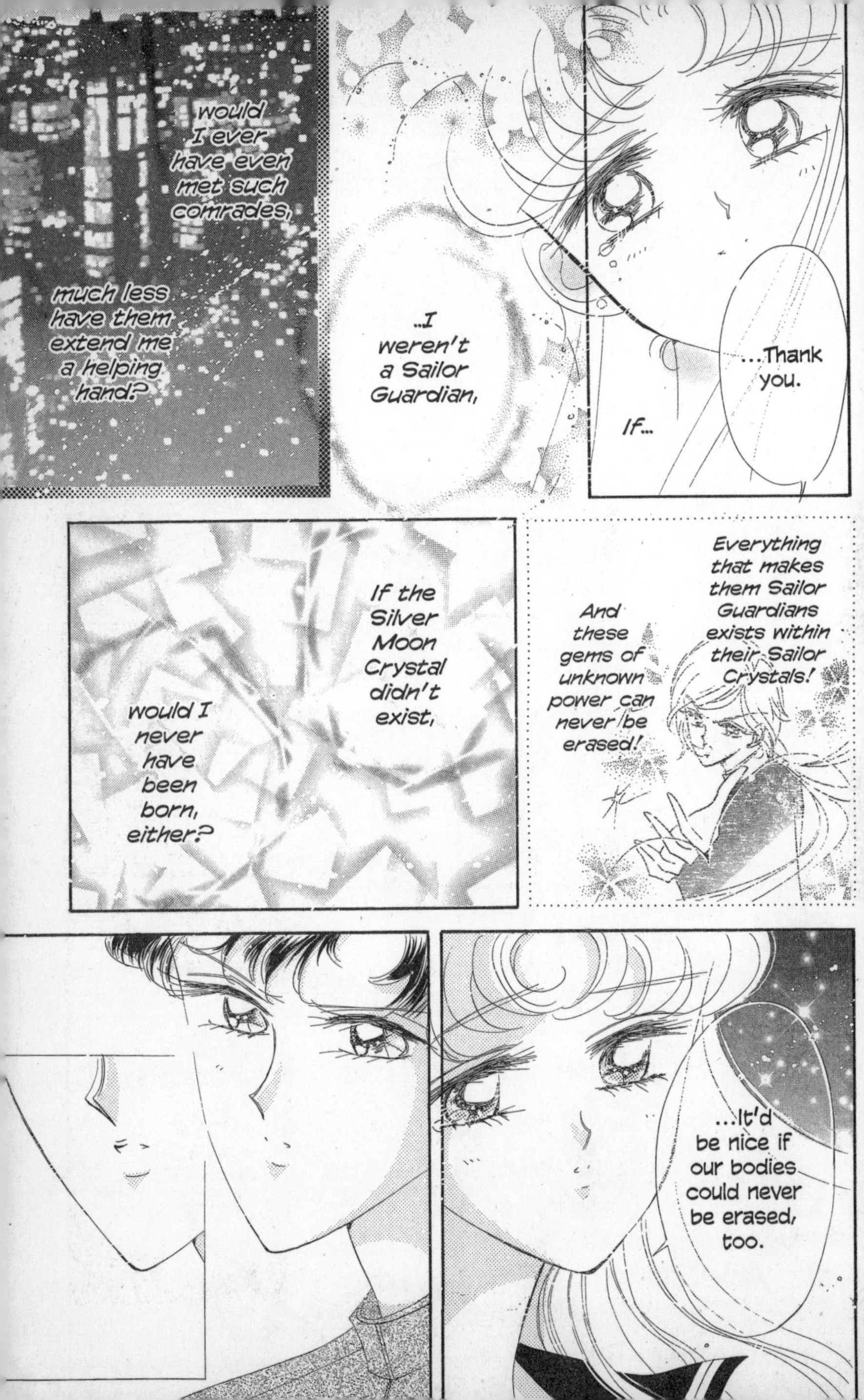
...Thank you.
If...
...I weren't a Sailor Guardian,
would I ever have even met such comrades,
much less have them extend me a helping hand?
Everything that makes them Sailor Guardians exists within their Sailor Crystals!
And these gems of unknown power can never be erased!
If the Silver Moon Crystal didn't exist,
would I never have been born, either?
...It'd be nice if our bodies could never be erased, too.

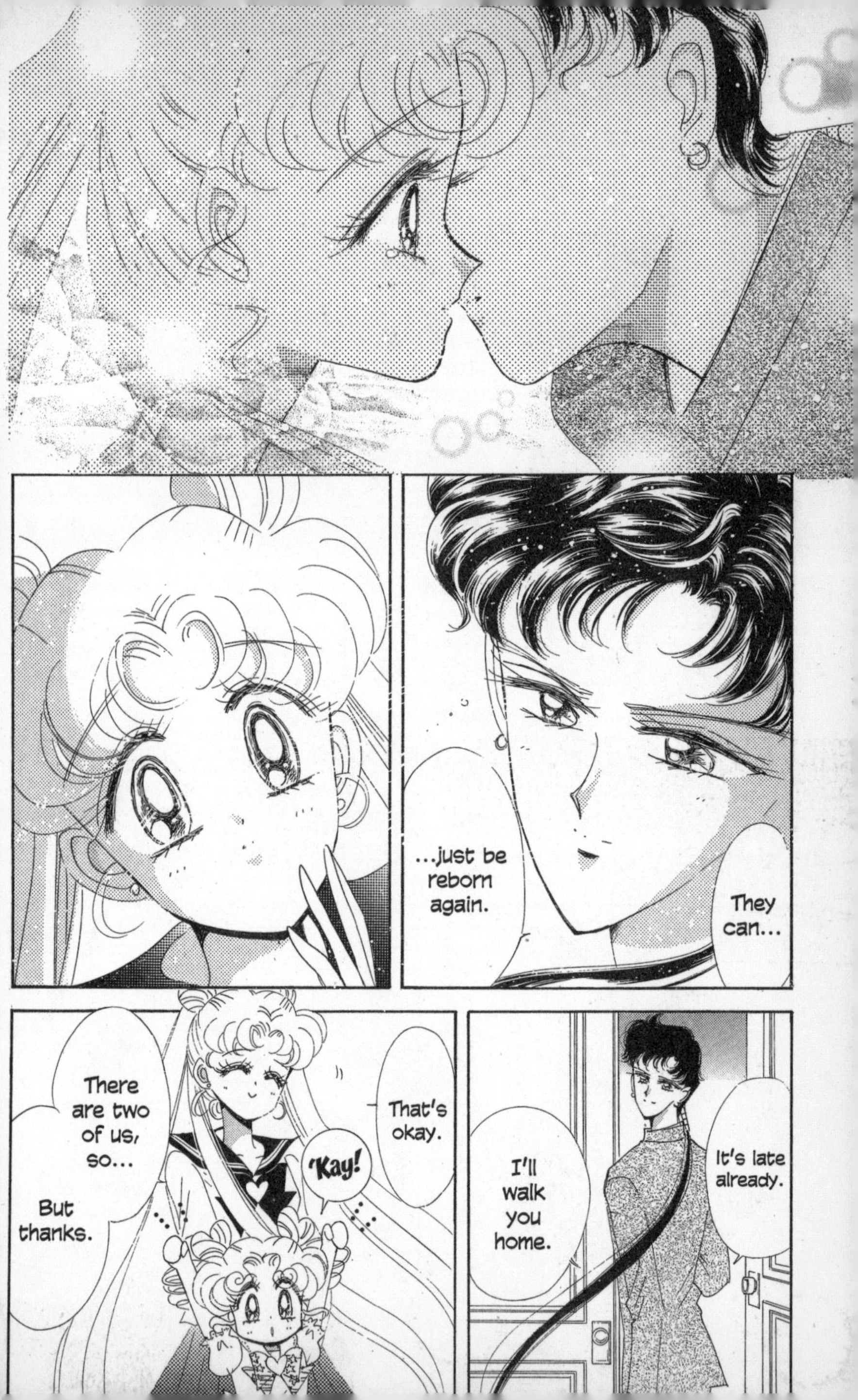
They can...
...just be reborn again.
It's late already.
I'll walk you home.
That's okay.
'Kay!
There are two of us, so...
But thanks.

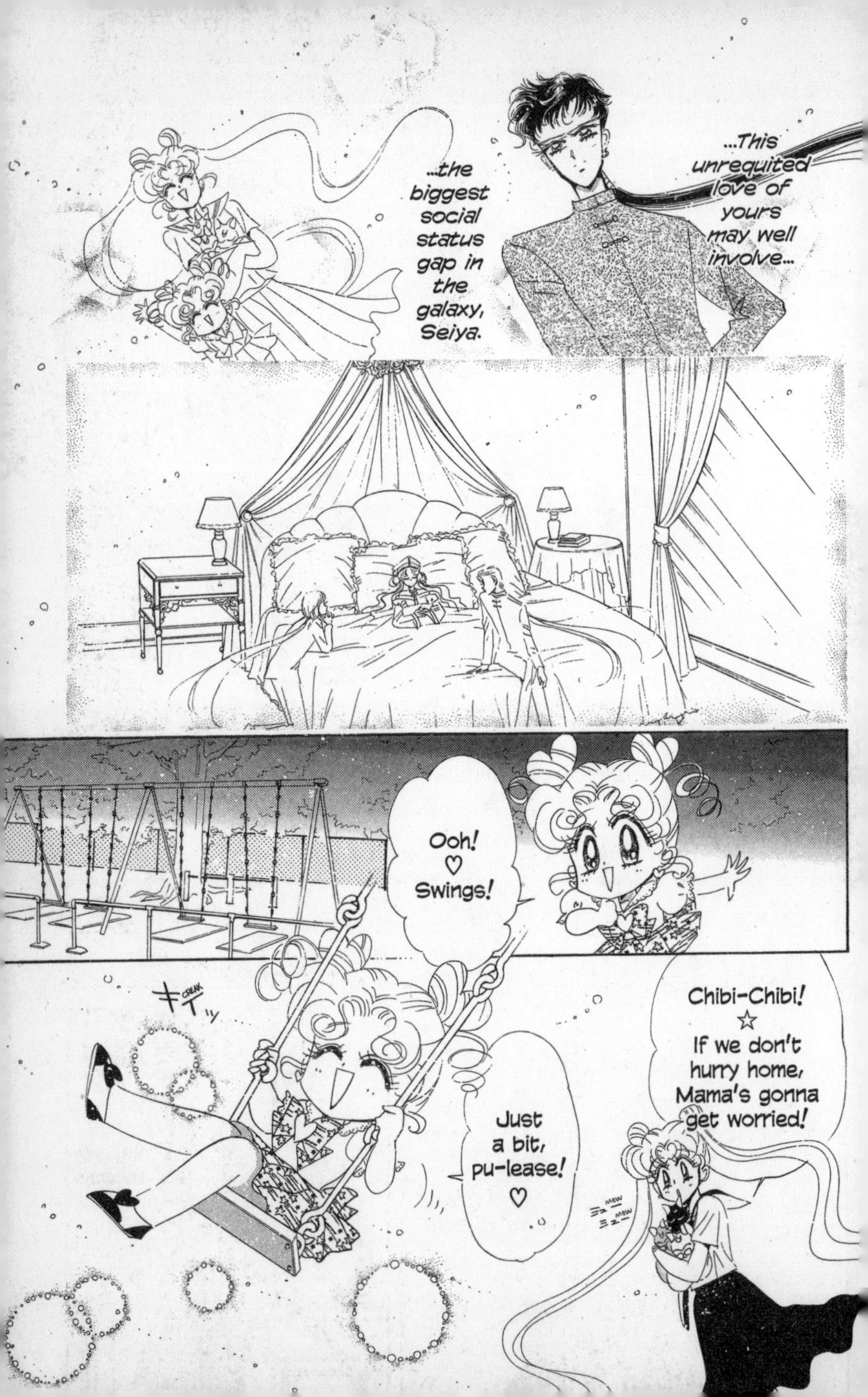
...This unrequited love of yours may well involve...
...the biggest social status gap in the galaxy, Seiya.
Ooh! ♡ Swings!
Chibi-Chibi! ☆ If we don't hurry home, Mama's gonna get worried!
CREAK
Just a bit, pu-lease! ♡
MEW
MEW

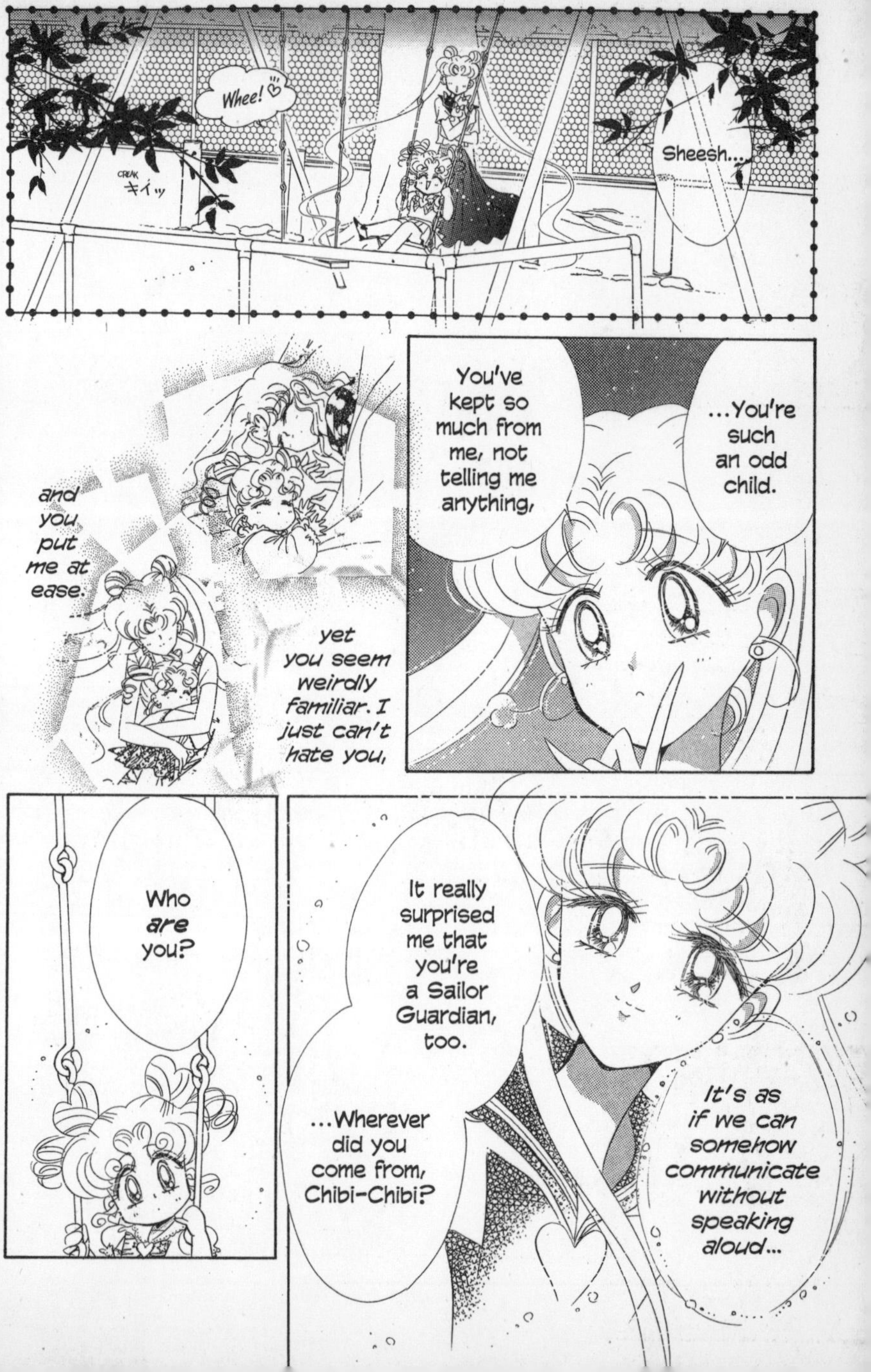
Sheesh...
Whee! ♡
CREAK
キイッ
...You're such an odd child.
You've kept so much from me, not telling me anything,
yet you seem weirdly familiar. I just can't hate you,
and you put me at ease.
It's as if we can somehow communicate without speaking aloud...
It really surprised me that you're a Sailor Guardian, too.
...Wherever did you come from, Chibi-Chibi?
Who are you?

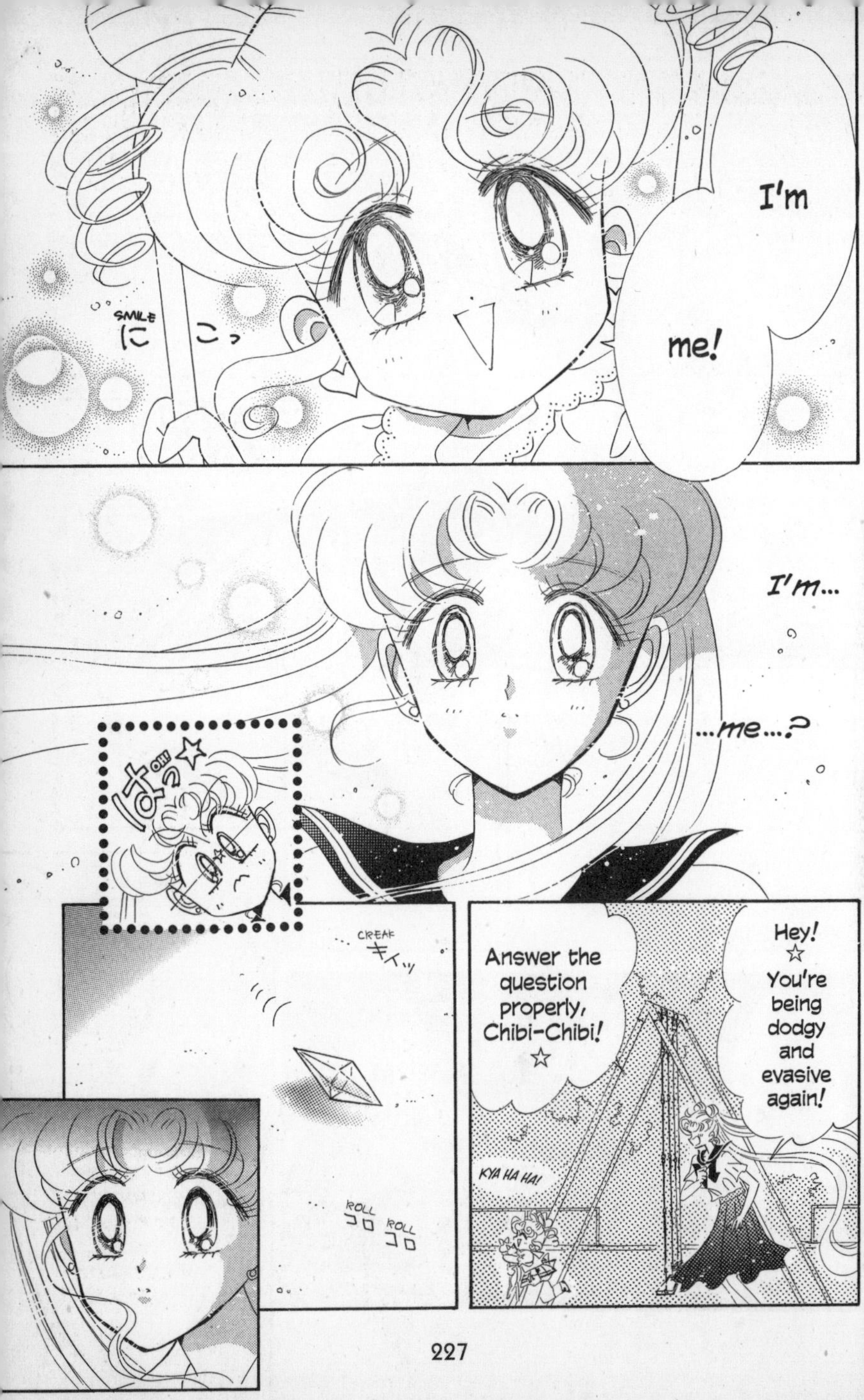
I'm me!
SMILE にこっ
I'm...
...me...?
OH! はっ☆
Hey! ☆ You're being dodgy and evasive again!
Answer the question properly, Chibi-Chibi! ☆
KYA HA HA!
CREAK キィッ
ROLL コロ ROLL コロ

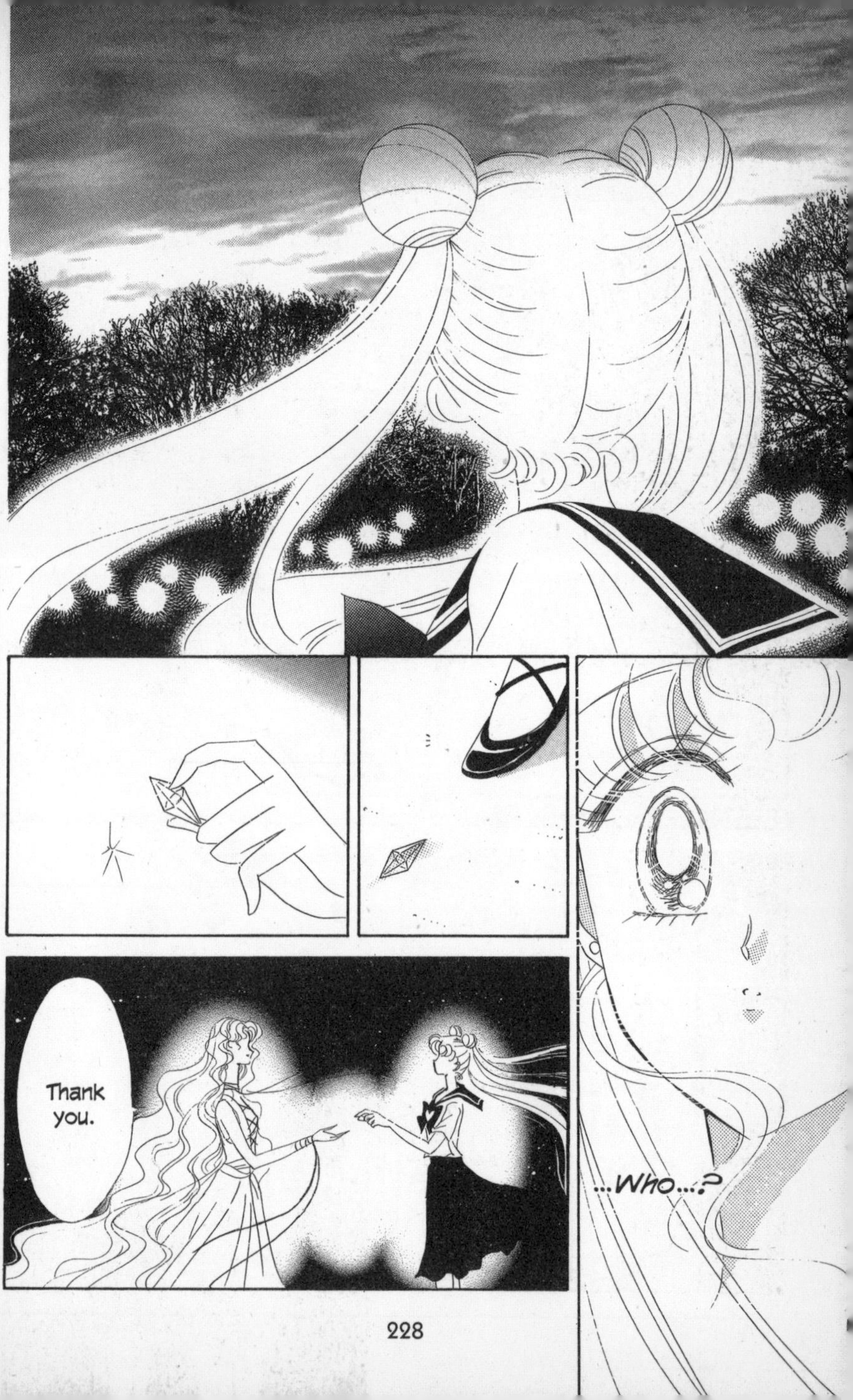
...Who...?
Thank you.

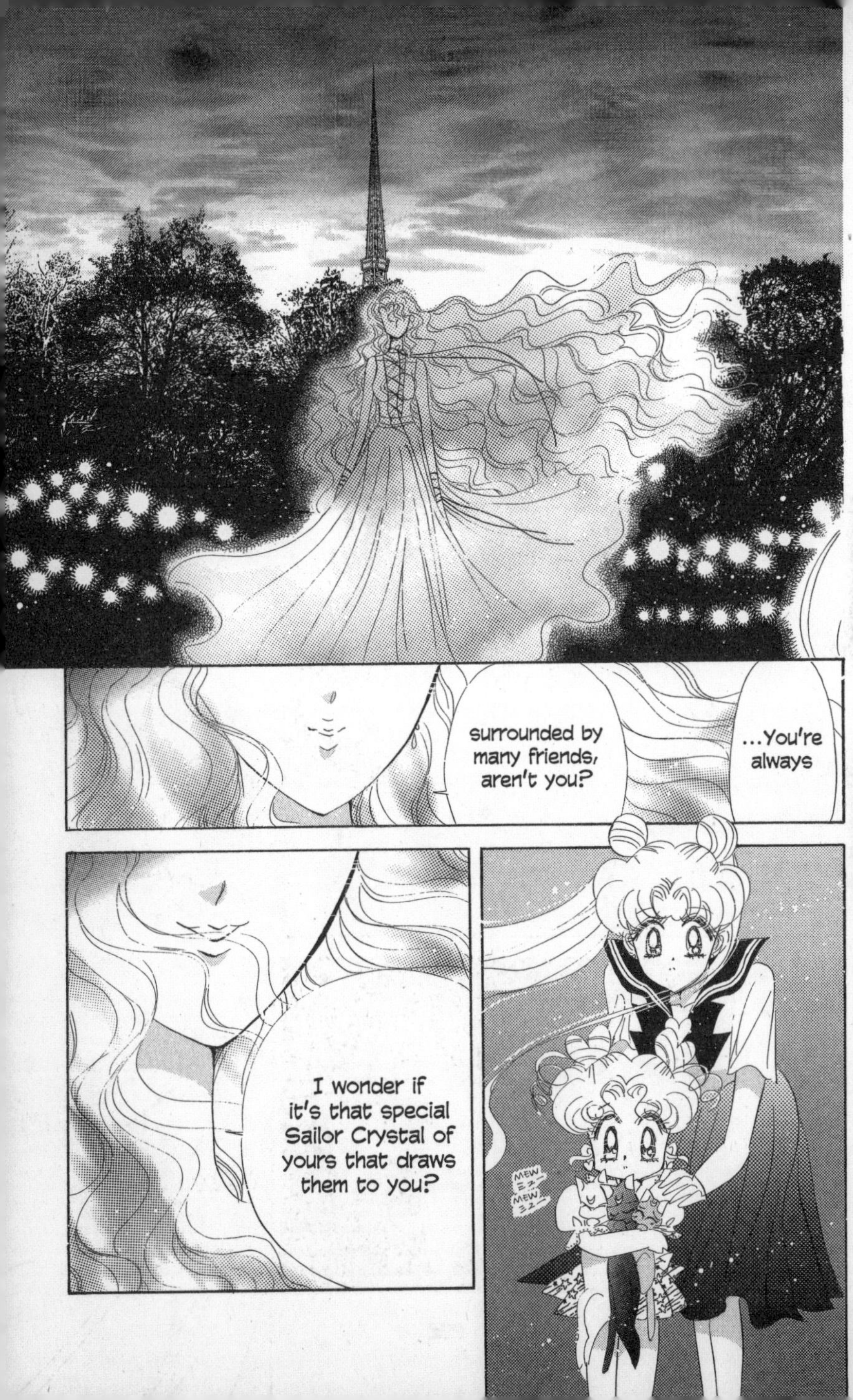
...You're always
surrounded by many friends, aren't you?
MEW
MEW
I wonder if it's that special Sailor Crystal of yours that draws them to you?

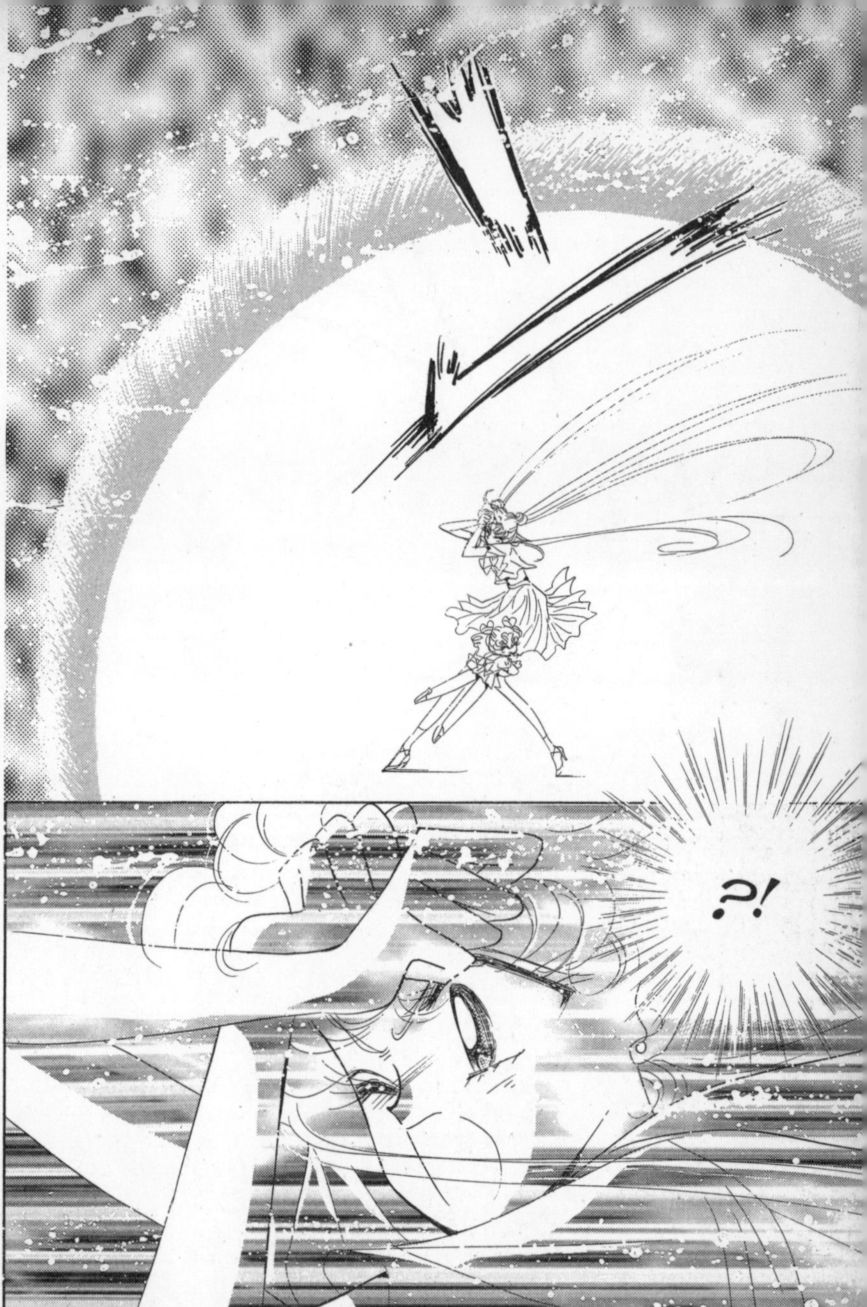
?!

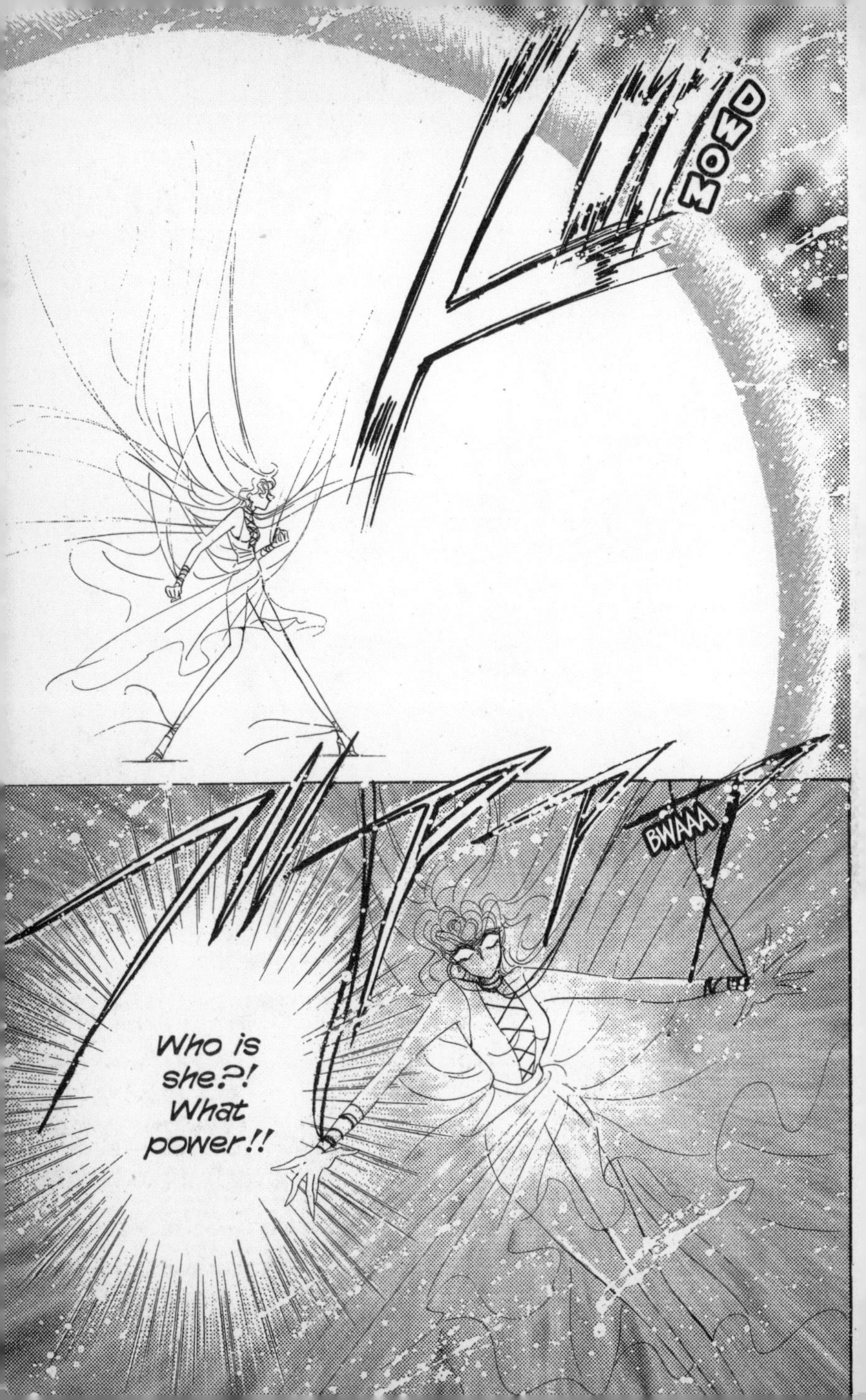
DOWM
BWAAA
Who is she?! What power!!

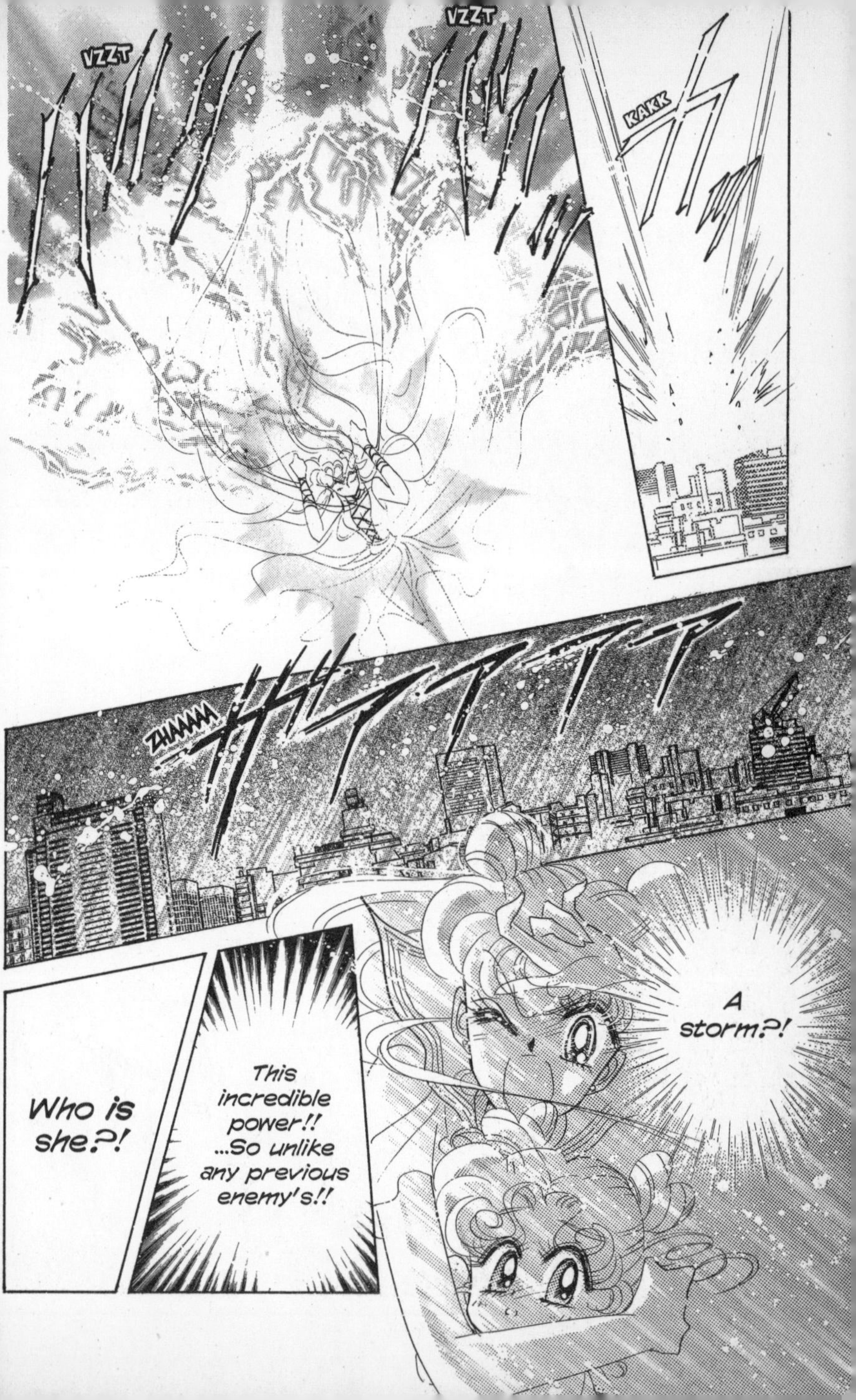
KAKK
VZZT
VZZT
ZHAAAA
A storm?!
This incredible power!! ...So unlike any previous enemy's!!
Who is she?!

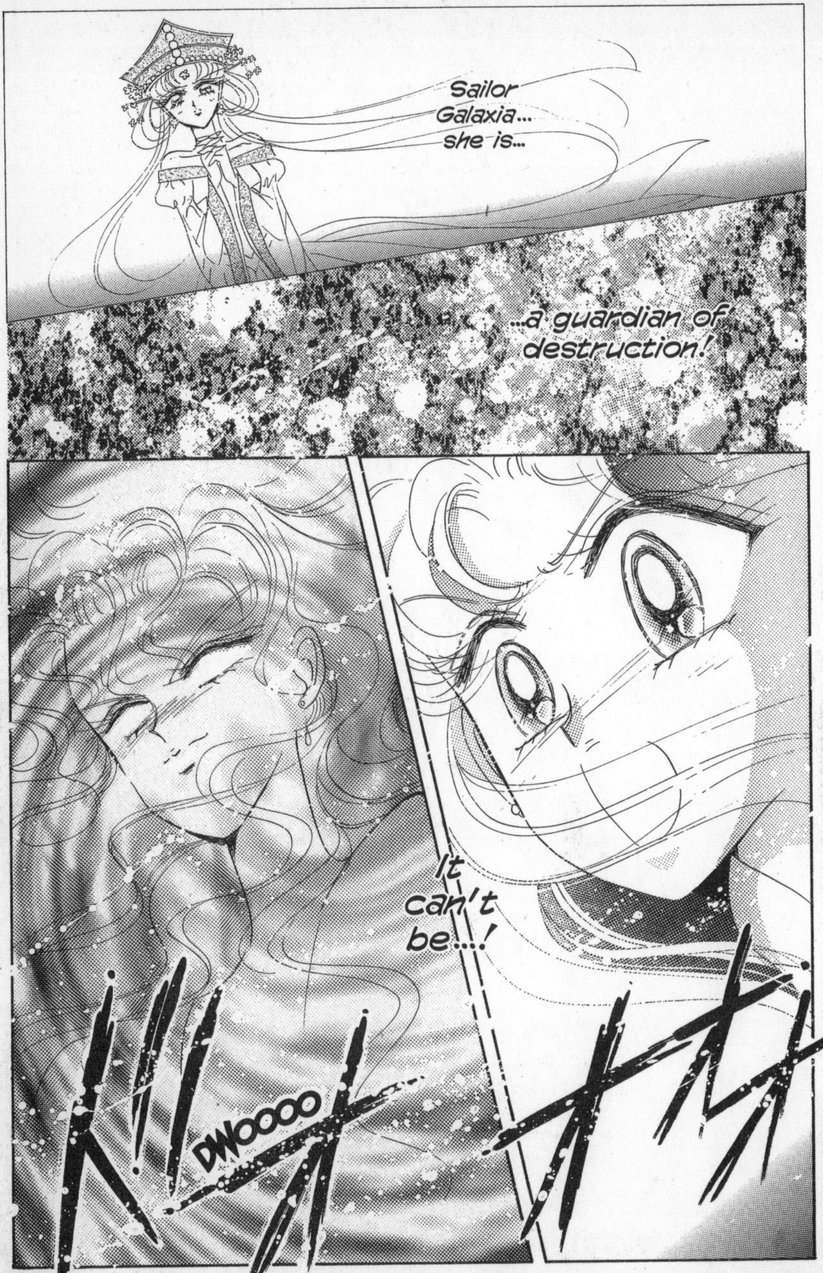
Sailor Galaxia... she is...
...a guardian of destruction!
It can't be...!
DWOOOO

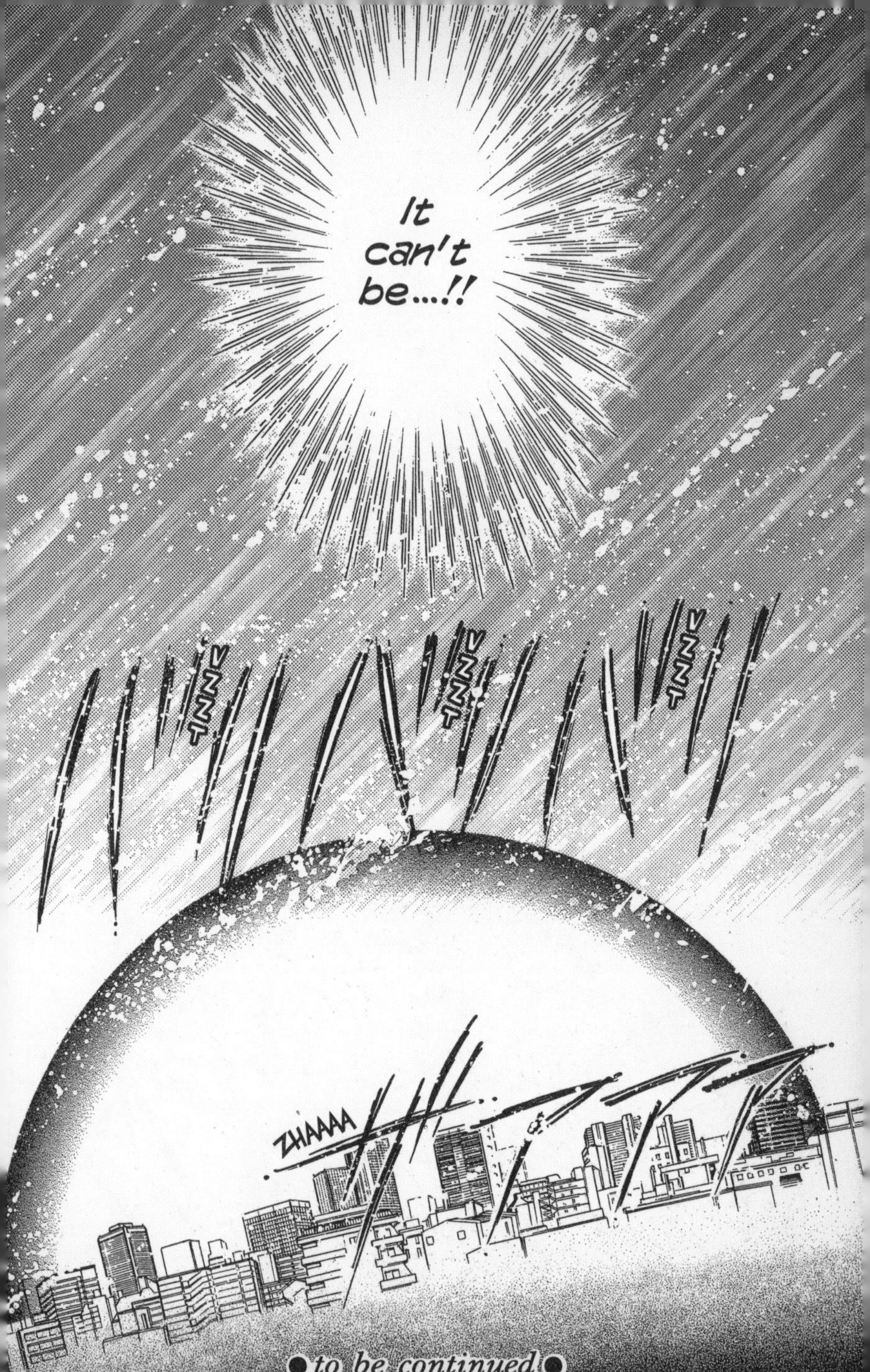
It can't be...!!
VZZT
VZZT
VZZT
ZHAAAA
●to be continued●

Translation Notes

Japanese is a tricky language for most Westerners, and translation is often more art than science. For your edification and reading pleasure, here are notes on some of the places where we could have gone in a different direction with our translation of the work, or where a Japanese cultural reference is used.

Sempai (page 16)
Sempai is a Japanese word that refers to someone senior to oneself in the context of academic year or office hierarchy, with some inference of a mentor-mentee relationship. Its opposite or counter term is *kôhai.*

Shoe cubby (page 16)
There are shoe cubbies located in the entryway of most schools in Japan, where students (and teachers) remove their street shoes and change into slippers or "inside shoes" only worn inside the building. As each slot is assigned a specific individual, these cubbies also often serve a locker-like function with students leaving notes and small gifts for each other.

School festivals (page 16)
School Cultural Festivals are annual events held by most schools from the nursery to university level in Japan, where, especially in middle and high schools, students get to showcase their talents and achievements to their parents and peers, as well as to prospective students and their families.

Sweet osmanthus (pages 34, 209)
Osmanthus fragrans, also known as sweet osmanthus, sweet olive, tea olive, and fragrant olive, is a species of flowering shrubs and small trees mostly native to Asia. Princess Kakyu's headdress is decorated with sweet osmanthus blossoms, and the trace scent of sweet osmanthus is what helps Seiya locate her hiding place. However, two other parts of the author's wordplay are lost in translation. The first is where the third and last kanji used to write the Japanese name for sweet osmanthus, "kinmokusei," is replaced with the kanji that means "star" or "planet" to denote the Princess and Three Lights' home planet, Planet Kinmoku. The second is the name of Kakyu's kingdom, "Tankei," which is written using the kanji for one spelling of "sweet osmanthus" in Chinese.

"Prodigy strikes when least expected" (page 64)
The actual proverb is "calamity (disaster) strikes when least expected," but Minako replaces "calamity" with the word "prodigy," both of which are pronounced *"tensai"* in Japanese but are spelled using different kanji.

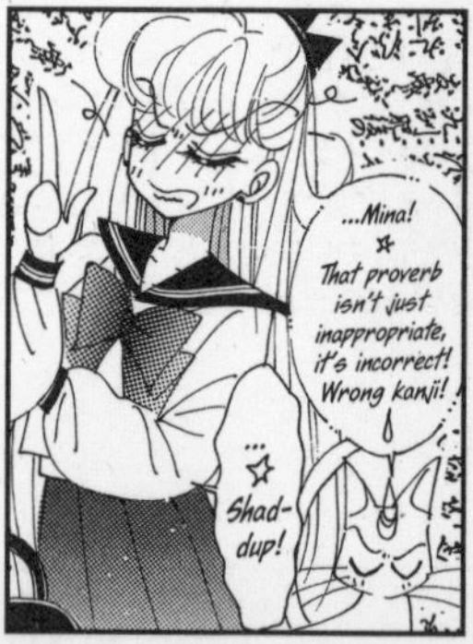
...Mina! ☆ That proverb isn't just inappropriate, it's incorrect! Wrong kanji!
... ☆ Shad-dup!

Three Sizes (BWH) (page 127)

An abbreviation for bust, waist, and hip, and denotes each respective circumference measurement. Originally intended for the purpose of aiding seamstresses make or fit clothes, it is currently also used by (mostly) women in their personal ads or profiles to describe their proportions to the viewer.

Direction of the Horse (page 138)

The seventh sign of the Eastern Zodiac, "Horse" is also used to denote the cardinal direction south. It is also used to denote the month May, and period of day from 11:00 AM to 1:00 PM.

Coronis (page 145)

There are a number of individuals named "Coronis" who appear in Greek mythology, several of which are either associated with or turned into crows, making it a fitting name for the home planet of Phobos, Deimos, and Lead Crow.

Nyanko Suzu (page 170)

"Nyanko" is a fictional girl's name created by adding the common Japanese girl's given name ender "-ko" ("child") to "nyan," the Japanese onomatopoeia for a cat's meow. The wordplay is extended further with the character's last name "Suzu," which with the kanji spelling used in this series means "bell," referring to the little bell Japanese people often put on their cat's collar so that the cat cannot sneak up on them or songbirds, but with a different kanji spelling can also mean "tin," which is Nyanko's Anima Mate chemical element.

Zuka fan (page 172)

"'Zuka" is short for "Takarazuka," which is in turn short for the Takarazuka Musical Revue, the most renowned all-female musical theater troupe in Japan. The actresses are selected, upon graduating from the music academy attached to the Revue, to exclusively play either male or female roles throughout the duration of their professional careers, and the male role ("otokoyaku") top stars tend to be more popular among the mostly female fan base. Usagi's classmate is querying her about that here, in response to Nyanko's comment about "girls dressing up as and acting like boys," though Nyanko is actually referring to Three Lights. In a way, this is likely also a tongue-in-cheek reference to the Takarazuka Revue's influence on Sailor Moon creator Ms. Naoko Takeuchi herself, who has said in an interview that the characters Haruka and Michiru were inspired by Takarazuka actresses. [Just as an aside, the Takarazuka Revue has also influenced many other anime and manga, most notably "Princess Knight" by Osamu Tezuka, who grew up in Takarazuka City watching many performances.]

Mau/Mautian (page 199)

The Egyptian Mau is a breed of shorthaired domesticated cat, so "Mau" is a fitting name for the home planet of Luna, Artemis, Diana, and Nyanko.

"-chama" (page 202)

"-chama" is baby speech for the honorific "-sama," used to indicate the young age of the person (or in this case, animal) speaking.

Sailor/Planet Chû (page 220)

"Chû" is the Japanese onomatopoeia for a mouse's squeaking, making it a fitting name for Iron Mouse's home planet.

Preview of *Sailor Moon 12*

We're pleased to present you with a preview from
Pretty Guardian Sailor Moon 12. Please check our
website (www.kodanshacomics.com) to see when
this volume will be available.

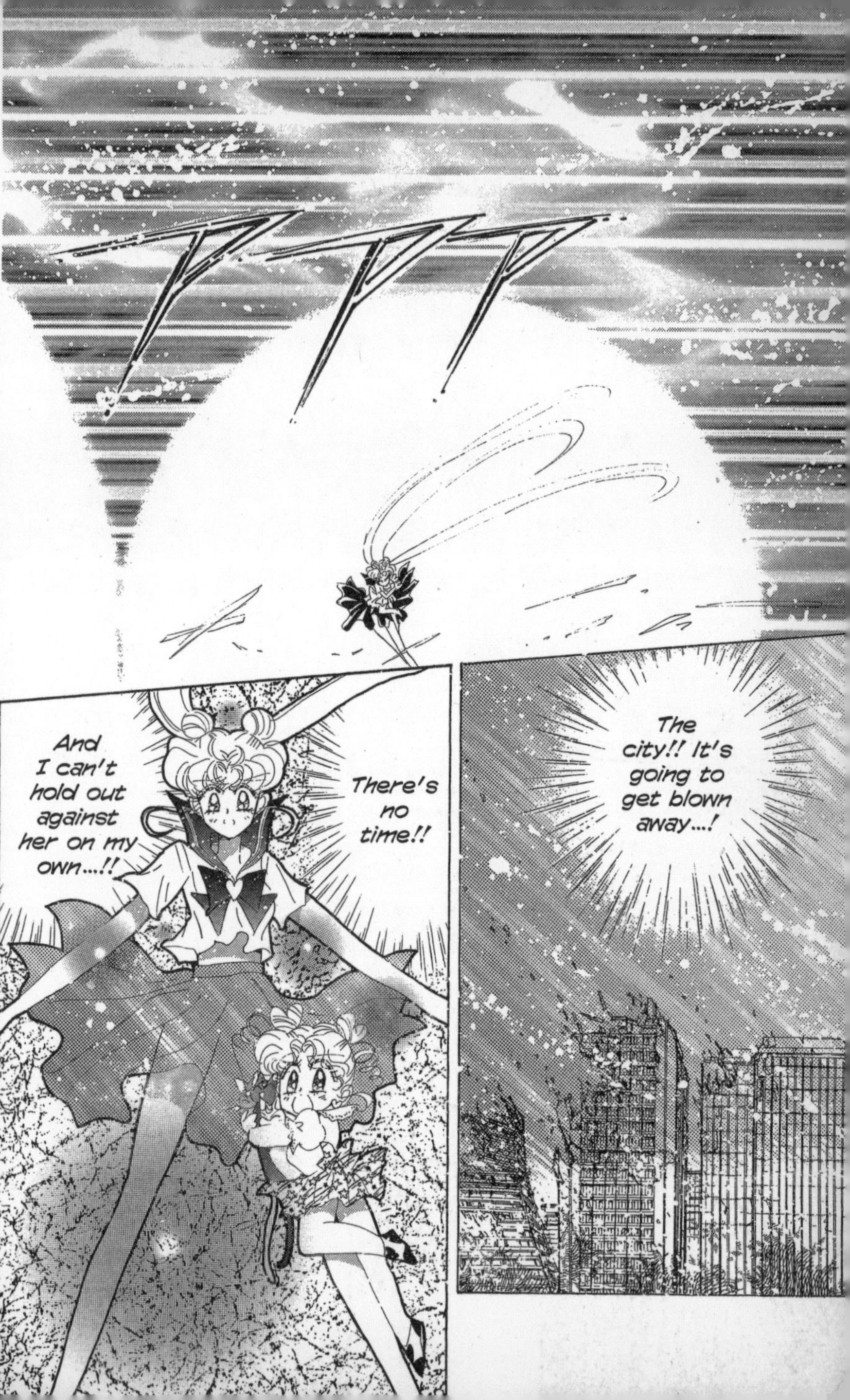
The city!! It's going to get blown away...!
There's no time!!
And I can't hold out against her on my own...!!

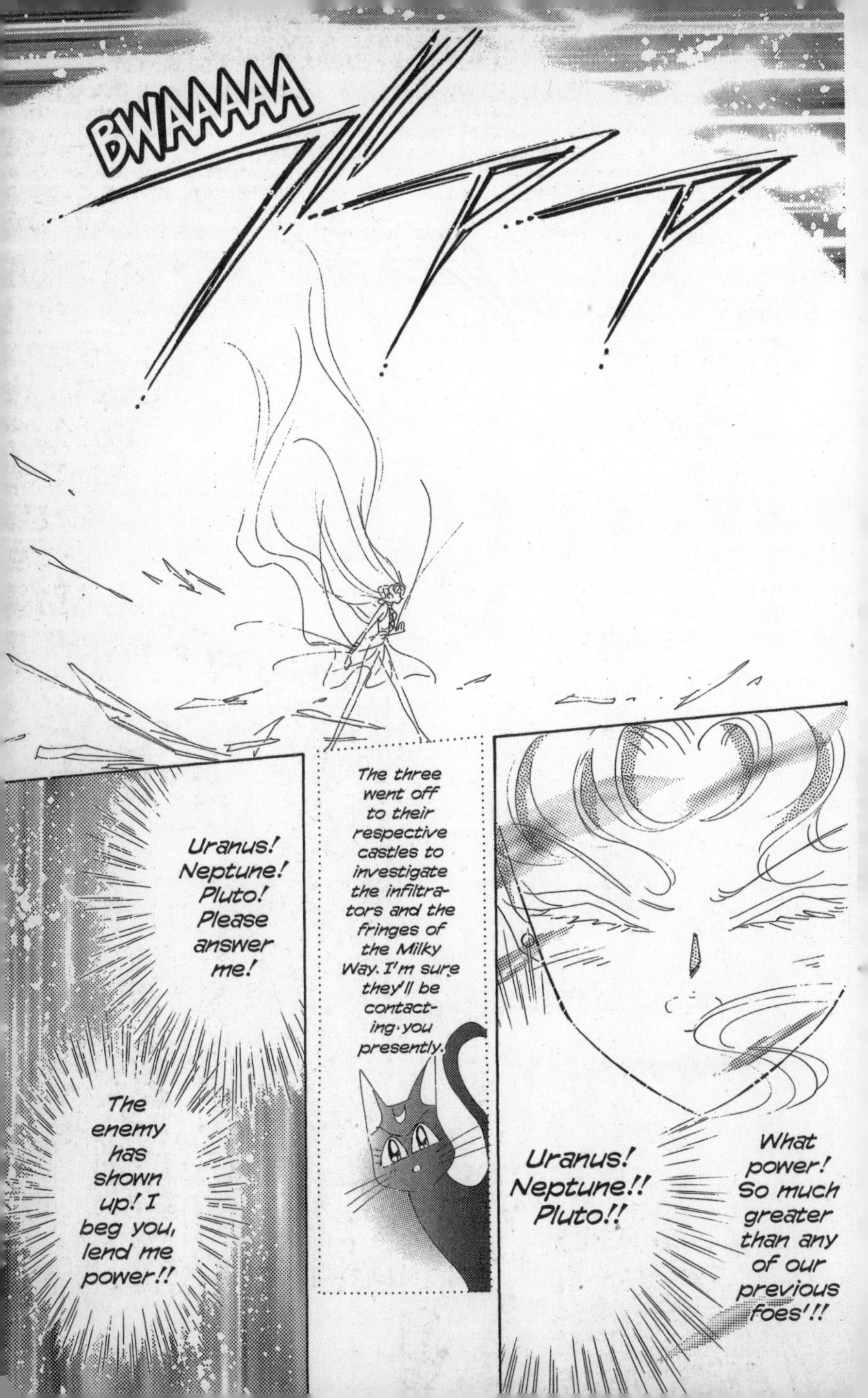
BWAAAAA
What power! So much greater than any of our previous foes'!!
Uranus! Neptune!! Pluto!!
The three went off to their respective castles to investigate the infiltrators and the fringes of the Milky Way. I'm sure they'll be contacting you presently.
Uranus! Neptune! Pluto! Please answer me!
The enemy has shown up! I beg you, lend me power!!

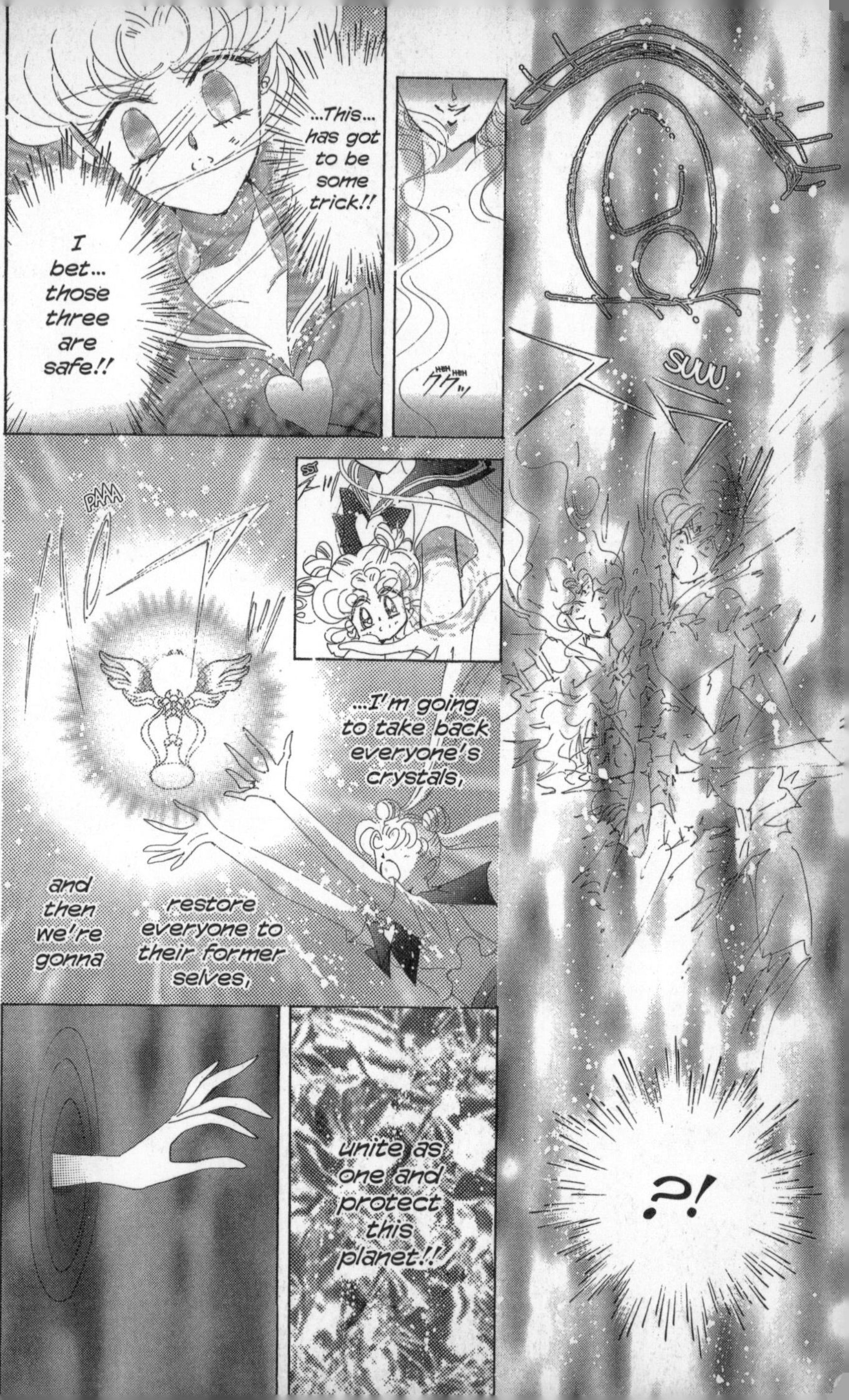
SUUU
?!
HEH HEH
...This... has got to be some trick!!
I bet... those three are safe!!
SST
PAAA
...I'm going to take back everyone's crystals,
restore everyone to their former selves,
and then we're gonna
unite as one and protect this planet!!

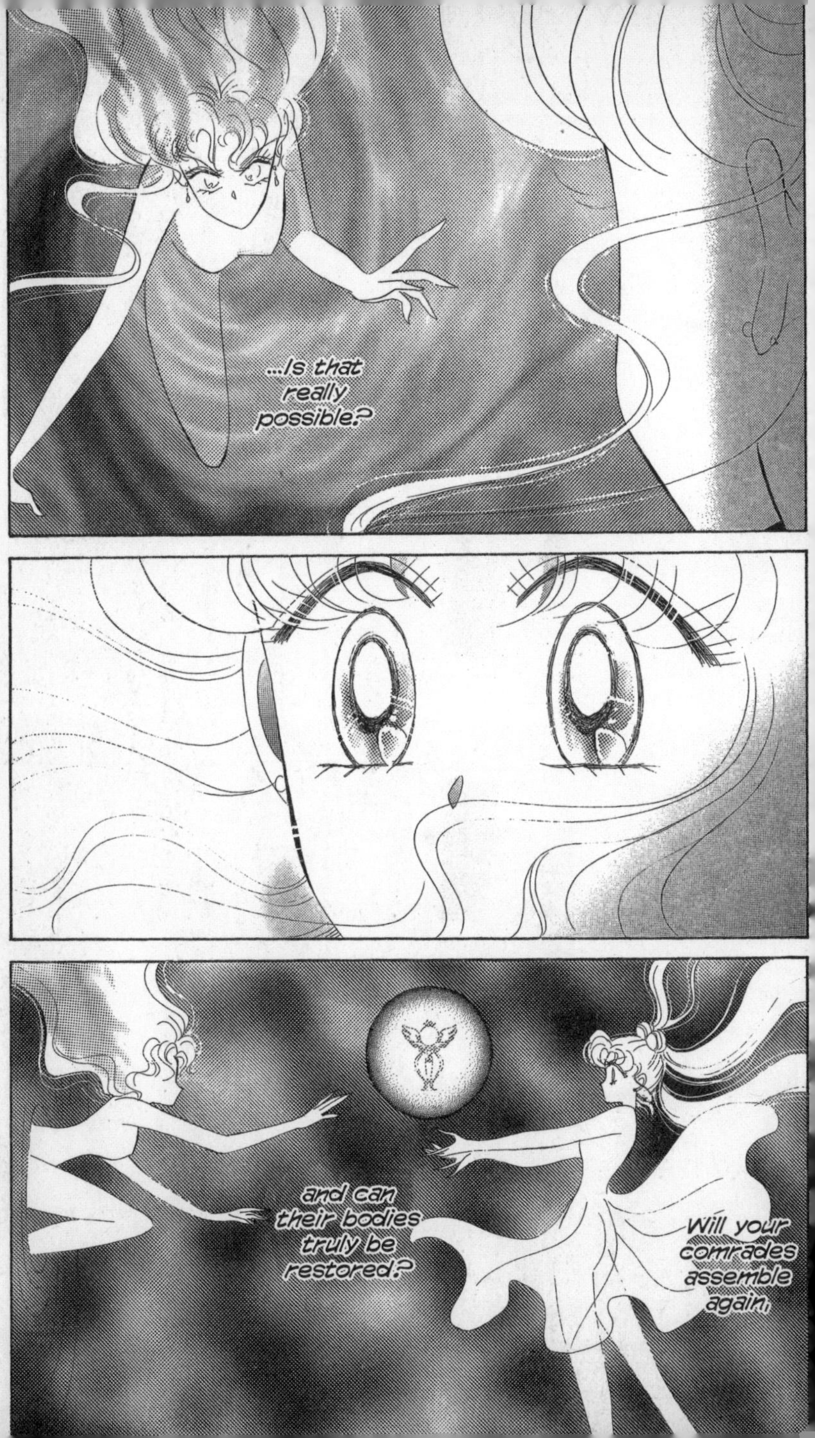
...Is that really possible?
Will your comrades assemble again,
and can their bodies truly be restored?

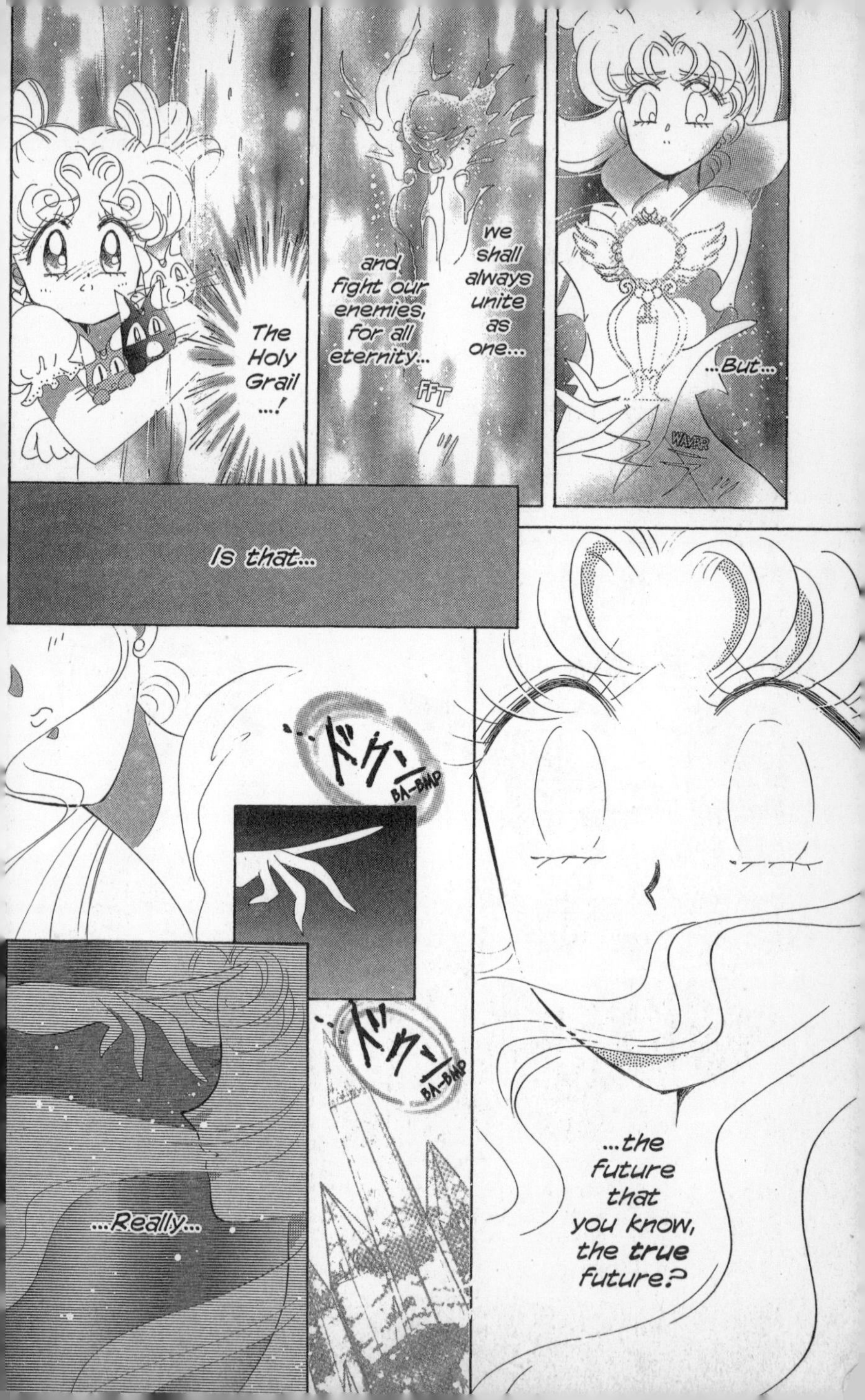
...But...
WAVRR
we shall always unite as one...
and fight our enemies, for all eternity...
FFT
The Holy Grail ...!
...the future that you know, the true future?
Is that...
BA-BMP
...Really...
BA-BMP

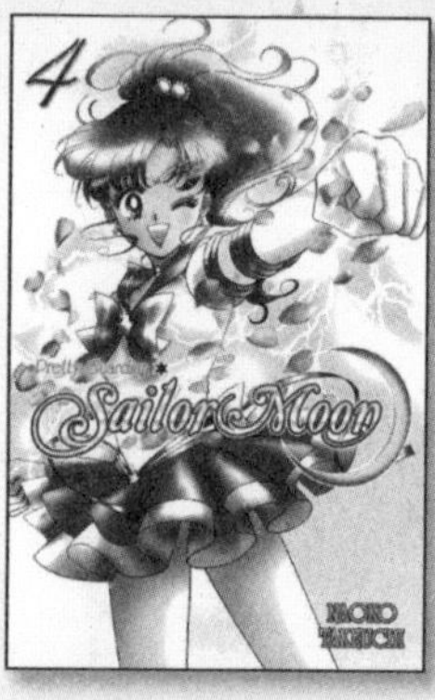
4
Pretty Guardian
Sailor Moon
NAOKO TAKEUCHI
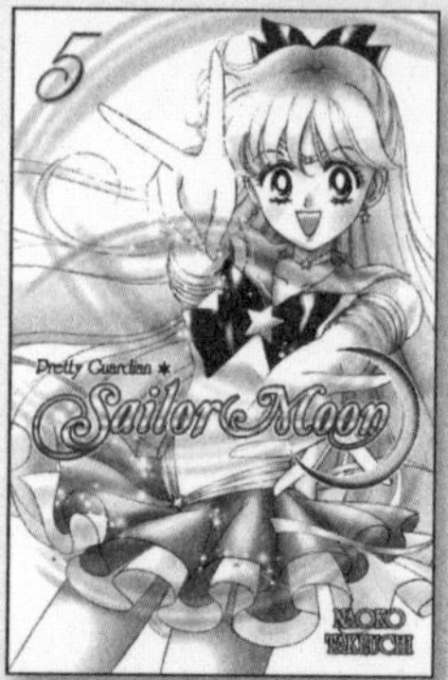
5
Pretty Guardian
Sailor Moon
NAOKO TAKEUCHI
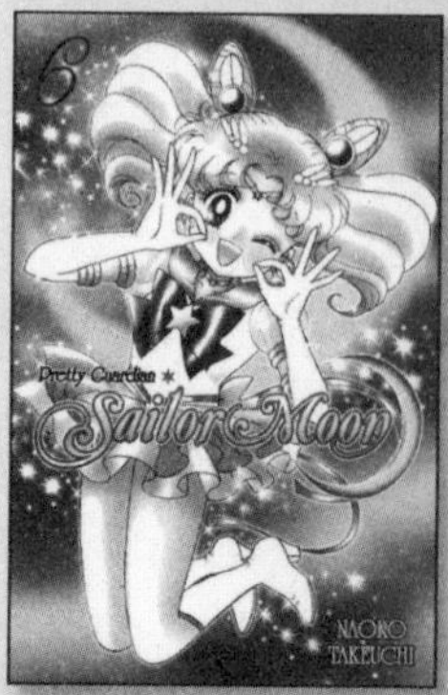
6
Pretty Guardian
Sailor Moon
NAOKO TAKEUCHI
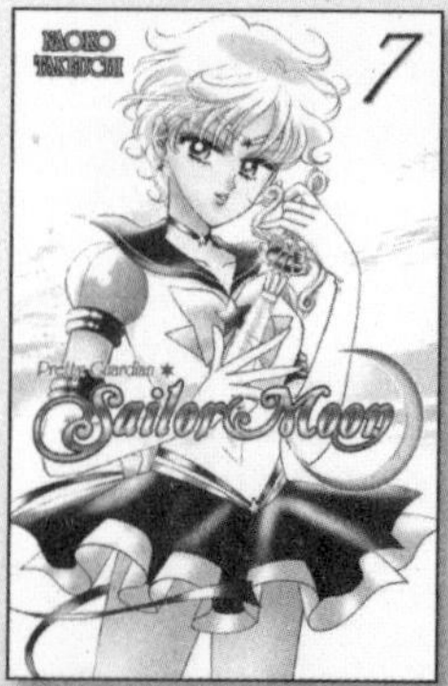
NAOKO TAKEUCHI
7
Pretty Guardian
Sailor Moon
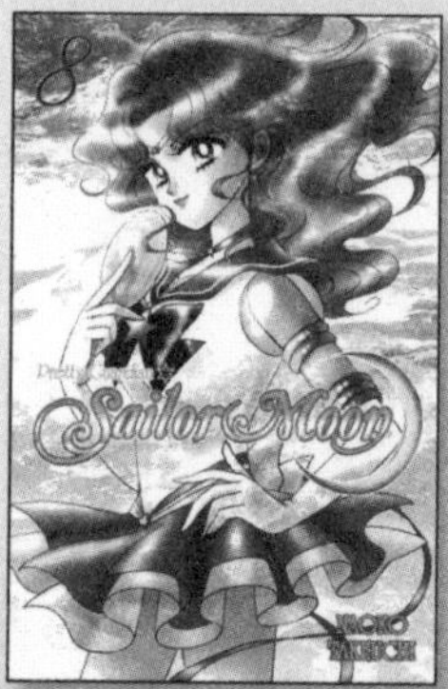
8
Pretty Guardian
Sailor Moon
NAOKO TAKEUCHI
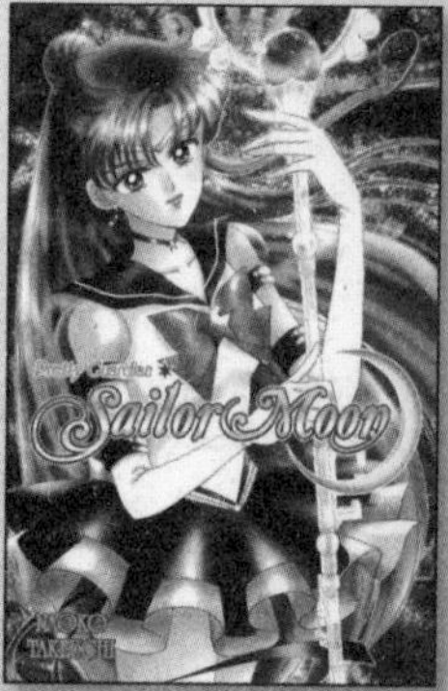
9
Pretty Guardian
Sailor Moon
NAOKO TAKEUCHI
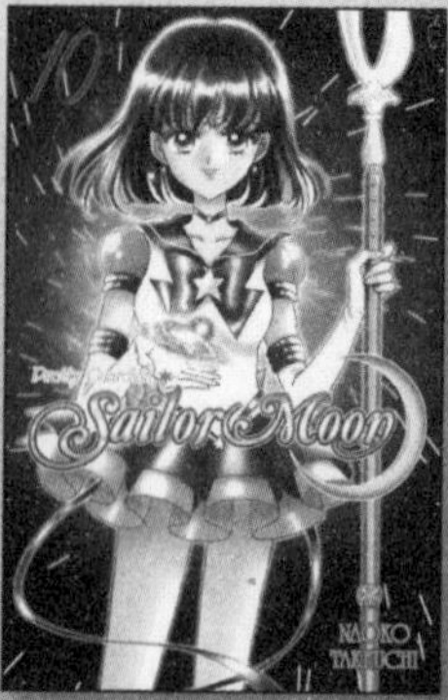
10
Pretty Guardian
Sailor Moon
NAOKO TAKEUCHI
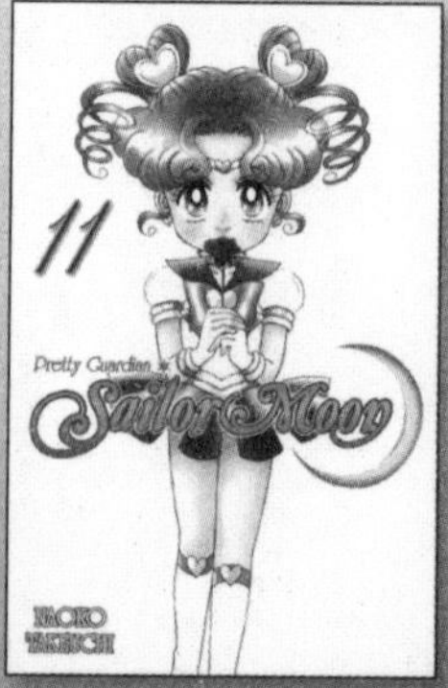
11
Pretty Guardian
Sailor Moon
NAOKO TAKEUCHI
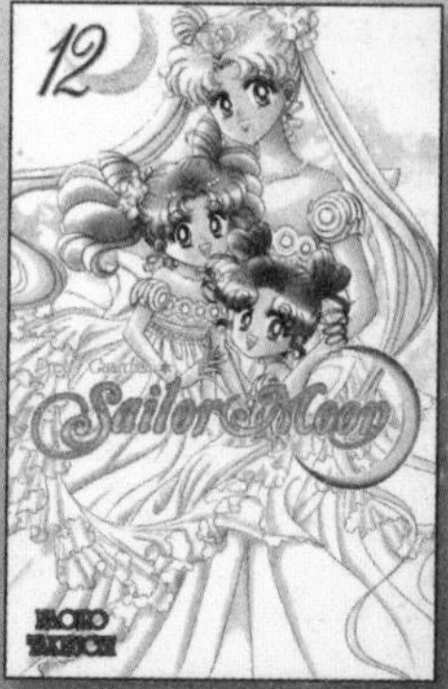
12
Pretty Guardian
Sailor Moon
NAOKO TAKEUCHI

Pretty Guardian Sailor Moon volume 11 is a work of fiction. Names, characters, places, and incidents are the products of the author's imagination or are used fictitiously. Any resemblance to actual events, locales, or persons, living or dead, is entirely coincidental.

A Kodansha Trade Paperback Original.

Published in the United States by Kodansha Comics, an imprint of Kodansha USA Publishing, LLC, New York.

Publication rights for this English edition arranged through Kodansha Ltd., Tokyo.

First published in Japan in 2004 by Kodansha Ltd., Tokyo, as *Bishoujosenshi Sailor Moon Shinsoban*, volume 11.

ISBN 978-1-61262-007-7

Printed in Canada

www.kodanshacomics.com

9 8 7 6 5 4 3 2 1

Translator/Adapter: Mari Morimoto
Lettering: Jennifer Skarupa

TOMARE! STOP

You're going the wrong way!

Manga is a completely different type of reading experience.

To start at the beginning, Go to the end!

! Authentic manga is read the traditional Japanese way— left, exactly the opposite of how American books are to follow: Just go to the other end of the book and read d each panel—from right side to left side, starting at ow you're experiencing manga as it was meant to be!

Pretty Guardian

Sailor Moon

11

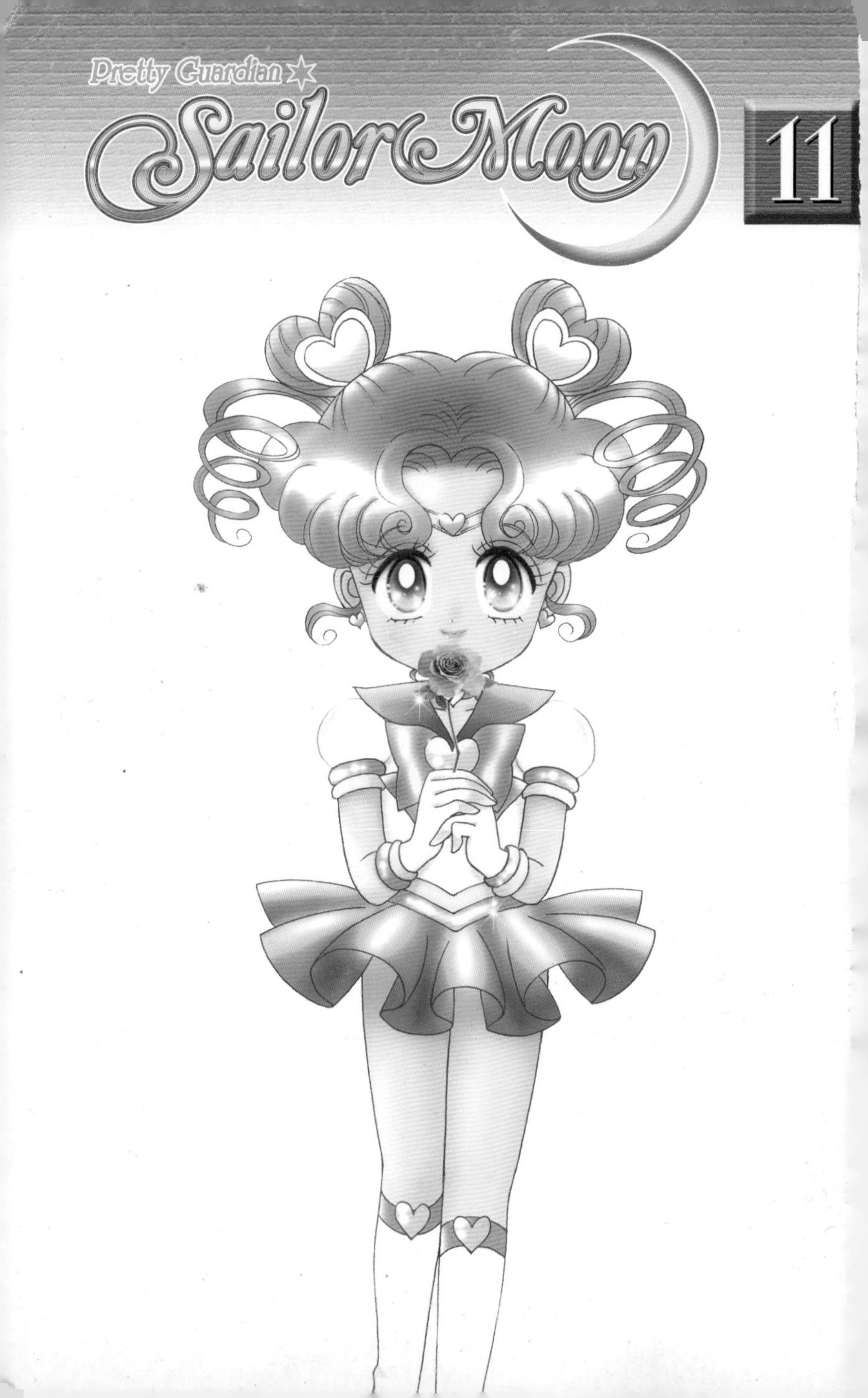

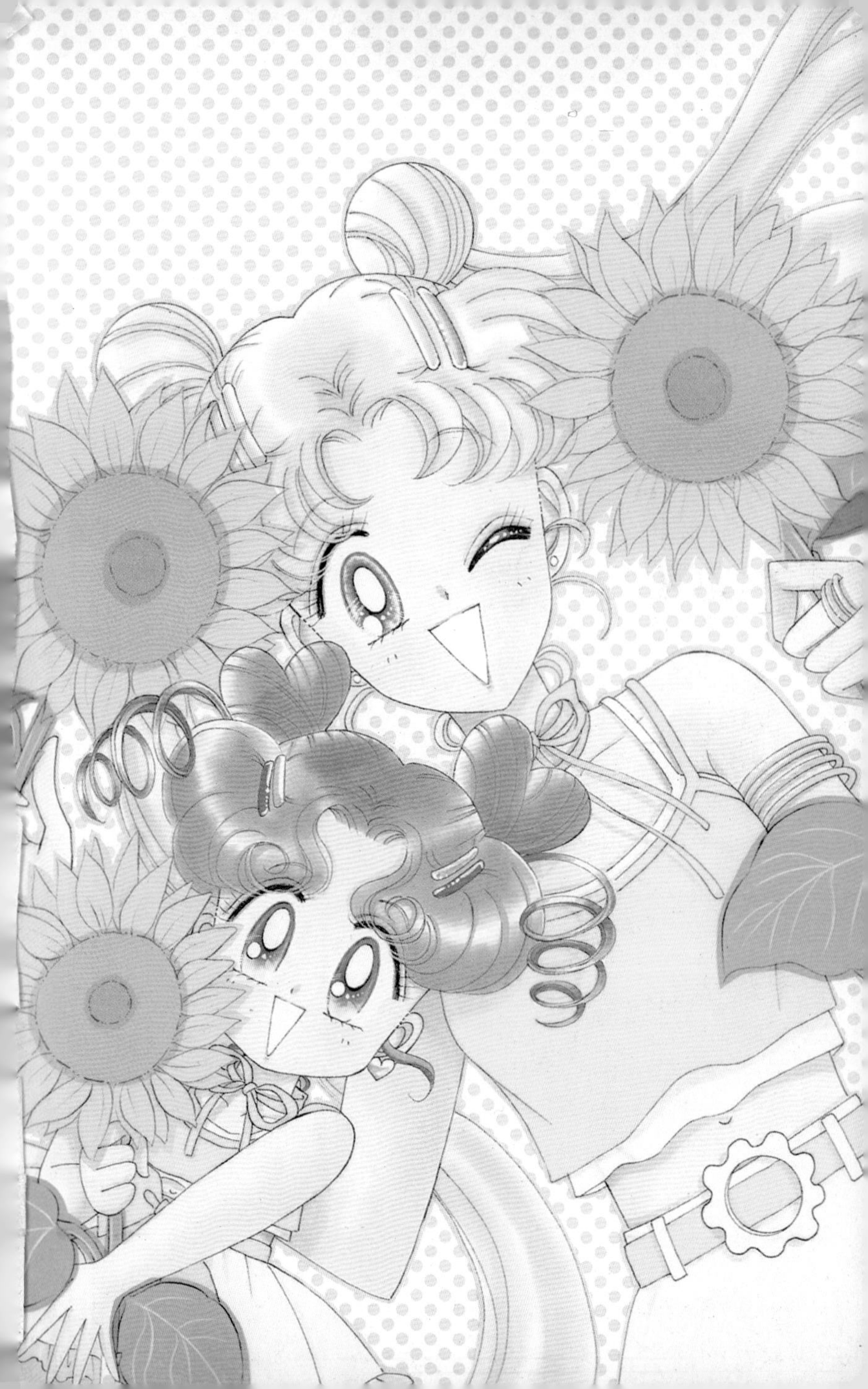